DATE DUE

The Norman Conquest

A New Introduction

Richard Huscroft

PEARSON

Longman

D0061173

Harlow, England • London • New York • Boston • San Francisco • Toronto
Sydney • Tokyo • Singapore • Hong Kong • Seoul • Taipei • New Delhi
Cape Town • Madrid • Mexico City • Amsterdam • Munich • Paris • Milan

PEARSON EDUCATION LIMITED

Edinburgh Gate
Harlow CM20 2JE
United Kingdom
Tel: +44 (0)1279 623623
Fax: +44 (0)1279 431059
Website: www.pearsoned.co.uk

First edition published in 2009

© Pearson Education Limited 2009

The right of Richard Huscroft to be identified as author
of this work has been asserted by him in accordance
with the Copyright, Designs and Patents Act 1988.

ISBN: 978-1-4058-1155-2

British Library Cataloguing in Publication Data
A CIP catalogue record for this book can be obtained from the British Library

Library of Congress Cataloging in Publication Data
Huscroft, Richard.
    The Norman Conquest : a new introduction / Richard Huscroft.
       p. cm.
    Includes bibliographical references and index.
    ISBN 978-1-4058-1155-2 (pbk.)
    1. Great Britain–History–Norman period, 1066–1154   2. Great Britain–History–William I,
1066–1087   3. Normans–Great Britain.   4. Great Britain–History–Anglo-Saxon period,
449–1066.   I. Title.
    DA195.H957 2009
    942.02'1–dc22

                                                                      2008039108

10   9   8   7   6   5   4   3   2   1
12   11   10   09   08

Set by 35 in 9.5/14.5pt Stone Serif
Printed in Malaysia (CTP-VP)

The Publishers' policy is to use paper manufactured from sustainable forests.

Contents

Preface   vii

Money and terminology   xi

References and abbreviations   xiii

Maps

1 England: shires and political divisions in 1066   xv
2 Scotland and northern England: regional divisions   xvi
3 Wales: regional and political divisions   xvii
4 Normandy in the eleventh and twelfth centuries   xviii

Genealogies

1 The kings of England: The West Saxon line (simplified) xix
2 The kings of England: The Danish line (simplified)   xx
3 The kings of England: The Norman line (simplified)   xxi

PART ONE Preliminaries

1 The principal sources   3
   Narrative sources 4
   Administrative sources 15
   Notes 18

2 Britain and Normandy in the eleventh century   21
   Lands and peoples 21
   Polities and power 31
   Military organisation 38
   Economies 49

The Church in pre-conquest Britain 55
Britain and the papacy before 1066 64
The Church in pre-conquest Normandy 66
Conclusion 69
Notes 69

3 The origins of conquest, 991–1066   75
Royal succession in England 75
Alliances and invasions, 991–1016 80
English, Danes and Normans, 1016–1042 82
The King and his earls, 1042–1045 85
Edward and the Normans 87
Edward and Godwine 89
The crisis of 1051 90
William of Normandy and the offer of the crown 91
The return of Godwine 95
Beyond England 96
The rise of the Godwinesons, 1053–1064 98
Harold and Wales 101
Harold and William 102
The Northumbrian rising 105
A fateful choice 107
Notes 109

PART TWO **The Norman Conquest**

4 Conquest, 1066   115
King Harold 115
The phoney war 116
The northern invasion 118
Duke William prepares 120
Invasion 122
The Hastings campaign 124
The Battle of Hastings 126
From Hastings to London 131
Notes 133

5 Conquest consolidated, 1067–1087   137
The establishment of Norman rule 137
England subdued, 1067–1072 138

Opposition: The next generation, 1072–1075 147
Frontiers and family, 1076–1084 150
Danes, Domesday and death, 1085–1087 155
Notes 157

6 Conquest confirmed, 1087–1100   159
William Rufus 159
Securing England, 1087–1088 160
Normandy, 1089–1091 162
Scotland and Wales in the 1090s 163
Conspiracy, 1095 166
Normandy and its frontiers, 1094–1099 167
A bolt from the blue 169
Notes 171

7 The English conquest of Normandy, 1100–1106   173
Henry, king of the English, 1100–1102 173
Henry, Wales and Scotland, 1102–c.1110 177
Duke Robert undermined 179
The Battle of Tinchebray 181
Notes 182

PART THREE **The impact of conquest**

8 Government and law   187
Kings and magnates 188
Household government 193
Cross-Channel government 196
Government in writing 198
Regional government 202
The royal forest 206
Royal wealth 207
Collecting the funds 212
The law 214
Conclusion 225
Notes 226

9 Lands and armies   231
A new aristocracy 231
Barons and below 233

Honours and incidents 235
The English survivors 239
The mechanics of settlement 241
Military power 247
Armies and fleets 249
'Feudal' England? 254
Wales and Scotland 258
Notes 266

10 Economies and families   273
Town and country 273
Families and female power 279
Notes 285

11 The Church   289
The post-conquest English Church 290
Questions of primacy 294
Parishes and councils 297
Conquest and cloister 300
Kings, archbishops and popes 303
Reconstruction 306
Wales, Scotland and Normandy 308
Conclusion 311
Notes 312

PART FOUR Conclusion

12 Britain and Normandy in 1106 – myths and reality   317
Notes 329

Suggestions for further reading   333
Index   347

Preface

The main purpose of this book is to introduce those new to the subject to one of the most important events in European history – the Norman Conquest of England. More specifically, my aim has been to describe and analyse the background to the Conquest, its principal events and characters, its consequences, and the debates which still surround it. The book does have some wider concerns, too, and I have tried to put what it describes in as broad a context as possible. After all, the Norman Conquest, whilst unique in many ways, was not an isolated or self-contained phenomenon; and the turbulent and transformative events of 1066 were one aspect of developments which had been affecting Western Europe since the tenth century and before. Moreover, the effects of the Conquest were not confined to England alone. All of the constituent parts of the island of Britain – England, Wales and Scotland – as well as Normandy and other parts of northern France, too, contributed to and were profoundly affected by the events which culminated in the experience of 1066 and its aftermath.

There are inevitably limits to my discussion, though. First, although the book does contain what I think are some fresh insights on specific matters, I have not attempted to say anything particularly new or innovative about the Conquest as a whole. Second, I have not tried to produce a comprehensive summary or synthesis of past and present thinking on the Conquest. The available sources are extensive, and the secondary literature on all aspects of the Conquest is vast. Perhaps for these very reasons, a full modern history of the Conquest in all its aspects remains lacking. One is certainly desirable, but it would be the work of a scholarly lifetime. Third, my analysis of the results of the Conquest stops, by and large, in 1106. I do not regard this as the definitive 'end' of the Norman Conquest; indeed, in many ways and in many parts of Britain and Normandy, it had only just begun by then. Nevertheless, the book has to end somewhere, and 1106 is an important date. By then, cross-Channel links of a political, economic and cultural kind were well established and strong; Normans were beginning to assimilate meaningfully into English society and their presence in Wales and lowland Scotland was significant. By 1106, there can be no doubt that what had happened in the decades after 1066 was irreversible: the Norman Conquest, if incomplete, was permanent. But that particular year is significant for other reasons, too. After Henry I's victory at Tinchebray, the idea, which had not been universally accepted before then, that England and Normandy, although they were sometimes divided in practice, should remain together under the rule of a single lord, became the guiding and settled principle which dictated the actions of twelfth- and, indeed, thirteenth-century kings of England. It was not until 1259 that the English king finally and formally abandoned his right to call himself Duke of Normandy. For over a century and a half after 1106, therefore, much of what the kings of England did arose from their urgent desire to keep England and Normandy together, or from their perceived duty to reunite them if they had drifted apart. Everything which had happened in the 40 years before 1106 culminated in the acceptance of this radical shift in Britain's political orientation.

Fourth, and finally, this book does not purport to be a general history of the British Isles during this period. The term 'Britain' meant different things to different medieval writers. It might mean 'the land of the Britons': modern Wales, in other words. It might also be used in a much more broadly geographical sense to describe the whole of the island: modern England, Scotland and Wales. And it might have more political overtones, too, and refer only to that part of the island, south of Hadrian's Wall, which had made up the Roman province of Britannia: a land which was occupied by Saxons, Scots and other peoples, as well as Britons. None of these usages allows Ireland to be considered part of Britain; and northern Scotland, beyond the Roman frontier, was only taken in by the second. It is usually, if not always, in the third sense that I have used the term in this book. Not, however, because Roman notions of 'Britannia' still had any political significance by the eleventh century, but because northern Scotland and Ireland contributed little if anything to the causes, timing and eventual shape of the Norman Conquest; and because they in turn were hardly affected by events in southern Britain until well into the twelfth century, where this book does not go. Having said this, whilst lowland Scotland, Wales and Normandy feature prominently throughout the book, England usually takes centre stage. I make no apologies for this; indeed it is inevitable for at least two reasons. The bulk of the source material comes from England and it views the events it describes from an overwhelmingly English perspective. More importantly, though, the emphasis on English politics and society is justified because the Norman Conquest affected England more immediately and more deeply than any of the other territories I consider. I have tried to avoid giving the impression that what happened in Wales, Scotland and Normandy before and after 1066 was merely incidental to what happened in England. Nevertheless, it bears repeating that this book does not set out to provide a full history of Britain and northern France in the eleventh century. It only tries to explain why the Norman Conquest happened and what form it took. Welsh, Scottish and Norman affairs are mentioned only to the extent that they are relevant to that primary concern.

I have incurred various debts whilst writing this book. I would like to thank Professor David Carpenter for reading through the whole manuscript at an early stage. His ideas as ever were insightful and illuminating. Closer to home, I cannot adequately thank Jo and Tilda for their patience and for the support and space they have given me. My time spent writing history is precious; but my time spent with them is priceless.

Money and terminology

Money

Monetary figures are expressed throughout this book in pre-decimal English units, namely pounds, shillings and pence. There was only one coin in circulation in England during this period, the silver penny. There were twelve pence in a shilling, 240 pence (twenty shillings) in a pound and 160 pence in a mark. A mark, therefore, was equivalent to two-thirds of a pound. However, shillings, pounds and marks were terms used for accounting purposes only; there were no coins with those values. For the sake of simplicity and ready comparability, I have converted all sums originally expressed in marks into pounds. Thus, for example, a payment of 1,000 marks would be referred to here as one of £666 13s 4d, or, in other words, 666 pounds, thirteen shillings and four pence.

Terminology

The different peoples of eleventh-century Britain had much in common. However, this was still a highly-regionalised environment, and the peoples of Wessex, Gwynedd and Strathclyde would have thought of themselves as in some senses different from the peoples of Northumbria, Powys or Galloway. Pinpointing the precise nature and reality of these perceived differences is difficult, of course; but even more problematic is defining the extent to which the inhabitants of these different regions would also have regarded themselves as English, Welsh or Scottish. Contemporaries described themselves, and were described by others, in many ways over time and in a range of languages. In the eighth century, for example, Bede used the Latin *Scotti* to describe the Irish; but by the tenth century, when another English writer referred to 'all the people of the Scots' (*eall Scotta Þeod*), he meant the inhabitants of Scotland. The latter, meanwhile, regularly called themselves *Gaídil*, or 'Gaels'.[1] Similar examples could be given to show the different ways in which the Welsh and English were described. The words used, moreover, are often subtly distinct, and to translate into modern English contemporary terms used to describe particular peoples is fraught with hazardous difficulties, and does less than justice to the complexities surrounding conceptions of national and local identities. It has rightly been said, for example, in the context of the relationship between Scotland and Ireland in the early Middle Ages, that 'it is impossible to use "Gaels", "Irish" and "Scots" as translations of contemporary terminology without appearing to have decided matters in advance'.[2] Nevertheless, and at the risk of over-simplification, some clarity is required in an introductory book of this kind. When I use the unmodified terms 'England', 'Wales' and 'Scotland', they refer to the territories which make up those modern countries. When I use the adjectives 'English', 'Welsh' or 'Scots' without further refinement, the intention is to describe things or people from within those territories. As for 'Normandy/Norman', I hope these terms are self-explanatory.

Notes

1 A.A.M. Duncan, *The Kingship of the Scots, 842–1292: Succession and Independence* (Edinburgh University Press, 2002), pp.3–5.

2 Dauvit Broun, *The Irish Identity of the Kingdom of the Scots in the Twelfth and Thirteen Centuries* (Woodbridge: Boydell Press, 1999), p.7.

References and abbreviations

I have tried to keep the number of references to a minimum by giving a citation only when a source or secondary work has been quoted or drawn from directly. I have used abbreviations only for those works I have referred to frequently. Details of other works are given in full when they are mentioned for the first time in the notes for each chapter; thereafter, shortened references are used.

I have used the following abbreviations in the references:

ANS	*Anglo-Norman Studies*, ed. R. Allen Brown *et al.* (Woodbridge: Boydell Press, 1979–)
ASC	*The Anglo-Saxon Chronicle*, ed. D. Whitelock (London: Eyre and Spottiswoode, 1961)
BT	*The Bayeux Tapestry*, ed. David M. Wilson (London: Thames and Hudson, 1985)
DB	*Domesday Book: A complete translation*, ed. A. Williams and G.H. Martin (London: Penguin, 2002)
EHD I	*English Historical Documents* I, *c.500–1042*, ed. D. Whitelock (London: Eyre Methuen, 1979)
EHD II	*English Historical Documents* II, *1042–1189*, ed. D.C. Douglas and G.W. Greenaway (London: Eyre Methuen, 1981)
EHR	*English Historical Review*
HH	*Henry of Huntingdon, The History of the English People*, ed. D. Greenway (Oxford University Press, 2002)
HN	*Eadmer's History of Recent Events in England*, trans. G. Bosanquet (London: Cresset Press, 1964)
JW	*The Chronicle of John of Worcester*, ii, ed. R.R. Darlington and P. McGurk trans. J. Bray and P. McGurk (Oxford:

Clarendon Press, 1995), and iii, ed. and trans. P. McGurk (Oxford: Clarendon Press, 1998)

ODNB *The Oxford Dictionary of National Biography*, ed. H.C.G. Matthew and B. Harrison (Oxford University Press, 2004)

OV *The Ecclesiastical History of Orderic Vitalis*, ed. and trans. M. Chibnall, 6 vols (Oxford University Press, 1969–90)

TRHS *Transactions of the Royal Historical Society*

Vita Edwardi *The Life of King Edward*, ed. and trans. F. Barlow (London: Nelson, 1962)

WJ *The Gesta Normannorum Ducum of William of Jumièges, Orderic Vitalis and Robert of Toriqni*, 2 vols, ed. and trans. E.M.C. van Houts (Oxford: Clarendon Press, 1992–5)

WMGP William of Malmesbury, *The Deeds of the Bishops of England*, trans. D. Preest (Woodbridge: Boydell Press, 2002)

WMGR William of Malmesbury, *The History of the English Kings*, 2 vols, ed. and trans. R.A.B. Mynors, R.M. Thomson and M. Winterbottom (Oxford: Clarendon Press, 1998–9)

WP *The Gesta Guillelmi of William of Poitiers*, ed. and trans. R.H.C. Davis and M. Chibnall (Oxford: Clarendon Press, 1988)

MAP 1 England: Shires and political divisions in 1066

Source: *Feudal Britain: The completion of the medieval kingdom 1066–1314*, pub. Edward Arnold;
reprinted by permission of the author (Barrow, G.W.S., reprinted 1971).

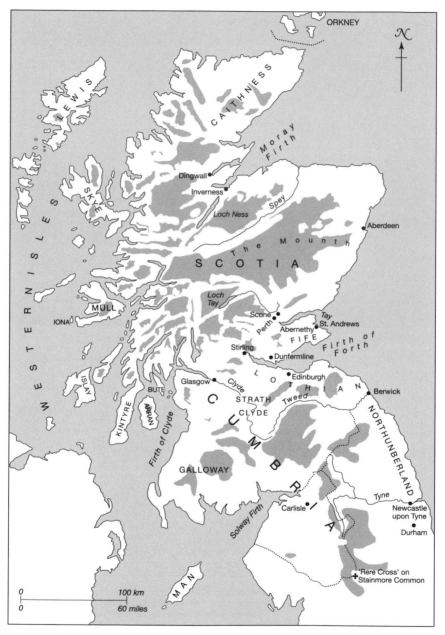

ORKNEY

𝒩

L
E
W
I
S

C A I T H N E S S

Moray
Firth

Dingwall

Inverness

Loch Ness

Spey

Aberdeen

The   Mounth

S C O T I A

W
E
S
T
E
R
N
I
S
L
E
S

SKYE

MULL

IONA

Loch
Tay

Scone

Tay

St. Andrews

Perth

Abernethy

F I F E

Firth of
Forth

Stirling

Dunfermline

Edinburgh

L
O
T
H
I
A
N

ISLAY

Glasgow

Clyde

STRATH

Tweed

Berwick

KINTYRE

BUTE

ARRAN

Firth of Clyde

C
U
M
B
R
I
A

CLYDE

NORTHUMBERLAND

GALLOWAY

Tyne

Newcastle
upon Tyne

Carlisle

Durham

Solway Firth

'Rere Cross' on
Stainmore Common

M
A
N

0   100 km
0   60 miles

MAP 2 Scotland and northern England: Regional divisions *c.*1100

Source: Adapted from G.W.S. Barrow, *Feudal Britain: The completion
of the medieval kingdoms* (London: Edward Arnold, 1956; repr. 1985).

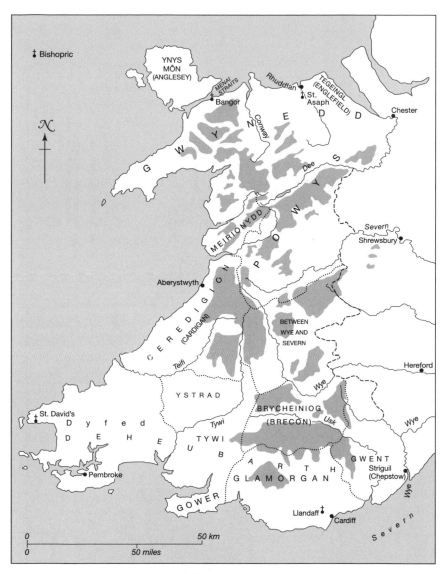

MAP 3 Wales: Regional and political divisions *c.*1100

Source: Adapted from G.W.S. Barrow, *Feudal Britain: The completion of the medieval kingdoms* (London: Edward Arnold, 1956; repr. 1985).

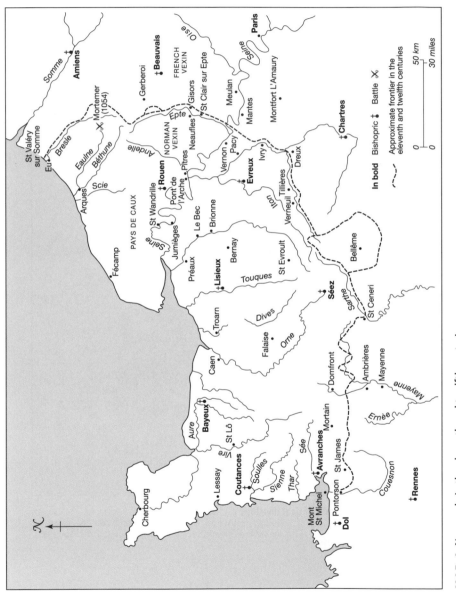

MAP 4 Normandy in the eleventh and twelfth centuries

Source: After van Houts, E. and Harper-Bill, C. (eds) 2003, *A Companion to the Anglo-Norman World*, pub. Boydell Press, p.xiii. Reprinted by permission of Boydell Press.

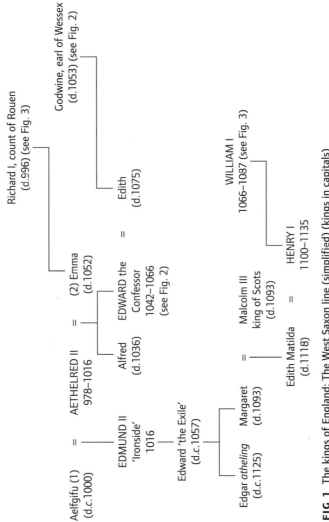

FIG 1 The kings of England: The West Saxon line (simplified) (kings in capitals)

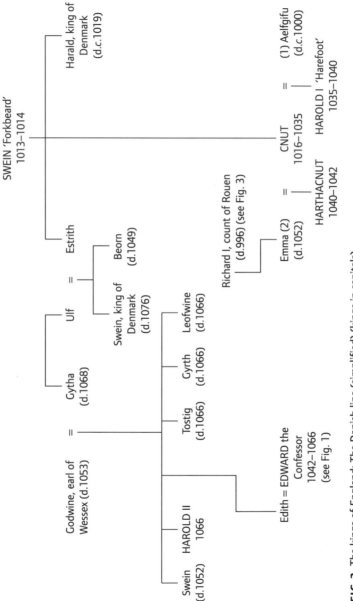

FIG 2 The kings of England: The Danish line (simplified) (kings in capitals)

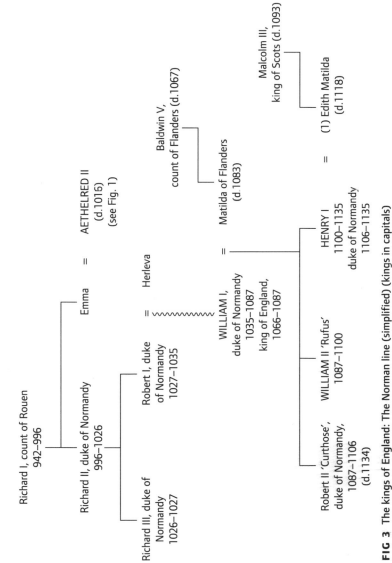

FIG 3 The kings of England: The Norman line (simplified) (kings in capitals)

PART ONE

Preliminaries

The principal sources

In Western Europe during the earlier Middle Ages, relatively little was recorded in writing and only a small part of that has survived. The Norman Conquest of England, however, because its significance was immediately understood by those who lived during or shortly after it, prompted more contemporary written discussion than many other medieval events. But whilst relatively plentiful, the surviving sources for the Conquest still present a far from complete picture. Huge gaps in absolute knowledge and clear understanding are bound to remain. Moreover, it is unrealistic for a twenty-first-century reader to apply modern standards of historical accuracy to what has survived from the eleventh and twelfth centuries. In the narrative sources, for example, an author's own preoccupations often blur the lines between truthful description on the one hand, and fable, myth and developing legend on the other. The words attributed to particular individuals are often designed to entertain rather than to inform; the reliability of simple statements of fact cannot be taken for granted. And as for the seemingly more objective administrative sources, specific doubts about their dating, or wider ones about their authenticity often allow only tentative conclusions over their significance. The contents of any one source need as far as possible to be compared with other available material to test their credibility and precision. But even where this is possible, definitive interpretations will usually remain elusive.

All of this makes studying the Norman Conquest a huge and exciting challenge. The scope for differing views and interpretations is enormous, as is the amount of space within which a lively historical imagination can wander and speculate. And it is the problems with the sources and the uncertainty they generate which make the Conquest such a fertile field for ongoing and probably endless scholarly cultivation. What follows here is only a brief introduction to the main sources for the period, and the true extent of that 'abundant material for writing many books', which is said to have been available at the court of William the Conqueror, can only be guessed at.[1]

Narrative sources

Contemporary or near-contemporary views on the Norman Conquest differed according to where, when, why and by whom they were written. In England soon after 1066 and into the twelfth century, the urge to record events was prompted by many different impulses. For some, it was necessary to explain why God had chosen to inflict the Norman invasion on the English people. For others, the intention was to preserve some knowledge and pride in English history and the kingdom's traditions in the face of a foreign onslaught which threatened to wipe out the old culture. In Normandy, by contrast, the earliest accounts of the Conquest had as their objectives the glorification of William the Conqueror and the justification of his invasion and subjugation of England.

The *Anglo-Saxon Chronicle* provides the most important narrative account of English history before the twelfth century. A year-by-year description of events (the *Chronicle* is technically an annal rather than a chronicle) that the compilers considered to be significant, it includes the only account of the Norman Conquest written in the native language of the English people. However, it is not one source, but several. Having been put together first of all in the 890s in Wessex (perhaps at the court of King Alfred (871–99)), the original manuscript of the *Chronicle* was copied and circulated around the country. The copies might then have been added to, amended or simply left alone by those who came into possession of them. It would then come down to chance to determine whether this extra information found its way into those copies which eventually survived. There are now eight surviving manuscripts of the *Chronicle* in all, labelled A–H by historians, but for this period C, D and E are the most important.[2] The original accounts, on which the surviving copies are based, were all written, using a common source, at different places and different times. Consequently they display different local interests and preoccupations. Therefore, each text of the *Chronicle*, whilst having much in common with the other versions, is very much an independent source. C is thought to have been compiled first in the early 1040s. It says nothing about the years 1056–65 but it may be a near-contemporary record of what it does describe, until it ends abruptly in 1066 with the Battle of Stamford Bridge still unfinished. The most recent analysis has suggested that, because of the text's preoccupation with Mercian affairs and the affairs of the earls of Mercia in particular, C was probably composed somewhere in the Midlands, close to the sources of the Mercian earls' power.[3] The pre-1066 parts of D are probably also contemporary, but they are more extensive than C. Manuscript D also provides the fullest account of the early years of the Conquest. It ends in 1079 and has a particular interest in the affairs of northern England, the west midlands and Worcester. The current consensus holds that D was probably compiled by persons close to Ealdred, archbishop of York (d.1069), and it is regarded as being particularly well informed about the deliberations of the kings and their councillors, of whom the Archbishop was one of the most important. Manuscript E continues until as late as 1154. Originally a northern compilation like D, it was continued at Canterbury after 1031 and until 1121 when its composition was carried on at Peterborough. The description in E of the events of the mid-eleventh century which, it is assumed, was written at the time of or very soon after the events it covers, is particularly well disposed towards Earl Godwine and his family.

The *Chronicle*'s varying accounts of the Conquest are permeated by a sense of doom and misery. The relevant parts of D and E were written in the aftermath of total English defeat, and they have little good to say about either the Normans or the English. The former were brutal and oppressive whilst the latter were sinful and corrupt: the Normans won at Hastings, according to D, 'even as God granted it to them because of the sins of the [English] people'.[4] Moral overtones aside, the *Chronicle*'s otherwise rather detached and straightforward tone should not be taken for objectivity, and its contents should not be assumed to be authoritative. Local and personal concerns often determined what was included in the surviving copies and what was left out. Nevertheless, the *Chronicle* is a remarkable source, and where the factual information it contains can be checked, it is usually corroborated. As a result, it provides our basic narrative of the important events, through the voices of the defeated in their own language.

All of the other narrative sources from England were written in Latin. One in particular, however, has a close connection with the *Chronicle*. The so-called *Chronicon ex Chronicis*, which was written at Worcester during the first half of the twelfth century, has traditionally been attributed to a monk of Worcester named Florence (d.1118). However, it is now generally thought that the author of this work was another Worcester monk, John. John wrote his history between *c*.1124 and *c*.1140, and his account of English history during this period was designed to fit into a much wider description of world events. He used a range of sources, but his principal one for events in England during this period appears to have been a copy of the *Chronicle* which has since been lost. This lost copy probably resembled D most closely, but it also differed significantly from it and other surviving versions of the *Chronicle*, so John's work is of great historical value in providing comments of his own as well as information not found elsewhere.[5]

Written in England much closer to the events of 1066 themselves was *The Life of King Edward* (*Vita Edwardi Regis*). This is an anonymous work, but the scholarly consensus now is that the author was probably a monk from the monastery of St Bertin in St Omer, Flanders. It was probably written in two parts either side of the events of 1066, the first part *c*.1065–6, and the second *c*.1067.[6] Part I provides a partial history of Edward the Confessor's reign, but is particularly concerned with the fluctuating fortunes of Earl Godwine of Wessex and two of his sons, Harold and Tostig. Such a focus is not surprising – the work is dedicated to the woman who commissioned it: Queen Edith, Godwine's daughter and the wife of Edward the Confessor, and the first half of the *Life* is decidedly pro-Godwine as a result. Part II is a more hagiographical account of the (by then) late King Edward's saintly qualities. Despite its rather partisan concerns, the *Life* is still an immensely valuable source. It gives fresh and specific insight into some of the most important events of the closing years of Edward the Confessor's reign: his building of Westminster Abbey, and the Northumbrian rising of 1065, for example.

It also contains the only written account of what happened at the bed-side of the dying king.

More talented and more engaging than any of the authors discussed so far was William of Malmesbury. He was certainly the best of all the English historical writers of the twelfth century, and perhaps the first truly great English historian since Bede, who wrote in the eighth century. William was born of mixed English and Norman parentage in about 1095 and he died in 1143. He was a Benedictine monk at the Wiltshire abbey of Malmesbury, but he was also an enthusiastic traveller in search of evidence and materials for his voluminous writings. He wrote histories and saints' lives, but two of his most important works, and those most relevant here, were *The Deeds of the Kings of the English* (*Gesta Regum Anglorum*), and *The Deeds of the English Bishops* (*Gesta Pontificum Anglorum*), both of which had been written by the middle of the 1120s.[7] The combination of William's perceptive analysis and his thorough and rigorous method has appealed greatly to later generations of historians. Nevertheless, William still shared the contemporary view that the Norman Conquest was God's judgement on an immoral and corrupt English nation. He has also been credited with introducing an English 'imperialist perception of Celtic peoples into history'. He regarded the Welsh, Scots and Irish as uncivilised 'barbarians' who lived in poor, primitive societies, whilst the English were 'prosperous, peaceful, law-abiding, urbanised and enterprising'. This notion of English superiority over their British neighbours has persisted to a greater or lesser degree ever since.[8]

Two of William of Malmesbury's contemporaries in England, Henry of Huntingdon and Eadmer, should also be introduced here. Like William, Henry of Huntingdon was of mixed Anglo-Norman parentage. He saw himself very much as an Englishman, however. Born in about 1088, he was taken as a boy to be educated at Lincoln in the household of Bishop Robert Bloet, who had been chancellor to William II and was a close adviser of Henry I. When his father died in 1110, Henry took his place as archdeacon of Huntingdon. Using a variety of written sources, including Bede and the *Chronicle*, as well as his own recollections and strong oral traditions, Henry wrote his *History of the English People* between 1123 and 1130 and revised it into the 1140s, and it includes stories not told by anyone else: about Cnut and the waves, for example, and the death of Earl Godwine.[9] The dominant theme of Henry's *History* was very much the resilience of 'our people', however, and the historical continuity which underlay the identity of the English as a separate race. The Norman Conquest was certainly a judgement from God on England's failings, Henry thought, but it did not wipe out the essential Englishness of the people. More than this, however, it has also been suggested that 'a developing sense of Englishness' can be traced in Henry's work. In other words, whilst his writings from the 1120s still show an awareness of the English as a 'subject' people, oppressed by their French conquerors, by the 1140s this feeling has gone and there is little distinction between Norman rulers and English subjects.[10] It should be remembered, nevertheless, that working as he did close to Bishop Robert and then to his successor Alexander (the nephew of Henry I's chief minister Roger, bishop of Salisbury), Henry's perspective on affairs was a rarefied one. He viewed his own time and the events which had preceded it from the summit of the Anglo-Norman political mountain, and his views on cultural and political assimilation may not have been shared lower down the social scale.

Eadmer was an Englishman, born in about 1064. He spent his career as a monk at Canterbury, where he served the two great post-conquest archbishops, Lanfranc and Anselm. Anselm was Eadmer's hero, however. Until Anselm's death in 1109, Eadmer was probably rarely absent from his master's side and it is his relationship with the saintly prelate which dominates all of his writing. As well as writing a biography of the Archbishop, Eadmer compiled the so-called *History of Recent Events* (*Historia Novorum*). On one level a history of his own times up to 1121, it was, despite its title, more an account of Anselm's public career.[11] It also describes, from a Canterbury point of view, the arguments between archbishops Lanfranc and Thomas of York over the primacy, an issue which also dominated the concerns of Hugh the Chanter's *History of the Church of York*, which was not written until after 1127.[12] Unlike William of Malmesbury and Hugh, Eadmer was a witness to many of the events he describes. He also gives different accounts of other significant episodes, Earl Harold's trip to Normandy in 1065, for example. He was a well-informed reporter with the ability vividly to describe a scene.

The earliest accounts of the Conquest from Normandy unsurprisingly contain none of the pessimism and defensiveness of the English commentators. Triumphalism and self-belief were the keynotes of the two works which do most to set out the highly partisan Norman view of the events either side of 1066. The first of these, *The Deeds of the Dukes of the Normans* (*Gesta Normannorum Ducum*) was written by William, a monk at the Norman abbey of Jumièges. William's plan was to continue a history of the Norman dukes (*De Moribus et Actis Primorum Normanniae Ducum*) which had been written by Dudo of St Quentin at the court of Duke Richard II (996–1026) by about 1015.[13] He therefore added to it accounts of the reigns of Dukes Richard II, Richard III, Robert I (1026–35) and William II, later King William I of England. His narrative ended in 1070 and the work was completed, it seems, in the following year. It was dedicated to William the Conqueror and William's intention was to legitimise and justify the conquest of England and to explain Duke William's conduct. This does not mean he is never reliable or trust-worthy, however. If he embellishes for rhetorical effect, he may well do so on factually sound foundations; and there is no reason to doubt that William's views about what happened were sincere and his ideas are probably representative of Norman opinion more generally. In the 1130s, a major revision of William's work was begun by the Norman Robert of Torigny (d.1184), prior of Bec and then abbot of Mont St Michel. He reinserted some passages from Dudo's *De moribus* which William had left out, and added passages of his own on William the Conqueror and Henry I.

Completed shortly after William de Jumièges's work (probably in the mid 1070s), but with a similar if even more ardent desire to glorify and justify Duke William's actions, was the *Deeds of William the Conqueror* (*Gesta Guillelmi ducis Normannorum et Regis Anglorum*) by William de Poitiers. First a soldier and then a priest, William de Poitiers later became Duke William's chaplain and archdeacon of Lisieux.[14] He was well informed, therefore, and well connected, and his account of the crucial decade of the 1060s is a detailed and immensely valuable one. William's description of the campaign of 1066 and the Battle of Hastings is the fullest narrative account, for example. Nevertheless, his work still needs to be treated with caution. No original manuscript survives, and what remains comes to a halt in 1067. Moreover, if William's self-confidence and directness are seductive, he is far from being objective by the standards of modern historical writing. William enjoyed putting long, grand speeches in the mouths of his characters, for example; and it is hard to believe that such a speech was designed to describe what actually happened when for instance William of Normandy addressed his troops before the start of the Battle of Hastings. But such passages served a purpose which a contemporary audience, one perhaps familiar with the styles and techniques of ancient Greek and Roman writers of history, would have understood – they were designed to entertain, to display a hero's eloquence, intelligence and moral virtue, and to identify him with the great men of the mythical past. Above all, William de Poitiers's purpose was to portray William the Conqueror as an epic hero in the classical mould and the English as wicked traitors to their true lord, and to do this as dramatically as he could. Now to demand from him precision in his use of detail and balance in his description of events would be to miss the point of William's work.

The works of William de Jumièges and William de Poitiers also need to be used carefully because of their relationship with each other. For the early history of Normandy, for example, both men used Dudo of St Quentin's (frequently unreliable) *De Moribus*, and for the later eleventh century there may have been other common sources which are now lost. Nevertheless, these two accounts remain important, not just because of their factual content, but because they express most fully the so-called 'Norman myth'. As will be seen in the next chapter, by the end of the eleventh century the Normans had developed a view of themselves as a separate and special people, the *gens Normannorum*; a people whose destiny it was to conquer and dominate others.[15] Such views colour and sometimes bring into serious question the reliability of what the Norman sources have to say about the Conquest. Nevertheless, later Norman writers picked up on and amplified these themes, none more impressively than Orderic Vitalis, who was born of mixed parentage in England in 1075, but who spent his adult life as a monk at the Norman monastery of St Evroult. In about 1114 Orderic began to write a history of the Norman Church; but over the next 30 years his *Ecclesiastical History* turned into something much more extensive and wide-ranging.[16] Despite living a cloistered existence for all of his working life, Orderic was able to acquire extensive knowledge about the affairs and histories of the leading Anglo-Norman families. At the same time, his cross-Channel sympathies gave Orderic's analysis of events a dimension lacking in the one-sided perspectives of William de Jumièges and William de Poitiers, whose work he used with discretion.[17] He was aware of what he perceived as the Normans' weaknesses as well as their strengths, and he was not afraid to criticise where he felt a need to do so. His huge work is thus of immense value as a guide to events on both sides of the English Channel up to 1141, when he stopped writing.

Not long after this, probably during the 1160s, another work was begun which covered the period from the origins of Normandy until 1106. The author was Wace and his long verse chronicle in Norman French is known as the *The Story of Rollo* (*Roman de Rou*). Born on Jersey around the start of the twelfth century, Wace tells us that he was taken to Caen as a small child and educated there and in France (probably Paris). On returning to Caen, he was granted a prebend (an endowment funded by the church in return for which the recipient had to live at the church and perform certain services there) at Bayeux. The patron of Bayeux was King Henry II himself, and it was Henry who commissioned Wace to write his history. Wace was heavily reliant on most of the authors who have already been mentioned – Dudo of St Quentin, William de Jumièges, William de Poitiers, Orderic Vitalis and William of Malmesbury. Like most of them, Wace employed the device of the long, concocted speech; and this makes much of what his characters say on these occasions difficult to credit. However, he also prided himself on his skills as a historian: by making use of monastic charters and oral traditions to supplement the standard narratives, for example, the *Roman de Rou* contains information about the events of the eleventh and early twelfth centuries not found elsewhere. It is a valuable source which, despite its distance from the events it describes, has a good claim to be taken seriously.[18]

As well as telling us nearly everything we know about the life of William de Poitiers, Orderic Vitalis also provides information about the man who may have been the author of another controversial source. According to Orderic, Guy, bishop of Amiens wrote a poem about the Battle of Hastings 'in imitation of the epics of Virgil and Statius, abusing and condemning Harold but praising and exalting William'. Guy was the brother of Count Hugh II of Ponthieu and well connected more widely to the aristocracy of northern France. He was close to Duke William and his family, and Orderic also recalls how he accompanied

Queen Matilda to England in 1068, by which time he had completed his poem.[19] If Guy did write an account of the battle, therefore, he was ideally placed to use eye-witness testimony and first-hand accounts to compile it, and when in the nineteenth century two twelfth-century manuscripts of a poem, one a copy of the other, describing the Battle of Hastings were found, it made sense to attribute them to Guy. This source, now known as the *The Song of the Battle of Hastings* (*Carmen de Hastingae Proelio*) contains one of the most detailed accounts of the battle.[20] Some of its scenes have become famous: the defiant antics of the Norman minstrel Taillefer at the beginning of the battle, for example. And the account of the death of Harold in the *Carmen* is unique: far from being killed by an arrow in the eye, Harold was spotted on the crest of a ridge, attacked, killed and dismembered by the counts of Boulogne and Ponthieu, accompanied by Duke William himself. The accuracy of these descriptions is questionable by modern standards, of course, and they contain a good deal of consciously mythical elements. These may have been the author's own descriptions, or reflections of rumours, stories and developing legends that he had picked up by the time he wrote. But it is the authenticity of the work as a whole which has given rise to most argument. It has been claimed that the *Carmen* is not the work of Bishop Guy at all, but a twelfth-century fabrication, a literary fantasy with no merit as a historical source.[21] More recently, though, strong arguments have been made once again that the poem was indeed written by Guy, and that the *Carmen* should be taken seriously. It is in the end impossible to be certain of its overall reliability as a source for the Norman Conquest, and it must be considered alongside other surviving accounts. In that respect it differs little from any of the other sources under discussion here.[22]

Just as contentious as the *Carmen* in its own way is the Bayeux Tapestry. It is not a conventional documentary source, of course, but this matchless survival provides its own distinctive narrative of the events it describes, beginning with the visit of Earl Harold of Wessex to France, which probably took place in 1064 or 1065. Technically an embroidery rather than a tapestry, its origins and purpose remain in the end obscure. During the eighteenth and nineteenth centuries, the myth developed that the Tapestry was the work of William the Conqueror's queen, Matilda. But there is no evidence to support this theory, and it is now discounted. It is generally accepted, however, that the Tapestry was made in the eleventh century, soon after the Norman Conquest, and that its production was closely connected with the city of Bayeux. The prevailing view, indeed (despite some recent attempts to bring it into question), continues to be that the Tapestry was probably commissioned by Odo, bishop of Bayeux and probably made in southern England.[23] Odo was William the Conqueror's half-brother and, after 1066, earl of Kent. Odo himself as well as the city of Bayeux feature prominently in the events depicted in the Tapestry, and he is one of the few individuals to be named in the Latin captions which briefly describe its scenes. If he was the Tapestry's patron, therefore, it must have been completed (at Canterbury, perhaps, within Odo's earldom, by some of those English seamstresses whose skills William de Poitiers praised in the *Gesta Guillelmi*) before Odo's fall from royal favour in 1082.[24]

The Tapestry is much more subtle and complex than this attribution might suggest, however. Its portrayal of the Battle of Hastings is extraordinarily dramatic, for example, and provides good evidence of eleventh-century military techniques and equipment. But, unlike the works of William de Jumièges and William de Poitiers, the conquest of England and the justice of William I's cause are arguably not its principal concerns. If the Tapestry was designed to be displayed in Bayeux cathedral (and most scholars still think that it was), this was not to pander to Bishop Odo's vanity, but rather to warn those who saw it of the spiritual power of relics, the significance of oaths and the dangers of breaking them.[25] This interpretation helps explain why the first third of the Tapestry's length is taken up with Harold's trip to France prior to the invasion of 1066 and why, throughout the Tapestry, Harold plays a more prominent role in events than William I. The scene in which Harold takes the oath to William is probably the formal climax of the work.[26] Everything depicted in the early part of the Tapestry is a prelude to the oath-giving ceremony, and everything which follows it is a result of Harold's failure to abide by what he had sworn and provides an object lesson in what happened to those who failed to appreciate the sanctity of oaths. For an account of 1065–6 which was sponsored by a leading Norman, the Tapestry is notably sombre and subdued in tone; and its attitude towards the vanquished Harold is almost neutral. In order to give as much prominence and clarity as possible to its moral message, it quite deliberately omits the rhetorical flourishes and angry hostility to Harold found in particular in the work of William de Poitiers.

Wales and Scotland produced little to compare with the copious narrative accounts of the eleventh and twelfth centuries which survive from England and Normandy. The native Welsh chronicle, *Brut y Tywysogyon* or *The Chronicle of the Princes* is of immense value and gives an account of the main events of Welsh political history from the seventh century to the 1330s; but the surviving versions are Welsh translations of a lost Latin original, which were compiled at the Cistercian abbey of Strata Florida at the end of the thirteenth century. The passage of time between the events described in the *Brut* and the compilation of its three extant texts needs to be borne in mind.[27]

Much of what is known about Scottish (and Welsh) affairs during this period comes from English sources, particularly the *Anglo-Saxon Chronicle* and the work of John of Worcester. The partiality they are likely to display should always raise questions about their accuracy and reliability. There are also scattered references of relevance to Scottish affairs in other places, too: in certain Irish annals or Norse sagas, for example. And later Scottish chronicles do deal with this earlier period to some degree.[28]

Authentic and contemporary Scots voices are certainly few and far between, however. Indeed, 'in the west the prize for poverty of native sources before the twelfth century surely goes to Scotland'.[29] Nevertheless, some English sources with northern preoccupations, such as Symeon of Durham's *Libellus de Exordio* and, to a lesser extent, his *Historia Regum*, can throw valuable light on the obscurities of border politics either side of 1066.[30] A monk at Durham from the early 1090s, Symeon composed the *Libellus* in the early 1100s. It presents a history of the ecclesiastical community at Durham from its origins in the seventh century until the death of Bishop William de St Calais (who was probably Symeon's patron) in 1096. The *Historia Regum* was also produced at Durham during the first half of the twelfth century, but it is in fact a composite volume which Symeon may simply have compiled from several different works, including those by William of Malmesbury and John of Worcester already in existence. If Symeon wrote any of it himself, it was probably only the last section, which covered the period 1119–29, and those earlier parts with specifically northern concerns.[31]

Another Durham monk, Turgot, was probably also the author of a biography of Queen Margaret of Scotland in the first decade of the twelfth century. Written at the request of Margaret's daughter, Matilda, Henry I's queen, it may have been designed principally to make the case for Margaret's canonisation, and so it needs to be used cautiously. Nevertheless, it does contain much information about Margaret's attempts to reform the Scottish Church.[32]

Administrative sources

Chronicles and histories form only part of the written evidence available to the historian of the Norman Conquest. Coins, for example, have been used to analyse the political and economic strength of late Anglo-Saxon England, to demonstrate the extent of its continental and Scandinavian connections, and to illustrate elements of continuity and institutional survival after 1066. Anglo-Saxon kings regularly issued law codes, too. They were often designed to serve as statements of royal ideology as much as practical, working texts. Fewer codes were produced in the eleventh century than the tenth, but after 1100 documents purporting to record the laws of Edward the Confessor and William the Conqueror were compiled. And some chronicles contain accounts of important legal disputes, such as the trial of William de Saint-Calais, bishop of Durham at the court of William II. Important lay and ecclesiastical magnates also issued documents of their own which cast light from time to time on the events of the Conquest. Barons might issue charters granting land or privileges to their vassals or a church, or they might prepare wills. And it has been said that 'students of the Anglo-Norman Church have reason to be grateful that Lanfranc was an indefatigable correspondent'.[33] Lanfranc's position as archbishop of Canterbury and chief adviser to William I gave him a unique insight into events, and his letters, dealing with such events as the Revolt of the Earls in 1075, cast invaluable light on some of the main events of the period.

The official documents produced by the main protagonists are of prime importance, too. Most such documents survive from England, a testimony to the administrative sophistication of royal government by 1066. The dukes of Normandy used writing in government, too;

and this despite Orderic Vitalis's observation that, until the middle of the eleventh century, the Normans 'devoted themselves to war rather than reading or writing books'. Originals or copies of over 230 ducal *acta* (documents produced in the name of the duke) survive from pre-conquest Normandy, although none from before the 960s.[34] The rulers of Wales and Scotland did not, so far as is known, issue their own documents before the twelfth century. As for England, developments in the nature and content of royal documents are discussed in Chapter 8, but it is worth noting here that approximately 350 writs and writ-charters survive from England after the beginning of the reign of Aethelred II in 978; most as later copies, but some in their original form. After 1066, writs, charters and diplomas continued to be produced by the royal administration in England; and many of these, of course, concerned Normandy. In Normandy itself, however, 'documents written according to the formulae of English writs' only came into regular use after 1106; and even then, their use was more limited than in England.[35] David Bates's monumental collection of the *acta* of William I runs to 1,000 pages and contains over 350 documents.[36] Over 200 of William II's *acta* survive in some form; and over 1,500 survive from the whole of Henry I's reign, the earliest of which concern the period covered by this book. Such documents, which might contain commands or records of transactions, were direct expressions of the royal will. They also show the king dealing with his important subjects, managing his economic, military and spiritual resources, and (through the witness lists attached to many of these documents) how the composition of the royal court changed over time. They reveal the power of English royal government in action.

So, too, does arguably the single most extraordinary record, official or otherwise, produced during the Norman Conquest – Domesday Book. In 1085, William I ordered a great survey of England to be carried out. According to John of Worcester, the king wanted to know 'how much land each of his barons possessed, how many enfeoffed knights, how many ploughs, how many villeins, how many animals and what livestock everybody had from the highest to the lowest in all his kingdom, and what rent could be obtained from every estate . . .' The results of this survey are preserved in two volumes now known as 'Great Domesday' and 'Little Domesday'. Great Domesday contains information about all the English shires south of the Tees except Norfolk,

Suffolk and Essex. The returns for these three counties make up Little Domesday; they were never written up in their final form. There are other gaps, too: London was never surveyed, for example, and nor was Winchester, probably because such projects were too complex to undertake in the available time. Despite this, the wealth of detail the survey gives about landholding in England both before and after the Norman Conquest is astonishing. It does not just describe the situation at the start and end of William I's reign, however; it tells us about the highly developed administrative systems of late Anglo-Saxon and early Norman England; it is our chief source of information about eleventh-century English society as a whole; and, for reasons discussed in Chapter 9, about how that society changed as a result of the events of 1066. It is no wonder that Domesday Book acquired its ominous name: contemporaries could think of nothing as final and conclusive other than the Last Judgement itself.

Writs, charters, diplomas and Domesday Book were the official products of English royal government during the period covered by this book. Another such product, the first so-called 'pipe roll', is also very important even though it dates from 1130.[37] Much more about this will be said in Chapter 8. It is enough to say here that the pipe roll is the record of an audit of the accounts of each sheriff held towards the end of 1130 at the royal exchequer which, by this time and from obscure origins, had developed into the chief financial department of royal government. The 1130 roll is the first of its kind to survive, and the only one from Henry I's reign. It sets out in great detail the amounts of money paid into the royal coffers by the sheriffs, and the amounts owed to the King from a whole range of sources. Estimates of income from the end of Henry I's reign need to be treated cautiously in any discussion of the 40 years before 1106, of course. However, the 1130 pipe roll is useful in revealing the likely sources of much of the revenue, and therefore power, available to William I and William II as well as Henry I.

Because they appear to deal with straightforward matters of fact (the appointment of an individual, the record of a payment or the grant of some land, for example), it is tempting to regard these administrative sources as objective and neutral evidence of what they record. They need to be treated, however, with just as much caution and care as the narrative sources described earlier. Writs, charters and the like are often difficult to date, for example; so they cannot be fitted into a chronology as neatly as might be desirable. Sometimes, too, there are doubts about the authenticity of a particular document: is it what it purports to be, a later revision or even a forgery? If it is one of the latter, in what circumstances was the document altered or invented? And even if a document is genuine and datable, its significance may be unclear without a clear appreciation of the wider context in which it was made; and this, because the narrative accounts are so often inconclusive, may be unavailable. All of the sources for the Norman Conquest will continue to raise as many questions as they answer.

Notes

1 *OV*, ii p.191.

2 B ends in 977; F is a version of the original of E; G is a copy of part of A; H is merely a fragment; and A has 'so many serious gaps in it as to be of little use': R. Allen Brown, *The Norman Conquest of England. Sources and Documents* (Woodbridge: Boydell Press, 1984), p.50.

3 Stephen Baxter, 'MS C of the *Anglo-Saxon Chronicle* and the Politics of Mid-Eleventh Century England', *EHR* 499 (2007), pp.1189–227.

4 *ASC* 'D'. s.a.1066.

5 *JW*, ii pp.xviii–xx.

6 *Vita Edwardi*, pp.xvii–lxxviii.

7 *WMGR*, ii pp.xxxv–xlvi.

8 John Gillingham, 'The Beginnings of English Imperialism', in *The English in the Twelfth Century: Imperialism, national identity and political values* (Woodbridge: Boydell Press, 2000), pp.3–18, quotation at p.13.

9 *HH*, pp.xiii–xxxii.

10 John Gillingham, 'Henry of Huntingdon and the Twelfth-Century Revival of the English Nation', in *The English in the Twelfth Century*, pp.123–44.

11 *HN*, pp.vii–xiii.

12 Hugh the Chanter, *History of the Church of York, 1066–1127* ed. and trans. Charles Johnson, rev. M. Brett, C.N.L. Brooke and M. Winterbottom (Oxford: Clarendon Press, 1990).

13 *WJ*, i ch.1; Dudo of St Quentin, *De Moribus et Actis Primorum Normanniae Ducum*, ed. J. Lair (Caen, 1865); translated as *The History of the Normans*, ed. E. Christiansen (Woodbridge: Boydell Press, 1998).

14 *WP*, pp.xv–xxxv.

15 Below, pp.29–30.

16 *OV*, i pp.1–115.

17 *WP*, pp.xxxv–xxxix.

18 *The History of the Norman People, Wace's Roman de Rou*, trans. Glyn S. Burgess (Woodbridge: Boydell Press, 2004), pp.i–xlvii.

19 *OV*, ii pp.184–7, 214–15.

20 *The Carmen de Hastingae Proelio of Guy Bishop of Amiens*, ed. and trans. Frank Barlow (Oxford: Clarendon Press, 1999).

21 R.H.C. Davis, 'The *Carmen de Hastingae Proelio*', *EHR* 93 (1978), pp.241–61.

22 *Carmen de Hastingae Proelio*, ed. Barlow, pp.xxiv–xl; M.K. Lawson, *The Battle of Hastings 1066* (Stroud: Tempus, 2003), pp.89–94, outlines the debate.

23 For statements of the standard view as expressed here, see, for example, *The Bayeux Tapestry, A Comprehensive Survey*, ed. F. Stenton (London: Phaidon Press, 1957) and N.P. Brooks and H.E. Walker, 'The Authority and Interpretation of the Bayeux Tapestry', *ANS* 1 (1978), pp.1–34. For alternative views about the authorship and purpose of the Tapestry see, for example, W. Grape, *The Bayeux Tapestry: Monument to a Norman Triumph* (Munich and New York: Prestel, 1994); S.A. Brown, 'The Bayeux Tapestry: why Eustace, Odo and William?', *ANS* 12 (1989), pp.7–28; A. Bridgeford, 'Was Count Eustace II of Boulogne the Patron of the Bayeux Tapestry?', *Journal of Medieval History*, xxv (1999), pp.155–85.

24 *WP*, p.177; *BT*, pls.25, 48, 67.

25 It has been suggested that the Tapestry was designed to be displayed in the hall of a great lord rather than in a large church: see S.A. Brown, 'The Bayeux Tapestry: A Critical Analysis of Publications, 1988–1999', in *The Bayeux Tapestry. Embroidering the Facts of History*, ed. Pierre Bouet, Brian Levy and François Neveux (Caen University Press, 2004), pp.27–47, and the works referred to on p.31.

26 *BT*, pls.25–6.

27 *Brut y Tywysogyon or The Chronicle of the Princes. Peniarth MS. 20 Version*, ed. and trans. T. Jones, 2 vols (Cardiff: University of Wales Press, 1941–1952), and *Brut y Tywysogyon or The Chronicle of the Princes, Red Book of Hengest Version*, ed. and trans. T. Jones (Cardiff: University of Wales Press, 1955).

Versions of the lost Latin original do survive: see *Annales Cambriae*, ed. J. Williams ab Ithel (Rolls Series, 1860) and *Chronica de Wallia*, ed. T. Jones (Cardiff: University of Wales Press, 1946).

28 *Early Sources of Scottish History, AD 500 to 1286*, ed. and trans. Alan Orr Anderson, 2 vols (Edinburgh: Oliver & Boyd, 1922; repr. with corrections, Stamford, 1990); Alan O. Anderson, *Scottish Annals from English Chroniclers, AD 500 to 1286* (London: D.N. Nutt, 1908; repr. with corrections, Stamford, 1991).

29 A.A.M. Duncan, *The Kingship of the Scots 842–1292: Succession and independence* (Edinburgh University Press, 2002), p.8.

30 Symeon of Durham, *Libellus de Exordio, Atque Procursu Istius, Hoc est Dunelmensis, Ecclesie. Tract on the Origin and Progress of this the Church of Durham*, ed. and trans. David Rollason (Oxford: Clarendon Press, 2000); Symeon of Durham, *Historia Regum* in *Symeonis monachi opera omnia*, ed. T. Arnold, 2 vols, Rolls Series 75 (London, 1882–5).

31 *Libellus de Exordio*, ed. Rollason, pp.xlviii–l.

32 Turgot of Durham, 'Vita sanctae Margaritae Scotorum reginae', in *Symeonis Dunelmensis opera et collectanea*, ed. J.H. Hinde, Surtees Society 51 (1868), pp.234–54; Lois L. Huneycutt, 'The Idea of the Perfect Princess. The *Life of St Margaret* in the Reign of Matilda II (1100–1118)', *ANS* 12 (1989), pp.81–97.

33 *EHD* II, p.7; *The Letters of Lanfranc Archbishop of Canterbury*, ed. Helen Clover and Margaret Gibson (Oxford: Clarendon Press, 1979).

34 *OV*, ii p.3; *Receuil des Actes des Ducs de Normandie (911–1066)*, ed. M. Fauroux (Caen University Press, 1961).

35 D. Bates, 'Normandy and England after 1066', *EHR* 104 (1989), pp.851–80 at pp.862, 872–3.

36 *Regesta Regum Anglo-Normannorum. The Acta of William I (1066–1087)*, ed. David Bates (Oxford: Clarendon Press, 1998).

37 *Pipe Roll 31 Henry I*, ed. J. Hunter (London: HMSO, 1833).

CHAPTER 2

Britain and Normandy in the eleventh century

Lands and peoples

O n 11 May 973, the *Anglo-Saxon Chronicle* records, Edgar, 'ruler of the English', was consecrated king in a ceremony at Bath. Immediately following this ritual, Edgar sailed with his fleet to Chester, 'and six kings came to meet him, and all gave him pledges that they would be his allies on sea and on land'.[1] Other sources state that there were in fact eight kings who met Edgar at Chester, including Kenneth, king of Scots, Malcolm, king of the Cumbrians, and Maccus, 'king of many islands'. Then,

[Edgar] boarded a skiff; having set them [the eight kings] to the oars, and having taken the helm himself, he skilfully steered it through the course of the river Dee, . . . [and] he is reported to have declared to his nobles at length that each of his successors would be able to boast that he was king of the English, and would enjoy the pomp of such honour with so many kings at his command.[2]

Many uncertainties surround these famous events. Edgar had been king of the Mercians since 957 and king of the English since the death of his brother Eadwig in 959. Why was he therefore being consecrated in 973? Edgar was 30 in that year, the same age as Christ when he began his ministry, and this may have been significant. The identities of the eight kings he met at Chester are open to some question, too, although the idea that John of Worcester's list is merely an invention has been largely discounted.[3] More generally, it is far from clear what the significance of these events was at the time. What did it mean when the eight British kings swore that they would be Edgar's faithful allies? Were they recognising his superiority over them, or accepting him as an equal? The fact that they rowed the boat whilst Edgar steered has usually been taken as an expression of their subordination to him; this seems to be what Edgar thought, too, but it may not have been the view held by the oarsmen.

In one sense, Edgar was simply building on the successes of his predecessors. In 927, following successful military campaigns in northern England, Aethelstan, king of the Anglo-Saxons, had received the submission of the Northumbrians and the Scots, the Welsh and the Britons of Strathclyde. In the words of the *Anglo-Saxon Chronicle*, 'he brought under his rule all the kings who were in this island'. Ten years later, in 937, he defeated the rebellious Scots and their Norse allies at the Battle of Brunanburh.[4] At some time between these two events, Aethelstan had also started to describe himself in his documents and on his coins, first as 'king of the English', and then as 'king of the whole of Britain' (*rex totius Britanniae*). And, to be fair, no king before him had a better claim to such an exalted title. However, what power Aethelstan had evaporated soon after his death, and no English monarch before the eighteenth century, not Edgar in 973 and not even Edward I at the end of the thirteenth century, was able convincingly to make another case for having direct control over the entire island of Britain.

These events are mentioned here, however, not to demonstrate the authority of the tenth-century English kings over their British neighbours (at best this was only ever intermittent and fragile), but to introduce the idea that Britain at the close of the first millennium was an island inhabited by different 'peoples' under the authority of different rulers. There were English, Scots and Welsh, but within these general classifications there were also Mercians, West Saxons, Northumbrians, Galwegians, men of Strathclyde, Lothian, Gwynedd, Powys and many more. These peoples had different origins; some had inhabited Britain for centuries, others for a much shorter time. The political, economic and social systems they lived under were of diverse kinds, languages varied from region to region, and local customs were distinctive. Nevertheless, these peoples shared with each other and with most of their contemporaries in continental Europe some basic assumptions: their societies were highly-stratified along lines of wealth and status; they relied on bonds of family and lordship for security and support; their lives were supported by an essentially non-monetary economy; and there was an all but universal acceptance of Christianity. It would therefore be wrong to imagine clear, defined boundaries separating the various peoples of Britain, either from one another, or from peoples elsewhere in most of Western Europe. And if the specific details of inheritance practices or methods of production diverged from area to area, and if the particular shapes of hierarchies of power contrasted, their essential features were often not radically dissimilar.

Most of the inhabitants of England in the eleventh century were descended from invaders who had begun to come to southern Britain from northern Europe following the end of the Roman occupation in the fifth century. These invaders had referred to themselves as 'Angles' and 'Saxons' after their areas of origin and had soon set up independent kingships at the expense of the indigenous population, the Britons, who were forced west by the newcomers. These British refugees, most of whom came to settle the area west of the great fortified dyke built by King Offa of Mercia in the eighth century, were known to their eastern neighbours as 'the Welsh'. Further north, and notwithstanding Aethelstan's and Edgar's efforts to bring the area under their authority, the local population remained largely untouched by these changes taking place in the south. However, eleventh-century Scotland bore only a partial resemblance to the country as we know it today. The kingdom of Scots proper (*Scotia*) stretched, broadly speaking, east of a line running from Glasgow to Perth up to the Moray Firth. It was mountainous nearly everywhere and widely covered by thick belts of pine forest. Surrounding *Scotia* were islands controlled by the descendants of Norwegian invaders, Orkney and Shetland to the north, and the Hebrides to the west. The Scandinavian influence also extended as far south on to the Scottish mainland as Dingwall. The rulers of Argyll and Caithness were effectively independent. Meanwhile, to the south of *Scotia* were the remnants of the old British kingdom of Cumbria or Strathclyde, which reached from Dumbarton in the north to the Lake District in the south. It had its own king until 1018, but became a Scottish client state thereafter. Finally, north of Cumbria to the west lay Galloway whilst to the east, between the rivers Tweed and

Forth, was Lothian, the northern part of the old English kingdom of Northumbria.

Lothian had been brought under the king of Scots' rule by the end of the 1020s, and thereafter the Tweed was usually accepted as the eastern border between the English and Scottish kingdoms. Despite this, there remained plenty of scope for uncertainty about where the dividing line lay between English and Scottish political power in the eleventh century. Such uncertainty was heightened by the linguistic, cultural and economic features which lowland Scotland and northern England had in common. A much sharper line divided the kingdom of Scots, where Scots and English were spoken, from the Gaelic-speaking, Scandinavian-influenced regions to its north and west. Offa's Dyke, by contrast, provided a somewhat firmer physical frontier between the English and the Welsh, and the gulf which separated them was deepened by the kind of clear differences in language, society and culture which did not exist to the north. The northern and western boundaries of the eleventh-century English kingdom may have had different characteristics, therefore, but they were alike in their political volatility; and it was along the fault lines between these areas of fluctuating English, Welsh and Scottish influence that much of the course of British history was to be played out for the rest of the Middle Ages and beyond.

The political and economic supremacy of the English amongst the peoples of Britain was always likely to be maintained, however. For one thing, whilst numbers alone were not sufficient to ensure dominance, there were always more English in Britain than Welsh or Scots. It is impossible to give precise estimates of population for this period, because the necessary evidence is so lacking; but it has been suggested that Britain as a whole is unlikely to have had a population of more than 4.5 million in the mid eleventh century. Domesday Book has been used to suggest that the population of England amounted to something between 1.1 million and 2.5 million in 1086, with most of these in the south and east. In Wales and Scotland, no equivalent information is available and highly speculative figures of 300,000 and 1 million respectively have been put forward. The combined population of Scotland and Wales, however, may have been anything between 1.5 million and 2 million.[5] These differences in population size are largely attributable to the fact that the lands inhabited by the English (about 60 per cent of the island) were so much more fertile, productive and profitable than those inhabited by the Welsh and the Scots. England was predominantly a lowland country suited to widespread arable farming, and this inevitably made its economy stronger than those of Wales and Scotland. Its landscape was also diverse, however, and offered more numerous and varied ways of working the land than elsewhere in Britain. It contained great forests, wooded plains and valleys, mountains, downs and moorland as well as marshes and fens.

One thing many of the different British peoples possessed, however, was their own particular sense of identity. The term 'English people' (*gens Anglorum*) had been coined by Pope Gregory the Great in the sixth century to describe the Germanic inhabitants of south-eastern Britain. It had been given more prominence, however, by Bede in his *Ecclesiastical History of the English People*, which was finished in the early 730s; and it had remained pervasive ever since.[6] For Bede, although there were differences between the Anglo-Saxon peoples who had settled in England, not least in the variety of their political arrangements, they were held together by the unifying power of their shared Christian faith. His work expressed in its clearest form the origin myth of the English people and 'gave Englishness a powerful ideological and moral foundation'.[7] The idea of the *gens Anglorum* was taken further by King Alfred at the end of the ninth century as part of his attempt to present a united front against Viking attacks. He promoted the use of the vernacular form of the Latin term, *Angelcynn*, to describe all those Christians under his rule.[8] Then, as the West Saxon kings built on Alfred's foundations to extend their rule across England in the tenth century, they were able to utilise a common language, a common currency and increasingly uniform political and ecclesiastical structures further to foster the development of the idea of a single people under a single king. It would be dangerous to press this too far, though, and regional differences remained obvious within England in 1000. Most evidently, large parts of eastern, central and northern England (collectively known to historians as 'The Danelaw') had been colonised by Scandinavian settlers during and after the Viking attacks of the ninth and tenth centuries; and these more recent arrivals in Britain had a profound influence on the political, economic and cultural history of these areas. Even so, it is probably fair to say that, by the second half of the eleventh century, few of those who lived south of the Tweed and east of Offa's Dyke would have denied that they were English.

Meanwhile in Wales, internal natural frontiers were provided by rivers, estuaries and mountain ranges. Travelling was difficult, so loyalties were primarily local and there was no central region or consistently dominant political power which might serve as foci for wider unity. Social structures, settlement patterns and agricultural practices also varied from region to region. But despite all this, the native Welsh still viewed themselves as part of *Cymry*, a people or community from the same region, and Wales was recognised by contemporaries either side of its borders in the eleventh century as a single, coherent unit in a cultural, linguistic and legal sense. The Welsh had a distinctive and different identity, therefore, which set them apart from the rest of the inhabitants of Britain. As early as the eighth century, they were conscious of their descent from a common origin, the Britons of old, and they took pride in their shared mythology and traditions, which were perpetuated by professional bards, poets and storytellers.[9] A common language was another unifying factor. It is worth stressing that the absence of political unity was no bar to the formation of a sense of national consciousness based on shared cultural, legal and linguistic patterns: as a result, in the eleventh century, 'The Welsh . . . by no means lacked the concept of themselves as a people and of their country as one.'[10]

In Scotland, by contrast, there was little if any developed sense of a distinctive 'Scottish' identity at the start of the eleventh century. There was a long-standing notion that the Scots and the Irish were a single people, the *Gaídil*, and it persisted into the fourteenth century.[11] However, the extent to which such ideas circulated beyond the circle of Scotland's 'men of letters' is unclear, and there were probably more obvious obstacles in the way of the development of 'Scottishness'. Like Wales, northern Britain was divided into regions by its landscape; and there was no obvious geographical, political or commercial centre, either. But unlike Wales, it was inhabited by a variety of different peoples (Scots, Picts and Norse, to name only a few) and there was no single language: Gaelic and Scots were the two 'native' tongues, but English would have been spoken in some lowland areas to the south, and various Scandinavian dialects in the north. The ceremonial centre of Scottish kingship was at Scone on the river Tay, although the core of the king's political strength lay across the lands which stretched north from Lothian up the east coast to the Moray Firth. However, in 1000 royal supremacy both within and beyond the king's area of immediate control was far from secure. Occasionally, Scottish royal power was extended at the expense of local rivals. In 1018, for example, Malcolm II won a famous and decisive victory over a Northumbrian army at Carham on the Tweed. As a result, Malcolm's possession of all of Northumbria as far south as the Tweed was formally recognised by the English authorities. Such successes were infrequent, however, and did little at the time to foster the growth of any distinct idea of 'Scottishness'. It was not until the second half of the eleventh century that royal control over Scotland began to extend more widely; and it was in the wake of this process that a clearer sense of a single Scottish identity began to develop. Important foundations were laid in this context when Malcolm III 'Canmore' became king of Scots in 1057. The dynasty he established lasted until the end of the thirteenth century and gave a sense of stability and tradition to Scottish politics; after all, 'it was as kingdom and then as community, that Scotland was put together'.[12] The Scottish Church, with its spiritual centre at St Andrews, was also to be instrumental in fostering ideas of 'Scottishness', when in the twelfth century it resisted the claims to ecclesiastical supremacy over Britain made by the archbishops of Canterbury and York. These developments had barely begun, however, when the Normans invaded England in 1066.

The duchy of Normandy at the start of the eleventh century, like the kingdom of England, was a very recent creation. Its origins are best understood in the wider context of French politics during the tenth and eleventh centuries. The early medieval Frankish monarchy had attained its widest extent and prestige under Charlemagne at the start of the ninth century. The empire he built did not survive intact for long after his death, however, and by the start of the tenth century there were separate monarchies for the east and the west Franks which, eventually and in broad terms, became respectively the kingdoms of Germany and France. By the early 900s, the west Frankish king was styling himself *Rex Francorum*, king of the Franks. Despite the grandness of this title, however, his power and authority continued to shrink during the tenth century, and new units of political authority began to emerge, which were eventually to become the great territorial principalities of northern France. Normandy was one of these; others included Flanders, Anjou and Aquitaine. A crisis for the Frankish monarchy came in 987 when a new royal dynasty, the Capetians, was established. Although the first Capetians were able men, it was not long before the area under direct royal control had contracted to a small area around Paris and Orléans. According to Bates, 'The Capetian monarchy in the eleventh century is therefore best considered as just another territorial principality, albeit one whose ruler bore the title of king.'[13]

It was not just the collapse of the Carolingian Empire which led to the emergence of the northern French principalities, however. From the end of the eighth century, north-western Europe had been under attack from the Vikings. King Alfred in England managed just to prevent a Scandinavian takeover of the whole of England during the 870s and 880s, although he was in no position to do anything about the significant Scandinavian settlement which took place in eastern, midland and northern England thereafter. Meanwhile, in north-western France, the persistence of the Viking raids combined with the lack of a strong, centralised authority to coordinate resistance to them led to local compromises being made with the invaders. One such agreement was made in 911, Dudo of St Quentin records, when Charles the Simple, king of the West Franks, agreed to grant an area of land in the region of the lower Seine, including Rouen, to the leader of one band of Viking invaders called Hrlófr (the Latinised version of his name, 'Rollo', is more commonly used). In return, Rollo agreed to be baptised and to help the French king repel other invaders. It is at this point that the history of Normandy truly begins.[14]

Rollo survived until the late 920s or early 930s. During the 20 years or so of his rule, he succeeded in colonising new lands up the Seine valley towards the sea, whilst his son and successor, William I 'Longsword', in the face of serious opposition from his Breton neighbours, managed to expand his control into the Avranchin and the Cotentin. By 942, when William was assassinated on the orders of the count of Flanders, the lands he controlled covered most of what was to form the duchy of Normandy. William was succeeded by his young son Richard I (942–96) who, after surviving a difficult minority and securing his inheritance, oversaw a period of relative stability and consolidation in Normandy. Economic and political connections with Scandinavia were retained, but at the same time the province became more and more assimilated into its Frankish, Christian environment. By the time Richard died in 996, Normandy's government, social structure and Church had developed; even the Scandinavian language had largely disappeared, and Normandy was 'accepted as one of the integral principalities which made up the greater realm of France'.[15] Even so, it is important to remember that whatever assimilation did occur amongst the peoples of northern France during this period was not total; Rollo's descendants were always Normans, never Franks.

Normandy had few well-defined geographical boundaries. In the north, of course, it was bordered by the sea, but to the south, east and west there was much less clarity about the precise position of the frontiers, and little by way of physical features to define an obviously 'Norman' area of influence. At the same time, within the expanding province, there was considerable ethnic diversity. Some Scandinavian settlement took place before and after 911, but the achievements of Rollo and his successors do not appear to have encouraged mass migration, and the indigenous population of the north-western French seaboard was far from overwhelmed. And there were probably as many newcomers to Normandy from other parts of France as there were from Scandinavia during this period. Nevertheless, by the end of the tenth century, outsiders were coming to accept the permanence of what was turning into Normandy; and the Norman people themselves, despite the differences between them, had also developed clear views about their special qualities as a distinct people (the *gens Normannorum*) with its own characteristics. The reign of Richard II was crucial in this context. As will be seen, his involvement with English affairs had a significant bearing on the course of events leading up to the Norman Conquest. In France, meanwhile, Richard was not a great conqueror, but his reputation as a ruler who preserved the peace and security of Normandy seems to have been deserved.[16]

What is more, the earliest forms of the very name 'Normandy', *terra Normannorum* ('the land of the Northmen') or just *Normannia* or *Nortmannia*, are recorded during Richard's reign, too; and he was the first ruler of Normandy regularly to style himself 'duke'. His predecessors had tended to refer to themselves as 'count of Rouen', but in taking steps to ensure the security of their frontiers they had appointed members of their own family to positions of responsibility and given them the title of count, too. A more prestigious designation was required for the ruler himself, and by referring to himself as duke, Richard II was expressing his desire to be seen as something more than first among equals.[17] Yet further coherence was given to the idea of 'Normandy' by Dudo of St Quentin, who wrote the first history of the Norman people at Richard II's court during the 1020s, and laid in the process the foundations of what historians often refer to now as 'the Norman myth'. He claimed that the Normans had two chief qualities: first, they were warlike and, second, they were shrewd in argument and had a propensity for cunning and deceit. In his hands, and in those of William de Jumièges and William de Poitiers later in the eleventh century, the events of early Norman history acquired a spurious precision and a misleadingly clear sense of direction which ignored the messy realities of tenth-century state-building. As Bede had done for the English, it was Dudo and his successors who most clearly expressed the origin myth of the Norman people and who 'laid down the written foundations for the Norman sense of the past'.[18] In reality, of course, there was nothing distinctively Norman about the dukes' drive to expand; this was a 'ubiquitous impulse' among the rulers of the principalities of northern France in the eleventh century.[19] Emphasis was deliberately given in the writings of Dudo, William de Poitiers and William de Jumièges to the idea that the Normans were extraordinary and special, however; quite simply, they claimed, the Normans were destined to triumph over their foes. This is certainly what William the Conqueror thought, according to Orderic Vitalis. As he lay dying in 1087, the king reflected on the singular qualities of his Norman subjects: 'if the Normans are disciplined under a just and firm rule, they are men of great valour, who press invincibly to the fore in arduous undertakings, and prove their strength by fighting resolutely to overcome all enemies'.[20] By 1066, therefore, the Normans had a strong sense of ethnic identity. Underpinned and helped to develop further by the institutions of ducal government and the Church, '*Normanitas* was no flimsy construct ready to crumble under the slightest pressure'.[21]

Polities and power

All the rulers of eleventh-century Britain and Normandy would have travelled constantly around their lands to see that they were being administered properly, to eat their produce, and to show their faces to their people. Medieval government was a very personal business, and the successful projection of a dominant, charismatic character was central to the way any prince asserted his power. All, too, would have spent their days and nights surrounded by the members of their own households: wives, children and extended family would have been present; domestic staff would have cooked, sewn and washed; huntsmen would have cared for the dogs and the birds; priests would have said mass and heard confession and, as the literate members of the household, handled their lord's administrative needs; military men would have provided hunting and feasting companions as well as a bodyguard and an élite force in times of military need. Beyond the household, however, the practical power of these different rulers varied. Most powerful within Britain was the king of England. As has been seen, there were differences between the regions of England, but in some fundamentally important ways it was a unified kingdom by 1066. This was the achievement of the kings of Wessex who, since the middle of the tenth century, had been acknowledged as kings of the English at least as far north as the Tyne and often as far as the Tweed, as far west as Offa's Dyke and as far south as Cornwall. These kings had the sole right to raise taxation for national purposes, to issue coins in their name and to publish laws which purported to apply to the whole kingdom. There was a single vernacular language, too, which the kings used in their official documents. Government in writing, by contrast, appears to have been unknown to the rulers of eleventh-century Scotland and Wales.

Further underpinning the English kings' power were comparatively robust systems and institutions. In return for their protection and patronage, the English Church gave the kings legitimacy and, through the ceremony of consecration at the start of their reigns, a unique position amongst laymen as God's designated agents on Earth. They also had at their disposal an administrative structure which covered most of the kingdom. By 1066, all of England, with the exception of the region north of the river Tees to the east of the Pennines and the river Mersey to their west, and the anomalous area of Rutland, was divided into shires, each under the control of a 'shire-reeve' or 'sheriff'. The sheriff was the king's principal representative on the ground, with day-to-day responsibility for supervising the collection of taxes, presiding over the shire court, and raising and perhaps leading military forces when required to do so. He also administered the king's lands in his shire and collected their revenues. The sheriff kept the latter in return for paying the king a fixed amount every year (the 'farm'). The shires were in turn subdivided into hundreds (in southern England) and wapentakes (in the Danelaw, that area which had been under the control of the Vikings until the mid tenth century), which were administered by reeves. Each hundred had its own court, which met once a month. Below the level of the hundred were the vills, which had their own reeves as well. There were plenty of regional customs and variations within this system, and neither its relative sophistication nor its comprehensiveness should be overstated. Nevertheless, it was sufficiently uniform and regular to give a significant degree of organisational cohesion to English local government in the mid eleventh century, and to provide a meaningful link between the royal centre and the regions.

The actual reality of royal power in eleventh-century England needs to be examined, however. To be sure, the English kings were the most powerful rulers in Britain, but even within their own kingdom their authority was not uniformly strong. They were significantly weaker in the north and the far west than in the south, primarily because they were unable or unwilling to spend much time there and rule directly, but also because, in northern England particularly, the Scandinavian element within English society, with its own traditions, culture and usages, had taken deep root since the ninth century. When William the Conqueror arrived in England, Orderic Vitalis records, he found that, 'in the northern and western extremities of the kingdom an unchecked savagery had ruled until now and, under Edward the Confessor and his predecessors, those areas had disdained to obey the king of England unless it suited them'.[22] Orderic's claims of 'savagery' may be exaggerated, but controlling their frontiers remained a problem for the English kings well beyond this period. And there were other constraints acting upon them, too. A ruthless and imaginative ruler such as Cnut could use the system he inherited to reinforce and extend his control. However, a less masterful character, such as Aethelred II or Edward the Confessor, might struggle to maintain his pre-eminence in practice. And as much depended on circumstances as on personalities: Cnut became king when England was exhausted after a quarter of a century of war, and he faced little by way of opposition. Edward the Confessor, meanwhile, had a problematic inheritance in 1042; he lacked a landed power-base of his own and an established network of supporters. Arguably he never recovered from his difficult start. What all kings had in common, however, was the need successfully to manage their most powerful subjects, collectively their *witan* ('wise men'). This was not a formal council with a fixed membership; the king could take advice from anywhere he chose. However, along with the leading churchmen, it was the earls and thegns of Anglo-Saxon England who mattered most politically, whose goodwill and support the king needed to keep and whose advice he needed to heed. A successful king was able to inspire loyalty and instil fear in his great men as circumstances required. This was a difficult task, however. Edward the Confessor failed to master his magnates and was in the end dominated by them.

England's earls ranked directly below the king in terms of authority. Their office derived ultimately from that of the *ealdormen* of ninth-century Wessex, most of whom had been responsible for enforcing royal rights and carrying out royal orders within an individual shire. By the end of the tenth century, however, individual ealdormen had become more powerful and tended to wield authority over several shires at once. Under Cnut, they came to be called earls (from the Old English *eorl* which roughly translates as 'noble'), and it was during his reign that Leofric, Siward and Godwine appear as holders of this title in Mercia, Northumbria and Wessex respectively. The number and size of earldoms was not fixed, and a fourth major earldom by the mid eleventh century was East Anglia. The powers of the earls were not clearly defined, either. In effect, they functioned as representatives of the king in the shires under their control. The king could not exercise his authority everywhere in person, and he needed men who kept the peace, administered justice and raised armies in his name. The earls could not carry out all of these duties on their own either, however, and they needed the help of the sheriffs within individual shires and the five thousand or so thegns who dominated English local society at this time. Many of these men were substantial landholders with property far in excess of the five hides of land (a medium-sized manor, perhaps) needed to qualify as a thegn. Domesday Book pulls back the curtain on a landed élite of about ninety men in England in 1066 who dominated local society and whose advice and assistance contributed to the conduct of affairs of state. Some of these would be so–called 'king's thegns' who served in the royal household and had the ear of the king. In turn these great men and other wealthy thegns would also have households of their own. In these would be lesser thegns, the holders of perhaps a single manor or two, who owed service and loyalty, albeit probably undefined, to their lord. They would serve with him in wartime. The thegns also carried out important administrative responsibilities in their localities, particularly in the shire court. Without their active participation and cooperation, the administrative and military systems on which the king relied would have collapsed.

The kingdom of Scots had been created as recently as that of the English. It was ruled in the eleventh century by the line established by Kenneth MacAlpin (840–58), who has traditionally been credited with destroying the last Pictish kings and imposing Gaelic customs and language throughout his lands. As a result, Kenneth holds a place in Scottish history comparable to that of King Alfred in England. Whether these developments were really down to Kenneth is difficult to say. And whatever the extent of his achievements, it remained the case that the powers of the eleventh-century Scots kings were significantly less extensive than those of their English neighbours. Whilst they went through an inauguration ritual at Scone on the river Tay, for example, they were not consecrated, which made their kingship less prestigious. There was also nothing remotely as mature as the English system of shires, hundreds and wapentakes to bolster the Scottish king's power. Having said this, and although evidence is not available from the mid eleventh century, it may be that already by then the Scots king's own estates had been divided into units known as thanages. This is certainly what was happening by the later twelfth century when these lands were being administered by officials called thanes. The thanes were responsible for collecting renders in kind from the occupants of the estates, and so in this sense at least, carried out similar duties to the sheriffs in England.

There were also sub-regions within the Scottish kingdom, something akin to the English earldoms, which were ruled over by *mormaers*. Traditionally there were seven *mormaers*, but in practice the number varied. Like the English earls, they were royal officers but, much more so than in England, there was the potential for them to become in effect largely autonomous local rulers. The power of the kings was strongest in the centre around Perth, in Fife and Gowrie, where the thanages were most densely collected. Beyond these areas and farther west, in Strathearn and Athol, and north into Buchan, the power of the *mormaers* tended to be greater because royal lands were less extensive.

At least in Scotland a single king would ultimately provide a focus for loyalty; unlike in Wales where local rulers dominated and political violence and fragmentation were the order of the day. There were three main 'kingdoms' in eleventh-century Wales: Gwynedd in the north, Powys in the centre and Deheubarth in the south. The boundaries between them and the smaller kingdoms were dictated to a large extent by rivers and mountain ranges; and because there was no central region which might serve as a focus for unity, loyalties were bound to be primarily to regional rulers. Each kingdom had its own ruler, but whilst these men might sometimes have styled themselves kings, they lacked most of the substance that title implies.[23] There is no evidence to suggest that they went through any inauguration or consecration ceremony, and they were usually little more than local warlords with a military following that depended on its leader for plunder through continuous raiding and ravaging of neighbouring areas. There are indications that Welsh kings occasionally had some sort of role in the law-making process, in giving judgements and in exacting tribute and other forms of taxation. However, securing power and keeping it was the limit of their ambitions for most Welsh rulers. The conventions about how a Welsh king was chosen also added to the unstable mixture. Sons were expected to succeed fathers, it seems; but if several sons succeeded in turn, there was the potential for disputes between their sons and 'in effect segmentation, that is alternation between different branches of the same family, became characteristic'. Political in-fighting and dynastic disputes (particularly between siblings and cousins competing for control) were therefore the norm in Welsh politics, and there was little by way of structures and institutions to make the kings' powers more wide-ranging or permanent. By the end of the eleventh century, each kingdom was gradually becoming divided into smaller areas known as *cantrefs* and even smaller units called *commotes*; but these were recent and unfinished developments. Overall, it has been said that 'the administrative machinery of early medieval Wales was extremely rudimentary'.[24]

The political dominance within Britain of the English kings was underpinned by the administrative structures just described; but it was based ultimately on their wealth. They made money from the operation of the legal system, and from their attempts to regulate internal and foreign trade, for example. Merchants paid tolls, and trading communities might pay lump sums for the privilege of being exempt from such dues. Certain trading activities could only take place at designated royal centres with royal officials overseeing the transactions. More significant, however, was the money the king made from his lands. He received an annual payment or 'farm' from the sheriff of each county, but he also made money from the lands he kept under his own direct control (his 'demesne'). Much of the king's demesne would have been leased out in return for rent, payable in cash, foodstuffs or services. Surplus produce could be sold by the king's agents at local markets. He therefore had a financial interest in the development of both the urban and rural economies. The administrative division of England into shires, hundreds and wapentakes also facilitated the levying of a land tax, or 'geld', across most of the country. The tax was originally levied during the reign of Aethelred II (978–1016) in order to pay off Danish invaders and protect the kingdom against fresh attacks. It was controlled at the centre, administered locally by the sheriff and assessed on property. The 'hide' was the basic unit of land measurement in Anglo-Saxon England; it originally represented the amount of land required to sustain a family for a year. The size of the hide, therefore, was not fixed, but varied according to the value and resources of the land involved. Geld was usually collected, perhaps as often as annually, at the rate of two shillings per hide. It has been estimated that the normal yield from such a tax would have been about £6,000, but it was also capable of raising much larger sums, as it did during the first half of the eleventh century. In 1051, Edward the Confessor appears to have suspended the levying of geld for the purpose of funding armies, although it is not clear why he did this.[25] It is also not clear whether he continued to collect the tax for other reasons, or whether he ever raised the unpopular army geld again during his reign. As will be seen, however, later kings certainly did so well into the twelfth century.

Linked to the king's wealth and England's system of taxation was the coinage. Neither the Scots nor Welsh rulers used coins in the eleventh century, but by 1042, the English coinage was superior to any other in north-west Europe, and the system for administering it was well established. The minting of coins was a royal monopoly. Dies were produced in London and silver pennies of standard design were then produced by some sixty mints, staffed by royally-licensed moneyers, located across southern and central England (the only northern mint was at York). The high quality and geographical spread of the coinage are important indicators of how far royal power was acknowledged across the kingdom; and the king's image and title on the coins were visible manifestations of royal power. But the importance of the coinage to the king was more than symbolic. He made money from it, too. Local moneyers would pay to acquire their centrally-struck dies, and a new coinage was regularly issued, sometimes as often as every three years, at which time weights and designs might be altered. Only coins of the current type were legal tender; so when the designs changed, old coins had to be brought to royal centres and exchanged for new ones. For this privilege, people might pay as much as 15 per cent of the value of their old coins. Some of this would be kept by the moneyer, but the bulk would be pocketed by the king.

The duke of Normandy also had at his disposal by 1066 well-established structures and institutions which can only have enhanced his power. By then, it has been said, Normandy 'was a polity which was well organised, administratively traditional, and politically centralised and coherent to a remarkable degree'.[26] Having said this, the ducal administration was less developed than the royal one in England. The dukes did issue charters and coins, but the quality of both was poor by English standards. What counted for more in the end, however, was the considerable wealth the duke derived from his lands scattered across the duchy and from a range of other fiscal rights and commercial strategies. Details of when and how taxes were levied are elusive, but several different types of tax are mentioned in the second half of the eleventh century. The eleventh-century dukes certainly do not seem to have been short of cash. William the Conqueror's generosity was famous and explains in part why he was able to recruit support for his invasion of England from areas outside Normandy.[27]

There was also a system of local administration within Normandy which allowed a masterful duke to intensify his control and look to extend it further. In the tenth century, the rulers of Normandy had relied on the counts they appointed (often close members of their family) to control exposed areas on the Norman frontier. In the eleventh century, however, new officials emerged, the *vicomtes*. Comparable to the English sheriffs, they had a range of financial and military responsibilities, and they were generally supposed to supervise the enforcement of ducal rights and customs. They were each responsible for an administrative district called a *pagus*, a remnant of the Carolingian administrative system. In the second quarter of the eleventh century, during a period of notable ducal weakness following the death of Duke Richard II and continuing through the turbulent minority of William II, control of the *vicomtes* passed into the hands of a number of powerful aristocratic families, amongst which were the Montgomerys, the Beaumonts and the Montforts. These families dominated eleventh-century Normandy and displayed their wealth and status by building castles and founding monasteries. Such developments could have led to the fragmentation of power and the enfeeblement of ducal authority within Normandy. Duke William II, however, was able to reassert his power in the years following his victory at Val-ès-Dunes in 1047. The judicious use of force, a clever cementing of kinship ties through marriage within the duchy, and the promise of reward by aggressive campaigning outside it enabled William to secure the loyalty and service of the *vicomtes* and of other leading Norman families. The Norman aristocracy by 1066 has been described as 'almost a hand-picked group' and as 'more than an aristocracy; first and foremost they were a family'. The help these men gave their duke was crucial in and after the invasion of England.[28]

Military organisation

The Scottish armies that regularly terrorised northern England in the eleventh and twelfth centuries were notoriously ferocious. They were not just disorderly savage bands, however, and there seems to have been some organised system of military service within the kingdom, super-vised by the *mormaers*, whereby specified numbers of men were pro-vided for the army. How far this worked in practice is impossible to say. From Wales, meanwhile, there is little to suggest the existence of any formalised obligation to serve a particular ruler. Nevertheless, Welsh or Scottish forces could occasionally overcome an English army, or inflict significant damage on English interests. In 1052, for example, Gruffudd ap Llewelyn raided Herefordshire and defeated local forces near Leominster; and in 1055, with the help of the exiled Earl Aelfgar of Mercia, he overcame local troops who had been made to fight on horse-back by their French earl, Ralph, and sacked Hereford. And no less than five times during his reign, Malcolm III launched expeditions south-wards from the kingdom of Scots. However, their successes were short-lived and there always remained a huge gulf between English military strength and that of the Welsh and the Scots. From across the Channel, however, the English king would face more formidable opponents.

Unfortunately there is little firm evidence that clearly demonstrates how English or Norman armies were raised and organised before 1066. In the seventh and eighth centuries, royal hosts in England were small and comprised mainly the king's own retainers and their followers. The obligation to serve derived from the personal bond between a man and his lord, and in some senses little had changed by the eleventh century. There was still no standing army as such, and the household retainers permanently with the king and each great magnate would have formed the nucleus of the national force or *fyrd*. These men might be called *housecarls* in the sources, but this Scandinavian term does not denote any difference of function or status from the English 'thegn'. Men might serve with their lords for a number of reasons. If they had been granted land by them, military service could have been expected in return, although this was not inevitably the case. Others might have served in the hope of being granted land or other rewards in due course. Others would serve with the king simply because it befitted their rank to do so; not necessarily as a result of any formal requirement based on landholding.

Developments had occurred during the eighth and ninth centuries, however, as a result of the Viking invasions of England and the intro-duction of a new form of land tenure, bookland. Bookland (land granted by a *boc* or diploma) was held in perpetuity by the recipient, rather than loaned for life as had hitherto usually been the case. The successors of the original beneficiary would not necessarily see themselves as personally bound to the original grantor of the land or his successors, and so military service might not continue to flow automatically from this new legal relationship. To deal with this, the Mercian kings of the eighth century introduced the concept of the 'common burdens': all those in Mercia who held bookland were obliged to assist in the performance of bridge and fortress work, and to serve in the *fyrd* on land or at sea. In the ninth and tenth centuries, firstly as a response to Viking attack and then as part of their attempts to conquer the Danelaw, the kings of Wessex extended the imposition of the common burdens to all those in their expanding kingdom who held by bookland. The amount of service owed by a particular individual was determined by the number of hides at which his lands were assessed; and this in turn was based on the value of the estate. Thus, in Edward the Confessor's day in Berkshire, according to customs recorded in Domesday Book, 'if the king was sending out an army anywhere, only one soldier went out from each five hides, and for his provision or pay four shillings for two months was given him from each hide'. This process of selection was probably designed to provide a better-trained and better-prepared force of troops. The members of this 'select' *fyrd* were probably provided for and equipped by those who stayed behind. There were also other forms of obligation in different parts of England: it was the custom in Chester, for example, for the walls of the city to be repaired by one man from each hide in the county.[29] It is impossible to gauge the extent to which such arrangements either existed or were enforced across the kingdom, but if England in 1066 was comprised of roughly 80,000 hides, as has been suggested, then the Berkshire arrangements applied throughout the kingdom would have recruited more than 15,000 men for the *fyrd*. Not all of these men would have been of thegnly status, and it is very unlikely that all of them would have served at the same time. Nevertheless, the performances of English troops against the Danish invaders during the opening quarter of the eleventh century, and their efforts in the battles of 1066 demonstrate that they were much more than just an ill-disciplined peasant mob.

There was more to the military system of pre-conquest England than ground troops, however.[30] First, there were also the *burhs*, fortified sites scattered throughout England which served as troop stations and refuges for local communities in the event of external attack. They had been established and used most effectively during the reign of King Alfred (871–99). During the 880s and 890s, he constructed a network of such sites, strategically placed throughout his kingdom of Wessex. They acted as a barrier to Viking invasion in the last decade of his reign and made it impossible for the invaders to penetrate into the heart of southern England. The *burh*s were also centres of population and trade. However, their military and political importance was reinforced during the first quarter of the ninth century, when Alfred's son Edward the Elder, and his daughter Aethelflaed, extended the rule of the kings of Wessex over most of central England. Wherever they went, their chosen tactic was usually to build a *burh* as a reminder of royal power and as a means of local control. How the burghal system developed after this is harder to say. Little is heard of it during the reigns of Aethelstan and Edgar; Exeter was destroyed by a Danish army in 1003, and only the resilience of London in the face of Danish attack towards the end of Aethelred II's reign serves as a reminder of how formidable these fortified sites could be.[31] Under Edward the Confessor and Harold II there is similarly little comment on the continuing effectiveness of the *burh*s. London was still sufficiently daunting for William of Normandy to avoid attacking it directly after Hastings, however, and the prolonged resistance to the Normans shown by the people of Exeter in 1068 may have been made possible by a reconstruction of the fortifications there after the events of 1003.

Despite all of this, however, it is difficult to argue that the burghal system was as integral to the Anglo-Saxon military system in 1066 as it had been in the 890s. Of much greater importance was sea power. There was nothing new about this in the eleventh century, although the trad-itional view that King Alfred was the effective founder of the Royal Navy is erroneous. He may have had ships built on a new design, but they do not appear to have been very successful; and, moreover, his predecessors had appreciated the importance of fleets, too.[32] There were probably professional sailors in any particular royal fleet; but beyond this, the obligation to serve at sea in the *scipfyrd* was as general as that of serving on land in the *fyrd*, and part of the common burdens. The *Anglo-Saxon Chronicle* contains plenty of references to the royal fleet in the eleventh century. In 1008, two years after the arrival of 'the great fleet' of Danish ships on English soil, Aethelred II 'ordered that ships should be built unremittingly all over England'. They were designed 'to protect this country from every invading army', and the chronicler's horrified reaction to their self-inflicted destruction in 1009 provides strong evidence of how central to the English defensive strategy they were thought to be, and suggests strongly that these ships were not just troop carriers: whilst they were probably better suited to blockading estuaries and coastline, and to coastal raiding, they had an offensive capacity, too.[33] Edward the Confessor also appears to have been a keen sailor. In 1045, the 'D' text of the *Chronicle* tells us, Edward 'collected a great naval force at Sandwich because of the threat of Magnus of Norway'. Then, in 1048, after Magnus's death and following attacks on the Isle of Wight by pirates, 'King Edward and the earls went out with their ships'. And in 1049, Edward 'went to Sandwich and stayed there with a large naval force' after a request for assistance against the count of Flanders from the Emperor Henry III.[34] In 1063, a fleet under Earl Harold's command intimidated the Welsh into submission as it sailed around the coast, and in 1066, in response to the threat of an imminent invasion from Normandy, King Harold 'assembled a naval force and a land force larger than any king had assembled before in this country'. One version of the *Anglo-Saxon Chronicle* hints at there having been a naval encounter between Harold and Duke William in 1066 before the latter's invasion. And according to William de Poitiers, Harold stationed a fleet of 700 ships in the English Channel to cut off a Norman retreat after William had landed.[35] Much attention is rightly given by historians to the perceived strengths and weaknesses of the English infantry in 1066; but it should not be forgotten how important naval power was to the security of Anglo-Saxon England.

In pre-conquest Normandy, meanwhile, military arrangements were probably even more flexible and less precisely defined than in England. It is important to emphasise this general point, because it was once thought that William I brought with him to England in 1066 a developed and fully articulated system of military obligations owed by his leading subjects to him, and that he simply imposed this extant system upon England after becoming king.[36] At the heart of this interpretation was the idea that pre-conquest Normandy was 'one of the most fully developed feudal societies in Europe'.[37] In other words, in return for their lands, Normandy's great men were obliged to supply the duke at their own expense with a fixed number, or quota, of armed men, who were obliged in turn to perform military service of some kind to the duke for a fixed period of time, probably 40 days. There is some evidence which lends some support to this view: having been captured at the Battle of Mortemer in 1054, for example, Count Guy of Ponthieu was only released from prison after agreeing to perform homage to Duke William and to perform military service for the Duke every year with a hundred knights. Wace describes how, during the discussions immediately prior to the invasion of England, William FitzOsbern reminded the Norman baronage of the military service they owed their duke for their lands; although the author may be displaying his twelfth-century expectations at this point.[38] And military service might be owed in terms of ships as well as land forces. A document which dates from the middle third of the twelfth century, but which may be a copy of one prepared originally in the late 1060s or early 1070s, provides a list of the number of vessels owed to Duke William in 1066 by 14 of his followers, as well as details of the knights owed by 4 of them. Robert of Mortain and Odo of Bayeux owed 100 and 120 ships respectively, and the total owed amounted to 776 ships and 280 soldiers. Wace's description of similar obligations is sufficiently different from the ship list to suggest that he was not relying on it for his information, and this tends to bolster the general reliability of the two accounts. However, it is not clear from either source how long-standing these obligations were, or how regularly they were enforced.[39] Moreover, whilst service in return for land is mentioned quite often in Norman documents of the eleventh century, the nature of the service in question is hardly if ever specified, and there is little to suggest that it was inevitably military in nature.[40]

Beyond this, conclusions in support of the idea that pre-conquest Normandy was a 'feudal' state have relied mainly on evidence which post-dates 1066, such as ducal charters issued after the invasion of England and records of obligations owed by Norman abbeys and monasteries as late as the 1170s. The leading modern authority on pre-conquest Normandy, David Bates, indeed, has shown that 'feudal' terminology was used loosely and imprecisely in the duchy before 1066 and that obligations were ill-defined and ties between individuals were of various kinds.[41] The duke had the right to call out a universal levy of freemen; but this was hardly likely to produce a body of well-trained, professional troops.[42] As in England, therefore, the core of his army would have been made up of household retainers and the military entourages of his leading vassals; paid troops from outside the duchy were also employed, most notably in 1066. Others would perform military service to the duke, perhaps because they had agreed to do so in return for land; but this was just one way amongst the many, varied and imprecisely defined ways in which the ties between the duke and his leading subjects might be expressed. In the end 'service was governed by need', and if the duke's expectations of his men were evolving by 1066, that was probably because it was simply not sensible to resist William's demands. Moreover, it has been suggested that it was the exigencies of the 1066 campaign which might finally have led to a clearer definition and regularisation of those military services which the vassals of the king-duke were supposed to provide on both sides of the Channel. The ship list referred to above may be an example of how vague and poorly-defined expectations of service were formalised into fixed obligations in order to meet the needs of a unique crisis.[43]

What did distinguish the military infrastructure of pre-conquest Normandy from that of pre-conquest England, it has been argued, was the presence of castles. As will be seen, the extent of this difference might have been exaggerated; nevertheless, it should not be ignored. There may have been some fortified structures in eleventh-century England more akin to castles than *burh*s, but there were certainly not many: mottes (large, man-made mounds of earth with flattened tops on which some kind of fortified structure could be built) were erected before 1066 at Hereford and Ewyas Harold, and there may have been another at Richard's Castle. However, all of these were in Herefordshire (the only other possible pre-conquest castle site is Clavering in Essex), an area dominated for a time during Edward the Confessor's reign by a Frenchman, Earl Ralph, who may have been responsible for introducing these continental devices as well as Norman cavalry techniques. The absence of castles in England before 1066 is attributable largely to the sustained period of peace the kingdom had enjoyed since 1016. This is not to say that England was untroubled by political arguments during this period, or that there was no violence between members of the aristocracy. However, the disputes of 1051–2 and 1064–5 were ended by compromise, and personal rivalries never spilled over into uncontrolled aggression. Therefore, there was simply no need for castles or for anything like them. When the Normans arrived, however, the lack of readily defensible sites contributed significantly to the English defeat. Orderic Vitalis's view about England's military shortcomings after 1066 was surely correct: 'the fortifications called castles by the Normans were scarcely known in the English provinces and so the English – in spite of their courage and love of fighting – could put up only a weak resistance to their enemies'.[44]

By contrast, it has been argued that there were castles in Normandy in the tenth century, and that 'in the eleventh there is ample evidence of new ones being built both by the duke and his magnates'.[45] The Bayeux Tapestry at least seems to support this, as does William de Jumièges, who describes how, during William II's minority 'many Normans built earthworks in many places and erected fortified strongholds for their own purposes'.[46] Castles, along with cavalry, it has been said, 'were integral to the intensely competitive military and political environment in France'.[47] Others have suggested, however, that the current state of knowledge about castle-building in pre-conquest Normandy does not support such conclusions. The Tapestry depicts several castles, but only one in Normandy, at Bayeux; and William de Jumièges did not mention any castles by name when he described how their numbers multiplied in the first half of the eleventh century.[48] Indeed, most of the few strongly defended sites which appear to have existed in Normandy before 1066 belonged to the duke or his kinsmen, and most members of the Norman aristocracy appear to have lived in a ringwork or a fortified enclosure, not a motte and bailey. There is also little evidence of building in stone in Normandy before 1066, and many Norman castles may in fact date from the late eleventh or early twelfth century. To be sure, political circumstances in Normandy during the 1020s and 1030s may have been turbulent enough to encourage some to defend their residences more strongly, but 'castle-building in pre-1066 Normandy was restricted to a small élite'.[49] Once again, it may have been the unique circumstances the Normans encountered in post-conquest England, rather than any desire simply to replicate what they were familiar with from home, which prompted the rash of castle-building in England after 1066.

Some of the best evidence of the different military tactics employed by English and Norman armies in 1066 comes from the Bayeux Tapestry. At Hastings, central to the English army's strategy, as it had been for centuries by then, was the shield wall. Designed to absorb the shock of enemy attacks, this defensive structure was made by men standing closely together in lines with their shields interlocked. The successful deployment of the shield wall and its maintenance in the heat of battle would have required discipline and confidence, and these could only result from training and practice. The Tapestry portrays almost all of the men in the English shield wall wearing mailshirts or hauberks and helmets and carrying kite-shaped shields and spears.[50] They appear to be acting as a coherently organised unit, although perhaps the evidence of the Tapestry should not be interpreted too literally here. Less formally engaged in battle are those mailed and helmeted English infantrymen shown in the Tapestry wielding axes and swords and holding round shields. It has been argued that these weapons were suited to the needs of those fighting in open rather than close order, and that their role in battle was quite different from that of the men in the shield wall.[51]

The Tapestry also shows other elements within the English army. Lightly armed infantry ferociously defend a hillock against a Norman onslaught at one particularly dramatic point in its depiction of the battle.[52] They wear no mail and are bare-headed; most carry spears and small kite-shaped shields, whilst one, with his sword hanging at his side, stands at the foot of the hillock swinging his two-handed axe. There are even suggestions on the Tapestry that the English employed archers at Hastings; certainly, a single bowman stands in front of the shield wall, and, given his position, it can be assumed that he is supposed to be English. Whether he really could be seen as 'representative of lines of missile troops who skirmished in front of the heavy infantry before retiring to the rear as the enemy approached', is more debatable, however. It is equally likely that the single archer is meant to show how few of Harold's troops had actually turned up by the time the battle began.[53] Nevertheless, it is fair to suggest that large English armies by the late eleventh century were probably made up of several different types of fighting unit, all of which had their own responsibilities on the battlefield. The level of organisation and range of experience required to recruit, deploy and control these armies were formidable, and the speed and extent of the English response to the military demands of 1066 were all the more remarkable given that the kingdom had been largely at peace since 1016. Of course, English armies were not always successful, but the very narrowness of Duke William's victory at Hastings, coming as it did for the English so soon after Fulford and Stamford Bridge, showed how tough and resilient they could be.

Whether the English ever fought willingly on horseback is another thorny question. In 1055, Earl Ralph of Hereford, Edward the Confessor's nephew but also a Frenchman, was defeated in battle by Earl Aelfgar and his Welsh ally Gruffudd ap Llewelyn: 'before any spear had been thrown', the *Anglo-Saxon Chronicle* records, 'the English army fled because they were on horseback'. John of Worcester adds that the English lost because they were ordered to fight on horseback 'contrary to custom'.[54] The conventional wisdom, indeed, holds that the English did not use cavalry in battle: they rode to the battlefield, fought on foot and remounted in order either to flee or to pursue a defeated enemy. This is what happened, according to William de Poitiers, when the English arrived at Hastings: 'At once dismounting from their horses, they lined up all on foot in a dense formation.'[55] And there is certainly little to suggest that the horse was seen by the late Anglo-Saxon military élite as anything much more than a sign of status and a means of transport. In this regard the Normans and their French allies were quite different, for troops of heavily armed cavalry were central to their tactics and to their ultimate effectiveness as a fighting force. Together at speed, the specially-bred horse and its rider, mailed and helmeted with a shield in one hand and a spear in the other, constituted an awesomely powerful projectile against which an individual foot soldier would have little chance. On the Tapestry, Harold's brothers Gyrth and Leofwine are killed by individual mounted warriors.[56] And if groups of these mounted troops operated together (and it is thought that this is how they trained, in units of five or ten known as *conrois*), the weight of a charge was potentially devastating. One late eleventh-century contemporary, who witnessed French cavalry in operation during the early stages of the First Crusade, thought the charging Frankish knights capable of piercing the walls of Babylon; and it was the shock from this sort of attack which, as the Bayeux Tapestry shows, the English shield wall was intended to absorb.[57] In the end, and with fateful consequences, it was unable to take the strain.

It would probably be wrong to think that the effectiveness of the French cavalry at Hastings was based simply on its weight and its speed, however. If William de Poitiers's account of the feigned retreats employed by the cavalry during the battle is to be believed, these troops were capable of carrying out difficult and sophisticated manoeuvres which must have required intensive training and regular practice.[58] Despite their obvious importance, though, and despite their prominence in the Tapestry, it would probably also be wrong to think that the heavy cavalry formed the overwhelming bulk of Duke William's forces during the battle. William de Poitiers places them in the third line of battle, behind the archers and the infantry.[59] There are few depictions of the latter on the Tapestry; but as Duke William lifts his helmet to show his troops that he is still alive, the lower margin of the Tapestry is filled with loosely-clothed, bareheaded bowmen getting into position for what proves to be the decisive phase of the battle.[60] Like the English armies of the eleventh century, therefore, French ones were composed of different kinds of fighting men. Each army at Hastings had its strengths: the English were well-suited to a defensive battle, whilst Duke William's cavalry allowed him to be more aggressive from the outset, as he needed to be. However, the closeness of the battle should always be borne in mind. Had Duke William rather than King Harold been killed at Hastings, as nearly happened more than once, the Norman invasion would have ended in disastrous failure; and had the English shield wall still stood as darkness gathered on 14 October 1066, William's chances of becoming king would have been seriously if not completely under-mined. As will be seen in Chapter 4, however, whilst good fortune contributed to Duke William's triumph at Hastings, his victory was ultimately attributable to the superiority of the Norman military machine. And if the duchy was not the equal of England in political, economic or cultural terms by 1066, a lucky, determined and superbly able Norman duke had resources at his disposal sufficient to present his English neighbour with an unstoppable military challenge. Indeed, it has been argued that, by the mid eleventh century, the Norman élite 'formed the most disciplined, cooperative warrior society in Europe, capable of a communal effort – the conquest and subjugation of England – that was not, and could not have been, mounted by any other European political entity'.[61]

Economies

This was an overwhelmingly agrarian age, and the majority of the British and Norman populations in the eleventh century supported themselves through farming of some kind. As a result, like all the peoples of northern Europe, they were vulnerable to the inconsistencies of the weather and the inevitability of disease. Technology was basic, as was scientific understanding of the climate and of animal husbandry. The means to avert disaster were simply not available; consequently, poor harvests, famine and sickness amongst livestock and people were common, and contemporary sources were understandably concerned to record and lament such things. According to the *Anglo-Saxon Chronicle*, for example, 'there was no one alive who could remember so hard a winter as that was [in 1046–7], both for pestilence and murrain'; whilst in 1054, 'there was so great a pestilence amongst cattle that no one remembered anything as bad for many years'.[62]

English land was still the most fertile in Britain, however, especially in the southern and central regions, where much of it was low-lying and used for arable cultivation. Here the population was at its most dense, and the farming of wheat in these areas was more profitable than the growing of hardier crops such as oats and rye and the pastoral farming which was prevalent on the generally higher pastures, moors and mountains of Wales and Scotland. This is not to say that there was no arable farming in these areas; far from it, and the best Scottish and Welsh land was able to support a mixed agrarian economy. Nevertheless, England's economy was the most developed in Britain, and whilst eleventh-century yields must generally have been much lower than modern ones, in a normal year England probably produced more grain than it needed to feed its population. Where arable farming was impossible, thousands of sheep and cattle (small and thin ones, admittedly, compared with later periods) grazed on good-quality grassland and produced meat, milk, cheese, hides and, above all, wool. Other natural resources were available in England, too: tin in Cornwall, lead in Cumbria and iron ore in the Forest of Dean, for example. And there was also a developing export trade, particularly with Scandinavian traders, who would have exchanged their furs for English wheat and cloth; with Flanders where the developing cloth trade was greedy for English wool; and with southern Europe where leather, silk, spices and gold might be found.

The foreign silver which was brought into England by such activity could be coined as money bearing the king's image. One indicator of the kingdom's wealth is the amount of money in circulation during the eleventh century. If the sources are to be believed (and there has been some dispute about their reliability in this context), huge sums were regularly paid out by the English government to deter the attacks of Danish invaders during the first half of the eleventh century, and the amounts involved suggest that there were mountains of silver pennies in the kingdom. According to the *Anglo-Saxon Chronicle*, for example, between 991 and 1012, £137,000 was paid by the English authorities to ward off the attacks of Danish invaders, and another £82,500 was raised by Cnut in 1018 immediately after he became king.[63] It has been estimated that, in 1086, there were approximately 9 million silver pennies in England, worth roughly £37,500.[64]

By contrast, there was no coinage in Wales, and none in Scotland until the kings there began producing one in the 1130s. The Welsh and Scottish rulers were generally much poorer than their English neighbour, too. They had less land to profit from and what they had was less fertile. Rents from their tenants tended to be paid in kind rather than cash. However, such comparisons should not be pushed too far. Even in England there was only one form of currency, the silver penny, and whilst this may have been useful for buying livestock or bulk supplies of goods, or for paying rents and taxes, it was too valuable for small-scale everyday transactions. For most of their basic needs, English people, like their Welsh and Scottish neighbours, were necessarily self-sufficient; and they would have bartered for much of what they were unable to produce themselves.

As for Normandy, 'the duchy possessed what was for the eleventh century a highly developed money economy'.[65] That is to say, the use of cash was common for everyday transactions, and payment in kind appears to have been unusual. The duchy was prosperous, too, as the prevalence of such practices would suggest. New towns were being established and earlier settlements expanded at places like Caen, Alençon and Falaise. The ducal centre of Rouen was well placed to take advantage of trading opportunities with Scandinavia as well as with

Western Europe and areas far beyond. The rural economy appears to have been thriving, too, and more land was being cultivated, presumably in response to the demands of a growing population. The number of churches both large and small built in the duchy during this period is further evidence of economic buoyancy. Overall, it has been said that eleventh-century Normandy should be placed 'among the wealthiest regions of contemporary western Europe'.[66]

A 'town' in this eleventh-century context has been defined as 'accommodation deliberately constructed for residents not involved in agriculture' and as a settlement with 'a permanent concentration of population, some hundreds at least, who made their living from a variety of non-agricultural occupations'.[67] There were no such places in Scotland in 1066 and, as far as Wales at this time is concerned, it has been said that 'the picture is not merely one of minimal urbanisation but also of minimal trend towards urbanisation'.[68] In the absence of centres of commerce and trade, economic growth was bound to be slow. The eleventh-century Norman dukes appreciated this; they encouraged the growth of Caen as a port and Rouen was already a noted trading centre by 1000. In England, too, probably between 6 and 10 per cent of the pre-conquest population lived in towns, making it a highly urbanised kingdom by contemporary standards. The two hundred or so years before 1050 had been a time of urban expansion in England: more towns were established and more people left the countryside to live in them. Sometimes a town had grown up around one of the fortified *burhs* established by King Alfred and his successors to meet the threat of the Vikings in the ninth and tenth centuries; others might have become established around a royal mint or minster church. Royal legislation stipulating that certain types of goods could only be traded in specific places under the supervision of royal officials might also lead to urban development. By 1066, England had more than a hundred towns, about thirty of which had populations of between 1,000 and 5,000. Most were concentrated in southern and particularly eastern England. The most northerly was York. The five most important towns in England in 1066 were: Winchester, Norwich and Lincoln, with populations of between 5,000 and 10,000, York with probably more than 10,000 inhabitants, and London with perhaps as many as 25,000. The range of occupations followed within these English towns was extensive. With their blacksmiths, leather-workers, potters, tailors, dyers and goldsmiths they were centres for manufacturing. Because there were also butchers, bakers, brewers and fishmongers among the inhabitants, they were centres of food distribution both for fellow townspeople and those of their country cousins who came to town to sell their surplus agricultural produce. Most trade was of this kind, locally-based. The towns required food and this led to increases in agricultural production. In return, the traders and craftsmen in the towns met the countryside's needs for professionally made tools, clothes and the occasional luxury.

Important though towns were, however, it remained the case that most of England's wealth in the eleventh century, as in the rest of Britain and beyond, was generated in the countryside. Any discussion of this area is fraught with technical and terminological difficulties. However, some general observations can be made. In Scotland and Wales, whilst there were certainly exceptions to this general pattern, most people lived in dispersed hamlets and farms – larger nucleated settlements were rare, and there were no recognisable towns before the middle of the eleventh century, as has been seen. In very general terms in this context, it has been said, 'the Celtic regions in the twelfth century looked rather like eighth-century England'.[69] Such comparisons should be treated with caution because the survival of Domesday Book allows so much more to be known about the pre-conquest English economy than either the Welsh or Scottish ones. And despite that economy's undoubted relative sophistication, the everyday lives of most English people in 1066 were probably not very different from those of most Welsh and Scots. Probably nine out of ten of them lived in one of the 13,000 villages or hamlets which are identified in Domesday Book, and worked in the surrounding fields. In Yorkshire, Lincolnshire, eastern England and Kent, and in much of Wales and Scotland, so-called 'multiple estates' predominated.[70] These comprised a central settlement under a lord's direct control, to which the inhabitants of outlying subsidiary settlements rendered goods, money and, less often, labour services. In parts of northern England, such areas of seignorial authority, by no means as large as a county, might confusingly be known as 'shires': Hallamshire in Yorkshire is one example. In the east, by contrast, they might be referred to as 'sokes'. In much of southern and midland England, meanwhile, most people lived on a 'manor'.[71] These varied in size, but a typical manor might consist of a number of houses grouped together, a church or chapel and perhaps a large house belonging to the lord. Such an arrangement constituted the classical 'nucleated' village. The village would have been surrounded by two or three large fields, one of which would be left uncultivated or 'fallow' every year to serve as grazing land for the villagers' livestock; the animals in their turn would restore its fertility with their manure. At the heart of a manor or a multiple estate was the lord's 'inland' – the core lands which he controlled directly and which gave him his regular supplies of food. He (or more accurately those peasants who were obliged to do so) would have farmed the inland to obtain his essential foodstuffs and some saleable surplus produce; whilst other estates would have been leased out to tenants. They would pay him rent, in cash, produce or labour. Where a manor had tenants, as it usually did, there was usually a court, too, presided over by the lord's bailiff. He could settle disputes between tenants there, collect debts, and generally police local affairs.

All of those who worked the land with their own hands in eleventh-century Britain can be described loosely as 'peasants', but there were different ranks within this general term.[72] Highest-ranked in England were the members of the free peasantry: freemen (*liberi homines*, Domesday Book calls them) and sokemen. Between them they accounted for approximately 14 per cent of the recorded population of England in 1086. It is hard clearly to distinguish between the meaning of these two terms, and in places the difference may have been purely one of nomenclature. In the end, it is probably fair to say that freemen and sokemen were similar kinds of peasants, ones who could give away or sell their land, and who were not obliged to perform extensive labour services to the lord who had given it to them. More strikingly, however, they were not found across the kingdom: sokemen appear to have been confined entirely to eastern and northern England in 1086, and there were few freemen south of the Thames. These were 'comparatively "unmanorial"' areas of the kingdom, and it has been suggested that this difference in the social and agrarian conditions prevailing in these parts of the country explains the relative freedom enjoyed by peasants there.[73]

Villani or 'villeins' made up more than 40 per cent of the rural population recorded in Domesday Book; in many parts of England, indeed, more than half of the people were villeins. It is often hard to know precisely what the term 'villein' means in Domesday Book; but a typical villein would perhaps hold a 'yardland' (thirty acres) or half a yardland (fifteen acres). He would produce enough food for himself and his family, as well as a small surplus which he could sell. The 'bordars' were the next largest group recorded in 1086 – about 30 per cent of the total. The word *bordarius* used in Domesday Book is probably a Latin translation of the Norman French term *bordier*. *Bordiers* 'were small-holders holding small allotments of land by particularly servile tenure . . . In Normandy, where there was no slavery, they were the bottom rank of a strictly hierarchical society.'[74] In England, they probably had a small amount of their own land, perhaps between five and eight acres; but when required to do so (and the burdens imposed on them were prob-ably quite onerous), they worked with their hands as general labourers for their lord, and carried out a range of dirty but essential jobs. The terms 'bordar' and 'cottar' (the latter is used to describe approximately two per cent of the population recorded in 1086) are sometimes used without distinction in Domesday Book, and in many places they may have meant the same thing. But 'cottar' might also signify a peasant of even lower and more servile status than the bordar, someone with no land other than the plot on which stood his small house or 'cot'.[75] It is unlikely that the bordars and cottars would have been self-sufficient; they would also hire themselves out to work on the lands of better-off neighbours.

At the bottom of the social and economic scale were the slaves, who made up just over 10 per cent of the recorded English population in 1086, and probably as much if not more of the Welsh and Scottish ones. There was an active slave trade based at Bristol and Dublin in the eleventh century – the undefended shores of south Wales provided tempting opportunities for pirates. But slavery has also been described as 'essentially the bottom of a long slippery slope which was a hazard for the economically insecure'.[76] The desperate poor could sell themselves or members of their family into slavery, a step which would at least give some security to those sold and relieve the sellers of the burden of feeding them. The slaves were the lord's chattels, they had to do what they were told and they were used by their lord as full-time workers on his demesne lands. If they did not follow orders, they could be pun-ished with mutilation or death. Given that they were expensive to buy and maintain, however, it has been suggested that slaves were most efficiently used when they were trained to do particular kinds of job, as stockmen, swineherds or ploughmen. Most English slaves, therefore, 'are more likely to have been skilled workers and specialists rather than general agricultural labourers'. Perhaps precisely because their housing and upkeep was so costly, however, and because the Church increasingly disapproved of enslavement, the number of slaves was probably already declining by 1066; and slavery had all but died out in England, if not in Wales and Scotland, by the middle of the twelfth century.[77]

Villeins, bordars and cottars were all 'unfree' to some extent, although not as unfree as slaves. The precise nature of their obligations would vary from place to place; but they are likely to have included compulsory attendance at the manorial court, presided over by the lord's bailiff, and work on the lord's inland, for perhaps two or three days a week and more at harvest time. Beyond this, however, things are less clear; and the condition of the English peasantry in 1066 is a matter of ongoing debate. The general idea that, by the time of the Conquest, 'the framework of rural England as we know it was already laid out' has recently been challenged.[78] The Anglo-Saxon countryside was not as extensively 'manorialised' as was once thought, the argument goes, and the heavily dependent and intensely servile populations of the inlands may not have been representative of the peasantry as a whole. The corollary of this interpretation, as will be seen, is that the Norman Conquest initiated a period of significant and sometimes devastating change for England's rural population.

The Church in pre-conquest Britain

Christianity had been the dominant religion in Britain since Roman times. However, religious practices and organisational structures developed differently in England, Scotland and Wales during the second half of the first millennium. When Pope Gregory the Great sent St Augustine and his followers to England to convert the Anglo-Saxons to Christianity in 596, he had in mind the establishment of an ecclesiastical structure which would encompass the whole of Britain: two provinces of 12 bishops, each with a metropolitan (an archbishop with authority over the bishops of his province), one based at London and the other at York. For various reasons, however, only elements of this blueprint were ever put into effect. An archbishopric was established at York; but Canterbury, not London, became the principal church of the southern province. Other bishoprics were established throughout the Anglo-Saxon kingdoms as time went on, but this was not a systematic process. As a result, of the 12 English bishoprics including Canterbury and York which existed by 1066, only 2 were in the northern province. Therefore, whilst in theory neither of the English archbishops was supposed to have precedence over the other, and because the southern province was in general terms much richer and more closely in touch with the political centre than the northern one, the archbishop of Canterbury saw himself as England's senior churchman.

Another legacy of the missionary activity of the seventh and eighth centuries was the development of so-called 'minster' churches across England. These were large churches staffed by secular, often married, clergy (rather than monks), whose responsibility it had originally been to serve the pastoral needs of a wide surrounding district. However, by the eleventh century, the influence of the minsters was beginning to wane. Some had never recovered from the damage inflicted on them by the Viking raids of the ninth century. More commonly, however, minsters had suffered at the hands of rapacious kings and other lay lords who had appropriated their lands.[79] Also, by 1066 English bishoprics were being gradually divided into more compact areas or parishes. This process had probably begun in the second half of the tenth century, and it was far from complete when the Normans arrived. It was well under way, however; and by then England 'was gradually filling up with solidly built little churches with their own priests', who ministered to the needs of small groups of people in their immediate neighbourhood.[80] These local churches may have been established by the bishop or even the king, but most would have been set up by a local nobleman, who would reserve the right to choose the priest who administered to the basic spiritual needs of his congregation – baptisms, marriages, burials and confession. The local church itself and the right to appoint its priest were regarded by those who controlled them as pieces of real property belonging to them as of right, and over which nobody else, even the local bishop, had any control. They were sources of profit, too, bringing in revenue from tithes, and fees for marriages, burials and other necessary religious services.

Existing alongside the kingdom's minsters and parish churches were England's monasteries. Monasticism had flourished throughout England during the age of conversion, but in the ninth century, Viking raids inflicted significant damage, to the extent that, by the tenth century, there may have been few functioning monasteries left in England. King Alfred took some steps to revive monastic life within his kingdom of Wessex, but a widespread revival did not take place until the reign of King Edgar (959–73). With no little royal assistance, the monks Dunstan, Aethelwold and Oswald, who were to become respectively archbishop of Canterbury (959–88), bishop of Winchester (963–84) and bishop of Worcester/archbishop of York (961–92/971–92) led the way in re-establishing England's monasteries. By c.1000 there were about forty monasteries and nunneries in England, although none north of the river Trent. From this time onwards, moreover, monks were chosen as bishops in England much more often than was generally the case elsewhere in Western Europe; and this led to the emergence of another peculiar feature of the Anglo-Saxon ecclesiastical system: the 'monastic cathedrals' at Canterbury, Worcester, Winchester and Sherborne. These were staffed by monks who lived secluded in their cloister, and the abbot was also a bishop. They should be distinguished from the other 'secular' cathedrals which were administered by canons who were supported by the revenues from the churches they ministered to outside their cathedral precincts.

England's ecclesiastical structure was reasonably well defined by 1066, although it continued to develop. The number of bishoprics and their territorial boundaries were mostly settled; monastic life had been revived; the parochial organisation of later centuries was also under construction. The same could not be said of Wales and Scotland. There was no meaningful sign of any sort of formalised parochial structure in either territory by the end of the eleventh century, for example. And in Wales by then, whilst there were plenty of religious communities which were described as monasteries, arrangements within them were far from consistent. Some were probably well ordered, on a more or less strict Benedictine model; but in others, practices and rules varied, and plenty had members who had not taken monastic vows at all. By about 1100, it has been said of Wales, 'communities which were considered monastic had practices which were not very "monastic" in the usually accepted sense'.[81] This is hardly surprising given that, at the higher level of ecclesiastical organisation, too, there was little clarity. For one thing, it was by no means obvious who was in charge of the Welsh and Scottish Churches. Because there was no British archbishopric north of York or west of Offa's Dyke, the archbishops of York and Canterbury continued to claim authority over the churches of Scotland and Wales respectively. Occasionally English ecclesiastical muscle was flexed in direct ways. In 1056, for example, the bishop of Llandaff was consecrated by the archbishop of York; but usually such claims meant little in practice, and the bishops of the eleventh-century Welsh and Scottish Churches were left largely to their own devices.[82] There was no settled number of bishops in either pre-conquest Wales or Scotland and no dioceses with fixed territorial limits. In Wales, an individual bishop, who might also be the abbot of a monastery as at St David's, might try to extend his authority from his 'mother church' or *clas* over as many smaller churches as possible. In doing so, he would have the help of the often hereditary and married secular canons who staffed their enclosed community whilst at the same time ministering in an unregulated way to the surrounding congregations. With each *clas* supervising the ecclesiastical and spiritual needs of an area of fluctuating size, within which the extent of episcopal control also varied, regional loyalties, often focused around the cult of a particular saint, such as St Tysilio in Powys, were fiercely cultivated and defended. The Welsh Church was thus highly fragmented and localised in 1066. In Scotland, there were some centres of monastic life, but they were few and far between and standards were not high. Elsewhere in Scotland in the eleventh century there were similar arrangements to those found in Wales. Again there was no fixed diocesan structure or organisation, Scottish bishops consecrated each other, and in some areas there were churches or 'culdees' analogous to the Welsh *clasau*. Unlike Wales, however, Scotland did have a fixed ecclesiastical centre by 1066, at St Andrews.

How well these systems dealt with the spiritual needs of the British people in the years immediately prior to the Norman Conquest is a matter of some debate. Norman writers in the years after 1066 had a vested interest in portraying the late Anglo-Saxon Church in particular, personified by the much-maligned Archbishop Stigand of Canterbury (1052–70), as backward and corrupt. He was probably from East Anglia, although his Old Norse name suggests Scandinavian descent. After serving as a priest of Cnut, Stigand became bishop of Elmham in 1043, bishop of Winchester in 1047 (he was succeeded at Elmham by his brother Aethelmaer) and archbishop of Canterbury in 1052 when Robert de Jumièges was expelled from England. He was also accused in the twelfth century of having had control of the revenues of several important monasteries, including St Augustine's at Canterbury, Winchester, Glastonbury, St Albans and Ely. Because he was a pluralist, and because his predecessor as archbishop was still alive when he assumed the title, Stigand's position was certainly irregular. However, he was also unlucky in having received his pallium, the symbol of his archiepiscopal office, in 1058 from Benedict X, an anti-pope whose own legitimacy was later rejected by the wider Church. He was also 'outstandingly worldly',[83] a politician first and foremost and a rich one, too, with an extensive personal landed estate. He showed no interest in the reform movement emanating from Rome, and he gave no meaningful spiritual lead to the English Church during his time as its leader. Nevertheless, he did have his better side: he was a patron of the arts, and generous to the churches he controlled. He was also an efficient administrator. Even William of Malmesbury conceded that, where Stigand's personal ambitions were not involved, 'he was not lacking in judgement or inefficient'.[84] He was not a good pastor, then, but 'he represented a fine example of the old unreformed order of the Church, primarily a capable administrator, appreciated as such by Edward and to some extent William in his early years'.[85] Nevertheless, he was an easy target for the Norman propagandists who were quick to identify him, most obviously on the Bayeux Tapestry, as the illegitimate archbishop who had crowned an illegitimate king.[86] Whether he actually did so is open to question. Harold must have known how irregular Stigand's position was, and how he might be tainted by association with him. John of Worcester at least is quite clear that it was Archbishop Ealdred of York who consecrated the last Anglo-Saxon king.[87]

Whatever Stigand's faults actually were, his fellow English bishops on the eve of the Conquest were, as a group, reasonably impressive. Several of the foreigners received a good press from contemporaries. According to the author of the *Vita Edwardi*, Giso of Wells and Walter of Hereford were both 'men most suitably and excellently trained in their office', whilst Herman of Ramsbury was a 'famous and well-educated bishop'.[88] Archbishop Cynsige of York was venerated as a saint by the monks of Peterborough, where he was buried. Leofric of Devon and Cornwall has been described as a 'conscientious and cultured bishop . . . an able administrator and a progressive force'.[89] And most outstanding of all, albeit for different reasons, were Ealdred, first bishop of Worcester (1046–62) and then archbishop of York (1062–9), and Wulfstan, Ealdred's successor at Worcester (1062–95). Ealdred, despite being a monk, enjoyed perhaps as worldly a career as Stigand. He defended the English border against the Welsh in the late 1040s, undertook royal missions to foreign courts and administered several dioceses at once in the 1050s. He wanted to hold York in plurality with Worcester after 1062 but was forbidden from doing so by the pope. However, he took care to receive his pallium from a legitimate pope, and the indications are that he was a better pastor than Stigand and took more interest in the affairs of his diocese and the standards of his diocesan clergy. His reputation was secure by 1066, and he was the obvious man to perform Duke William's coronation. As for Wulfstan, his reputation has been founded largely on the *Life* written by his chaplain Colman in about 1095 and preserved by William of Malmesbury. Wulfstan was a monk, too; but unlike Ealdred, he was holy, ascetic, unworldly and reluctant to become a bishop. However, having accepted his appointment in 1062, he was relentlessly energetic about carrying out his duties and ministering to his flock. He is said to have performed miracles during his lifetime, and more took place at his tomb after his death. His reputation for sanctity soon spread, although he was not canonised until 1203.

Nevertheless, in so far as the English Church is concerned, it probably remains fair to describe the period between 1000 and 1066 as 'the slack water between two tides of reform'.[90] Indeed, in all parts of Britain in 1066, clerical marriage was common, lay influence over the Church was considerable, and ecclesiastical posts were regularly hereditary. In Wales, great ecclesiastical dynasties were founded by Herewald, bishop of Llandaff (1056–1104) and by Sulien, bishop of St David's (1073–8 and 1080–85), both of whom were married. And at the end of the twelfth century, Gerald of Wales still felt able to complain about the Welsh practice of hereditary succession to benefices.[91] In Scotland, where the influence of the Irish Church was still strong, marriage customs were lax, confession and communion were infrequent and the observance of Easter was irregular. It has been said that the Welsh Church on the eve of the Norman Conquest was 'archaic and backward-looking' and that the Scottish Church in the eleventh century 'was characterised by secularisation and even decay'.[92] However, such criticisms should not be pushed too far, and the Churches of late eleventh-century Britain should be judged by the standards of their own time rather than by those of earlier or later periods of reform. It suited post-conquest writers to portray the late Anglo-Saxon Church as backward and corrupt, just as it came naturally to clerical writers based in England to look with contempt on the behaviour of their Welsh and Scottish colleagues. But in the third quarter of the eleventh century, the 'abuses' they criticised would have been prevalent across Europe. Most priests were almost certainly not well educated, and many would have been married with families; but there is no reason to doubt that they carried out their duties responsibly. And where there was simony, as in the case of Bishop Sulien of St David's and his family, there was not necessarily a decline in standards: the great *clas* church at Llanbadarn Fawr over which he, his sons and his grandsons presided was a noted centre of Latin learning.[93] Archbishop Stigand was accused after 1066 of having bought offices and churches, but such charges might be expected from those who sought to discredit him for their own political purposes. Stigand was also a pluralist in that, from 1052, he was simultaneously bishop of Winchester and archbishop of Canterbury. And there were other noted pluralists, too. Earl Leofric's nephew and namesake was simultaneously abbot of Burton, Coventry, Crowland, Thorney and Peterborough. Herman was bishop of Ramsbury and Sherborne from 1056. Between 1055 and 1058, Bishop Ealdred of Worcester also administered the dioceses of Hereford and Ramsbury, and, when he became archbishop of York in 1061, he was only prevented from jointly holding the archbishopric along with Worcester when the pope refused him permission to do so. It had become traditional by this time for these two sees to be held together; no less a figure than St Oswald had done this, for example, less than a century before. However, the pope's decision in 1061 gave a clear signal that such practices were no longer acceptable in the eyes of the reform papacy. But such a signal was novel, and it was still not long since one of the greatest of the reforming popes, Leo IX (1049–54), had retained his diocese of Toul after succeeding to the see of St Peter.

Architectural evidence also suggests that England, at least, was far from being an ecclesiastical backwater in the mid eleventh century. William of Malmesbury's famous assertion that new churches were built throughout England after the arrival of the Normans does not preclude the possibility that churches of all kinds were being constructed in wood and stone in England before 1066. When Bishop Herman of Ramsbury visited Rome in 1050, he is reported to have told the pope that England 'was being filled everywhere with churches which daily were being added anew in new places'.[94] Hard evidence of such activity at a local level is inevitably lacking, but, as has been seen already, the parish church was almost certainly an increasingly common sight in the English landscape by 1066. There is better evidence for the building or redevelopment of great churches. Aelfwold, bishop of Sherborne (1045/6–58) rebuilt the monastery there, Cynsige of York (1051–60) built the tower at Beverley and further buildings were erected and lavishly decorated there by his successor, Ealdred. Laymen and women built churches, too. Earl Leofric of Mercia founded Coventry Abbey in about 1043 (and was later buried there), and he generously patronised several other monasteries including Worcester and Evesham. Queen Edith founded a nunnery at Wilton, and Earl Harold built a great church at Waltham in Essex where, it is generally thought, his remains were interred after Hastings.

Because so little of their fabric remains, it is difficult to know what these and other late Anglo-Saxon churches looked like. The prevalent style across the Channel in the eleventh century was 'Romanesque', but there is little indication that England's church builders were influenced by these trends before 1066. The majority of pre-conquest English churches probably tended to be smaller than their post-conquest replacements, simpler in form and rougher in detail. However, several dozen sites remain which still contain eleventh-century elements; they suggest that, whilst this generalised picture is probably fair, late Anglo-Saxon ecclesiastical architecture still had its sophisticated side. The huge crossing arches at Stow in Lincolnshire (c.1050) suggest a taste for the monumental. Towers both square and round were becoming increasingly widespread after 1000 as well. The best surviving examples are the square towers at St Peter's Church, Barton-on-Humber (c.990), and Earl's Barton church in Northamptonshire (c.1020–50), both decorated with pilaster strips and blind arcading.[95] And inside the churches there would have been decoration, although its extent would depend on the wealth of the individual church and the generosity of its patrons. Walls would have been plastered, painted with biblical scenes or hung with the embroideries or tapestries for which the English were famous in the eleventh century. English sculptors would have played their part, too: crucifixes, reliquaries, chalices, patens, portable devotional scenes and individual figures, and much more, would have been made out of metal, ivory or wood. The two ivory figures of the Virgin and St John the Evangelist, which survive from a larger crucifixion group carved in about 1000, reveal the heights attainable by the craftsmen of eleventh-century England.[96] As do the decorated or 'illuminated' manuscripts of the period produced in the workshops of England's monasteries. Book production (the writing, decoration and binding of manuscripts) had been given a huge boost by the monastic revival of the tenth century, and by 1000 the quality of English illumination was internationally renowned. The manuscripts produced during the century before the Norman Conquest are often referred to as having been executed in the 'Winchester style', although they came from monastic centres across southern England. They tended to be richly decorated with ornamental designs, often of acanthus leaves, in the borders; but figurative representations were often delicately and elegantly drawn, too. The former characteristic can best be seen in the Benedictional of St Aethelwold, produced at Winchester between 971 and 984; the latter in pages from the Tiberius Psalter (Winchester, c.1050), and the Old English translation of the first six books of the Old Testament, the 'Hexateuch' (Canterbury, c.1025–50).[97]

The one outstanding example of a late Anglo-Saxon church which consciously imitated the latest continental trends was Edward the Confessor's Westminster Abbey. Some sort of foundation already existed on the marshy and inhospitable 'Isle of Thorns' in the Thames in the first half of the tenth century, and St Dunstan's patronage may have given it greater prominence in the 960s or 970s. By the 1050s, Edward had decided completely to rebuild it, with the intention of making it his burial place. Very little of Edward's church now survives, but something of its appearance can be gleaned from the depiction of it on the Bayeux Tapestry and from the description of it in the *Vita Edwardi*.[98] It was built in the latest Romanesque style, and perhaps it was modelled in part on Archbishop Robert's abbey of Jumièges. It has also been suggested, however, that it was Westminster which provided the model for Jumièges. The Confessor's abbey was built of Reigate stone with a long nave of six double bays, and a central lantern tower overlooking the crossing. The abbey was consecrated on 28 December 1065, and its first ceremonial was the funeral of its patron about a week later. Edward did not live to see his great church functioning, but his legacy to his successors was the establishment of Westminster, with its abbey and its palace, as the heart of royal government in England.

Britain and the papacy before 1066

In 1050 Macbeth had left Scotland and embarked on a pilgrimage to Rome, where he 'scattered money like seed to the poor'. Earl Thorfinn the Mighty of Orkney made a similar journey, too.[99] Such striking episodes aside, however, there is little to suggest sustained, meaningful contact between Rome and either the north or west of Britain before 1066. Prominent Englishmen also went on pilgrimage to Rome, most notably King Cnut in 1025 and the brothers Harold and Tostig Godwineson in 1061; but such visits took place at a time when papal involvement in the business of the English Church was steadily increasing. Until the 1050s, the papacy had been dominated by powerful Roman families and it had been used by them as a tool of faction. Consequently, the popes themselves had been unable to exercise any meaningful authority either within Rome or outside it. However, from the 1040s, this began to change. The reforming popes who took charge in Rome were determined to have their authority as leaders of the Western Church acknowledged across Europe. They set about doing this in various ways, but principally by travelling widely, holding synods and pronouncing judgement on local disputes. Such policies were bound to bring them into conflict with lay rulers. This happened most obviously in Germany, but England was not untouched. England paid an annual tribute to the papacy, 'Rome-scot' or 'Peter's Pence'. The origins of this payment are obscure, but it was already a time-honoured custom by the eleventh century. Whilst the popes were weak, the English kings could regard it as nothing more than a polite courtesy; but once they were strong it might be interpreted in Rome as a sign of English subjection to the papacy. Another potentially compromising tradition for the king dictated that, whilst the king might appoint his arch-bishops, no archbishop was entitled to govern his province or consecrate and preside over the bishops of that province unless he had received the symbol of his office, the woollen stole known as the pallium, from the pope himself. Thus Robert de Jumièges travelled to Rome in 1051, as did Cynsige and Ealdred of York in 1055 and 1061 respectively. Stigand was sent his pallium by Benedict X in 1058. The failure properly to com-ply with these formalities could have personal repercussions for the authority of the individual concerned, as Stigand found to his cost: Giso of Wells and Walter of Hereford travelled to Rome in 1061 to be con-secrated by the pope because of Stigand's incapacity. There could also be political consequences for the king or even, as Harold discovered, for a claimant to the throne. English bishops and abbots might leave the kingdom for other reasons, too. For example, several English prelates attended Pope Leo IX's councils at Rheims in 1049 and at Rome and Vercelli in 1050; here they would have been exposed to the progressive ideas of one of the great reforming popes. And there are other signs that reforming ideas were gaining ground in England before 1066. Two of the bishops imported by Edward from Lotharingia (modern Lorraine), Herman of Ramsbury and Leofric of Devon and Cornwall began the practice, later accelerated by William I and Lanfranc, of bishops estab-lishing permanent diocesan centres and their accompanying cathedrals, in major towns – Leofric in Exeter (from Crediton, with papal approval) and Herman in Sherborne.

The popes also interfered in the affairs of the English Church in other ways which directly impinged upon the authority of the king. When Robert de Jumièges moved from the see of London to become archbishop of Canterbury in 1051, Edward nominated as his successor his own goldsmith, Abbot Spearhafoc of Abingdon. On his return from Rome, however, perhaps because rumours had reached Leo IX that Spearhafoc had obtained his position through simony, Archbishop Robert refused to consecrate the royal nominee. In the short term the king was not disadvantaged significantly and the royal priest, William, a Norman, was consecrated instead. But such acts of assertiveness by an archbishop acting under papal influence were significant indicators of the extent to which papal authority was beginning to spread across Europe. It was exercised again in 1061. Archbishop Cynsige of York died in that year and Ealdred, already bishop of Worcester, was chosen as his successor and travelled to Rome for his pallium. However, Nicholas II was not only unwilling to give the pallium to Ealdred; he went as far as to depose him entirely as a bishop because he had moved from one bishopric to another without papal consent. It was not until he had been attacked by robbers and fled back to Rome to acknowledge his offence that Ealdred was given his pallium; and even then only on the strict understanding that he surrendered his claims to the bishopric of Worcester. The king's absolute freedom to choose his own bishops, therefore, and their own freedom to hold more than one see at a time, was beginning to be whittled away by a foreign power. By 1066, papal influence in England was still limited and exercised only occasionally; no major conflict arose under Edward the Confessor or Harold and there was no fundamental clash between king and pope. But it was perhaps only a matter of time before the tension inherent in their rival claims to authority over the English Church erupted into conflict.

The Church in pre-conquest Normandy

Writing at Canterbury in the early twelfth century, the monk Eadmer claimed that, in so far as ecclesiastical matters were concerned, William I's aim after Hastings was 'to maintain in England the usages and laws which he and his fathers before him were accustomed to have in Normandy'.[100] What this meant in practice was tight, centralised control over the running of the Church, which was a source of patronage and funds for the Duke, as well as a source of political, military and divine support. In Normandy as in England, the stark reality for William was that 'unless he could rule his ecclesiastical as effectively as his lay subjects, his power would be much diminished'.[101]

The Church in Normandy had been reinvigorated during the first half of the eleventh century. Established monasteries which had suffered at the hands of the Vikings were revived with ducal assistance at places like Fécamp (which prospered and led the way under the leadership of its abbot from 1001, William of Volpiano), Mont St Michel and Jumièges; and new ones were founded by the dukes. Duke William himself and his wife made a 'double foundation' at Caen in the years before 1066, William's monastery dedicated to St Stephen and Matilda's convent to the Holy Trinity. Particularly after 1035, moreover, when ducal authority was weak, the emergent Norman aristocracy played a decisive role in the monastic revival within the duchy. According to Orderic Vitalis, great Norman families competed with each other in the founding of religious houses, and 'each magnate would have thought himself beneath contempt if he had not supported clerks and monks on his estates for the service of God'.[102] The twenty or so monasteries established in Normandy between 1035 and 1066 by the likes of Herluin, *vicomte* of Conteville, his wife Herleva and his son Robert, count of Mortain (Duke William's half-brother) at Grestain, William FitzOsbern at Lire and Cormeilles and by the Montgomery family at Sées, Troarn and Almenèches bear witness to his claim. Most famous of all was the monastery of Le Bec, founded in 1041 by Herluin, a knight of Count Gilbert de Brionne. Two of the most important participants in the Norman Conquest of Britain, Lanfranc and Anselm, were both monks there before they became archbishop of Canterbury. In 990, there were six monasteries in Normandy; by 1070 there were 27 monasteries and six nunneries. Within less than a century, Normandy had become an internationally famous centre of monastic life and practice.

Beyond the cloister, the Norman Church also underwent a radical reorganisation during William's reign. The borders of the duchy of Normandy coincided roughly with the limits of the ancient ecclesiastical province of Rouen, within which, in addition to the archbishopric of Rouen itself, there were six bishoprics or dioceses. The duke's right to appoint to bishoprics was acknowledged well before 1066. Some candidates came from the ranks of the ducal chapel, others (Mauger, archbishop of Rouen, Odo, bishop of Bayeux and Hugh, bishop of Lisieux, for example) were related to the dukes or (like Geoffrey, bishop of Coutances and Yves, bishop of Sées) were members of leading Norman families. These men were worldly and 'many of them were lamentably lacking in spirituality'.[103] And to be sure, by later standards, their qualifications for episcopal office were lacking: Geoffrey of Coutances was accused of acquiring his bishopric by simony, and Archbishop Mauger was actually deposed in 1054, although this was probably a result of his support for the rebellion of his brother, Count William of Arques. However, from the late 1040s, the character of the Norman episcopate began to change under William II's firm rule. Well-trained and well-educated men were appointed to bishoprics, and by 1080, it has been said, the Norman episcopate had 'acquired a professional quality which was outstanding in contemporary northern France'.[104] Perhaps the most important appointment of all was that of Maurilius, archbishop of Rouen (1054–67). His appointment to such an eminent position was unusual given that, although he had been a monk at Fécamp, he was a Lotharingian by birth and not aristocratic. Nevertheless, he and Duke William, who may have presided over them (they certainly met 'at his command and by his encouragement', William de Poitiers claimed[105]), summoned a series of councils of the Norman Church, at Lisieux (1054 and 1064), Caen (1061) and Rouen (1063), with the aim of streamlining its organisation and improving its discipline. The intensity of such conciliar activity in Normandy contrasts sharply with the situation in Britain during this period, where no such reforming councils met.

By 1066, therefore, the Norman Church was tightly organised and well regulated, with the Duke in overall control of it. It was central to the way William ruled his duchy. It was also a centre of religious reform, a state of affairs gratefully recognised in Rome. As duke and then king, William was properly respectful towards the papacy, but he always remained clear about his own dominant position within the Churches he controlled. And until about 1075, the popes went along with this. In 1061, therefore, Pope Alexander II (1061–73) acknowledged that William should be allowed to appoint the archbishop of Rouen and, in the same year, when the Duke refused to allow papal legates to examine the case of the abbot of St Evroult, whom William had deposed, the papacy meekly submitted. Papal approval of William's rule is best evidenced, if William de Poitiers is correct about this, by the banner provided for him by the pope on the Hastings campaign.

Conclusion

Despite the obvious and multiple differences between them, the peoples of eleventh-century Britain and Normandy had much in common. They were all to a greater or lesser degree part of the same Latin Christian world; and whilst economic, social, religious and political structures and norms differed from region to region, they remained connected through networks of travel, trade and cultural exchange which ignored frontiers and bred familiarity. The relations between these peoples were not always harmonious, of course, and it would be unwise to play down the extent to which they regarded each other with hostility and suspicion. Their ruling élites, in particular, were politically ambitious and intensely competitive. The events of the eleventh century were to show this time and again, and it is to those events that attention should now turn.

Notes

1 *ASC*, 'C', 'D', s.a.973.

2 *JW*, ii pp.423–5.

3 F.M. Stenton, *Anglo-Saxon England*, 3rd edn (Oxford: Clarendon Press, 1971), pp.369–70.

4 *ASC* 'D', s.a.927; 'C' s.a.937.

5 Richard Britnell, *Britain and Ireland 1050–1530: Economy and society* (Oxford University Press, 2004), p.110; David Carpenter, *The Struggle for Mastery. Britain 1066–1284* (Oxford University Press, 2003), pp.31–2, 37–8. John S. Moore says just under two million for England: ' "Quot homines?": the Population of Domesday England', *ANS* 19 (1996), pp.307–34.

6 *Bede's Ecclesiastical History of the English People*, ed. Bertram Colgrave and R.A.B. Mynors (Oxford: Clarendon Press, 1969).

7 Hugh M. Thomas, *The English and the Normans: Ethnic hostility, assimilation and identity 1066–c.1220* (Oxford University Press, 2003), p.22.

8 Sarah Foot, 'The Making of *Angelcynn*: English Identity before the Norman Conquest', *TRHS*, 6th series, 6 (1996), pp.25–49.

9 Wendy Davies, *Wales in the Early Middle Ages* (Leicester University Press, 1982), pp.81–2.

10 R.R. Davies, *The Age of Conquest. Wales 1063–1415* (Oxford University Press, 1991), p.19.

11 Dauvit Broun, *The Irish Identity of the Kingdom of the Scots in the Twelfth and Thirteenth Centuries*, (Woodbridge: Boydell Press, 1999), passim.

12 A.A.M. Duncan, 'The making of the kingdom', in *Why Scottish History Matters*, ed. R. Mitchison (Edinburgh: Saltine Society, 1991), p.13.

13 David Bates, *Normandy Before 1066* (London: Longman, 1982), p.47.

14 Dudo of St Quentin, *History of the Normans*, ed. Eric Christiansen (Woodbridge: Boydell Press), pp.48–50.

15 David Crouch, *The Normans: The history of a dynasty* (London: Hambledon, 2002), pp.16–17.

16 Bates, *Normandy Before 1066*, pp.65–8; Crouch, *The Normans*, pp.32–9.

17 Crouch, *The Normans*, pp.18–20; Bates, *Normandy Before 1066*, pp.148–51.

18 Thomas, *The English and the Normans*, p.35.

19 D. Bates, 'Normandy and England after 1066', *EHR* 104 (1989), p.853.

20 *OV*, iii pp.98–9, iv pp.82–3, v pp.24–7.

21 Thomas, *The English and the Normans*, p.40.

22 *OV*, ii p.210.

23 The rest of this paragraph draws heavily on Davies, *Wales in the Early Middle Ages*, ch.5.

24 Davies, *Wales in the Early Middle Ages*, pp.124, 134.

25 *ASC* 'D', s.a.1052.

26 Bates, *Normandy Before 1066*, p.182.

27 *The History of the Norman People, Wace's Roman de Rou*, trans. Glyn S. Burgess (Woodbridge: Boydell Press, 2004), pp.162–3.

28 R. Allen Brown, *The Normans and the Norman Conquest*, 2nd edn (Woodbridge: Boydell Press, 1985), p.31; Bates, *Normandy Before 1066*, pp.176–9; Eleanor Searle, *Predatory Kinship and the Creation of Norman Power, 840–1066* (Berkeley: University of California Press, 1988), p.233.

29 *EHD* II, pp.929, 932.

30 For much of what follows in the next two paragraphs see Matthew Strickland, 'Military Technology and Conquest: the Anomaly of Anglo-Saxon England', *ANS* 19 (1996), pp.353–82.

31 *ASC* 'C' s.a.1003, 1013; *JW*, ii pp.465, 473.

32 *ASC* 'C', 'D', s.a.896.

33 *ASC* 'C', s.a.1008, 1009.

34 *ASC* 'D', s.a.1045, 1049; 'C' s.a.1048.

35 *ASC* 'D', s.a.1063; 'C', 'E', s.a.1066; *WP*, p.125.

36 C.H. Haskins, *Norman Institutions* (Cambridge, Mass.: Harvard University Press, 1918), Chapter I; below, pp.251–2.

37 Haskins, *Norman Institutions*, p.5.

38 *OV*, iv, pp.88–9; *History of the Norman People*, trans. Burgess, pp.158–9.

39 E.M.C. Van Houts, 'The Ship List of William the Conqueror', *ANS* 10 (1987), pp.159–83; *History of the Norman People*, trans. Burgess, pp.159–60.

40 Emily Zack Tabuteau, 'Definitions of Military Service in Eleventh-Century Normandy', in *On the Laws and Customs of England. Essays in Honour of Samuel E. Thorne*, ed. Morris S. Arnold, Thomas A. Green, Sally A. Scully, and Stepen D. White (University of North Carolina Press, 1981), pp.18–59, at pp.41–51.

41 Bates, *Normandy Before 1066*, pp.122–8 at pp.125, 168–9 at pp.168, 258–9.

42 Bates, *Normandy Before 1066*, p.122.

43 Marjorie Chibnall, 'Military Service in Normandy Before 1066', *ANS* 5 (1983), pp.65–77; repr. in *Anglo-Norman Warfare: Studies in late Anglo-Saxon and Anglo-Norman military organisation and warfare*, ed. Matthew Strickland (Woodbridge: Boydell Press, 1992), pp.28–40, at pp.35–6; Tabuteau, 'Definitions of Military Service in Eleventh-Century Normandy', argues at pp.18–21 and 58–9 that obligations in Normandy were probably not defined clearly until after 1100.

44 *OV*, ii p.219.

45 Brown, *The Normans and the Norman Conquest*, pp.36–7.

46 *WJ*, ii p.93.

47 Carpenter, *The Struggle for Mastery*, p.75; Brown, *The Normans and the Norman Conquest*, pp.36–8.

48 *BT*, pl.25.

49 Judith A. Green, *The Aristocracy of Norman England* (Cambridge University Press, 1997), pp.173–4; Bates, *Normandy Before 1066*, p.115.

50 *BT*, pls.61–2.

51 *BT*, pl.72; M.K. Lawson, *The Battle of Hastings 1066* (Stroud: Tempus, 2003), pp.153–4.

52 *BT*, pls.66–7.

53 *BT*, pls.61–2; Lawson, *The Battle of Hastings,* p.154.

54 *ASC* 'C', s.a.1055; *JW*, ii p.577.

55 *WP*, pp.127–9.

56 *BT*, pls.63–4.

57 *The Alexiad of Anna Comnena*, trans. E.R.A Sewter (London: Penguin, 1969), p.416; *BT*, pls.61–2.

58 *WP*, pp.129–33.

59 *WP*, p.127.

60 *BT*, pl.68.

61 Searle, *Predatory Kinship*, pp.1–2.

62 *ASC* 'C' s.a.1046, 'E' s.a.1054.

63 For the debate over the reliability of the *Chronicle's* figures, see M.K. Lawson, 'The Collection of Danegeld and Heregeld in the Reigns of Aethelred II and Cnut', *EHR* 99 (1984), pp.721–38; J. Gillingham, ' "The Most Precious Jewel in the English Crown": Levels of Danegeld and Heregeld in the Early Eleventh Century', *EHR* 104 (1989), pp.373–84; and Lawson's response, 'Danegeld and Heregeld Once More', *EHR* 105 (1990), pp.951–61.

64 N.J. Mayhew, 'Modelling Medieval Monetisation', in *A Commercialising Economy; England 1086–1300*, ed. R.H. Britnell and B.M.S. Campbell (Manchester, 1995), pp.55–77 at p.62.

65 Bates, *Normandy Before 1066*, p.96.

66 Bates, *Normandy Before 1066*, p.97.

67 Britnell, *Britain and Ireland*, pp.73–4; Christopher Dyer, *Making a Living in the Middle Ages: The people of Britain 850–1520* (London, 2003), p.58.

68 Davies, *Wales in the Early Middle Ages*, p.58.

69 John Gillingham, 'The Beginnings of English Imperialism', in *The English in the Twelfth Century: Imperialism, national identity and political values* (Woodbridge: Boydell Press, 2000), pp.3–18, p.12.

70 Britnell, *Britain and Ireland*, pp.58–61.

71 Britnell, *Britain and Ireland*, pp.533–4.

72 The figures in this and the following two paragraphs are taken from H.C. Darby, *Domesday England* (Cambridge University Press, 1977), pp.61–74, 337–45.

73 Reginald Lennard, *Rural England, 1086–1135: A study of social and agrarian conditions* (Oxford: Clarendon Press, 1959), pp.218–26; quotation at p.226.

74 Rosamund Faith, *The English Peasantry and the Growth of Lordship* (Leicester University Press, 1997), p.71.

75 Darby, *Domesday England*, pp.69–71; Britnell, *Britain and Ireland*, pp.529, 530.

76 Faith, *The English Peasantry and the Growth of Lordship*, p.61.

77 Faith, *The English Peasantry and the Growth of Lordship*, pp.64–5; Britnell, *Britain and Ireland*, pp.229–30.

78 In Faith, *The English Peasantry and the Growth of Lordship*. The quote is from Lennard, *Rural England*, p.3. See below, pp.276–7.

79 John Blair, *The Church in Anglo-Saxon Society* (Oxford University Press, 2005), ch.6, esp. pp.323–41.

80 Blair, *The Church in Anglo-Saxon Society*, pp.368, 498–504.

81 Davies, *Wales in the Early Middle Ages*, p.149.

82 John Edward Lloyd, *A History of Wales from the Earliest Times to the Norman Conquest*, 2 vols (1911), ii p.449.

83 Frank Barlow, *The English Church, 1000–1066: A constitutional history* (London: Longman, 1963), p.78.

84 *WMGP*, p.25.

85 H.R. Loyn, *The English Church, 940–1154* (Harlow: Longman, 2000), pp.60–1.

86 *BT*, pl.31.

87 *JW*, ii p.601.

88 *Vita Edwardi*, pp.35, 47.

89 Barlow, *The English Church, 1000–1066*, p.84.

90 Barlow, *The English Church, 1000–1066*, p.27.

91 Gerald of Wales, *The Journey Through Wales*, trans. Lewis Thorpe (Harmondsworth: Penguin, 1978), p.263.

92 Davies, *The Age of Conquest*, p.179; A.A.M. Duncan, *Scotland, The Making of the Kingdom* (Edinburgh: Oliver & Boyd, 1975), p.105.

93 Davies, *The Age of Conquest*, p.178.

94 *WMGR*, i p.461; Blair, *The Church in Anglo-Saxon Society*, p.368.

95 *The Golden Age of Anglo-Saxon Art*, 966–1066, ed. Janet Backhouse, D.H. Turner, Leslie Webster (London: British Museum Publications, 1984), p.141, figures 4–5.

96 *The Golden Age of Anglo-Saxon Art*, 966–1066, pp.118–19, and colour plate XXVII.

97 Michelle P. Brown, *Anglo-Saxon Manuscripts* (London: British Library, 1991), pls. 54, 72, 76.

98 *BT*, pl.29; *Vita Edwardi*, pp.67–71; R.D.H. Gem, 'The Romanesque Rebuilding of Westminster Abbey', *ANS 3* (1981), pp.33–60.

99 *Early Sources of Scottish History, AD 500 to 1286*, ed. and trans. Alan Orr Anderson, 2 vols (Edinburgh: Oliver & Boyd, 1922; repr. with corrections, Stamford, 1990), i p.588; *The Orkneyinga Saga. The History of the Earls of Orkney*, trans. Hermann Pálsson and Paul Edwards (London: Hogarth Press, 1978), pp.74–5.

100 *HN*, p.9.

101 Frank Barlow, *The English Church, 1066–1154* (London: Longman, 1979), p.275.

102 *OV*, ii p.11.

103 David C. Douglas, *William the Conqueror* (London: Eyre & Spottiswoode, 1964), p.122.

104 Bates, *Normandy Before 1066*, p.212.

105 *WP*, p.83.

CHAPTER 3

The origins of conquest, 991–1066

Royal succession in England

Put most simply, the Norman Conquest happened because there was a dispute about which man should succeed Edward the Confessor as king of England in 1066. The rules governing the royal succession in late Anglo-Saxon England were far from settled or clear. There was no fixed principle of male primogeniture (succession by the eldest son or the eldest surviving male relative), for example. Lineal descent from father to son might be desirable as far as most kings were concerned; but several eleventh-century kings (Harold 'Harefoot', Harthacnut and William II) did not leave a son to succeed them. And further, where there was more than one surviving son, as in 1087 and 1100, the eldest did not automatically take precedence over his younger brothers. Before the events of the eleventh century can usefully be described, therefore, it is important to grasp how controversial and problematic the choice of a new English king could be, and to understand what factors might lead to the success of one claimant to the throne and the failure of others.

In the spring of 1002, Emma, the sister of Duke Richard II of Normandy, crossed the Channel to England and married King Aethelred II (978–1016). The King was in his mid-thirties; he had been married before and had children. The new queen was probably about 20 and the English king was her first husband. By the twelfth century, this episode was already regarded as the first link in a long chain of events which ended with the Norman Conquest. According to Orderic Vitalis, it was through Emma that the Normans 'won power in England'. And Henry of Huntingdon stated that 'from this union of the English king with the daughter of the Norman duke, the Normans were justified according to the law of peoples, in both claiming and gaining possession of England'.[1] It is certainly correct to say that, whatever hereditary claim Duke William of Normandy had to the English throne in 1066, it derived ultimately from the marriage of 1002. But matters were not as straightforward as this as far as succession to the throne in eleventh-century England was concerned. Aethelred II was succeeded by Edmund, his eldest surviving son by his first wife, not by Emma of Normandy. Edmund in turn was replaced by a Danish invader, Cnut, whose two sons by different partners (the second of whom was the same Emma who had married Aethelred) succeeded him. With the failure of the Danish line, Emma's surviving son by Aethelred, Edward, became king, and, when he failed to leave an obvious heir of his own, he was followed as king by a nobleman, Harold Godwineson, who was linked to the royal family through marriage rather than descent. Harold was viewed as a usurper by Duke William of Normandy, who claimed that Edward the Confessor had chosen him as his heir. He defeated Harold in battle and took his place as king in 1066. Two of William's sons, neither of whom was the eldest, followed him on to the throne.

England was not alone in tenth- and eleventh-century Western Europe in lacking clearly established principles of royal succession. Indeed, dynastic instability was the norm in Britain and beyond; and only the kingdom of France, where between 996 and 1316 sons succeeded fathers as kings in an unbroken line, stood apart from the general pattern. Sons, brothers, uncles, cousins and even more distant relations might all be contenders for royal power, and selecting a king usually involved making a choice between rivals. The deceased king might ideally have wished to pass on his throne to his eldest son, if he had one; but, in England between 1016 and 1100, this only happened twice (in 1016 and 1035). More often, the throne passed from a king to a relation who was not his son at all. Both Harold 'Harefoot' and William II were succeeded by their brothers; Edward the Confessor was only a cousin of his predecessor in 1042; and when Edward himself died in 1066, the throne passed to his brother-in-law. There was also much more to becoming king than family ties to the previous incumbent.

These were important, but so was designation by the previous king. Edward the Confessor was almost certainly named as his successor by Harthacnut; Edward in turn appears to have designated Harold Godwineson on his deathbed; and William the Conqueror probably did the same for his son William Rufus, although there is some uncertainty about this. There is no evidence that Edmund 'Ironside', Harold 'Harefoot', Harthacnut or Henry I were designated by their predecessors, and to complicate matters even more, William the Conqueror claimed that he had been designated as heir to the throne by Edward the Confessor before any such designation was given to Harold Godwineson. If two separate designations were indeed made by Edward (and there is much doubt about this, as will be seen), did one made in the expectation of imminent death trump another made 15 years earlier in very different circumstances?

In both England and Normandy, it seems, a so-called *post obitum* bequest, one designed to take effect on the death of a donor, was binding. For two reasons at least, however, Duke William's claim to be the rightful successor of King Edward could have been regarded in England as deficient. First, according to English custom, the donor's *verba novissima* (the 'last words' made in the expectation of imminent death) were regarded as particularly forceful and superseded previous *post obitum* grants of the same property. And second, in England a *post obitum* grant was regarded as effective only when the recipient had also been given possession of the property bequeathed. This could be done by crowning the heir during the lifetime of his predecessor or by sharing kingship in some way. Something like this may have happened when Edward the Confessor returned to England in 1041; but neither of these things happened in William of Normandy's case and so, even if he had been promised the succession by King Edward in 1051 and again in 1064, and even if Edward had not designated Harold on his deathbed, the English could reasonably have viewed the late king's bequests to William as incomplete. In Normandy, by contrast, Edward's *post obitum* grant to William (formally made before high-status witnesses, according to William de Poitiers) was considered conclusive and irrevocable under any circumstances. This Norman custom may also have been behind King William's reluctant acceptance in 1087 that his son Robert, to whom he had earlier promised the duchy of Normandy, would have to succeed him.[2] In 1066 meanwhile, both Harold and William were able to base their claims to the throne on the testamentary customs of England and Normandy respectively. Both claims had their merits and, in the end, only the judgement of God on the battlefield could decide between them.

But whilst a kinship link with the previous ruler and designation by him were essential in establishing a right to succeed, they were not sufficient, even together, to guarantee the accession of one candidate rather than another. Most claimants to the English throne during this period lacked at least one of these requirements as they sought power; and even when a claimant had both, as Harold Godwineson and William of Normandy said they had, at least one was weak and thinly based. What all the ultimately successful claimants did have, however, was the support of a sufficiently large proportion of the English secular and ecclesiastical aristocracy. An element of election is strongly hinted at in accounts of the ways that all of the eleventh-century English kings came to power. According to John of Worcester, for example, whilst Harold Godwineson had been appointed by Edward the Confessor as his successor, it was just as important that he 'was elected by the primates of all England to the dignity of kingship'.[3] 'Election' is probably too precise and formal a word, however, for what actually happened in the days and weeks following a king's death. In the absence of an obvious heir (and there was only rarely one of these), the most important task for someone who considered himself 'king-worthy' was to convince the political élite that he rather than his rivals had the ability to do the job: 'the king was the man who in practice could command the allegiance of the ealdormen and thegns'.[4] To an extent, what this entailed depended on the circumstances of a particular interregnum. Support was not always given enthusiastically, and both Cnut and William the Conqueror became king because an exhausted and demoralised English aristocracy saw little alternative to accepting them. Edward the Confessor became king in 1042 in part because he had no obvious rival, but also because he had the support of Earl Godwine of Wessex, England's most powerful man, who may have seen a chance to dominate the recently-returned exile and further tighten his family's hold on the kingdom. William II and Henry I, too, struggled to establish themselves as king in 1087 and 1100; but having managed to recruit more powerful and extensive support than their brother Robert, they eventually prevailed. They had managed to prove that they, amongst all the other potential kings of England, were best qualified to rule.

Rulers across eleventh-century Europe were expected to be pious, just, generous, brave and responsive to advice. In the end, however, the English magnates, like magnates elsewhere, were likely to throw their support behind the man who seemed most capable of protecting and furthering their own interests. Edward the Confessor probably had to promise his leading subjects that he would do nothing to upset the status quo established by Cnut before they agreed to his accession in 1042. The defeated English submitted to William I without more of a fight in 1066 because they had concluded that this was the best hope they had of keeping their lands; Henry I made extensive promises in 1100 about how he would rule in order to broaden the base of his support. And Harold Godwineson stood out clearly from the other claimants to the throne in 1066. Edgar *atheling* was an inexperienced boy, Tostig Godwineson was in exile, and neither Duke William of Normandy nor King Harald Hardrada of Norway was welcome. More than this, however, the Earl of Wessex was a proven warrior, and he presided over a vast landed empire and patronage network. He was the obvious candidate to defend England and the assets of the kingdom's landed élite against foreign attack. It has been said of eleventh-century Scotland that 'the provincial leaders who accepted and backed a new king looked for his patronage, gifts and success in war, for the promise of which they might overlook a defect in his lineage'.[5] These observations apply equally well to eleventh-century England; and, in the end, Edward the Confessor's marriage to Harold's sister and the late king's designation of Harold as his successor probably counted for relatively little in the minds of those who accepted the Earl of Wessex as their king in January 1066.

On one level, therefore, the Norman Conquest was little more than the result of yet another of the many succession disputes which characterised English high politics in the eleventh century and beyond. Admittedly, it was more involved than most because there was a larger number of claimants to the throne than usual, a consequence of the way England's links with both France and Scandinavia had developed during and since the reign of Aethelred II; and because the leading contenders were prepared to defend their claims to the death. But none of this altered the essential nature of the basic question at stake, or the complex set of calculations which always went into determining who the next king should be. One thing was clear, however: if negotiation and other less overtly violent methods failed to do so, force was an acceptable way of reaching a clear resolution.

Alliances and invasions, 991–1016

The 50 years or so prior to Edward the Confessor's accession to the English throne in 1042 do not just provide colourful background to the events of the Norman Conquest. They are of great significance in their own right. It was during this period that the first meaningful contacts between England and Normandy were established. As we have seen, Emma's Norman descendants acquired a hereditary claim, albeit a remote one, to the English throne. More important, however, must have been the experience Edward himself had of Norman hospitality and support during his difficult and uncertain youth. He would remember how well he had been treated by his cousins across the Channel when he came to look for an heir of his own. This period also saw the conquest of England by Cnut of Denmark. Direct Danish control of England was short-lived; but its legacy for later non-Danish rulers of England was a system of regionalised government with the potential fundamentally to affect the relationship between the English king and his subjects. More broadly, and long after the last Danish king of England had died, the Scandinavian dimension in English and, indeed, British politics was still significant.

Diplomatic relations between the kingdom of England and the duchy of Normandy appear first to have been established in the early 990s. The context for this was provided by the Viking raids on England which, after 70 years or so of relative freedom from external attack, had recommenced in the 980s. In 990–1, with papal assistance, an agreement was made between Aethelred II and Duke Richard I of Normandy, Emma's father. It is not clear why this agreement was made, but it probably had something to do with Norman willingness to provide a refuge for the Viking raiders who were menacing England.[6] How successful this deal was in the short term is unclear, but it certainly seems to have collapsed by 1000–1 when, the *Anglo-Saxon Chronicle* records, a Viking fleet which had been raiding England took refuge in 'Richard's kingdom'.[7] And it is against this background of worsening relations between England and Normandy that Aethelred's marriage to Emma should be viewed – as another formalised attempt to prevent Norman ports being used as offshore bases for Viking attacks on England.

The marriage notwithstanding, the relationships between England and Normandy continued to be troubled. William de Jumièges describes a failed English attack on Normandy which took place soon after 1002. This may have been Aethelred's response to an agreement made between King Swein Forkbeard of Denmark and Richard II to the effect that the Danes would sell their plunder only in Normandy in return for a Norman promise to shelter Swein's wounded.[8] As for Queen Emma, she frequently witnessed her husband's charters, which suggests that she was influential at court; but events in south-western England in 1003 may not have helped the newly-weds. Exeter had been part of the collection of lands granted to Emma by the King in 1002. In 1003, according to the *Anglo-Saxon Chronicle*, the city was attacked 'on account of the French *ceorl* Hugh, whom the queen had appointed as her reeve'. John of Worcester was even more explicit: Exeter, he alleged, fell 'through the evil counsel, negligence and treachery of the Norman Earl Hugh, whom Queen Emma had put in charge of Devon'.[9] It is not clear what Hugh is supposed to have done, or whether he was singled out because of the harshness of his governing style or because of his nationality. There are strong hints here, however, of the kind of ethnic tension between English and Norman which would surface repeatedly as the eleventh century went on.

Nevertheless, and in the teeth of such continuing difficulties, Aethelred continued in need of Norman help against Scandinavian attack. The King asked Duke Richard for advice and help in 1009, probably because of the arrival in England of 'the immense raiding army' under Thorkell the Tall in the same year.[10] Then, when another fleet, this one under the command of King Swein of Denmark, landed in England in the summer of 1013, Aethelred looked to Normandy once again. Swein travelled freely across northern, midland and western England, receiving submissions wherever he went, and whilst Aethelred remained in London for the time being, his wife and their children, the *athelings* Edward and Alfred, crossed the Channel to take refuge at the Norman court. The King himself had moved to the Isle of Wight by Christmas 1013 but soon after that he, too, travelled to Normandy to rejoin his family.[11]

Aethelred had abandoned his kingdom, but Swein's sudden death in February 1014 gave Aethelred an unexpected chance quickly to recover his throne. He negotiated a return to England for himself and his family with various promises to govern better and more justly than he had done before his exile. But after campaigning energetically against Swein's younger son, Cnut, in the late summer of 1015, Aethelred died, on 23 April 1016, with the situation in England far from resolved. He was succeeded as king by his eldest surviving son from his first marriage, Edmund 'Ironside', who was eventually defeated by Cnut at the Battle of Ashingdon on 18 October 1016. For a few weeks the kingdom was divided between the two adversaries, with Edmund holding Wessex and Cnut taking charge of Mercia and Northumbria. But after Edmund's death on 30 November 1016, Cnut succeeded peacefully to the entire kingdom.

English, Danes and Normans, 1016–1042

Links with Scandinavia had been crucial to England's political, economic and cultural life since the Viking invasions of the ninth and tenth centuries, and the extensive Danish and Norwegian settlement which had followed in their wake. After 1016, however, with the deaths of Aethelred and Edmund, and the establishment of a Danish king on the English throne, England's political orientation shifted even more firmly towards the North Sea and Scandinavia, and the kingdom's relationship with Normandy entered a new and difficult phase. A marriage with Emma was still at the heart of things, however, because in the summer of 1017, Cnut 'ordered the widow of King Aethelred, Richard's daughter, to be fetched as his wife'.[12] It is unlikely that this marriage was part of a negotiated pact between the Norman and English rulers. With the English *athelings* still protected in Normandy, Emma's brother across the Channel could still cause trouble for the new Anglo-Danish regime. William de Jumièges's description of how Emma was seized by Cnut whilst still in London and of how they were married only a few days later is more convincing; and it has been suggested that Cnut might have acted in this way, with little apparent regard to Emma's own wishes or those of Duke Richard, 'to secure his position against any threat from the surviving *athelings*', Edward and Alfred.[13] That is to say, if he could marry Emma and have children with her, the claims of her children by Aethelred would lose much of their significance, and Emma would be bound to support her new children against her old ones. In the end, it is impossible to know precisely what Cnut's motives were in marrying Emma, or, indeed, what Emma made of the prospect of her power in England being revived. Another source, admittedly one commissioned by the Queen and written ostensibly in praise of her, describes how, far from being forced to marry Cnut, it was Emma who kept him waiting, agreeing to the union only once it had been agreed that only a son of theirs would succeed to the English throne.[14] The weight of evidence tends to suggest that Emma was prepared to abandon her sons by Aethelred, and to break her links with Normandy, in order to return to England as the new king's consort.

Meanwhile, those same sons were strengthening their Norman connections. The *athelings* Edward and Alfred were 'educated at the court of the dukes of the Normans, [and] they were treated with so much honour by the duke, Robert, after the death of his father Duke Richard [in 1026], that bound to them by great love he adopted them as his brothers'.[15] Then, at some time during his reign, probably during the first half of the 1030s, Robert sent envoys to Cnut demanding that the *athelings* should return to England from their Norman exile. Cnut rejected this request, and in response Robert prepared a fleet and set sail for England, only to have his invasion plans ruined by the weather. William de Jumièges is the only authority for this story, and the truth behind it is impossible to establish, but there is evidence from charters of the early 1030s which strongly suggests that Edward at least was regarded as the rightful king of England by his Norman cousins.[16] Despite this, Edward was not in a position immediately to get involved in the power struggle which followed the death of Cnut in 1035. Two of Cnut's sons vied for the English throne: Harold 'Harefoot', his son by his first wife, Aelfgifu of Northampton (although his enemies claimed that Harold had less distinguished parents), and Harthacnut, his son by Emma. The latter was in Denmark securing his position there against King Magnus of Norway, however; and Harold was soon regarded as 'full king over England'.[17]

It is against this background of instability and division amongst the Anglo-Danish aristocracy that stories of the *athelings'* return to England from Normandy in 1036 make best sense. According to William de Jumièges, Edward returned to England when he heard of Cnut's death, defeated an English army at Southampton but then went back to Normandy, having realised that he would get nowhere without a larger force behind him. More certainly, according to the *Anglo-Saxon Chronicle*, the *atheling* Alfred arrived in England in 1036 to see his mother, who was in Winchester. Emma had probably decided to desert the fading cause of her absent son, Harthacnut, and throw her weight behind a challenge to the throne by one of the sons of her first marriage.[18] The sources are by no means clear-cut about what happened after Alfred's arrival. They all agree that he died horribly, but there is no consensus about how this happened or about who was responsible. Those authorities hostile to Earl Godwine and his son Harold suggest that Godwine forcibly prevented Alfred from seeing Emma, took him into captivity, and killed or mutilated his companions. Alfred was then blinded and finally died under the care of the monks at Ely. Other sources describe Alfred's death but do not mention Godwine by name; implicitly they blame King Harold. The death of Alfred is important, however, because the course of much of the politics of Edward the Confessor's reign was dictated by the King's relationship with, first, Earl Godwine, and then his son, Harold. It has been regularly suggested ever since that Edward was prejudiced against the Godwine family from the start because of its role in the shocking murder of his brother.[19]

After the landings had come to nothing, in 1037 Harold 'was chosen as king everywhere, and Harthacnut was deserted because he was too long in Denmark'. Queen Emma, moreover, went into exile in Flanders.[20] This was almost certainly a reflection of Harold's anger at Emma's scheming on behalf of his half-brothers. Meanwhile, Harthacnut had made peace for the time being with Magnus of Norway and was able finally to turn his attention to England. There was little sign that he or Emma, whom he joined at Bruges in 1039, would be able to do anything about the situation there whilst Harold ruled; but obligingly, Harold died, suddenly and unexpectedly, in 1040 and, on his arrival in England, a bitter Harthacnut had him 'dug up and thrown into the fen'.[21] Earl Godwine, too, according to John of Worcester, had to buy the new king's goodwill with a ship manned by 80 fully-armed warriors; he was also required to swear that he had not played any part in the death of Alfred in 1036, and that the whole thing had been King Harold's idea.

Harthacnut was not a popular king. Immediately after arriving in England, he imposed 'a very severe tax', and in 1041 he ravaged Worcestershire after two of his tax-collectors had been killed there.[22] It was in these circumstances that Edward *atheling* returned to England from Normandy once more. This time, however, unlike in 1036, he was welcome; indeed, he must have received an invitation, and Emma was probably responsible for this. She and Harthacnut may have been trying to build a wider base of support for the latter's unpopular regime. Harthacnut may also have wanted someone to act as his deputy in England whilst he dealt with affairs in Denmark, or he may already have been ill and thinking about the succession. Whatever the reason for his return, however, Edward 'was sworn in as king; and he thus stayed at his brother's court as long as he lived'.[23] This probably meant that Edward and his half-brother were to reign together to some extent (it is not clear how this would have worked in practice; perhaps Edward would act as regent whilst Harthacnut returned to Denmark, as he must have planned to do) and that Edward was Harthacnut's designated successor. In the event, Harthacnut 'did nothing worthy of a king as long as he ruled', and when he died in June 1042 at the wedding ceremony of one of his prominent nobles, nobody mourned. Without any hesitation, it seems, and even before Harthacnut was buried 'all the people received Edward as king, as was his natural right'.[24]

The King and his earls, 1042–1045

When he had left England in 1013, Edward *atheling* was on the run; and when Cnut was at the height of his power, with sons to spare, Edward's chances of becoming king were remote. And even though Edward may have been recognised as the rightful king of England in Normandy during the 1030s, the events of 1041–2 amounted to a remarkable reversal of fortune for him. Nevertheless, in 1042 his inheritance was not a straightforward one, and his position was weak from the start. He was at least 38 in 1042; arguably his best years were already behind him. What is more, having spent only a year in England before becoming king, its geography, traditions, governmental structures, perhaps even its language, would have been unfamiliar to him. He had no established network of followers within England on whose support he could rely, and there can have been few close to the royal court who remembered the regime of Edward's father. The lay and ecclesiastical élites had been largely created by Cnut, and they owed their loyalty and their fortunes to the Danish kings. Nevertheless, Edward would need their backing if he was to have any chance of succeeding as king.

According to most of the sources, such support came from Earl Godwine of Wessex who took the lead in reconciling his fellow magnates to their new king.[25] The Earl was determined to take the new king under his wing, perhaps so that he could put himself in a position to dominate him, or perhaps to convince Edward of his loyalty and get his powers confirmed. After all, Godwine was deeply implicated in the murder of Edward's brother, Alfred, in 1036, and he had spent his life fighting for the Danish kings. His father, Wulfnoth, had betrayed Edward's father, Aethelred, in 1009.[26] If Edward regarded Godwine with suspicion in 1042, this is understandable. At the same time, Edward was in no position in 1042–3 to alienate his most powerful subject; and anyway, Edward may have wanted to make use of Godwine's Danish links. Through his wife Gytha, Cnut's former sister-in-law, Godwine was a kinsman of King Swein Estrithson of Denmark. Swein was struggling in 1042 against King Magnus of Norway, who almost certainly had his own designs on the English throne; so Edward had a vested interest in Swein's victory. Distasteful as Edward and his leading subject might have found such an idea, they needed each other as the new reign began.

A good deal of political bargaining probably took up the ten months or so between Harthacnut's death and Edward's consecration in April 1043. All three great earls, Godwine, Leofric and Siward, remained in position; but the new king's relationship with Earl Godwine and his family soon began to assume ever greater significance. In or shortly after 1043 Godwine's two eldest sons, Swein and Harold, were given their own earldoms in the west midlands, and in East Anglia, Cambridgeshire, Essex and Middlesex respectively. Godwine's nephew, and Swein of Denmark's brother, Beorn, was granted an earldom in the east midlands in 1045; and, to set the seal on the relationship, Edward married Godwine's daughter Edith in the same year. She was at least 15, if not 20 years younger than Edward; and, according to the *Vita Edwardi*, she was beautiful, intelligent, modest and chaste.[27] This last quality was stressed much later by writers seeking to explain the childlessness of the royal couple and emphasise Edward's saintly qualities. When the marriage took place, however, there can be little doubt that it was intended to produce sons; the next king was supposed to have Godwine blood.

Another consequence of this early bargaining may have been the humiliation of Queen Emma in 1043. According to the *Anglo-Saxon Chronicle*, soon after his coronation Edward, in company with Leofric, Godwine and Siward, rode to Winchester where his mother was living. There they 'deprived her of all the treasures which she owned . . . because she had formerly been very hard to the king, her son, in that she did less for him than he wished both before he became king and afterwards as well'.[28] Her adviser, Stigand, who had recently become bishop of East Anglia, was also removed from his position. Edward may have felt aggrieved by his mother's inconsistent treatment of him over the preceding 25 years (although the choices Emma had to make in pursuing her children's best interests were never straightforward); and perhaps this was his attempt to cut her down to size and assert his ability to rule independently of her. But the great earls also stood to benefit if Emma was prevented from exercising any influence over the new king. That she was later restored to royal favour may suggest that Edward acted rather hastily in 1043. When Emma died at Winchester in 1052, she was buried there, significantly alongside her second husband, Cnut.

Edward and the Normans

Despite confirming and, in Godwine's case, extending, the powers of the established great families at the start of his reign, Edward did not completely cast off his Norman influences. According to the *Vita Edwardi*, when Edward returned from Normandy,

. . . quite a number of men of that nation, and they not base-born, accompanied him. And these, since he was master of the whole kingdom,

he kept with him, enriched them with many honours, and made them his
privy counsellors and administrators of the royal palace.[29]

However, apart from Robert de Jumièges, who became bishop of London
in 1044 and archbishop of Canterbury in 1051, and Ralph of Mantes,
Edward's nephew by his sister's marriage, who became earl of Hereford
before the end of the 1040s, there is little trace of these Normans.
Neither the witness lists to Edward's charters (which show who was with
the King when the charter was granted) nor Domesday Book (which
records who held land across most of England when Edward was king)
suggest either that Norman influence was strong at the English court
after 1042 or that Edward lavishly endowed his Norman friends with
English lands. Indeed, the witness lists to Edward's charters 'show
massive continuity of personnel between Cnut's and Edward's courts'.[30]
Other foreigners, such as Robert FitzWimarc and Ralph 'the Staller',
received small grants of land from Edward, but they were both Bretons,
not Normans.

Edward did promote Normans to influential positions within the
English Church, but it is hard here as well to interpret his actions as
evidence of a thoroughgoing preference for Normans over English.
Edward appointed three Normans to bishoprics: Robert de Jumièges;
and two royal clerks, Ulf and William, who became respectively bishop
of Dorchester in 1049 and bishop of London in 1051. Other new
bishops were Englishmen apart from Herman of Ramsbury and Sherborne (appointed in 1046), Giso of Wells, and Walter of Hereford (both
appointed in 1060), all of whom were from Lotharingia. Lotharingia was
a centre for the reforming ideas which were spreading through the
Western Church in the second half of the eleventh century, so such
appointments may testify as much to Edward's desire to keep up to date
with the latest developments in the Church as to a deliberate plan to
create a Norman or at least a non-English episcopate. There is certainly
little evidence to suggest, from either the lay or ecclesiastical side,
that Edward was intent on filling the kingdom with Normans from the
moment he became king. Having said that, the Normans who came to
England in the 1040s did become unpopular; and especially at moments
of national crisis, their 'foreignness' could work against the King. In
1051, for example, the castle which had been built by 'the foreigners' in

Herefordshire was a cause of friction and critical comment.[31] These men came to have a political importance belied by their mere numbers.

Edward and Godwine

Between 1046 and 1050, the relationship between King Edward and Earl Godwine began to deteriorate. In 1046, whilst campaigning on the Welsh border (part of his normal responsibilities as earl in that area), Swein Godwineson abducted Eadgifu, the abbess of Leominster in Herefordshire. John of Worcester suggests that Swein had wanted to marry the lady in question and that the King had refused him permission to do so. It is more likely that he was interested in the lands of her abbey in Herefordshire. Either way, having surrendered her, Swein went into exile, first in Flanders and then in Denmark.[32] The limits of Godwine influence were also evident in 1047 when the Earl tried to persuade Edward to send ships to help Swein of Denmark in his struggle against Magnus of Norway. The Earl's suggestion was dismissed as it seemed a 'foolish plan to everybody', and by 1047 Edward was apparently happy to let the Scandinavian kings thrash things out between themselves. This was a risky strategy, but it paid off when the immediate threat to England was removed with Magnus's death in October 1047. He was succeeded by Harald Hardrada, a Viking warrior with a legendary reputation.[33]

The association between Edward and Godwine was perhaps further undermined in 1049 when the King received a request for naval assistance from the Holy Roman Emperor, Henry III, in a campaign against Count Baldwin V of Flanders.[34] Baldwin regularly allowed his harbours to be used by Scandinavian pirates who preyed upon English ships in the North Sea. Importantly, too, Flanders was the regular first port of call for exiles from the English court. Emma had gone there in 1036, and in 1046 Swein had fled to Baldwin's court before going on to Denmark. Godwine himself was to take refuge there in 1051, and in the same year Tostig Godwineson married Judith, Count Baldwin's sister. Edward never had to use the fleet which he gathered at Sandwich in 1049, as Baldwin and the Emperor came to terms, but the hostile stance he adopted towards a friend of Godwine cannot have gone unnoticed by the Earl and his followers.

After Swein Godwineson's exile, his lands in England were shared out between his brother, Harold, and his cousin, Beorn. Not surprisingly, they were not pleased to see him return to England in 1049. Swein, however, asked them to help him regain the King's favour. Harold refused, but Beorn prevaricated with fateful consequences. On meeting Swein, he was abducted and murdered. Swein had added a crime of international significance (Beorn was the king of Denmark's brother) to his already lengthy list of previous convictions; Edward and his councillors declared him *nithing*, an outcast irrecoverably disgraced, and he fled into exile, once more in Flanders. His lands were given to the King's nephew, Ralph.[35] In 1050, however, Swein returned to England once more and, remarkably, Edward pardoned him again.[36] This event has usually been seen as further evidence of Edward's weakness in the face of Godwine family power. On the other hand, perhaps Edward thought that Swein's return might sow further dissension amongst his wife's kin: it was unclear what status the returning exile was to have, after all, and at whose expense. Edward may already have been plotting the downfall of his kingdom's most powerful clan.

The crisis of 1051

In 1051, there was open confrontation between the King and his most powerful family. Whether Edward deliberately manufactured the crisis or took advantage of events as they arose is unclear. It has been suggested, for example, that, his marriage to Edith having failed to produce an heir, Edward's first concern in 1051 was to find himself a new wife. Divorcing her, the theory goes, meant that the whole family had to be destroyed.[37] The lack of an obvious successor may indeed have been an element in Edward's calculations in 1051; but his wider concern was probably to rid himself once and for all of Godwine influence.

Two events provoked the clash. First, on the death of Archbishop Eadsige of Canterbury in October 1050, the monks of Canterbury elected one of their number, a relative of Godwine's named Aethelric, as his successor. Edward, however, was determined not to allow such an important appointment to slip out of his control and he named his Norman friend and adviser, Bishop Robert de Jumièges of London, as his candidate for the archbishopric. Robert was subsequently blamed by sources close to Godwine and his family, principally the *Vita Edwardi*, for turning the King against the Earl.[38] It is more credible to suggest, however, that in pulling rank over Godwine, whose power and influence in Kent were considerable, the King had insulted the Earl's dignity and undermined his authority. Second, when Count Eustace of Boulogne, Edward's brother-in-law, arrived in Kent at the beginning of September 1051, his men quarrelled with Godwine's in Dover, and there were casualties. When Eustace complained to the King about the incident, Edward ordered Godwine to go to Kent and discipline his people, but the Earl refused. Edward then ordered his council and army to meet at Gloucester on 7 September. Both sides, the King supported by earls Siward, Leofric and Ralph, and Godwine by his sons, armed themselves.

A new date for the summit meeting was then arranged. Godwine agreed to answer the charges against him on 21 September at London, and he provided hostages to guarantee his conduct in the meantime. On his way to London, however, the Earl's support began to evaporate. When he reached the south bank of the Thames he was told by the King's messengers that he could regain royal favour when he produced Alfred *atheling* and his companions.[39] The message was clear – the King was implacable, there was no chance of a fair hearing and Godwine's only option was to flee abroad. Along with his wife Gytha, and his sons Swein, Tostig and Gyrth, he went to Flanders; Harold and his brother Leofwine went to Ireland. Sentences of outlawry were pronounced against them all. As for Queen Edith, she was sent to live as a nun at Wherwell in Hampshire.

William of Normandy and the offer of the crown

By the end of 1051, Edward's triumph over Godwine and his family seemed complete. The King was quick to redistribute their confiscated lands. Aelfgar, the son of Earl Leofric, was granted Harold's earldom of East Anglia, and lands in the south-west were granted to another of Edward's loyal supporters, Odda of Deerhurst. Wessex was probably retained by the King himself. Edward may have taken steps to formalise his succession plans, too, because, according to one version of the *Anglo-Saxon Chronicle*, which was later followed by John of Worcester, at this point Duke William of Normandy 'came from overseas with a great force of Frenchmen, and the king received him and as many of his companions as suited him, and let him go again'.[40] The purpose of this visit is not made clear in these sources; nor is it certain that it happened at all. But it has often been suggested that, determined to take advantage of his new-found freedom to act, Edward designated William of Normandy as his heir during this visit. Such a claim is of obvious significance, and it, along with the early career of the man to whom the offer was allegedly made, is worth investigating more closely.

Born probably in 1027 or 1028, Duke William II of Normandy, later King William I of England, was the illegitimate son of Duke Robert I of Normandy. His mother, whose name was Herleva, has been variously identified as the daughter of an undertaker or a tanner of Falaise, and as a woman from the ducal household. William's illegitimacy was not yet the bar to succession it was later to become; he was formally designated as his father's heir in 1035, and became duke in the following year when Robert died on his return from a pilgrimage to the Holy Land. William was no more than eight or nine at the time, however, and for the next few years he was reliant, not infrequently for his very survival, on the loyalty of supporters from his father's regime. By the late 1030s, their control of the duchy was slipping away, and aristocratic feuding made Normandy a violent and dangerous place for the young duke. He survived this turbulent period, however, and by the early 1040s he was old enough to assert his power in person. Nevertheless, when in 1046–7 William had to face serious and coordinated opposition from within his duchy, he looked for help to King Henry I of France, to whom he had performed homage in 1035–6. Accordingly, in January 1047 King Henry led his forces into Normandy and came face to face with the rebels at a place called Val-ès-Dunes. The battle appears to have been a messy and uncoordinated one, but the rebels were defeated, and William was secure.

In the years immediately following Val-ès-Dunes, William's authority within Normandy continued to develop. His half-brother Odo, one of Herleva's sons by Herluin de Conteville, the Norman magnate she had married after William's birth, became bishop of Bayeux in 1049 or 1050. This appointment helped to extend ducal influence in western Normandy; and by 1049, too, it seems that William was negotiating his own marriage to Matilda, the daughter of Count Baldwin V of Flanders. Despite papal objections to it (Pope Leo IX argued that William and

Matilda were too closely related to each other), the marriage took place, probably in 1050. This prestigious union followed hard upon a successful campaign William and Henry I had jointly conducted against Count Geoffrey of Anjou in 1049. By 1050, therefore, William had begun to consolidate his authority within Normandy and assert himself over his neighbours. Then, at around this time, according to William de Jumièges and William de Poitiers, Archbishop Robert of Canterbury travelled to Normandy and on King Edward's behalf told William that he would be the English king's heir. As security for this promise, William de Poitiers alleged, Edward sent to William the son and grandson of Earl Godwine, Wulfnoth and Haakon, as hostages. English sources do not mention this embassy, however, and its timing is unclear. William de Jumièges's suggestion that the offer was made before the fall of Godwine and his family is unpersuasive.[41] Still dominant and strong prior to their exile, the Earl and his relatives stood to lose considerably by it: their ambitions were predicated on the assumption that the next English king would be of Godwine blood.

It was central to the Norman case after 1066, however, that William was Edward the Confessor's legitimate heir. If such a view was to carry any weight, and given that William's hereditary claim to the English throne was weak, and that his support within England was non-existent, a valid *post obitum* designation by Edward was essential to buttress the legality of William's actions in 1066. William de Poitiers argued that Edward made William his heir out of gratitude for the support he had received during his exile, and in securing the English throne in 1042.[42] But William was only about 15 by then; and, more importantly, the turbulent politics of Normandy in the late 1030s and early 1040s are likely to have prevented the Duke from giving his English cousin much by way of practical help. It is also remarkable that no Norman source before Wace in the late twelfth century mentioned the visit by William to England in 1051 which is referred to in the 'D' text of the *Anglo-Saxon Chronicle*. If this meeting between King and Duke did happen, it could considerably have strengthened Norman arguments about William's claim to the English throne.[43] This gives rise to the strong possibility that the 1051 visit never took place at all, and that, even though the 'D' text of the *Chronicle* was compiled before 1066 and is generally well informed, it may simply be mistaken about what happened.

Alternatively, if the *Chronicle* is correct about the meeting having taken place, it may have been wiser for the Norman writers to overlook it because it reflected less well on their Duke than they would have liked. King Edward 'received' as many of William's companions 'as suited' him, the *Chronicle* records; and it has been pointed out that the Old English word translated as 'received' (*underfeng*) carries implications of overlordship.[44] In other words, with Edward at the height of his power late in 1051, and William still emerging from a period of sustained instability within his duchy and on its borders, he may have come to England to seek the English king's military, financial and diplomatic support as much as to be designated Edward's heir. He could have been a needy supplicant rather than a feted successor.

On the other hand, there are sound reasons to think that, in the flush of his triumph over Godwine and his family, King Edward might have turned to Duke William. By the end of 1051, Edward was separated from his wife, he was unlikely to have children soon if at all, and William of Normandy was his closest male relative on his mother's side. Moreover, if the Norman chroniclers protest a little too much about Edward's attitude to his Norman relatives, there is no reason to doubt that he felt some gratitude for the way he had been treated there as a youth. At the same time, given that relations between England and Flanders in the mid eleventh century tended to be problematic, William's marriage to Matilda may have made the English king uneasy. However, the marriage was at least a sign of William's growing reputation and standing. Also, by the end of 1052, William's erstwhile ally, King Henry I of France had joined forces with Count Geoffrey of Anjou against the Norman duke. The prospect of a union between Normandy and Flanders may have had something to do with this; but the idea of a Norman on the English throne would have been even more threatening and could have convinced them that Norman power was growing too fast at their expense and that something needed to be done to check it. Henry and Geoffrey failed to impose such a check, of course, most notably at the battles of Mortemer in February 1054 and at Varaville in 1057, both of which were decisive Norman victories.

None of this conclusively proves that Robert de Jumièges went to Normandy and promised the succession to Duke William and that William of Normandy came to England in 1051 to have that offer confirmed. At best, the evidence of the *Anglo-Saxon Chronicle* is ambiguous and the accounts of Edward's designation of Duke William given by William de Jumièges and William de Poitiers are suspect. There is also no compelling reason to think that Edward's leading subjects saw Duke William of Normandy as a desirable heir to the English throne in the early 1050s; and William de Poitiers's claim that Edward made this offer 'with the assent of his magnates' is difficult to accept. However, Siward, Leofric and the rest may have gone along with Edward's plan if the offer of the crown was only provisional. It has already been seen how a *post obitum* grant, in order to be binding in England, needed to involve some kind of transfer to the recipient of the property bequeathed. There is nothing to suggest that William was crowned in 1051 or that he shared kingship in some way with Edward thereafter. Indeed, there is no sign that William took any interest in English affairs for more than a decade after 1051. Any designation of William in 1051 may have been no more than an interim measure, therefore, made on the understanding that Edward might later change his mind. This, after all, is what he appears to have done.

The return of Godwine

King Edward had little time to enjoy his liberation from Godwine's influence. His exile and that of his sons proved only temporary, and their return to England dealt a mortal blow to Edward's authority. Despite his attempts to consolidate his position in 1051–2 by redistributing the exiles' lands and by fortifying the coast against any attempted return by them, in June 1052 Godwine landed in Kent and then sailed on to Sussex. He soon returned to Bruges, but this preliminary sortie had probably reassured him about the amount of support he still retained within his earldom. Meanwhile, Harold and Leofwine had crossed from Dublin and ravaged in Somerset and Devon. Eventually they met up with their father, who had left Flanders again, on the Isle of Wight, probably in August 1052. Together, they then sailed around the coast to Sussex and on to Kent. Finally they began their voyage up the Thames and towards London, where the King, with a large naval and land force, awaited their arrival.

Battle and even civil war were serious possibilities in the late summer of 1052. In mid-September, Godwine sent messengers to the King from his base at Southwark asking for the restoration of all that he and his sons had been deprived of in the previous year. Edward refused and appears to have been prepared to fight. But so was Godwine, and the King found that his support had begun to waver. The prospect of civil war was too much for those advising him, in particular for earls Siward and Leofric, and a truce was soon negotiated and terms of settlement were agreed. Godwine and his sons declared their innocence of any crime of which they had been accused, and they were then restored to their lands and titles. Queen Edith returned to court, too. Many foreigners, Robert de Jumièges amongst them, who were widely blamed for having provoked the crisis in the first place, fled the country after having been outlawed. Robert himself was replaced as archbishop of Canterbury by Stigand, who had played a leading role in negotiating the peace. He was already, and continued to be, bishop of Winchester.

King Edward's bold attempt to free himself from the control of Godwine and his kin had failed. He was powerless to prevent them reasserting their power when 'it was hateful to almost all of them [the English nobles] to fight against men of their own race . . . and they also did not wish the country to be laid the more open to foreigners through their destroying each other'.[45] These were serious considerations, of course, although perhaps a little disingenuous. Godwine and his sons may have lost their lands and titles in 1051, but their influence was deeply entrenched, and they probably returned to England before their vast network of supporters had begun to break apart. Those defeated in a conflict with them would have had much to lose. What is more, the revival of Godwine power would probably have been seen by a relieved English élite as dealing a fatal blow to any claim William of Normandy might have had to the English throne. As for King Edward, after the events of 1052 his meaningful power was more circumscribed than ever before. For the rest of his reign, as he concentrated on hunting and on building Westminster Abbey, control of England lay in the hands of others.

Beyond England

In continental Europe, Scotland and Wales during the mid-1050s, events took place which helped to shape the Norman Conquest. In 1054, Bishop Ealdred of Worcester travelled to the court of Emperor

Henry III in Cologne. John of Worcester later explained that he was on a royal mission to make contact with Edward *atheling*, or Edward 'the Exile', the son of Edmund 'Ironside', and bring him back to England. Edward had spent most of his life in Hungary since fleeing England in the wake of the Danish conquest of 1016; he had married Agatha, a German-Hungarian princess and he held a distinguished position at the Hungarian court. He finally returned to England in 1057 but, for reasons which are unclear and mysterious, he never managed to see the King.[46] He died soon afterwards, leaving in England two daughters, Margaret and Christina, and a son Edgar, who was to pursue his own claims to the throne during a long and adventurous career.

It has usually been assumed that this episode was connected with the succession, and that Edward and Edgar were to be installed as King Edward's heirs. It is hard to think of any other reason why they would have returned to England at this time. William of Normandy's claim to the English throne, such as it was, had probably been overtaken in English minds by the events of 1052, and the King had not produced any sons of his own since Queen Edith's return to court. In such circumstances, and as the King entered his fifth decade, the question of who would succeed him must have begun more and more to preoccupy the English political élite. Edward and Edgar were the surviving representatives of the native English dynasty and the King's nearest male relatives on his father's side. In that sense their hereditary claims were strong. Like Edward in 1042, however, they had no established power-base in England when they returned, and their support amongst the Anglo-Danish aristocracy must have been limited. They may have been Edward's preferred heirs by 1057, but this was not enough to clear a way to the throne.

Also in 1054, King Edward had ordered Earl Siward of Northumbria to march into Scotland. Malcolm II had been succeeded as king of Scots in 1034 by his grandson Duncan I. Duncan himself was murdered and succeeded in 1040 by his rival, the *mormaer* of Moray, Macbeth. Siward's campaign of 1054, therefore, had two principal objectives: the first was to depose Macbeth, and the second was to replace him with a friendly client ruler. Duncan's two sons, Malcolm and Donald Bàn, had fled into exile following their father's death, and Malcolm had found refuge at Siward's court and at King Edward's. If he could be installed as king in Macbeth's place, his English sponsors would expect him to be a pliable ally who accepted that he owed his throne to English help. Despite being assisted by Normans who had fled to Scotland in the aftermath of 1052, Macbeth was defeated in battle by Siward, probably near Dunsinane in Perthshire, and fled. In the process, Siward also seems to have brought Cumberland (Cumbria south of Solway) under English control. By 1058, both Macbeth and his step-son and heir, Lulach, were dead and Malcolm III 'Canmore' was acknowledged as king of Scots both north and south of the frontier with England. The English king's strategy appeared to have worked, therefore; but its success came at a cost. During the campaign against Macbeth, Siward's eldest son and his nephew were killed. His younger son Waltheof was still very young. When Siward died in 1055, therefore, a new earl of Northumbria was appointed from outside his family: this was Tostig Godwineson, and the consequences of his appointment were profound.

By this time a new star had also risen in Wales. In 1039 Gruffudd ap Llewelyn became ruler of Gwynedd and Powys. He spent the next decade and a half fighting to extend his control over south Wales, and by 1055 he had succeeded in establishing himself as ruler of Wales. Gruffudd was also determined to make life as difficult as possible for his English neighbours. In 1039 he defeated a Mercian army near Welshpool (amongst the dead was Edwin, Earl Leofric's brother), and in 1052, whilst raiding near Leominster in Herefordshire, he was confronted by a force made up of 'natives' (Englishmen) and 'Frenchmen' (Normans).[47] These Normans may have come to Herefordshire with Edward's nephew, Earl Ralph, who appears to have introduced some Norman military methods into the area, including the building of a new castle, in order to keep the Welsh at bay. Meanwhile, in 1049, Gruffudd had recruited the help of Danish pirates from Ireland and defeated Bishop Ealdred of Worcester in battle, and in 1053 he invaded Westbury on Severn. Gruffudd was becoming more than just a nuisance to the English authorities, and in due course they would need to find a way of dealing with him.

The rise of the Godwinesons, 1053–1064

In April 1053, Earl Godwine of Wessex died after having celebrated Easter with his sons and the King at Winchester. According to William of Malmesbury and Henry of Huntingdon, in what reads more like a morality tale than a description of actual events, the Earl choked to death on his food after assuring Edward that he had never been disloyal towards him.[48] Suitably, he was buried near his patron, Cnut, at Winchester. His son Harold succeeded him as earl of Wessex, whilst Harold's earldom of East Anglia was given to Aelfgar, the son of Earl Leofric of Mercia. Harold Godwineson was to be the dominant figure in England for the rest of the reign.

Events on the Scottish and Welsh frontiers now began to combine to cause problems for the English government. According to *Vita Edwardi*, the appointment of Tostig Godwineson as earl of Northumbria following the death of Earl Siward in 1055 was an eminently sensible move. Edward was particularly fond of Tostig, who was courageous, wise and shrewd. It made perfect sense to give him the great earldom in the north when Harold was already dominant in the south: these two men were the twin pillars on which English security rested.[49] These arguments, however, underpinned as they are by the *Vita Edwardi*'s need always to speak in positive terms about Queen Edith and her relatives, are less than convincing. With Tostig's appointment, indeed, the power of the Godwinesons was dangerously extended and the balance of power within England was imprudently upset. Moreover, Tostig can have known little if anything of the people, structures and traditions of northern England. He was almost certain to be received there with suspicion and hostility, and Tostig's appointment also caused problems elsewhere.

Soon after it, Earl Aelfgar of East Anglia, Leofric's son, was exiled; probably because he voiced his unhappiness at Tostig's promotion. He may have been afraid that he too would be overlooked when his own father died. In exile he joined forces with Gruffudd ap Llewelyn and raided into Herefordshire. The English defenders under Earl Ralph failed to withstand the assault and 'before any spear had been thrown the English army fled because they were on horseback'.[50] In other words, they were using Norman tactics to fight (traditionally English armies rode to battle and fought on foot), and Ralph's attempt to impose these alien techniques was disastrous; it earned him the damning nickname 'the Timid'. Hereford and its cathedral were destroyed and even when Earl Harold arrived with reinforcements the best he could do was negotiate a truce. A more lasting peace was only established when

King Edward himself travelled to the river Severn in 1058 to accept Gruffudd's formal submission, presumably in return for an English acceptance of Gruffudd's gains and status.

Even this did not bring stability to the Welsh border, however. In 1058 Earl Aelfgar was exiled for the second time. Having been received back into royal favour after his first collaboration with Gruffudd, and having succeeded to the earldom of Mercia in 1057 following the death of his father Leofric, Aelfgar may have overplayed his hand when his daughter Ealdgyth married his old Welsh ally shortly afterwards. It was probably this formal union with the ruler of Wales that prompted his second banishment. He returned almost immediately, however, 'by violence through Gruffudd's help', and he and Gruffudd were associated with a naval force which came from Norway in the same year under the command of Magnus, the son of King Harold of Norway.[51] Whatever his role in this rather obscure episode, little is heard of Aelfgar after it. He appears once more to have been rehabilitated, but he was dead by 1062. Having struggled with only limited success to maintain some sort of parity between the power of his own family and that of the Godwinesons, he was succeeded as earl of Mercia by his teenage son Edwin.

Aelfgar became increasingly marginalised as Godwineson power across England continued to grow from the end of the 1050s. Following Aelfgar's succession to the earldom of Mercia in 1057, Harold Godwineson's brother Gyrth took over from him in East Anglia, and another brother, Leofwine, was granted an earldom in the south-west. And when Earl Ralph of Hereford died in December 1057, Harold himself took control of his lands in the west. By 1058, therefore, all of England, with the exception of Mercia, was covered by earldoms in the hands of the Godwinesons. One family dominated English affairs as never before. According to Domesday Book, in 1065 the Godwinesons held twice as much land as the descendants of Earl Leofric and 17 times as much as those of Earl Siward. They also held more land than the next 70 wealthiest landholders combined. Such extensive estates gave the Godwinesons great wealth, but it also enabled them to recruit and find support across England. Between them, they and their followers probably controlled about a third of all the land in the kingdom by 1066. More significantly still, the estates of Harold, his brothers and their mother in 1065 were worth about £7,500, whilst the King's lands at the same time were worth a little under £6,000.[52] In other words, they were arguably more powerful than the King himself. Edward has been criticised by some for allowing this state of affairs to develop. According to one historian: 'If the Confessor approved of the family's rapid aggrandisement and its vast network of allies he was a fool; if he acquiesced he cannot have been in full control of his kingdom.' Others, however, have been more sympathetic towards Edward and argued that, given the events of 1051, he cannot have wanted Godwine to become as powerful as he did; and that, thereafter, in relying on the Godwinesons, many of whose estates were in vulnerable coastal and frontier areas, 'he showed himself a realist. The power of the Godwins, when at the disposal of the king and queen, provided the monarchy with stability.'[53] These two positions are hard to reconcile; but whilst it is correct that England was relatively free of internal strife and foreign attack between 1053 and 1066, it must also be right to say that Edward's over-dependence on a single family had serious implications for the English monarchy. In the short term, it threatened a serious diminution of royal authority; and had anyone but a Godwineson succeeded Edward, they would have found it hard to assert themselves against Harold and his brothers. In the longer term, however, because Harold united his lands with the royal demesne when he became king, his power was potentially far greater than that exercised by any of his predecessors. Unfortunately for Harold, the main beneficiary of this development was William I.

Harold and Wales

Earl Aelfgar's death by 1062 and Harold's acquisition of Ralph's old earldom gave the earl of Wessex a chance to deal with Gruffudd ap Llewleyn once and for all. Late in 1062, Harold made a raid on Rhuddlan in north Wales, only for Gruffudd to escape by sea. Then in the early summer of 1063, determined this time to leave nothing to chance, Harold and Tostig launched a full-scale campaign designed to destroy the Welsh prince. Whilst Harold sailed along the coast of south Wales ravaging as he went, Tostig invaded from the north. Eventually, in August, seeing the direction in which events were going, Gruffudd's own men killed him and took his head to Harold. It was later delivered to King Edward. Gwynedd and Powys were given to Gruffudd's half-brothers, Bleddyn and Rhiwallon, who were to rule as client kings of their English neighbour, and in south Wales the old dynasty of Deheubarth was restored. The unity Gruffudd had briefly brought to Wales ended with his death, and the old order of local rivals competing for power was restored. This suited the English as it meant that the Welsh became preoccupied once more with fighting each other. One ambitious Welsh princeling, Caradog ap Gruffudd, still found time in 1065 to destroy the hunting lodge that Harold built at Portskewett in Gwent after his victory; but the fall of Gruffudd ap Llewelyn was ominous for Wales. It left the country vulnerable and exposed once the Normans arrived on the other side of the frontier.

In the short term, however, the Welsh campaign of 1063 was a stunning personal success for Earl Harold. His conduct of the campaign had been sophisticated and ruthless; the military reputation it secured for him, and which was spoken of until well into the next century in awed terms, seems to have been genuinely deserved.[54] His victory also reinforced his position as the leading figure in England after the King. 'No subject of the English Crown had ever been at once so powerful in relation to other noblemen and so great a figure in the country at large', and with the succession probably becoming more of an issue with every passing day, the list of Harold's qualifications for kingship was getting longer.[55]

Harold and William

By 1064 at the latest, Earl Harold was determined to succeed Edward the Confessor as king. The trip Harold is said to have made to Normandy shortly after his campaign in Wales, probably in 1064, needs to be considered with this in mind. No contemporary English source mentions this trip, and the main narrative accounts of it are given by William de Jumièges and William de Poitiers. Characteristically and unsurprisingly, they use it to blacken Harold's name, dismiss the legitimacy of his claim to the English throne and justify Duke William's. The Bayeux Tapestry also devotes a good deal of its length to describing the visit, but the questions it leaves unanswered are tantalising to say the least.

The core of the story can be pieced together from these three versions.[56] Having sailed into the English Channel, Earl Harold landed in

Ponthieu, just to the north of the Norman frontier. There he fell into the hands of the local count, Guy, who took him prisoner. Harold was handed over to Duke William of Normandy by Guy and taken to Rouen. Harold then accompanied William on a campaign against Count Conan of Brittany, during which he may have demonstrated his valour and military skill. Harold then publicly swore an oath to William, undertaking to act as William's agent in England pending King Edward's death and to support William's claim to the English throne thereafter. He also promised to place various important military strongholds (not least Dover) in the hands of William's men, presumably as a bridgehead in anticipation of William's eventual arrival in England. In return for all this, William confirmed Harold in all his lands and powers.

If the essential elements of these accounts are relatively easy to list, however, their accuracy is open to serious question. On the assumption that Harold did indeed go to Normandy, it is far from clear why he did so. The Bayeux Tapestry simply shows him taking leave of King Edward, but it does not explain what the purpose of his mission might have been; nor does it make clear the terms of the oath Harold is later vividly shown making to William.[57] By contrast, the Norman narrative sources stress that Harold travelled to Normandy to confirm the offer of the English throne which King Edward had made to Duke William earlier in his reign. Such an explanation clearly served their purposes very well, but the accounts of the Norman writers are not convincing. It is hard to see why Harold would have agreed to carry out a plan which was so detrimental to his own interests. And after all, once Harold had eventually arrived at William's court, he was at the Duke's mercy unless he did what was required of him. He may have been threatened with a more violent fate if he did not fall into line with William's plans, and the value of an oath given under duress was at least questionable.

Other sources certainly suggest rather different motives for Harold's trip from those put forward in the 'official' Norman versions. William of Malmesbury, for example, alleged in the twelfth century that Harold ended up in France only after being blown off course during a fishing trip in the English Channel. In other words, he never intended to go to France at all.[58] The Canterbury monk, Eadmer, writing after 1090, states that Harold visited Normandy to procure the release from captivity of two of his relatives, namely Wulfnoth (Harold's brother) and Haakon (his nephew).[59] However, it is hard to credit the idea that Harold under-took such a potentially dangerous mission purely for the sake of these two relatives. Indeed, there is no obvious reason why he would want them back in England anyway. Wace, writing in the second half of the twelfth century, agrees that the release of his relatives was Harold's main reason for crossing the Channel. He goes further, however, and rather incredibly suggests that Harold may have left England despite the King's express orders not to do so.[60] That Harold went further on his mission than Edward had wanted is possibly suggested by the scene in the Bayeux Tapestry which portrays Harold's return to the English court. Harold is depicted in a submissive posture before the King, who might be rebuking him. The meaning of this scene is far from clear, however.[61] Eadmer also states that Harold was unaware that Edward had ever offered the throne to William until the latter himself revealed to his guest that this offer had been made whilst Edward was still an exile in Normandy. William suggested that Harold should support his claim, garrison Dover for him and make a double marriage (Harold to William's daughter Adeliza, and Harold's sister to one of William's vassals). In return, one of the hostages would be freed, and the second released when the rest of the agreement had been complied with. Harold duly swore and took his nephew home.[62]

Given the nature of the evidence, the truth about the time Harold spent in Normandy in 1064 or 1065 can never be established. But it is reasonable to inject a dose of practical realism into a mystery otherwise dominated by a slightly unconvincing emphasis on the rights and wrongs of oath-taking and breaking. The Norman sources may show Duke William 'rescuing' Harold from Count Guy, but it is more likely that Guy simply handed over his captive to another, more powerful gaoler. It is worth remembering, therefore, that Harold never actually travelled to Normandy itself other than as a prisoner of Duke William. Thereafter, whilst the giving of an oath was a serious business, any promises Harold made to William were almost certainly forced out of him and therefore, as far as Harold was concerned, not binding. On balance, it seems likely that Harold had already decided to try to make himself king before 1064, that he never intended to go to Normandy and ended up there by accident, and that, by the time he returned to England, his determination to resist Duke William's claim to the throne can only have been strengthened by the unpleasant treatment he had received at his rival's hands.

As for Duke William, Harold's fortuitous arrival may have prompted him to start thinking seriously about seizing the English throne. William's hereditary claim was weak, and if he had ever been formally designated by King Edward, he must have known that there would still be opposition to any attempt by him to become king. Certainly since 1051 there is little to suggest that William had taken much of an interest in English affairs; and plenty to indicate that Edward changed his plans for the succession more than once. However, Harold's plight presented William with an opportunity which was arguably too good to miss. By compelling England's most powerful man to swear an oath to support him, William may have thought that he had gone some way towards acquiring that aristocratic backing which, in the end, was essential for the success of any claimant to the throne. He would have been naive to think this would suffice, of course.

The Northumbrian rising

Events in England soon conspired to render whatever had happened in Normandy increasingly irrelevant as far as Harold was concerned. In the autumn of 1065, the thegns of Northumbria rose up against the rule of Earl Tostig. Whilst Tostig was absent at the royal court, his *housecarls* were attacked and killed at York, and Morcar, younger brother of Earl Edwin of Mercia, was chosen as earl in his place. The rebels, with Morcar at their head, advanced as far south as Lincoln and then on to Northampton, the southern limit of the northern earldom. Here they joined forces with Earl Edwin (who had Welsh support as well as Mercian) and met Earl Harold. Harold negotiated with them and took their demands (principally the outlawry of Tostig and the recognition of Morcar as their earl) to King Edward at Oxford. The King reluctantly gave in to the rebels' demands and Harold returned to give the rebels the news. Morcar was confirmed as the new earl and Tostig fled with his wife and followers to the court of his father-in-law in Flanders.

Local grievances dominated the northern rebels' concerns. Tostig's relationship with King Malcolm of Scotland, for example, may have been causing unease for some time. *Vita Edwardi* describes how, in the late

1050s, Tostig had responded to Scottish raids southwards with diplomacy rather than military force. Malcolm and Tostig became sworn brothers and the former acknowledged the superiority of King Edward. However, Malcolm's unreliability as an ally was demonstrated in 1061 during Tostig's absence from England on a pilgrimage to Rome. With northern England leaderless, Malcolm raided again, and influential members of England's northern élite may well have felt that Tostig was neglecting his primary duty of defending his earldom from Scottish attack. If so, their disquiet can only have been compounded after Tostig's return from Rome when, in 1062, he travelled to Scotland and made peace with Malcolm, reaffirming his earlier agreement with the Scots' king and effectively accepting the latter's possession of Cumberland. This was 'a serious setback for the security of the North'.[63]

According to John of Worcester, moreover, Tostig's rule was brutal and cruel: he was responsible for the deaths of two prominent Northumbrian noblemen, whilst his sister (Queen Edith, no less) had ordered the killing of the Northumbrian thegn Cospatric 'for her brother's sake' at the King's Christmas court in 1064. Cospatric was the son of Earl Uhtred of Northumbria, who had died in 1016. He therefore had his own claim to the earldom, and his death may hint at the political tensions which remain largely hidden behind the scenes in northern England during Tostig's rule. That rule was also oppressive for other reasons: Tostig 'unjustly levied on the whole of Northumbria' a 'huge tribute'; and even the pro-Godwine *Vita Edwardi* concedes that he had repressed the Northumbrian nobility 'with the heavy yoke of his rule because of their misdeeds'.[64] It is possible that the harshness of Tostig's regime is overstated in these sources, but the particularly northern concerns of the rebels cannot be overlooked. One of their demands was for the restoration of the 'Laws of Cnut'. The laws themselves were not important for their detail as much as for what they were seen to represent, namely 'the pattern of northern rule which Tostig's government had subverted'.[65] This strongly suggests that Tostig had been trying to impose southern laws and, in particular, southern (that is, higher than usual) levels of taxation in the north.

The *Vita Edwardi* reports a rumour that Earl Harold had actually instigated the rising against his brother. The author takes care to dismiss this possibility (perhaps out of deference to the feelings of his patron, and Harold's sister, Queen Edith), but clearly states that Tostig himself believed it and that he publicly charged his brother with this treachery before the King. Harold certainly had a great deal to gain from a successful rising. Having recently returned from Normandy, he knew about Duke William's designs on the throne, and he must have been thinking about the best course to pursue so as to ease his own path to power on Edward's death. In this context, the support of Earl Edwin of Mercia and his family would have been extremely helpful, and there was perhaps no better way to secure this than by quietly supporting Morcar's claim to the earldom of Northumbria. In other words, by supporting Morcar, 'Harold aligned himself with both Mercians and Northumbrians, a political gain which overrode any familial feelings for a brother whose rule had led to disorder in the north.'[66] Harold's marriage at around this time to Ealdgyth, the sister of earls Edwin and Morcar and the widow of Gruffudd ap Llewelyn, was probably designed to set the seal on this newly-established amity between England's two most powerful families. On balance, it is probably going too far to suggest that Harold stirred up the northern rising; and he may, as the *Anglo-Saxon Chronicle* claimed, have tried but failed to reconcile his brother with his opponents.[67] The fallout from the events of 1065 nevertheless benefited Harold greatly in the short term; although by abandoning Tostig he created problems which eventually contributed to his own downfall.

For King Edward, the way in which the Northumbrian rising was brought to an end amounted to a personal humiliation. Tostig had been a royal appointee to the earldom of Northumbria in 1055, and it would have been understandable had Edward perceived the rising as a challenge to his own authority. He had wanted to crush the rebels by force, but, as in 1052, his leading subjects effectively ignored him. According to the *Vita Edwardi*, a furious and raging Edward felt that he had been betrayed and he fretted himself into an illness from which he never recovered. News of Edward's poor health must soon have reached William of Normandy.

A fateful choice

King Edward was too ill to attend the consecration of his great new abbey church at Westminster on 28 December 1065, and he died on

5 January 1066, only a few months after the Northumbrian rising. There are two accounts of what happened at Edward's deathbed. A scene in two parts in the Bayeux Tapestry depicts the King, first upright and conscious, talking with four of his confidantes, one of whom is a woman, presumably Queen Edith. In the second image, Edward is shown dead and being readied for burial. Unfortunately, the Tapestry gives no clue about what Edward and his companions were discussing.[68] The *Vita Edwardi* purports to fill in the details with information which may have come from Queen Edith herself.[69] The four individuals at Edward's bedside were Edith, Harold, Archbishop Stigand of Canterbury and Robert FitzWimarc, the King's steward and kinsman. On briefly recovering consciousness, the King gave orders that his household should be gathered together, and recounted to the assembled company an ominous vision he had just had. Then the dying king finally made known his decision about the succession:

And stretching forth his hand to his governor, her brother, Earl Harold, he said, 'I commend this woman and all the kingdom to your protection. Serve and honour her with faithful obedience as your lady and sister, which she is . . .'

If this is indeed what happened, it hardly amounts to an unambiguous statement that Edward bequeathed the throne to Harold. In the twelfth century, William of Malmesbury for one doubted that any such thing had happened, arguing that Edward was hardly likely to leave the kingdom in the hands of a man he had always distrusted; and for Orderic Vitalis, Harold was an unpopular usurper who stole the English throne in a coup. It was only the lack of an alternative candidate which compelled the unhappy English to accept 'his tyranny which daily grew worse'. 'In a short time', Orderic went on, 'the kingdom which he had nefariously seized was polluted with crimes too horrible to relate.'[70] Other evidence, however, suggests strongly that Edward did indeed make Harold his heir. John of Worcester states that Edward appointed Harold as his successor, as does the *Anglo-Saxon Chronicle*.[71] Most compellingly, perhaps, the near-contemporary Norman sources, whilst they strongly disapproved of him doing so, do not deny that Edward nominated Harold as his successor. They get around this rather awkward fact by arguing that Edward's earlier promise to William could not be overridden by a deathbed bequest and that Harold could not accept it in any event, except by perjuring himself.[72]

There can be little doubt, therefore, that on his deathbed Edward designated Earl Harold as his successor. In doing so, he ignored or over-looked any arrangements he may previously have made involving other potential successors such as William of Normandy and Edgar *atheling*. However, it is likely that Edward's announcement of Harold as his heir did little more than implement a plan which had been made some time, probably some years, before 1066. There certainly appears to have been little argument on the English side of the Channel about the merits of Edward's choice: John of Worcester (admittedly in the 1130s) states that Harold 'was elected by the primates of all England to the dignity of kingship', and even the imagery of the Bayeux Tapestry suggests that he had the support of the English nobility and the English Church.[73] He was, it would seem, a popular choice, and the dissenting accounts of other writers were concocted to stress the illegitimacy of Harold's accession for the benefit of a post-conquest audience.

Notes

1 *OV*, vi p.169; *HH*, p.6.

2 *WP*, p.121; Ann Williams, 'Some notes and considerations on problems connected with the English royal succession, 860–1066', *ANS* 1 (1978), pp.144–67, esp. pp.164–7; John S. Beckerman, 'Succession in Normandy, 1087, and in England, 1066: The Role of Testamentary Custom', *Speculum* 47 (1972), pp.258–60.

3 *JW*, ii p.601.

4 Williams, 'Some notes and considerations', p.163.

5 A.A.M. Duncan, *The Kingship of the Scots 842–1292: Succession and independence* (Edinburgh University Press, 2002), p.34.

6 *WMGR*, i pp.277–9; *EHD* I, pp.894–5.

7 *ASC* 'C', s.a.1000.

8 *WJ*, ii pp.11–17.

9 *ASC* 'C', s.a.1003; *JW*, ii p.455.

10 *HH*, p.9; *ASC* 'C', s.a.1009.

11 *ASC* 'C', s.a.1013.

12 *ASC* 'C', s.a.1017.

13 *WJ*, ii p.21; Simon Keynes, 'The Aethelings in Normandy', *ANS* 13 (1990), pp.173–205, at p.183.

14 *Encomium Emmae Reginae*, ed. A. Campbell, Camden Society, 3rd series, 72 (London, 1949; repr. Cambridge University Press, 1998), p.33.

15 *WJ*, ii pp.77–9.

16 Keynes, 'The Aethelings in Normandy', pp.188–94.

17 *ASC* 'E', s.a.1035.

18 *WJ*, ii pp.105–7; *WP*, pp.3–5; *ASC* 'C', s.a.1036.

19 The contradictory accounts are more fully discussed in Frank Barlow, *Edward the Confessor* (Berkeley, Cal.: University of California Press, 1970), pp.44–6.

20 *ASC* 'C', s.a.1037.

21 *ASC* 'C', s.a.1040.

22 *ASC* 'C', s.a.1041.

23 *ASC* 'C', s.a.1041.

24 *ASC* 'C', s.a.1042.

25 *JW*, ii p.535; *Vita Edwardi*, p.15.

26 *ASC* 'C', s.a.1009; *ODNB*, 'Godwine, earl of Wessex'.

27 *Vita Edwardi*, pp.23–5.

28 *ASC* 'D', s.a.1043.

29 *Vita Edwardi*, p.29.

30 Barlow, *Edward the Confessor*, p.75.

31 *ASC* 'E', s.a.1051.

32 *ASC* 'C', s.a.1046; *JW*, ii p.549.

33 *ASC* 'D', s.a.1047.

34 *ASC* 'C', 'D', s.a.1049.

35 *ASC* 'C', 'D', 'E', s.a.1049; *JW*, ii pp.549–51.

36 *ASC* 'C', s.a.1050.

37 Pauline Stafford, *Queen Emma and Queen Edith: Queenship and women's power in eleventh-century England* (Oxford: Blackwell, 1997), pp.262–6.

38 *Vita Edwardi*, pp.33–5.

39 *Vita Edwardi*, pp.35–7.

40 *ASC* 'D', s.a.1051; *JW*, ii p.563.

41 *WJ*, ii p.159; *WP*, pp.21, 121.

42 *WP*, pp.21, 121.

43 *The History of the Norman People, Wace's Roman de Rou*, trans. Glyn S. Burgess (Woodbridge: Boydell Press, 2004), p.151.

44 Eric John, 'Edward the Confessor and the Norman Succession', *EHR* 94 (1979), pp.241–67, at pp.253–5.

45 *ASC* 'C', 'D', s.a.1052.

46 *ASC* 'D', s.a.1057.

47 *ASC* 'D', s.a.1052.

48 *WMGR*, i p.355; *HH*, pp.21–2.

49 *Vita Edwardi*, pp.49–51, 59.

50 *ASC* 'C', s.a.1055.

51 *ASC* 'D', s.a.1058.

52 Robin Fleming, *Kings and Lords in Conquest England* (Cambridge University Press, 1991), ch.3 *passim*, esp. pp.60–83.

53 Fleming, *Kings and Lords in Conquest England*, p.102; Frank Barlow, *The Godwins: The rise and fall of a noble dynasty* (Harlow: Longman, 2002), p.61.

54 Gerald of Wales, *The Journey Through Wales*, trans. Lewis Thorpe (Harmondsworth: Penguin, 1978), p.266.

55 F.M. Stenton, *Anglo-Saxon England*, 3rd edn (Oxford: Clarendon Press, 1971), p.577.

56 *WJ*, ii pp.159–61; *WP*, pp.69–77; *BT*, pls.1–28.

57 *BT*, pls.1, 25–6.

58 *WMGR*, i p.417.

59 *HN*, pp.6–8; *WP*, p.21.

60 Wace does accept that there are other versions of this story, however, and concludes: 'I do not know which is the correct explanation, but we can find both in writing': *History of the Norman People*, p.153.

61 *BT*, pl.28.

62 *HN*, p.8.

63 William E. Kapelle, *The Norman Conquest of the North. The region and its transformation, 1000–1135* (London: Croom Helm, 1980), p.93.

64 *JW*, ii p.599; *Vita Edwardi*, p.77.

65 Patrick Wormald, *The Making of English Law: King Alfred to the Twelfth Century* (Oxford: Blackwell, 1999), p.133.

66 Ann Williams, *Kingship and Government in pre-Conquest England, c.500–1066* (Basingstoke: Macmillan, 1999), p.148.

67 *ASC* 'C', s.a.1065; *JW*, ii p.599.

68 *BT*, pl.30.

69 *Vita Edwardi*, pp.117–27.

70 *WMGR*, i p.421; *OV*, ii pp.135–9.

71 *JW*, ii p.601; *ASC* 'C', 'D', s.a.1065.

72 *WP*, p.119.

73 *JW*, ii p.601; *BT*, pl.31.

PART TWO

The Norman Conquest

CHAPTER 4

Conquest, 1066

King Harold

Harold II was the first king to be crowned in Westminster Abbey; and this on the same day, 6 January 1066, as his predecessor, Edward the Confessor, was buried there. Harold lacked royal blood, although he was married to Edward's sister; but he was the late king's choice and there was popular and influential support for his accession. He was properly consecrated, too, and the claims made by William de Poitiers and in the Bayeux Tapestry that Harold was anointed by another usurper, Stigand, the archbishop of Canterbury, are not convincing. The new king was no fool and he would have appreciated the importance of legitimacy. There is therefore no reason to doubt John of Worcester's claim that Harold was consecrated by Archbishop Ealdred of York.[1] Harold was also mature, he had extensive political and military experience and he was richer than ever, having now added the royal lands to his own. Any new king should have been delighted at such a combination of circumstances, and confident about dealing with the problems which were bound to occur. According to the *Anglo-Saxon Chronicle*, however, and despite all his advantages, Harold 'met little quiet in it as long as he ruled the realm'.[2]

For post-conquest Norman writers, Harold's difficulties were easy to explain: he was an illegitimate usurper who had perjured himself. John of Worcester's assessment of Harold, however, whilst itself perhaps rather overstated, is a useful corrective to the pro-Norman accounts: he was good to the Church and 'he soon, when he had undertaken the government of the realm, destroyed iniquitous laws, and set about establishing just ones; . . . he ordered the earls, ealdormen, sheriffs and his own officers generally to seize thieves, robbers and disturbers of the realm, and to exert themselves by land and sea for the defence of their country'. And even William of Malmesbury, who thought Harold was a usurper, grudgingly acknowledged that 'he might well have ruled the kingdom, to judge by the figure he cut in public, with prudence and fortitude, had it come to him lawfully'.[3] It is certainly difficult to hack a way through the thicket of propaganda and prejudice to see what sort of ruler Harold really was and how he set about dealing with the problems he faced during his nine months as king. No charters and only one writ survive from his reign, and whilst the quality of the coins issued in his name was high, there was only time for one issue and on its own this does not provide enough of a basis for solid conclusions about the quality of his rule.

The phoney war

Following his coronation, Harold spent the first weeks of his reign in northern England. He was probably reassuring the leading men of Northumbria that the settlement of the previous year still held, and that Tostig would not be allowed to return. He had returned to Westminster by Easter, and shortly after that, Halley's Comet appeared over England and remained visible for a week from 24 April. The comet was depicted in the Bayeux Tapestry and spoken of in the *Anglo-Saxon Chronicle* and by William de Jumièges, but what contemporaries really made of it at the time is hard to say. It would certainly have been perceived as an omen, but whether it was a good one or a bad one probably remained to be seen.[4]

In May, Tostig Godwineson, the deposed earl of Northumbria, returned to English shores, and landed on the Isle of Wight where he had lands and followers. Tostig's motives at this point are obscure. He may have had his own designs on the throne; after all, in many ways he had just as good a claim as his brother. Tostig's movements since his banishment are also unclear. Scandinavian sources from the late twelfth century suggest that he travelled to Denmark and Norway to secure assistance from kings Swein and Harald. It is also possible, if rather unlikely, that he had visited William of Normandy in an attempt to construct a coalition against Harold.[5] Both William and Tostig certainly had reason to resent the new English king. They also had in common family links to the ruling house of Flanders (Tostig was married to Judith, the daughter of Baldwin IV of Flanders, and William to Matilda, the daughter of Baldwin V, Judith's half-brother), and Tostig may have been hoping to make political capital out of their wives' kinship. And sure enough, when Tostig did return to England, he was accompanied by a fleet of uncertain size which had been supplied to him by Count Baldwin. This enterprise was probably designed to ascertain the degree of support Tostig might expect if he reasserted himself more forcefully. He raided along the south coast, but appears to have gathered little momentum or support. And when he heard that his brother, the new king, was advancing against him, he turned northwards. Having made some forays into Lindsay as he travelled up the eastern coastline and down the river Humber, Tostig was eventually seen off for the time being by King Harold's new brothers-in-law, earls Edwin and Morcar. Tostig fled as a result to Scotland, to the court of his old ally King Malcolm. Malcolm was still keen to add Northumbria between the Tees and the Tweed to his lands, and he knew that the prospect of political instability in England which Tostig represented was his best hope of achieving his aims.

Tostig's flight left Harold free to deal with what he probably perceived as a far more serious threat, the one posed by William of Normandy. According to the *Anglo-Saxon Chronicle*, Harold '. . . assembled a naval force and a land force larger than any king had assembled before in this country, because he had been told that count William from Normandy, king Edward's kinsman, meant to come here and subdue the country'.[6] And there is no reason to doubt that, by the summer of 1066, the prospect of a Norman attack on England was imminent. William de Jumièges describes how, on hearing news of King Edward's death and Harold's seizure of power, Duke William sent envoys to Harold 'urging him to renounce this act of folly and with worthy submission keep the faith which he had pledged with an oath'.[7] Such a description allowed William's supporters to portray him as the aggrieved victim of deceit standing firmly on the moral high ground. In reality, such diplomatic niceties were irrelevant. The Duke was determined to stake his claim to the English throne, and he began the construction of an invasion fleet which was ready, at the latest, by early August 1066. It did not set sail until the end of September, and William's delay of several weeks has traditionally been attributed to adverse winds in the English Channel. There may be some truth in this, but it seems very unlikely that the winds remained against him for such a long time. As will be seen, there may have been other reasons why William chose to wait.

Expecting a Norman attack, King Harold kept his forces on stand-by along the Channel coast for the whole of the summer. No invasion materialised, however; and, according to the English sources, by 8 September 'the provisions of the people were gone, and nobody could keep them there any longer. Then the men were allowed to go home, and the king rode inland.'[8] These events have sometimes been interpreted as demonstrating the shortcomings of the late Anglo-Saxon military system. That Harold had managed to keep his forces in the field at all for upwards of four months, however, was a significant achievement. And the decision to disband, a temporary measure perhaps, may have been as strategic as it was forced. Harold may have concluded, after waiting so long for Duke William to arrive, that he was not coming at all, at least not until the following year. It is hard to believe he would not have had intelligence about William's movements, however, and the English king may simply have made a terrible mistake.

The northern invasion

News soon arrived of an invasion of England, but it was not on the south coast and not by the Normans. In the north-east Tostig had returned; this time with a new and fearsome ally, King Harald Hardrada of Norway. As has been seen, Tostig may have contacted King Harald during his Scottish exile and Harald, an experienced and battle-hardened warrior with a large fleet of anything between three hundred and five hundred ships at his disposal, probably liked his chances, especially in view of the fact that English eyes were directed towards Normandy.[9] Had he wanted to, Harald could have staked a claim to the English throne on the basis of an agreement allegedly made between King Magnus of Norway (Harald's nephew, who had died in 1047) and Harthacnut in about 1040, whereby each had agreed to succeed the other if they died without natural heirs. But he probably did not concern himself with such legalities. England was rich and, he may well have thought, there for the taking.

The English sources suggest that news of the northern invasion came as a complete surprise to King Harold.[10] Tostig and Harald appear to have met up at the mouth of the river Tyne at the start of September 1066, just as Harold was disbanding his troops in the south. Their joint forces then sailed down the coast and up the rivers Humber and Ouse towards York, the chief city of the north. Meanwhile, King Harold rushed to confront the invaders. However, before he reached York, the first of this year's three battles had already taken place (on 20 September) outside the city at Gate Fulford between the invaders on one side and the forces of earls Edwin and Morcar on the other. The battle appears to have been hard-fought, long and bloody. There were heavy casualties on both sides, but eventually the invaders won the day and York was theirs.

Why the midland and northern earls chose to confront the invaders when they probably knew that the King was on his way is an important question. On the one hand, Harold could have been pleased at the readiness of his new allies to confront Harald and Tostig: Edwin and Morcar clearly thought that their best interests lay with the continuance of the new regime. On the other hand, had they waited only a few days more for Harold to arrive, the outcome of the battle might have been very different. As it was, Harold arrived in Yorkshire on 24 September, only four days after the battle. By 25 September the bulk of the invasion force was encamped at the village of Stamford Bridge, to the north-east of York. Harold advanced through the city on the 25th, came upon the invaders 'by surprise' and immediately engaged them in battle.[11] Harald and Tostig were almost certainly unprepared for battle; but they still managed to put up strong resistance, and the encounter lasted most of the day. Harald Hardrada and Tostig were both killed, along with scores of their followers.

Taken together, the northern campaigns of 1066 had demonstrated the effectiveness of England's military systems. Edwin and Morcar had managed to recruit enough men to take on Tostig and Harald Hardrada within days of hearing of the latter's arrival on English shores, and although they had been defeated, the Battle of Fulford can only have drained the invaders' energies and resources and benefited Harold at Stamford Bridge. As for Harold, he had marched north within ten days of the invaders' arrival, recruited an army substantial enough to take on the still considerable invasion force, and fought a long, arduous battle immediately after a forced march of 16 miles. This was an impressive performance by any standards. And on the political level, Stamford Bridge was a crushing, decisive victory, and the greatest moment of Harold's reign. Two potential rivals for power (Tostig and Hardrada) had been removed at a single stroke. Most significantly, perhaps, Harold had confirmed his military reputation and justified his elevation to the throne earlier in the year. If he had been chosen because of his capacity to protect England from invasion, contemporaries must have thought that their choice had been a legitimate one after all. Harold must have felt secure in his kingship on the evening of 25 September 1066. Unfortunately for him, however, it was only three days later, on 28 September 1066, that Duke William of Normandy's fleet landed at Pevensey in Sussex. The scene was set for the last and most decisive campaign of the year.

Duke William prepares

After Edward the Confessor's death, Duke William spent nearly nine months preparing for his attack on England. According to William de Poitiers, the Duke first called a meeting of his leading magnates to discuss his options and, initially, many of his most influential subjects expressed their misgivings about any plans for an invasion. Such a plan was 'too arduous and far beyond the resources of Normandy'. Moreover, they said, Harold was rich enough to recruit powerful assistance, he had a large fleet, 'and both in wealth and numbers of soldiers his kingdom was greatly superior to their own land'.[12] William de Poitiers may have overstated the degree of opposition William faced at this stage, in order to make his ultimate success seem all the more remarkable. Nevertheless, caution was not misplaced: William's plans would involve the construction of a large fleet, a risky sea crossing and an opposed landing in a hostile country. Success was far from guaranteed.

Unlike Harold, William had no ready-made fleet upon which to call. He had to rely on his vassals to provide him with some ships, and build the rest from scratch. This must have been a time-consuming business and the Bayeux Tapestry's depiction of the fleet being built probably makes the process look easier than it really was. William de Jumièges's assertion that the fleet eventually contained 3,000 vessels can almost certainly be dismissed; but it does at least suggest that the fleet was large.[13] William needed ground troops, too, however, and again he had to rely on his vassals to provide most of these. He also recruited volunteers from outside Normandy, from Brittany, Ponthieu, Flanders and even further afield, who filled the ranks of this expanding force.

The fleet was probably ready to set sail by the end of July or early August, but adverse winds played a part in keeping it at home. Until they were able to set sail, William's troops had to be accommodated and fed; their horses, too, had to be provided for. William de Poitiers's estimate that William fed 50,000 men at his own expense for the whole of this period is certainly a wild exaggeration. Nevertheless, it has been calculated that, in a month, an army of the sort William had recruited, even if it was made up of no more than 14,000 men (including non-combatants) and 2,000–3,000 horses, would have used up 9,000 cart-loads of grain, straw, wine and firewood; the horses, moreover, would have produced 700,000 gallons of urine and 5 million pounds (lbs) of manure, which would have had to be taken away by 5,000 more carts. The logistical problems were huge, but they seem to have been managed successfully.[14]

William was making preparations of another kind, too. According to William de Poitiers, he secured influential support for his plans to seize the English throne. Both the Holy Roman Emperor, Henry IV, and King Swein of Denmark backed him. So, most famously, did the pope, Alexander II, who also, we are told by William de Poitiers, supplied William with a papal banner, 'by following which he might attack the enemy with greater confidence and safety'.[15] Such claims should be treated with caution, however, and they were probably made to further strengthen William's claims to legitimacy. King Swein is much more likely to have favoured Harold over William, as this would have made possible the resurrection of English support for the Danish king against his Norwegian adversary; this is the line Harold's father, Earl Godwine, had pursued. And Henry IV was still a minor in 1066. As for the Pope, it is possible that William de Poitiers was manipulating the papal support which was given to the conquest after it had already taken place and succeeded. After all, William de Jumièges does not mention Alexander II's involvement, and whilst the Bayeux Tapestry might depict a papal banner, this is not certain.[16]

Whatever the true extent of international support for William's invasion, in the event none of these new allies provided him with meaningful military help. And of much more importance in the immediate context of September 1066 was William's ability to leave his duchy without fear of external attack. Both King Henry I of France and Count Geoffrey of Anjou, who had worked together to restrict further Norman expansion since the early 1050s, had died in 1060. A succession dispute had followed Geoffrey's death in Anjou, whilst Henry I had left only a young son, Philip I, to succeed him. Until he came of age in 1067, he had as his regent Count Baldwin V of Flanders, Duke William's father-in-law and ally. Another ally, for the time being, was Count Eustace II of Boulogne. These events enabled William to increase his own power in northern France and to make Normandy the dominant power there. Most importantly, however, in 1063 William's forceful military tactics helped him to secure the succession to the county of Maine of himself and his eldest son, Robert. And prior to his invasion of England, the campaign William led into Brittany, on which he may have been accompanied by Earl Harold of Wessex, served to bully the count of Brittany into accepting William's regional supremacy, and probably also served to recruit significant numbers of Bretons into the Duke's invasion force. His security at home assured and unthreatened, William was free to concentrate on England.

Invasion

William of Normandy's sea crossing to England was as significant in its own way as those of the Emperor Claudius in the first century and the Anglo-Saxons in the fifth. Its timing was crucial. Having been ready to sail since early August 1066, the fleet did not set sail until late in September. This delay requires explanation. William de Jumièges states that the fleet had been constructed at St Valéry-sur-Somme and that it sailed for England from there. Most scholars today, however, accept William de Poitiers's version of events which explains how the fleet, which had been constructed at the mouth of the river Dives in Normandy, was blown north to St Valéry whence it finally sailed for England.[17] According to William, the fleet had been prevented from sailing by adverse winds; and perhaps the wind had changed whilst the fleet was in its original location, the fleet had set sail when the wind did change, but was blown off course by yet another change in the wind direction. Such a scenario would provide one explanation for William's delay in setting out for England.

Two other reasons for this delay should be considered, however. William must surely have known, through spies and informants, something of what was happening on the English side of the Channel during the late summer of 1066. Perhaps the Duke moved his fleet north when he heard that Harold had disbanded his forces on 8 September. The crossing from St Valéry was much shorter than that from the Dives and William had perhaps planned to do this all along: now was the right time. Second, it was surely no coincidence that the fleet finally set sail when Harold was still in northern England dealing with Harald Hardrada and Tostig at Stamford Bridge. William would not have known the outcome of the Battle of Stamford Bridge when he set sail, and so he would not have known whom he would be fighting for control of England; but he must have been aware that the south coast of England was largely undefended.

William de Poitiers's emphasis on wind direction in determining the precise moment the Norman fleet set sail for England placed the ultimate responsibility for William's fate in God's hands, and provided evidence of divine approval for William's plans. And indeed, it was in response to the Duke's prayers, William says, that the direction of the wind finally changed. Immediately, the ships were boarded and during the night of (probably) 27–8 September they set sail. William did not want to arrive in England before daybreak, however, and ordered the other ships to anchor close to him in the Channel until they saw a lantern lit on board his ship: that was the signal to sail on. William then lost contact with the fleet whilst in mid-Channel and he had to reassure his shipmates that they would be found. And sure enough, the fleet regrouped and eventually landed, unopposed, at Pevensey on the morning of 28 September 1066. Once at Pevensey, William erected an earthwork bank within the old Roman fort to give his troops some protection, but after a few days he moved his whole force along the coast to Hastings where he ordered the construction of a castle of earth and timber. He was digging himself in.

The Hastings campaign

News of William's arrival in England can have reached Harold, at the earliest, by 1 or 2 October. He immediately began his return to London, a journey of nearly 200 miles, which was probably carried out between 2/3 and 9/10 October. The core of the force Harold had with him when he left Yorkshire would have been made up of his surviving *housecarls*. To supplement this, he probably sent mounted messengers around the shires with orders to raise yet more troops for immediate assembly at London. When he arrived there, Harold probably spent a couple of days organising his resources, gathering reinforcements and making his final plans. The decisions he made at this point were arguably the most important of his career, and Harold probably left London on the 60-mile march to Hastings on 11 October at the latest. He was criticised by John of Worcester in the 1120s for having rashly moved off before his whole army had gathered.[18] Orderic Vitalis also describes how the King had angrily rejected the advice of his brother Gyrth to wait before advancing further. Gyrth even offered to fight William in his brother's place. When Harold's mother, Gytha, also tried to hold him back, he kicked her away. This may be just another of Orderic's concocted set-pieces, heavy with hindsight and designed to demonstrate Harold's impetuosity and foolhardiness. Gyrth is said to have told Harold, rather too presciently, perhaps, that he would struggle to defeat William because he had broken his oath to him.[19] It has also been suggested more recently that Harold simply underestimated the seriousness of the Norman threat: 'He seems to have come away from Normandy [in 1064–5] with the idea that the French warriors were ineffectual posers, and that a determined front would send them back in disarray across the sea.'[20] It is unlikely that Harold was so dismissive of his rival's abilities. Nevertheless, still in the flush of his victory at Stamford Bridge, perhaps Harold's over-confidence did lead him to reject well-meant advice and act more hastily than was prudent.

It is more likely, however, that Harold felt he had little choice but to respond as quickly as possible to the Norman threat. The Bayeux Tapestry shows Duke William's men burning and plundering after their landing.[21] Of course they needed supplies, but there was more to their terror tactics than this. William's plan, in fact, seems to have been to goad Harold into coming to him. Mindful of the difficulties of keeping an army supplied in hostile territory, William certainly seems to have gone out of his way to provoke an early response from the English king. William had arrived in Harold's heartland and had set about systematically despoiling his rival's family estates. This imposed upon Harold a responsibility, not just as king, but as the lord of this area, to come to the aid of his people. If his standing as a good lord was to be maintained, and if he was not to lose the support of his followers, Harold arguably had no choice but to act quickly, even if this meant he was not as fully prepared for battle as he would like to have been. Moreover, Harold must have been aware of the dangers of William later leaving the south coast and travelling inland, where he would have been much more difficult to pin down. William de Poitiers also claims that Harold had sent his fleet into the English Channel to cut off William's retreat, and it would have suited Harold best to keep William bottled up in Sussex with no chance either of advance or retreat.[22] As much as anything else, however, after the events of 8 September, Harold must have been well aware of the need to act quickly and deal with William before his own troops became restless and hungry. Speed was essential, and numbers were not the most important thing.

Having got within a few miles of William's army by nightfall on Friday 13 October, Harold probably planned to engage the enemy as soon as possible once dawn broke. He had surprised Hardrada and Tostig at Stamford Bridge, so it was not unreasonable to think that the same tactic would work once more. Alternatively, although this seems less likely, he could have planned to confine William in his south-coast pocket, deprive him of supplies, wait for the rest of his own force to arrive and then strike the final blow. Whatever his plans were, however, he did not have the chance to put them into operation. William's scouts had warned him of Harold's approach, and it was now the Duke's turn to act quickly. Having marched north from Pevensey or Hastings, probably in darkness, it was William who in the event surprised Harold in the early hours of Saturday 14 October 1066.[23]

The Battle of Hastings

The sources for the Battle of Hastings are abundant but problematic. The full and detailed accounts offered by the Bayeux Tapestry and William de Poitiers are evocative and compelling; however, they are also tainted by their central assumptions, namely that Harold was a perjurer and a usurper who deserved to be defeated, and that William was an inspirational leader who almost single-handedly secured victory. Questions about its date and authorship also make it difficult to rely confidently on the third major narrative account of the battle, the *Carmen de Hastingae Proelio*. The English documentary sources are brief and far less detailed; whilst the battlefield itself gives rise to as many questions as answers.

The battle took place about six miles north-west of Hastings along the London road. The town of Battle was later to develop around the abbey which was built by William in thanks for his victory; and the high altar of the abbey was reputedly placed on the spot where King Harold eventually fell. According to William de Poitiers, the battle began at the third hour of the day, nine o'clock, and it lasted all day. It may have been preceded by negotiations of some kind, but these were probably more ritualistic gestures than serious attempts to reach a settlement. By this time, both sides were probably fixed on fighting as the only way to resolve their differences. Arguments have continued about the size of the two armies but, in the end, certainty on this, as on most aspects of the battle, is elusive. The consensus currently holds that there were probably about six or seven thousand troops on each side; although the most recent study of the battle has urged a reminder that the numbers could have been much greater.[24] However, if Harold and William had roughly the same number of troops at their disposal, the armies they commanded were organised very differently. The English army at Hastings was made up largely of infantry, some lightly armed with spears and shields (in the Bayeux Tapestry, the English shield wall is made up of such men wearing mail coats and helmets), others heavily armed with axes, who perhaps fought in looser, more mobile order. The

English had archers, too, although the Tapestry only shows one of these in action, and it is not clear whether significant numbers of English bowmen took part in the battle.[25] The Norman army at Hastings, by contrast, consisted of infantry, cavalry and archers. As a result, 'the Normans had more effective means of killing', but only if they were able to break through the English lines.[26]

The swift Norman advance may have surprised Harold, but it did not prevent the English army taking up a strong defensive position along a wooded ridge running east to west which looked down a steep slope. Grouped around the royal banners (a dragon according to the Bayeux Tapestry; an 'armed warrior' according to William de Poitiers), the English were thus able to get a good view of their enemy and form themselves into their traditional shield wall.[27] The wall was designed to soak up the Norman attacks and gradually to sap Norman strength and morale. The chances of this happening were enhanced because William would have to keep driving his forces uphill. The English were certainly in a strong position as the battle began, therefore, although there are hints in the sources that they were rather cramped on the ridge, with little room to manoeuvre. Nevertheless, Harold may have calculated that, whilst only total victory would suffice for William, avoidance of defeat would be enough for him. And indeed, 'had the English been content to stand on the defensive all day it is doubtful whether they could have been defeated'.[28]

Battle was joined when Norman missiles were launched at the English line. This was followed up by an infantry and then a first cavalry attack, neither of which managed to make any significant impression. Initially, therefore, the English tactics worked well; but the first crisis of the battle soon came as the left wing of William's army, made up largely of Breton troops, panicked and fled in disorderly retreat. This was a chance for Harold, but it was also the moment at which the limitations of his army and of his tactics became apparent. Had he ordered a full counter-attack at this moment, he might have been successful. Had he had cavalry at his disposal, too, horsemen could have pursued the retreating French troops down the hill and turned a flight into a rout. Lacking such troops, however, he decided to stay where he was, presumably in the hope that his enemy would fail to regroup. Having opted for this course, he also had to make sure that his men kept to the script and did not begin to act on their own initiative. Stuck in the middle of his army, however, perhaps invisible and inaudible to any but those closest to him, it was probably very difficult indeed for Harold to communicate quickly and effectively with his troops. Consequently, some of them decided to break ranks and pursue the Bretons as they fled. They were easily surrounded and slaughtered by the Norman cavalry. Twice more the Normans actually simulated retreat to draw more of the English down from the hill, and twice they fell for the ruse. Harold was a fine soldier, and, whilst he may have had an impatient streak and ideally desired a decisive victory, it seems very unlikely that he would have ordered these piecemeal attacks had he had the chance to do so. It is much more likely that, in the heat of battle, Harold was simply unable to control his troops as tightly as he would have liked.

The Normans by contrast were ultimately able to turn near defeat into victory. William de Poitiers and the Bayeux Tapestry naturally attribute this success to the leadership qualities of Duke William. When the Bretons fled, rumours also circulated that William himself had been killed. Only when he rode shouting through his troops and raising his helmet so that they could see his face, a scene famously depicted on the Bayeux Tapestry, were they reassured enough to regain their composure.[29] In reality, things were probably more complicated than this. After all, the fighting lasted most of the day, which suggests that the outcome of the battle was in doubt for much of that time. William, too, whilst he was almost certainly able to play a more active role than Harold in the organising and deployment of his troops after the battle had begun, would still have been reliant on his lieutenants to control the contingents under their command. And by late afternoon, and perhaps after a long pause in the fighting, the pressure on William was mounting. If he did not secure victory by the end of the day, his chances of ever doing so would perhaps be fatally damaged. Harold could expect reinforcements; William could not. Any chance of a strategic withdrawal may already have been destroyed by the arrival of an English fleet in the Channel.

Unfortunately, the afternoon of the battle is less well documented than the early phase. Fierce fighting continued, but it may be that the Normans' feigned retreats and repeated cavalry assaults gradually chipped away at the English line, weakening it and creating gaps which might be exploited once a clear breakthrough had been made. William de Poitiers's narrative all but ignores this part of the battle, however, and recommences its description of events only after the death of Harold and his brothers. William de Jumièges claims that Harold was killed at the start of the battle, but no other source agrees with this. According to the *Carmen*, Harold was struck down and dismembered by William himself, who was accompanied by Eustace of Boulogne and two other knights. This description has not generally been given much credit by historians, however. Most famous, of course, is the scene in the Bayeux Tapestry, beneath the words *Hic Harold rex interfectus est* ('Here King Harold has been killed') which has often been taken as showing Harold being struck in the eye with an arrow and then being cut down by a Norman knight. There are many problems about interpreting the scene in this way, not least that the first of these figures may originally have been depicted holding a spear aloft not clutching at an arrow. By the twelfth century, however, the idea that Harold had been killed by an arrow which struck him in the head was current.[30]

However it happened, Harold's death was, it seems, the decisive event which finally broke the resolve of the English and swung the battle in the Normans' favour. When rumours of William's death had spread through his ranks earlier in the day, he had been able to quell the panic. According to William de Poitiers, however, the English 'knew that they had been weakened by the loss of many troops; that the king himself and his brothers and not a few of the nobles of the kingdom had perished; that all who remained were almost at the end of their strength, and that they could hope for no relief'.[31] They therefore started to flee from the battlefield, only to be pursued remorselessly and probably through the night by their opponents. Some English troops made a valiant last stand, William records, but it was futile. Their defeat was complete because their king was dead.

Any attempt to explain Duke William's victory at Hastings is fraught with interpretative difficulties; and what follows here is a far from definitive reading of sources and events. Attention should be focused, however, on what happened during, not before, the battle. Of course, William and his troops were well prepared and highly motivated, and he appears to have planned a strategy which worked well in luring Harold into Wessex. By contrast, the weeks prior to the battle could not have been more demanding for the English king. His march to and from Stamford Bridge, combined with the effects of the vicious battle itself can only have served to reduce the number of troops available to him and to tire those he managed to retain. It is also right to point out that if Harold's plan was to take William by surprise, he failed. Perhaps, too, he can be criticised for impetuousness in attacking before he was as strong as he might have been. Nevertheless, none of these factors was decisive in determining the outcome of the battle. And it is worth repeating that the sheer length of the battle shows how hard fought it was and how unpredictable its outcome was until close to the end. Harold's plan was to hold out for the entire day in the hope that this would be enough to deal a mortal blow to William's cause, and he very nearly succeeded. The darkness was probably beginning to gather when Harold was finally struck down. And, indeed, it does seem that the luck was with William rather than Harold. If William de Poitiers is to be believed, the Duke had three horses killed under him during the course of the battle; Harold may just have looked up at the wrong time. Of course, William de Poitiers would not have considered this to be simply a matter of 'good luck', but as a sign of the *fortuna* which attached to those favoured by God. If William was spared during the battle, it was because his cause was just.

Beyond this, however, there were more rational explanations for the English defeat. William was a more experienced battlefield general than Harold, but Harold still had a chance to secure victory when the left flank of William's army collapsed early in the battle. However, he may have been too cautious a commander to take advantage of this. Alternatively, even if he wanted to pursue the enemy, he may have appreciated that the English infantry would have been hard-pressed to handle the Norman cavalry on open ground. Either way, his capabilities were limited, whereas the Norman army, which could fight on horseback as well as on foot, provided William with more options and greater tactical flexibility. When the English needed horsemen to pursue the retreating Bretons early in the battle, none were used; and the lack of English cavalry at Hastings has rightly been described as 'a fatal deficiency'.[32] Harold staked everything on being able to remain where he was until the Normans could no longer fight on. However, when English losses and fatigue began to tell later in the day, William's archers and cavalry were well placed and ideally equipped to pick off their increasingly demoralised opponents. The Battle of Hastings was, indeed, a close-run thing, but in the end, and whilst William had his share of good luck, Harold and the English were out-thought and out-fought by a better commander and a superior military machine.

From Hastings to London

On the morning after the battle, William returned to the scene of his triumph to bury his dead. The English bodies were left where they lay as a reminder of what happened to those who had defied the victorious Duke and ignored the will of Heaven. Harold's body, surrounded by the bodies of his brothers and his *housecarls*, its face mutilated and unrecognisable, was eventually identified from markings on his body or armour. His mother, Gytha, offered William her son's weight in gold for the privilege of having the body; but William refused. He ordered the corpse to be taken and buried on the cliff overlooking the harbour. Whether this happened, indeed what happened to the body in the end, is unclear. By the 1170s, tradition at the abbey founded by Harold at Waltham claimed that his body had been interred there after having been identified on the battlefield by his first wife, Edith Swan-neck.

Meanwhile, the general surrender which William had probably hoped for after his victory at Hastings failed to materialise. He still had work to do before he could call himself king. After leaving a garrison at Hastings he went first to Romney in Kent, where he punished the inhabitants for the way they had treated some of his soldiers who had arrived there after landing and lost their way. He then went on to Dover, where the citizens, perhaps already informed of William's uncompromising methods, surrendered as he approached. Then, dysentery in his army notwithstanding, William refortified the town, left another garrison behind, and went on to Canterbury, where he himself fell ill. He did not reach Southwark until late November. Meanwhile, he sent a detachment of troops to Winchester to secure the city, the royal treasury which was based there and the surrender of Queen Edith, Harold's widow. William did not cross the Thames when he reached Southwark, however, and, burning as he went, he marched his troops around the south and west of London through Surrey, Hampshire and Berkshire before finally crossing on to the north bank of the Thames at Wallingford in early December.

William's strategy during these weeks was clear and direct. He wanted to impose his presence on the south-east, the traditional heartland of royal authority in England, and he went about doing this methodically and patiently. Winchester, Dover and Canterbury were not random targets: the first was where the royal treasury was based; the second had to be taken in order to secure safe access to England for Norman reinforcements, and the third was the ecclesiastical centre of the kingdom. There was no point rushing to London before these vital financial, military and religious centres were secured. And the violence William inflicted as he went was not a mindless tactic either. In ravaging and burning the lands he passed through, William was attempting to intimidate and demoralise the English people into submission and to make it clear to them that continued support for their traditional lords, who were demonstrably no longer able to help them, was pointless. He was the only power that counted now, so they might as well accept him if they did not want the devastation to get even worse.

It was partly because William showed himself to be so ruthless so quickly that English resistance to his continued progress round the south-east was so ineffectual. After Harold's death, according to the *Anglo-Saxon Chronicle* and John of Worcester, Archbishop Ealdred of York (William de Poitiers says it was Archbishop Stigand) and earls Edwin and Morcar nominated as king the teenage Edgar *atheling* 'as was his proper due'.[33] Such backing as the *atheling* received was lukewarm, however, and despite their early promise of support, Edwin and Morcar seem to have been less than enthusiastic about his chances of successfully challenging Duke William and soon deserted his cause. William had shown himself to be assertive, bold and determined to succeed; Edgar, by contrast, was later described by Orderic as 'handsome in appearance, eloquent, generous and nobly born . . . but indolent too'.[34] Orderic's assessment was given with the benefit of hindsight, of course, and it may be unfair; Edgar was not helped in 1066 by the confusion and consequent indecision which must have gripped the surviving English nobility after Harold's defeat. But it also seems right to say that his youth (he was probably about 14 in 1066) and inexperience counted against him and that, both at this time and in the following years when he was still involved in English politics, the *atheling* lacked the dynamic and forceful personality required to impose himself on events.

At Wallingford the major English submissions to William began. Archbishop Stigand did homage to William and renounced Edgar, and soon afterwards at Berkhamsted, Edgar himself, Archbishop Ealdred and earls Edwin and Morcar submitted. For the *Anglo-Saxon Chronicle*, it was 'a great piece of folly that they had not done it earlier, since God would not make things better, because of our sins'. Then, as William moved back towards London itself, according to William de Poitiers, 'the chief men of the city came out to meet him; they submitted themselves and the whole city to him'.[35] At this point William took the counsel of his leading followers, all of whom urged him on towards his coronation in London. In advance of this, however, William sent a force into the capital to erect a fortress (this probably became the Tower of London), and by Christmas 1066, all of two months since his victory at Hastings, William was finally ready to be crowned. In Edward the Confessor's great church at Westminster on Christmas Day 1066, Archbishop Ealdred of York asked the assembled English if they would have William crowned and 'all gave their joyful assent without hesitation, as though heaven had given them one mind and one voice'. Not everything went smoothly, however. When the Norman soldiers assembled outside the abbey during the coronation heard the loud shout from inside in a foreign tongue, they feared the worst, assumed treachery was afoot and torched the neighbouring houses. Most of the congregation fled from the church in panic and confusion and the ceremony was completed by the bishops and clergy with the new king trembling from head to foot.[36] This was a far from auspicious start to the reign, and it could almost be read as a portent of the difficult times to come.

Notes

1 *WP*, p.101; *BT*, pl.31; *JW*, ii p.601.

2 *ASC* 'C', 'D', s.a.1065.

3 *WMGR*, i p.421; *JW*, ii p.601.

4 *BT*, pl.32; *ASC* 'C', 'D', s.a.1066; *JW*, ii p.601.

5 *OV*, ii p.141.

6 *ASC* 'C', s.a.1066.

7 *WJ*, ii p.161.

8 *ASC* 'C', s.a.1066.

9 300 according to the *Anglo-Saxon Chronicle* ('D', s.a.1066), 500 according to John of Worcester (*JW*, ii p.603).

10 *ASC* 'C', s.a.1066.

11 *ASC* 'C', 'D', 'E', s.a.1066.

12 *WP*, pp.101, 107.

13 *BT*, pls.35–7; *WJ*, ii p.165.

14 *WP*, p.103; Bernard S. Bacharach, 'Some observations on the military administration of the Norman Conquest', *ANS* 8 (1985), pp.1–25.

15 *WP*, p.105.

16 *BT*, pl.68.

17 *WJ*, ii pp.165–7; *WP*, pp.109–11.

18 *JW*, ii p.605.

19 *OV*, ii pp.170–3.

20 David Crouch, *The Normans: The history of a dynasty* (London: Hambledon, 2002), p.90.

21 *BT*, pls.50–1.

22 *WP*, p.127.

23 *ASC* 'D', s.a.1066.

24 M.K. Lawson, *The Battle of Hastings 1066* (Stroud: Tempus, 2003), pp.150, 191.

25 *BT*, pls.61–2.

26 David Carpenter, *The Struggle for Mastery: Britain 1066–1284* (Oxford University Press, 2003), p.73.

27 *BT*, pl.71; *WP*, p.153.

28 Lawson, *Battle of Hastings*, p.219.

29 *BT*, pl.68; *WP*, p.131.

30 *BT*, pl.71; Lawson, *Battle of Hastings*, pp.207–12.

31 *WP*, p.137.

32 Carpenter, *The Struggle for Mastery*, p.73. For an alternative view, see Matthew Strickland, 'Military Technology and Conquest: The Anomaly of

Anglo-Saxon England', *ANS* 19 (1996), pp.353–82, at p.382: the English were defeated in 1066 'not because of any technological inferiority or the absence of crossbows, cavalry or castles, but because of an unusually decisive victory which annihilated effective dynastic members, paralyzed the remaining leadership and resulted in a rapid and widespread political submission'. This of course, begs the question why the victory was so decisive.

33 *WP*, p.147; *ASC* 'D', s.a.1066.

34 *OV*, v pp.271–3.

35 *ASC* 'D', s.a.1066; *WP*, p.147.

36 *WP*, p.151; *OV*, ii p.185.

CHAPTER 5

Conquest consolidated, 1067–1087

The establishment of Norman rule

Between 1067 and 1075 the Norman rulers of England faced opposition from all over their new kingdom and beyond. Its eventual suppression owed much to the leadership and drive of William I. Archbishop Lanfranc acknowledged his importance in 1072 or 1073 when he wrote to Pope Alexander II and claimed that 'while the king lives we have peace of a kind, but after his death we expect to have neither peace nor any other benefit'.[1] The Norman chroniclers' accounts of these years are also focused on the conduct and personality of the King; indeed they portray him almost as some kind of superman, dealing often single-handedly with one threat to his rule after another. There is no doubt that King William went to great lengths to secure his hold on England. However, the resistance he faced was unfocused and uncoordinated. There was no unity among the insurgents, no dominant figure for them to unite around (Edgar *atheling* was the obvious candidate for this position) and no single coherent plan for rebellion. William's task in subduing the opposition he faced was still a hugely difficult one, and he faced setbacks along the way. Nevertheless, he and his deputies were able to pick off their opponents one by one.

Yet there was more to the events of these years than simply holding the line against English counter-attack. Their course dictated to a large extent the shape that Norman England would eventually assume and the style of rule its new lords would eventually adopt. There is every reason to believe that William intended to conciliate his new English subjects when he became king. However, his early good intentions soon came to nothing. The occupation of England quickly became a massive ongoing military enterprise which required heavy taxation, the dispossession of the native aristocracy and the granting of their lands to men who were, in effect, Norman military governors of particular areas. The chronic instability current in England until the early 1070s also presented tempting opportunities to the adventurous rulers of Scotland and Denmark, who were keen to try to win lands and treasure at William's expense. In the end, reluctantly or not on William's part, England could only be subdued by the relentless, single-minded use of force. Scotland, Wales and Normandy were inevitably affected by these turbulent upheavals, too.

England subdued, 1067–1072

After his coronation at Christmas 1066, King William remained in England until March 1067. During that time, rather than removing the remaining members of the old Anglo-Saxon aristocracy he first tried to reconcile them to the new regime. Edwin, Morcar and Waltheof (earls of Mercia, Northumbria and Northamptonshire respectively), having submitted to the new king, had their lands and titles confirmed. According to William de Poitiers, Edgar *atheling* was also given lands by William; the King's niece, Judith, married Earl Waltheof, and a marriage between Earl Edwin and William's daughter also appears to have been discussed. In the Church, too, continuity was preserved: Archbishop Stigand, for example, remained in office for another four years after 1066. On the administrative side also, the keynote was continuity. A new coinage was issued – it bore William's image, but the Anglo-Saxon system was used to produce it; and royal writs sent from central government to the localities continued to be written in English until Latin took over as the language of government in the early 1070s. One such writ confirmed the ancient privileges of the City of London.[2] William was looking for an accommodation with the old regime; but whilst this may have been an attractive idea in theory, practical reality dictated that it was almost inevitably bound to fail.

Signs of continuing tension between Normans and English soon began to surface. When William returned to Normandy in March 1067, he took with him Archbishop Stigand, Edgar *atheling*, and earls Edwin, Morcar and Waltheof. Whilst he was prepared for these representatives of the old regime to retain their ranks and positions, the new king also wanted to show them who was now in charge. These men were also the natural magnets for any opponents of the new regime, and it was a prudent move for William to keep them at his side where he could watch them closely. According to William de Poitiers, indeed, he took with him to Normandy those Englishmen 'whose loyalty and power he particularly suspected'.[3] They were also the spoils of victory, and he displayed them (humiliatingly, it can be supposed, for the Englishmen concerned) along with all his other loot when he processed solemnly yet victoriously through Rouen and Fécamp.

Whilst William was in Normandy, England was left in the hands of his half-brother, Bishop Odo of Bayeux, who was based at Dover, and another of his closest followers, William FitzOsbern, who was based at Winchester. William de Poitiers's too rosy view was that Odo and William FitzOsbern 'were administering their prefectures in the kingdom, each praiseworthy in his own, working sometimes together, sometimes separately'.[4] The *Anglo-Saxon Chronicle*'s view of their methods is more convincing: they 'stayed behind and built castles far and wide throughout this country, and distressed the wretched folk, and always after that it grew much worse'.[5] It may be no coincidence, therefore, that the first signs of overt opposition to Norman rule in England appear during their guardianship of the kingdom. In 1067, Count Eustace of Boulogne, who had fought alongside William at Hastings, but who was, perhaps more significantly, Edward the Confessor's brother-in-law, attempted to land in England only to be seen off by the garrison at Dover. Eustace may have been dissatisfied at the amount of land he had been given by the new king and decided to assert his own claim to the throne, but it is impossible to know. Perhaps more seriously, William de Poitiers emphasised the English habit of sending envoys to the Danes 'or some other people from whom they might hope for help'. Again, it is impossible to know how much truth there was in these allegations, but it was almost certainly a deteriorating situation in England that led to William's return from Normandy at the end of 1067.[6]

At this stage, however, whilst the challenges William had to face were serious, they were largely confined to one area, the south-west of

England. The leading English noblemen were still, at least superficially, loyal to the new king. One challenge to Norman authority was launched by the mysterious figure known as Eadric 'the Wild', who attacked Hereford with the support of the ruler of Gwynedd and Powys, Bleddyn ap Cynfyn, who had been installed by Harold Godwineson in 1063.[7] Most serious, however, was the opposition William was forced to confront in Exeter. Harold's mother Gytha appears to have been based there, and she provided a natural focus for discontent with the new regime. Early in 1068, William marched into Devon at the head of a large force and laid siege to Exeter. The inhabitants were determined in their resistance, however; they tried to recruit support from a wide area and they strengthened the town's defences in anticipation of William's assault. Interestingly, Orderic states that this was the first time that William called out Englishmen to fight for him, and after a long and apparently bloody siege he managed to obtain the town's surrender. William was generous to his opponents, and all he did after accepting their submission was to begin the construction of a castle within the town walls. His conciliatory approach may have been dictated by a need to secure support in the south-west, and after leaving Exeter he travelled into Cornwall to show his strength and then returned to Winchester for Easter. It must have been soon after this that William summoned his wife Matilda from Normandy. She was crowned and anointed queen at Westminster in May 1068. This was an important moment for the royal couple and more than simply a gesture on William's part. Matilda was the daughter of a count and the grand-daughter of a French king (Robert the Pious). Her status therefore trumped that of her husband, and having her acclaimed as queen was designed to add further lustre to his own image.[8]

The troubles of 1068 were far from over, however. At the same time as William had been besieging Exeter, an invasion fleet led by three of King Harold's sons had been launched from Ireland and had landed in south-west England. It is conceivable that this invasion was supposed to reinforce the rebellion at Exeter, but there is no proof of this. In any event, part of this force went to Bristol where it was seen off, and it was defeated again by another survivor of the old regime, Eadnoth the Staller, Edward the Confessor's former steward, who was killed in the encounter. It is worth stressing that Bristol did not open its gates to these invaders and that they were defeated by an Englishman on William's behalf: this was not a simple case of old versus new. Similar patterns were at play in 1069, too, when the sons of Harold chanced their arms again. This time they landed at Exeter and ravaged much of Devon; they were joined by supporters from Devon and Cornwall but Exeter, the town which had given the king such trouble only a year before, this time remained loyal to the new regime. The garrison William had left behind was probably crucial in this respect and showed the wisdom of his policy of building castles at places of strategic importance almost wherever he went in his new land.

More serious for William in 1068, however, was the decision of earls Edwin and Morcar to defy their new king. Their reasons for doing so at this point are obscure. Edwin may have rebelled because the marriage which had been arranged between him and William's daughter had not taken place, and because the authority which William had granted Edwin 'over his brother and almost a third of England' was more illusory than real.[9] Certainly, the appointment of Roger de Montgomery as earl of Shrewsbury, which had probably happened by 1068, undermined Edwin's position as earl of Mercia. To complicate matters further, there was upheaval in northern England at the same time. To avert the possibility of the earls' supporters joining up with the northern rebels, and to remind them of his power, William marched into the heart of the earldom of Mercia and ordered the building of a castle at Warwick. Edwin and Morcar immediately surrendered. The King then proceeded to Nottingham where the construction of another castle began. Finally in the north, he went to York where, again, a castle was built. Then, on his way back south, William set in train the construction of yet more castles at Lincoln, Huntingdon and Cambridge. Loyal Normans were placed in charge of all these new fortifications: William Malet in York, William Peverel at Nottingham and Henry, son of Roger of Beaumont, at Warwick.

The suppression of these first revolts seems to have brought to an end forever any idea William might have had of establishing a genuinely Anglo-Norman polity in England. Such a policy was always bound to cause tension. The Normans remained an alien, occupying force within England; they were not trusted and remained unwelcome. At the same time, William was under pressure from his Norman followers to redistribute English lands to them, both as rewards for their service and as a more immediately effective way of enforcing his rule and protecting his new frontiers. From their bases at Chester, Shrewsbury and Hereford, new French lords controlled the border between England and Wales by the early 1070s. One of these men, William FitzOsbern ('the first and greatest oppressor of the English', according to Orderic Vitalis[10]), also exercised authority over wide stretches of western and southern England, probably those which had made up Harold Godwineson's earldom of Wessex. But in Herefordshire his job was to guard against the attacks of the Welsh and to do this he rebuilt the castle at Hereford and began the construction of the enormous keep at Chepstow. On the south coast of England, too, more of William's loyal Norman followers, Roger de Montgomery, William de Warenne and others, were given large blocks of territory in Sussex called 'Rapes', to guard the English Channel. Castles were constructed by these men at Arundel, Bramber, Hastings, Lewes and Pevensey. Authority in other strategically important areas was placed in the hands of some of William's closest supporters. Odo of Bayeux, for example, was made earl of Kent and held Dover against Eustace of Boulogne in 1067.

The building of castles, the steady influx of Norman lords and the heavy taxation which was also characteristic of these years were probably necessary if the new regime was to survive. But these developments must also have convinced many amongst the English that they had little to lose in continuing to oppose the newcomers. Northern England, always less integrated into the English king's sphere of authority than the centre or the south of his kingdom, provided William with his greatest challenge. His first attempts to deal with the north had led to the appointment by him as earl of Northumbria of Copsi, a former associate of Tostig, who had gone into exile with the earl in 1065. This imprudent step demonstrated William's ignorance of politics and tradition in the further flung parts of his new kingdom, and Copsi was murdered by his local rival Osulf of Bamburgh as soon as he arrived in the north to take up his post early in 1068. His successor, Gospatric, another survivor of the old regime, was not appointed on merit, although his family did have strong Northumbrian connections. Rather, he paid William for the privilege of taking control in the north, and in 1068 he became involved in a serious rising there. This followed an attack on Durham, in which Robert FitzRichard, who had been given general responsibility for Yorkshire by the King, was killed along with many of his men, and during which the castellan of York, William Malet, was besieged in his castle by Gospatric and Edgar *atheling* amongst others. The king returned from Normandy, marched north early in 1069 and destroyed the rebel army at York. A second castle was built there and, to demonstrate how seriously William considered the situation to be, he left William FitzOsbern in charge.

Following William I's campaign, Gospatric fled to Scotland and was succeeded as earl by Robert Cumin who was slaughtered along with his knights on the first night after their arrival in Durham in January 1069. Somehow, Gospatric then seems to have been reinstated as earl in the north. Such events highlight the very real difficulties William had in asserting his control over northern England in the early years after 1066. The problems of governing a distant, unfamiliar region, one with its own traditions, customs and power structures, were exacerbated by other factors too, however. There was always the possibility that the leading men of Northumbria might form a coalition with that arch-opportunist, King Malcolm III. Extra fuel might also be poured on the flames of opposition by Edgar *atheling*, who had fled for refuge at the Scottish king's court at around the same time as Edwin and Morcar were staging their revolt against William in 1068. The links between the king of Scotland and the remaining representative of England's pre-conquest ruling house were strengthened further when Malcolm married Edgar's sister, Margaret, in 1069 or 1070.

Yet another potential threat to William's position in England came from further north still. King Swein Estrithson of Denmark maintained a claim to the English throne as the son of Cnut's sister and the cousin of Harthacnut, and by Easter 1069 the arrival of a large invasion fleet in England from Denmark was imminent. When it reached the banks of the Humber in the summer, it was led by Swein's brother, Osbern, and three of his sons, and it is said to have consisted of 240 ships. Edgar *atheling*, Earl Waltheof, Earl Gospatric (no more loyal to the new regime than before, it seems), and other rebels then joined forces with the Danes and moved south to besiege and brutally capture York in September 1069. King William responded by travelling north once again; and after a difficult crossing of the river Aire near Pontefract he reached York. He ordered his crown to be brought from Winchester and wore it in great ceremony amidst the ruins of the city on Christmas Day 1069.

The Danish army, meanwhile, had retreated to the north bank of the Humber and had agreed to leave England in the spring. It may be that this force, although large by all accounts, was designed mainly to prepare the way for a later invasion by King Swein himself. However, such tactics played into William's hands. He removed the possibility of their making any contact with potential rebels in southern England and slowly began to encircle them. In the process began one of the most notorious episodes of William's reign, the so-called 'Harrying of the North'. According to the *Anglo-Saxon Chronicle*, the king went north 'with all his army that he could collect, and utterly ravaged and laid waste that shire'.[11] Orderic's account was more graphic: according to him, William 'continued to comb forests and remote mountain places, stopping at nothing to hunt out the enemy hidden there. His camps were spread over an area of 100 miles. He cut down many in his vengeance; destroyed the lairs of others; harried the land and burned homes to ashes.' Orderic even becomes critical of William at this point:

Nowhere else had William shown such cruelty. Shamefully he succumbed to this vice, for he made no effort to restrain his fury and punished the innocent with the guilty. In his anger he commanded that all crops and herds, chattels and food of every kind should be brought together and burned to ashes with consuming fire, so that the whole region north of the Humber might be stripped of all means of sustenance. In consequence so serious a scarcity was felt in England, and so terrible a famine fell upon the humble and defenceless populace, that more than 100,000 Christian folk of both sexes, young and old alike, perished of hunger . . .[12]

Orderic's assessment of the number of people who died as a result of William's conduct in the north is surely exaggerated. If true it would mean that something approaching five per cent of England's population died in the winter of 1069–70. It is a pardonable overestimate, however, and reveals the shock contemporaries felt at what can only be described as William's terror tactics.

There has been much debate about the true extent of the destruction caused by the Harrying of the North, and about its long-term effects on the lands and people of northern England. In Domesday Book, hundreds of vills in Yorkshire were described as 'waste', with no population or value. The conventional wisdom has tended to hold that these areas were devastated during the events of 1069–70.[13] It is impossible to be sure that this was the case, however, and more recently it has been argued that major destruction was probably confined to the more remote upland areas of northern England and that only a relatively limited area in Yorkshire was affected. Lands in Yorkshire might later have been described as 'waste' simply because they were worthless.[14] Perhaps they had been ravaged by a ferocious army; but they may have lacked value for other reasons, too. Further questions have been raised about the capacity of William's army, working in winter and for only three months, to inflict the sort of damage traditionally associated with the Harrying. It has been suggested that the purpose of the campaign was limited, that is 'to seek out and secure the submission of those native leaders who had assisted the Danish capture of York'. It is more likely, however, that, in late 1069, the king's intention was to make as much of northern England as uninhabitable as he could, at least temporarily, so as to 'make it impossible for the North to revolt after his departure'.[15]

In this respect, the Harrying of the North was successful, but it did not put an end to opposition elsewhere. In January or February 1070 William travelled west to deal with a rising on the Welsh border, new castles were constructed at Chester and Stafford and arrangements were made for the security and government of the Welsh borders with the appointment of more Normans to positions of power. Roger de Montgomery had already become earl of Shrewsbury by this time, and Hugh d'Avranches earl of Chester; then, in 1071, on the death of William FitzOsbern, his son Roger was granted his English manors and became earl of Hereford.

By Easter 1070, William may have thought that the storm of English opposition had blown itself out. Papal legates attended his court at Winchester and crowned him once more in what was almost certainly a consciously symbolic assertion of the legitimacy of Norman rule in England. In the same year, the hierarchy of the English Church was remodelled. Stigand was the most prominent of a number of English prelates dismissed from their posts, although the prospect of getting hold of his extensive estates may have tempted William to depose him as much as any concern for the condition of the Church. At the same time formal penances were announced for those who had taken lives in and since the Battle of Hastings. For King William, there was more to winning a kingdom than success on the battlefield: he understood that he owed his victory to divine support, and he wanted to make sure he kept God on his side. Nevertheless, Orderic Vitalis's description of the condition of England by about 1070 is too glowing. According to him, 'by the grace of God peace reigned over England; and a degree of security returned to its inhabitants . . . English and Normans were living peacefully together in boroughs, towns and cities, and were intermarrying with each other'.[16] There were still threats to William's authority which needed to be dealt with.

In the spring of 1070, as William sat re-crowned at Winchester, King Swein of Denmark finally arrived in England to join up with those of his countrymen who had never left England as they had agreed to do at the end of the previous year. In the view of the *Anglo-Saxon Chronicle*, there was a genuine expectation at the time that Swein was going to conquer the country. It is hard to assess the accuracy of this claim, but there can be little doubt that this was potentially the most serious threat that William had faced since becoming king.[17] In the end, however, it came to nothing. Swein sent part of his army to Ely where its forces combined with some remaining English resistance under the leadership of a figure of later legend, Hereward. His origins and grievances are obscure, but Hereward was probably a Lincolnshire thegn who lost lands in the aftermath of the Conquest, and he set up his rebel base in the Fens. He appears to have been the leader of an assault on Peterborough Abbey launched by the abbey's tenants, of whom Hereward was one, resentful of the appointment of the Norman Turold as abbot there. Soon after this, however, the Danes made their own peace deal with William and finally returned home with their loot. Hereward was then joined by Earl Morcar, presumably by now desperate for a cause to attach himself to, and his brother Edwin was killed by his own men at the same time, either during an attempt to flee to Scotland, or whilst trying to recruit support for the rebels in the north. The King then besieged the rebels on the Isle of Ely, constructing in the process a huge causeway across the marshes, another impressive military feat; and when they finally surrendered, Earl Morcar was imprisoned for life.

Hereward by contrast, a nuisance rather than a threat, was given back his lands by the King.

By this time, it must have been clear to those Englishmen who continued to oppose the new regime that there was little hope of success in the absence of concerted external support, from the Scots perhaps, but ideally from the Danes. King Swein's return to Denmark, however, almost certainly amounted to an acknowledgement by him that William could not be dislodged, and Hereward's surrender was a sensible move in hopeless circumstances. William set the seal on this phase of his reign by marching north to Scotland in 1072, presumably intending to intimidate King Malcolm, to make him aware of the dangers of his continuing support for Edgar *atheling*, and to warn him about further meddling in the affairs of northern England. This was yet another considerable military undertaking, involving a land army and a fleet travelling farther north than any English royal force had done since Aethelstan's reign. The two kings reached an agreement in 1072, known as the Peace of Abernethy: Malcolm acknowledged William's superiority (he became the 'man' of the English king) and expelled Edgar from his court.[18] The situation was stabilised for the moment, although Scotland and Edgar were to give William more trouble in years to come.

Opposition: the next generation, 1072–1075

By 1072, the Norman hold on England was secure if not untroubled. However, since 1067, Norman pre-eminence in northern France had come under threat. In part this was because William I had been forced to spend so much time in his new kingdom; but it was also because, by the early 1070s, a new generation of assertive and ambitious French opponents had come of age. In William's absence, Normandy had been governed by a number of his advisers and family members. His wife Matilda had acted as regent until she came to England in 1068, probably in collaboration with her son Robert Curthose and sometimes under the guidance of Roger de Montgomery and Roger de Beaumont. After that, however, in 1070–1, Norman authority in Maine had collapsed under pressure from a local uprising, and early in 1071 a succession dispute in Flanders resulted in some serious political and personal losses for the King. On the death in 1070 of Count Baldwin VI, Queen Matilda's brother, the claims of his children were challenged by their uncle, also Matilda's brother, Robert the Frisian. When King William sent a force to intervene under the leadership of William FitzOsbern, it was defeated in February 1071 and FitzOsbern was killed. A hostile prince now ruled Flanders, and William had lost one of his closest friends and allies. To make matters worse, William now faced maturing opponents on his other frontiers, namely King Philip I of France, who offered his support to Edgar *atheling* in 1074, and Count Fulk IV of Anjou. The number of William's French enemies was growing fast, and this partly explains why, from 1072 onwards, he spent the bulk of his time in Normandy (about 130 out of the 170 months between his probable crossing in 1072 and his death).[19] The first real manifestation of these disturbing developments, however, appeared in England.

Following William FitzOsbern's death, the King had divided his lands between his friend's two sons. William de Breteuil received the Norman lands, and the younger son Roger was given his English lands and the title earl of Hereford. By 1074, however, Earl Roger was frustrated at the amount of real power he had; confined as it was to Herefordshire, it was significantly less than the much wider authority his father had wielded across England. He particularly resented losing authority over the sheriffs of the south-west: 'he had the rank of an earl without the substance of an earl's power', it has been suggested.[20] Matters came to a head in the autumn of 1074 when a plan to defy the King and to force concessions from him was formulated at a wedding feast held to celebrate a marriage between Roger's sister Emma and the recently appointed earl of East Anglia, Ralph de Gael, the son of Earl Ralph the Staller. They were joined in the conspiracy, to some degree, by Earl Waltheof of Northumbria. Their motives, especially Waltheof's, are obscure. Ralph's authority seems to have been confined to East Anglia (and perhaps to Norfolk), whereas the earldom of East Anglia had once embraced the whole of the east midlands. For his part, Waltheof may only have been guilty of failing to tell the King of the other conspirators' plans for revolt; he does not appear to have played an active role in it. There was a generational element to the rebellion, too. Roger and Ralph had not shared with the King the traumas and upheavals of the 1040s and 1050s; nor had they taken part in the events of 1066. There was little to bind them to William, and there was little sympathetic appreciation on either side of respective interests and ambitions.

The 1075 revolt against Norman rule in England was potentially very serious indeed. Waltheof, had he participated more fully, might have attracted support from the dispossessed English majority; and Earl Ralph could use his strong Breton connections (his mother was a Breton and he had been based there until after 1066) to call on support from France and from those Bretons who had come to England in 1066. The plotters even appealed for help to the Danes. In the event, however, the earls were unable to raise significant support from within or outside England; and King William, who was in Normandy when the revolt broke out, left it to be dealt with by his deputies. Both Roger and Ralph attempted to rally the men of their earldoms, but Roger was prevented from crossing the Severn by a force under Wulfstan, bishop of Worcester. He retreated into Wales and took refuge at the court of Caradog ap Gruffudd, who had become ruler of Glamorgan in 1072 by defeating his rival in battle with the help of Norman cavalry. In East Anglia meanwhile neither the castle garrisons nor the local levies supported Ralph and he was cornered at his manor of Fawdon by Geoffrey, bishop of Coutances, and other barons loyal to the King. His army was scattered and Ralph fled to Norwich, then abroad, leaving his new wife to hold the castle at Norwich. She eventually arranged safe conduct for herself and her men, joining her husband in Brittany.

In the autumn of 1075, having left Normandy in the hands of Queen Matilda, Archbishop John of Rouen and Roger de Beaumont, King William returned to England to deal with the Danish invasion, which was still likely. However, when the Danes finally arrived with a fleet of 200 ships, under the command of King Swein's son Cnut, the rising was all but over; they sacked York Minster and retired to Flanders. William proceeded to deal with the rebels. Roger de Breteuil was dispossessed and imprisoned for life. Earl Waltheof, after travelling to Normandy, threw himself on William's mercy. This did him little good, though: he was brought back to England, tried for treason and beheaded at Winchester in May 1076. How much the King was involved in Waltheof's trial, and whether he was present at the execution, is unclear. The earl's estates were given to his wife Judith, the King's niece, and a cult soon grew up around his tomb at Crowland Abbey, where he was venerated as a martyr. Walcher, bishop of Durham, was allowed to purchase the vacant office of earl of Northumbria. Lesser prisoners who were not exiled were blinded and mutilated instead. Had the Danes arrived before the threat posed by the earls had been neutralised, then matters might have turned out differently. The speed of the reaction to the revolt was impressive, however, as was the range of individuals, both English and Norman, who stood up to challenge the rebels.

Frontiers and family, 1076–1084

Orderic Vitalis claimed that, following the execution of Earl Waltheof, King William never again enjoyed peace in his lands.[21] There is some justification for this view. William's ability to leave the crushing of the 1075 revolt to his deputies in England reflects well on the security of his position there; but his troubles were still far from over. And at the same time, William's position in France continued to deteriorate. When he returned to Normandy in the spring of 1076, William's main objective was to deal with the threat posed to his western border by the presence of the fugitive Earl Ralph in his castle at Dol in Brittany. He was besieged there as William terrorised the surrounding countryside. However, in November, William was attacked and decisively defeated at Dol by the French king, Philip I. This was the first major military setback of William's career, and contemporaries noted its significance. William was said to have lost many men and horses, and much treasure; and he was also forced to retreat into Normandy. The defeat at Dol was only a temporary reversal, however, and William soon recovered. But he was dealt another blow in May 1077 when Simon, count of Amiens, Valois and the Vexin retired to a monastery and handed over the French Vexin to Philip I. Simon held this territory as a vassal of the abbey of St Denis, so William had no obvious right to intervene or object to what Simon had done. However, he is said to have been very close to the count, and the loss of an ally whose lands formed a buffer zone between Normandy and the lands of the French king was a major blow. William made truces with King Philip and with Count Fulk of Anjou in 1077 and 1078 respectively, but the pressure on his frontiers was mounting.

These pressures were only increased by conflict within William's own family; more specifically by the deterioration of his relationship with his eldest son, Robert. Born soon after his parents' marriage in the early 1050s, Robert was, according to Orderic Vitalis, 'very courageous in battle', but he was also 'talkative and extravagant, reckless . . . round-faced, short and stout, he was commonly nicknamed "fat-legs" or "curt-hose"'.[22] Orderic Vitalis had a low opinion of Robert, and his descriptions of his personality and of events in which he was involved should be treated cautiously. Having been promised the succession to Normandy by his father well before 1066, a promise which had been restated at least once after the victory at Hastings, Robert must have enjoyed a certain degree of paternal approval. But by the late 1070s, he was a mature man with his own followers to satisfy, and he must have been keen to start exercising authority in his own right. There was little sign, however, that William was preparing to cede any measure of meaningful authority over England or Normandy to his son. Even after 1066, when Robert might have expected to take the lead in governing Normandy during his father's absences, the indications are that power was usually exercised during these periods by Queen Matilda and particularly trusted associates of the King. Robert's discontent may have been sharpened further after 1072 when his father began once again to spend the bulk of his time in Normandy, leaving him with even less room for independent manoeuvre.

Robert may therefore have been considering his options before 1078, but in that year he made a concerted bid for independence. It was a quarrel between him and his two younger brothers which provoked Robert into action. Whilst he was staying in a house in Laigle on the southern Norman border, Robert was visited by William Rufus and Henry. Robert stayed downstairs whilst the others went to the upper storey to play dice. They soon began to taunt Robert from above and pour water down on him and his companions who, enraged at such disrespectful conduct, demanded that Robert take action. He ran upstairs to confront his brothers, and the quarrel was only prevented from degenerating further by the intervention of the King himself, who had heard the noise from where he was staying. The next night, however, Robert and his companions left the royal army and attempted to seize the castle at Rouen. Their attempted coup failed and they fled from Normandy to avoid the King's 'terrible rage'.[23] Orderic's description of these events is difficult to credit in all its detail. His depiction of the relationship between the brothers supports his consistently held view that Robert was the weakest and least able of the three. Nevertheless, there must have been tensions between them, albeit over more than a fraternal prank gone wrong, and between Robert and his father.

The quarrel between Robert, his father and his brothers divided the Anglo-Norman aristocracy as much as it did the royal family. Robert attracted plenty of powerful support, especially from ambitious young Normans of his own age, who were themselves desperate to take power from their elders. Robert de Bellême, the son of Roger de Montgomery, and William de Breteuil, the son and Norman heir of William FitzOsbern were amongst his confederates. The sound of such internal discord was also picked up outside Normandy and England. By the end of 1078, Robert was based at the castle of Gerberoy, south-east of Normandy, which had been given to him by King Philip of France, from where he made raids into Norman territory. William laid siege to the castle for three weeks at the start of 1079 and eventually saw his army attacked when Robert and his troops left the castle in an attempt to break the siege. Robert even fought his father during the ensuing battle and wounded him in the hand. His brother William was wounded, too. An uneasy peace between father and son, mediated by senior members of the Norman aristocracy and by Queen Matilda, was not established until Easter 1080; and although precisely what was agreed is unknown, it is likely that William had little choice but to confirm Robert's status as his heir to Normandy.

Meanwhile, during the King's long absence from England, his half-brother Odo had acted as regent there. He had had to deal with another invasion of Northumberland by Malcolm III in 1079, as well as the murder of Bishop Walcher of Durham, Waltheof's successor as earl of Northumbria, who fell victim to factional squabbling within the northern aristocracy and became the tenth earl of Northumbria since 993 to meet a violent end. Odo travelled north and carried out reprisals, but a more personal reassertion of royal control was badly needed. In the autumn of 1080, William sent Robert Curthose north to bring King Malcolm to heel. He managed to secure a confirmation of the terms of the Peace of Abernethy, but nothing more permanent except the building on his way south, and by way of frontier defence, of the 'new castle' on the Tyne, close to the site of Walcher's murder.

King William wore his crown at Gloucester at Christmas 1080 and at Winchester at Whitsun 1081. It was also in 1081 that William made his only known visit to Wales. He travelled across south Wales as far as St David's, a route which led Welsh sources to describe William's expedition as a pilgrimage. It is much more likely, however, that this was a military expedition with clear political aims. In the same year as William went to Wales (unfortunately it is not known precisely when these events took place), the Battle of Mynydd Carn (somewhere north of St David's) brought an end to the turbulence which had characterised Welsh political affairs since the death of Gruffudd ap Llewelyn in 1063. Three aspiring native princelings, including the ruler of Glamorgan Caradog ap Gruffudd, were killed, enabling the two victors to become the new dominant forces in the north and south of Wales, Gruffudd ap Cynan in Gwynedd and Rhys ap Tewdwr in Deheubarth. It is almost certain, therefore, that William's campaign in 1081 was a response to these developments, and that his plan was to secure Rhys's submission; he may have envisaged something similar to his Scottish expedition of 1072. Caradog ap Gruffudd had been a compliant prince (Domesday Book shows him paying an annual tribute of £40 to the English king), even if he had been prepared to give shelter to the fugitive earl of Hereford in 1075. Caradog had fought with the help of Norman knights in 1072 and 1081, and William must have hoped that Rhys would also appreciate the benefits that might result from submission to him. By these means, William penetrated further into Wales than any Norman had hitherto and his influence in Wales was more widely felt than that of any pre-conquest king. Prior to 1081, after relatively rapid progress in the north and the marches, Chepstow and the river Wye had marked the practical limits of Norman control in the south. After 1081, the whole of southern Wales was added to the Normans' sphere of influence.

By the end of 1081, King William was back in France. Count Fulk of Anjou had attacked the castle of La Flèche in Maine, but William's arrival led to a truce whereby Fulk acknowledged Norman control of Maine and accepted Robert Curthose's homage for it. Having spent Christmas 1081–2 at Le Mans, and most of 1082 in Normandy, William returned to England late in that year to be confronted with a series of family crises. The first was caused by the ambitions of his half-brother Odo of Bayeux. One account of what happened alleged that Odo was plotting to seize the English throne on William's death. The version of events given by several writers of the early twelfth century, who claimed that Odo had hatched a plan to buy the papacy for himself, is more generally accepted, however.[24] Pope Gregory VII was certainly having difficulties with Emperor Henry IV in the first half of the 1080s, and Odo may have planned to use his vast wealth and the help of his fellow Normans in southern Italy to pursue his goal. The King disapproved, however, and accused Odo of trying to take knights out of the kingdom for his private purposes when they were needed to defend it. Odo was seized and imprisoned at Rouen for the rest of the reign.

Queen Matilda died in Normandy in November 1083. Her death and Odo's imprisonment were serious personal and political blows for the King. There is no reason to doubt that the royal marriage had been a successful and happy one. There is certainly no sign that William had mistresses or illegitimate children – an unusual state of affairs for a medieval king. He also relied heavily on Matilda for help with governing England and Normandy during his absences. She was a trusted lieutenant as well as a beloved partner. There was one cause of friction between husband and wife, however – their eldest son Robert. Matilda never lost her particular fondness for him, and during Robert's quarrels with his father and his exile, she supported him and sent him large sums of money. The King stopped at punishing the messenger who carried the cash, however, rather than the woman who had sent it. As for Odo, it is hard to know what the King's personal feelings towards him were. He was extravagant, worldly and regularly accused of tyrannical and overbearing conduct (his seal revealingly depicted him as a bishop on one side and a mounted warrior on the other). Nevertheless, it is clear that he was also forceful, determined and ruthless, and that he along with his brother Robert, count of Mortain, had played a central role in the government of William's cross-Channel lands and particularly in the Norman resettlement of England after 1066. William would not have made Odo earl of Kent or regent of England if he had not been a man of significant ability. As for Robert Curthose, the death of his mother and the imprisonment of his uncle removed his two closest allies in the royal family and probably allowed the differences still in existence between him and his father to resurface. Robert was exiled again in 1084, although it is unclear what happened to cause this.

Danes, Domesday and death, 1085–1087

Also in 1084, William had to deal with opposition in Maine and, more importantly, with the threat of a fresh Danish invasion led by King Cnut VI and his uncle, Count Robert of Flanders. William returned to England in 1085 with what was, by all accounts, a huge army. The King and his forces remained on standby during the latter part of 1085 and the first half of 1086 until news that Cnut had been murdered removed the threat of invasion. During this period, however, as William's mercenary troops ravaged the coastline and lived billeted on the kingdom, the *Anglo-Saxon Chronicle* noted the sufferings, hardship and heavy taxation inflicted on the English people.[25] William was certainly paying particular attention to what his kingdom could produce at this point, because it was at Christmas 1085, at Gloucester, after having 'much thought and very deep discussion with his council about this country – how it was occupied or with what sort of people', that he gave orders for an investigation into England's resources to be carried out.[26] This survey, which was soon given the name 'Domesday' because of its thoroughness and finality, was completed at the latest by autumn 1086, and the returns were brought to the King before he left for Normandy. He probably had them with him on 1 August 1086 at Salisbury when 'all the people occupying land who were of any account over all England, no matter whose men they were' appeared before him, 'bowed to him and became his men and swore hold oaths to him, that they would be loyal against all other men'.[27] This was probably the stage-managed climax of the whole Domesday process: an authoritative record of landholding had been made and the oaths amounted to an acknowledgement of what that record contained. The results of the Norman Conquest had been formally set down and confirmed. Soon, perhaps early in the next reign, the returns were edited, standardised and rebound into the volumes still known as Domesday Book.

Following the ceremony at Salisbury, William returned to Normandy for the last time, to deal with further threats from his neighbours, in particular King Philip, who had taken advantage of William's absence in England to make raids across the Norman border from the territory he had acquired from Count Simon of the Vexin in 1077. In July 1087, the King and his troops headed for the town of Mantes in the French Vexin, which had been the base for the raids. Whilst sacking the town, however, William, who by this time had grown excessively fat, was taken ill and carried back to Rouen. He may have been ill already and afflicted further by the heat; or he may have sustained a stomach injury from the pommel of his saddle. After a slow decline which lasted six weeks, William died on 9 September 1087. He was 59 years old. His body was carried back to Caen and buried in the church of St Stephen which he had founded in 1063. His body was too big for its sarcophagus, however, and as attempts were made to squeeze it in, the bloated corpse burst. It was an undignified and confused end to the reign of the greatest ruler of his day, a man who had changed the political shape of Western Europe.

There is no definitive account of what happened when William made his bequests just prior to his death. The two principal descriptions of the scene at the Conqueror's deathbed are difficult to interpret. Orderic Vitalis's account is long and characterised by flowery verbatim speeches.[28] It is clearly intended as a sermon on the insubstantial nature of worldly achievement and the morality of the conquest of England. It is shot through with hindsight, too: for example when the dying King predicts that his eldest son Robert 'will have long to suffer severe misfortune', and when he predicts that his third son Henry will one day 'succeed to all the dominions which belong to me'. The anonymous *De obitu Willelmi* ('The Death of William'), which may have been written in the 1090s, was probably not designed as an accurate historical record at all; it is more a description of how a great king was expected to die.[29] Derived almost entirely from two Carolingian sources, only a small number of names and phrases were changed to fit the circumstances of 1087. However, if they are used carefully, these descriptions make it clear that William sought atonement through extensive gifts to the Church and to the poor. There was an amnesty for prisoners, although, according to Orderic, William tried to exclude his brother Odo from this. As for the succession, William reluctantly, and after some persuasion from those around him, kept his promise that the absent Robert would succeed him as duke of Normandy. He may have felt obliged to do this, given Norman views on the permanence of *post obitum* gifts.[30] The sources are less clear about the English succession. It is possible that the King made no express provision for this kingdom at all, but this seems unlikely.[31] *De obitu Willelmi* records that William gave his crown, his sword and his jewel-encrusted gold sceptre to his second surviving son, William. Orderic by contrast has the King leaving the English kingdom in God's hands, while at the same time expressing the hope that William would be the next king and sending a letter to Archbishop Lanfranc ordering him to receive him. The King's third surviving son, Henry, was given £5,000 but no land.[32]

On balance, it is reasonable to argue that William I did designate William Rufus as his heir to the English crown. However, as Harold had found in 1066, a deathbed designation by no means guaranteed an undisputed transfer of power. As later events were to show, and despite what his father appears to have wanted, Robert Curthose continued to covet England. He might occasionally have been led to believe that he would inherit both England and Normandy; when he commanded the 1080 expedition against the Scots, for example. However, no express promise appears ever to have been made and Robert spent too little time in England to take his succession there for granted. In the second half of William I's reign, moreover, the divisions and disagreements within the ruling family had probably made a definitive settlement impossible. In 1087, whatever William I tried to do, another disputed succession beckoned.

Notes

1 *The Letters of Lanfranc Archbishop of Canterbury*, ed. Helen Clover and Margaret Gibson (Oxford: Clarendon Press, 1979), no.1 (p.35).

2 *EHD* II, p.1012.

3 *WP*, p.167; *ASC* 'D', s.a.1066.

4 *WP*, pp.181–3.

5 *ASC* 'D', s.a.1066.

6 *ASC* 'D', s.a.1066; *WP*, p.183.

7 *ASC* 'D', s.a.1067.

8 *ASC* 'D', s.a.1067; *OV*, ii pp.211–15.

9 *OV*, ii pp.215–17.

10 *OV*, ii pp.318–19.

11 *ASC* 'D', s.a.1069.

12 *OV*, ii pp.231–3.

13 See, for example, H.C. Darby, *Domesday England* (Cambridge University Press, 1977), pp.248–52; W.E. Kappelle, *The Norman Conquest of the North: The region and its transformation 1000–1135* (London: Croom Helm, 1980), pp.117–9, 173–4.

14 Paul Dalton, *Conquest, Anarchy and Lordship: Yorkshire, 1066–1154* (Cambridge University Press, 1994), pp.23–5.

15 Dalton, *Conquest, Anarchy and Lordship*, p.24; Kappelle, *The Norman Conquest of the North*, p.117.

16 *OV*, ii p.257.

17 *ASC* 'E', s.a.1070.

18 *ASC* 'D', 'E', s.a.1072.

19 David Bates, *William the Conqueror* (London: G.Philip, 1989), p.133.

20 C.P. Lewis, 'The Norman Settlement of Herefordshire under William I', *ANS* 7 (1984), pp.195–213, at p.212.

21 *OV*, ii p.351.

22 *OV*, ii p.357.

23 *OV*, ii p.359.

24 *ODNB*, 'Odo, earl of Kent'; *WMGR*, i p.507; *OV*, iv pp.39–45.

25 *ASC* 'E', s.a.1085, 1086.

26 *ASC* 'E', s.a.1085.

27 *ASC* 'E', s.a.1086.

28 *OV*, pp.81–95.

29 *EHD* II, pp.303–5.

30 Above, pp.77–8.

31 Barbara English, 'William I and the Anglo-Norman Succession', *Historical Research* 64 (1991), pp. 221–36.

32 William of Malmesbury claims that Henry received only 3,000 marks: *WMGR*, i pp.711–13.

CHAPTER 6

Conquest confirmed, 1087–1100

William Rufus

William II was in his late twenties when he became king – he was born perhaps as early as 1058, and certainly by 1060. He probably acquired his nickname of Rufus ('the Red' in Latin) because of his florid complexion. Equally he might have had a red beard, although twelfth-century commentators tended to describe him as having blonde or fair hair. William of Malmesbury portrayed the King as short, stocky and strong, with a large belly. He had 'eyes of no colour but spangled with bright specks' and a habit of stammering when he got angry.[1] His courtiers were criticised for their effeminate ways, immoderate dress and sexual immorality, thus suggesting to subsequent generations of historians that Rufus himself was a homosexual. That he never married and is not known to have had any children may lend support to this view, but such considerations are far from conclusive.

Rufus was also described by some of his contemporaries (mostly monks and clerics) as irreligious. He was accused of keeping churches in his custody vacant in order to milk their revenues; it was even alleged that he flirted with the idea of converting to Judaism. He certainly appears to have had a facetious, flippant streak and a rather casual attitude to the expected proprieties of his day. Nevertheless, there are also indications that he was not completely oblivious to spiritual concerns: his promises to rule more justly and to appoint Anselm as archbishop of Canterbury suggest he was not heedless of the fate of his soul as he lay close to death in 1093. He was also recognised even by his critics as a fine soldier and a generous lord. He pursued his vision of an extended and reunited Anglo-Norman realm with ruthless determination and sometimes brutal ferocity. And despite his tendency to appear boorish, he possessed the strategic vision and tactical subtlety of an expert politician.

Securing England, 1087–1088

In the late summer of 1087, however, the English throne still had to be secured. On his deathbed, the Conqueror had sent Rufus to England with a letter addressed to Archbishop Lanfranc of Canterbury. He made for Winchester, seized the royal treasury and, on 26 September 1087, was crowned king by Lanfranc in Westminster Abbey. Rufus had acted with decisive urgency, and for good reason. He must have known that his elder brother Robert had a perfectly viable claim to the English throne, and that he was likely to challenge his right to succeed. He must also have known that there were plenty of barons with lands on both sides of the English Channel who supported Robert and who would prefer to serve one lord rather than two. Orderic Vitalis expressed the concerns of the Anglo-Norman baronage in a concocted speech which almost certainly reflects contemporary attitudes:

What are we to do? Now that our lord is dead, two young men have succeeded and precipitately divided the lordship of England and Normandy. How can we properly serve two lords who are so different and so distant from each other? If we serve Robert . . . worthily, we will offend his brother, William, and we will be stripped by him of our great revenues and large estates in England. On the other hand, if we obey King William fittingly, duke Robert will deprive us of all our inherited lands in Normandy.

As a result, by the beginning of 1088 Rufus faced a coalition of leading magnates, led by Odo of Bayeux (who had been released from prison by Rufus after the Conqueror's death), Odo's brother Robert, count of Mortain, Roger de Montgomery, earl of Shrewsbury and Geoffrey, bishop of Coutances. In northern England, too, Rufus's friend William of St-Calais, bishop of Durham, had been lured over to the rebels' side after being convinced that the new reign was bound to be short. The rebels' strategy was to consolidate their position in the south-east (they held the castles of Tonbridge, Rochester and Pevensey) whilst awaiting Duke Robert's arrival from Normandy. This played into Rufus's hands, however. With promises of good government and low taxation, he recruited support from his new English subjects, who had little sympathy for the Norman conspirators and no reason to think that the creation of a single Anglo-Norman realm was a particularly good idea, and moved into Kent. Tonbridge surrendered to the King, prompting Bishop Odo to leave Rochester and join Count Robert at Pevensey. Rufus was thus able to besiege them both in the same castle. Odo submitted after six weeks and undertook to persuade the garrison at Rochester to surrender, too. When he went back there, however, he was taken prisoner by his own men who were determined to make a last stand. In July, they eventually capitulated.

With victory secured in the south-east, the risings in other parts of the kingdom soon collapsed. Bishop Wulfstan of Worcester had held the line for William in the Severn Valley whilst the King had been occupied in Kent and Sussex. Only the bishop of Durham continued to hold out, until he came to the royal court at Salisbury under a safe conduct in November 1088. Bishop William denied that a secular court, even the king's, had any jurisdiction over a bishop. Archbishop Lanfranc, however, insisted that 'We are not judging you about your bishopric, but about your fief', and William was tried for treason as a vassal of the king.[2] He was only released from royal custody and allowed to leave England for Normandy once his castle at Durham had been surrendered.

The 1088 rising had been very serious. It had a wide geographical base and of the ten greatest baronial landholders in Domesday Book, six had been on the rebels' side. Rufus had dealt with it impressively, however. Although he was assisted by his brother Robert's failure to come to England, it was his own vigorous military efforts which secured England for the new king. And with such a conclusive victory behind him, Rufus could begin to pursue his own plans, first amongst which was the conquest of Normandy. There was an element of retribution about this, of course – revenge for Robert's part in the rebellion of 1088. But Rufus may also have thought that, unless he reunited his father's dominions, the threat of Robert trying to do so again would never go away. One of them would have to overcome the other.

Normandy, 1089–1091

Rufus did not rush headlong into a military campaign, however. His preferred tactic at this stage was to buy the support of the Anglo-Norman baronage, either with lands and titles (one of his chief supporters at the start of his reign, Henry de Beaumont, was made earl of Warwick in 1088), or with cash. For raising the money to do this the King was indebted to the man contemporaries viewed as his evil henchman, Ranulf Flambard, a man who 'skinned the rich, ground down the poor, and swept other men's inheritances into his net', according to William of Malmesbury.[3] The son of a priest from the diocese of Bayeux, Flambard made his way into the royal administration during the reign of William I. He must have caught Rufus's eye, however, because he became his most trusted servant; his nickname, according to Orderic Vitalis, meant 'torchbearer' and was bestowed as a result of his fierce support for the King in all areas of policy.[4] His unpopularity with the chroniclers is probably good evidence of his effectiveness as a minister, particularly as a fundraiser; as is the pocket of support Rufus was able to build up through bribes in and around Rouen by the end of the 1080s. In October 1090 these partisans rebelled and their rising had to be put down by the King's younger brother, Henry. An able and ambitious young man in his own right, who may already have set his sights on overcoming both his elder brothers in time, Henry had used £3,000 of the money his father had left him to buy the Avranchin and the Cotentin in western Normandy from Duke Robert in 1088, and had taken the title of 'count of the Cotentin'.

Meanwhile, as Count Henry consolidated his position and acquired friends such as Hugh d'Avranches in western Normandy, Rufus was widening the base of his support in the north-east of the duchy. The counts of Aumale and Eu became his allies, and Normandy began to break apart. At this important moment, in February 1091, Rufus crossed the Channel and set up headquarters at Eu. More defections to his side followed. Duke Robert was compelled to negotiate, and when he met Rufus at Rouen he had no choice but to accept his brother's control over upper Normandy: all those Norman lords who had pledged their support for the English king were recognised by the Duke as Rufus's men; Fécamp and Cherbourg, both useful ports for entering the duchy, were also surrendered to him. Robert and Rufus also agreed to become each other's heirs, partly as a way of excluding and disinheriting Count Henry, against whom they campaigned together later in the year. More significantly, however, the terms agreed at Rouen were clear indicators of the new reality in Normandy. Rufus may not have been duke, but he was controlling events and dominating the political landscape.

Scotland and Wales in the 1090s

In August 1091, King William and Duke Robert returned to England together. The immediate priority was to deal with Malcolm III, who, not for the first time, had taken advantage of the English king's absence abroad and ravaged the northern counties almost to Durham. A combined land and sea operation along the east coast was launched, and in October 1091 a deal was negotiated through the mediation of Duke Robert's long-time friend, and King Malcolm's brother-in-law, Edgar *atheling*. Malcolm performed homage and swore an oath to Rufus and gave him his son Duncan as a hostage. In return Malcolm was granted the lands and privileges he had enjoyed in England during the Conqueror's reign; it is possible that Malcolm also received Rufus's permission to continue ruling Lothian.[5] Duke Robert, however, perhaps aggrieved at what he may have perceived as his brother's lack of gratitude for his efforts on his behalf, returned to Normandy in December. As for Rufus, he had to travel north again in 1092 to deal with disruption in Cumbria, an area ruled hitherto by Dolfin, a lord dependent on the king of Scots, and probably the son of the former earl of Northumbria, Gospatric. It was during this campaign that the English king began the construction of a castle at Carlisle. Also, according to the *Anglo-Saxon Chronicle*, he sent from the south 'many peasant people back there with their wives and cattle to live there to cultivate the land'.[6] Political and military domination was therefore combined with colonisation to extend the frontiers of the English kingdom.

Soon after this, however, in 1093, the King was struck down with a sudden and painful illness, and appeared to be dying. In this desperate condition, he attempted to atone for at least some of his sins by promising to mend his ways and govern better if he was spared and, most importantly for the future of the English Church, by giving the archbishopric of Canterbury (which had remained scandalously vacant since the death of Lanfranc in 1089) to the saintly and unwilling Anselm, abbot of the great Benedictine monastery of Bec. On his recovery, of course, Rufus was left with an archbishop whose personality and outlook could not have been less like his own. Nevertheless, in the short term, the King probably thought that his promises had secured at least some divine goodwill. In November 1093, for example, Malcolm III was killed in an ambush near Alnwick by Earl Robert de Mowbray of Northumbria. Rufus's actions in Cumbria in 1092 must have fostered anxiety in Malcolm's mind about his future plans; and then, in the summer of 1093, Rufus summoned Malcolm to Gloucester only to refuse to see him once he had arrived. This may have been a calculated insult, designed to remind Malcolm of his subordinate status. It certainly infuriated him. Malcolm returned home to plan his fifth invasion of northern England, and it was during this expedition that he was killed. A large and very sharp thorn had finally been extracted from the English kingdom's side.

Malcolm's death was followed by political chaos in the kingdom of Scotland, the consequences of which were profound. The late king's eldest son from his second marriage to Queen Margaret, Edward, had been mortally wounded in the Northumbrian ambush, and within days of hearing what had happened to her husband and son, the saintly Queen herself died of shock. The throne was seized by Malcolm's brother, Donald Bàn, who immediately expelled all the English and Normans from his court. However, this was also Rufus's chance to establish a client ruler in the northern kingdom, and he had the perfect candidate, namely Duncan, the eldest son of Malcolm III by his first marriage. Duncan had long been a hostage at the English court and he had been brought up and trained in their ways by his Anglo-Norman captors. Rufus supplied Duncan with an army, at the head of which he marched north and ousted his uncle. He was king for only a single uneasy year, however, before he was murdered and Donald Bàn was restored. It was not until 1097 that Rufus tried again to install his own man as king of Scots. On this occasion, an army taken north by Edgar *atheling* was able to force Donald Bàn into exile and install Edgar, Malcolm III's eldest surviving son by Queen Margaret, and Edgar *atheling*'s nephew, as king. He ruled for ten years as a dependent and compliant subordinate of the king of England, until his death in 1107.

The 1090s was also a crucial decade in Wales. Since the turbulent events of 1081, Anglo-Welsh relations had been relatively stable. In Gwynedd, Norman influence had been extended at the expense of the native claims of Gruffudd ap Cynan by ruthless adventurers such as Robert of Rhuddlan, the cousin of Earl Hugh d'Avranches of Chester, who dominated northern Wales from the castle which gave him his name and another at Deganwy. In the south, Rhys ap Tewdwr had proved to be the accommodating client ruler of Deheubarth that William I had intended him to be. The speed and scale of the Norman penetration into Wales certainly increased significantly in the early 1090s: in central Wales, Ceredigion and Brecon had fallen under Norman influence, and a new castle was under construction in the south-west at Pembroke. It has been suggested that William Rufus, his appetite for expansion perhaps whetted by his success in Cumbria, was directly involved in making this enterprise much more coordinated than it had hitherto been.[7] It was probably no coincidence, for example, that the most significant Norman gain of the decade in Wales, the lordship of Glamorgan, was made by one of Rufus's closest associates, Robert FitzHaimon, whose power, previously based in Bristol and Gloucestershire, was extended into south Wales from his new castle at Cardiff.

The Welsh actively resisted such aggressive Norman assaults, and the view of the native Welsh chronicle, *Brut y Tywysogyon*, that after Rhys ap Tewdwr's death in 1093 'fell the kingdom of the Britons', is too simplistic.[8] Orderic Vitalis alleged that Gruffudd ap Cynan was behind the ambush which resulted in Robert of Rhuddlan's death, also in 1093; and that event seems to have been the signal for risings against Norman rule across Wales. They were uncoordinated, but they continued until 1098 and had in common the desire to throw off 'the rule of the French'.[9] Inconclusive expeditions to Wales by the King himself in 1095 and 1097 (when Rufus got as far as St David's) failed to prevent the Welsh pushing the Normans back beyond the river Conwy in the north and taking all the Norman outposts except Pembroke in Dyfed and Ceredigion. Then, in 1098, the earls of Chester and Shrewsbury invaded Gwynedd, forcing Gruffudd ap Cynan and his ally Cadwgan ap Bleddyn ap Cynfyn of Powys to flee to Ireland. However, soon afterwards off Anglesey, the earl of Shrewsbury was killed in battle with the king of Norway, Magnus Barelegs, the grandson of Harald Hardrada; the Normans were forced to retreat once more and Gruffudd and Cadwgan were able to return and make peace. At this point the Normans, on one view at least, 'seem to have sensed that they had overreached themselves in Gwynedd and Powys, and that an alternative to their policy of harrying the country and seeking to subjugate it by force was to strike a bargain with the Welsh princelings and to install them as clients'.[10] However, Rufus soon granted the lands and title of the late Earl Hugh of Shrewsbury to Hugh's elder brother Robert de Bellême. According to contemporaries, Robert was a gifted military architect and leader, but he was also cruel and remorseless. His appointment suggests that the King had not completely abandoned his aggressive approach towards Wales.

Conspiracy, 1095

After campaigning in Wales early in 1095, Rufus then had to deal with a major conspiracy in England. The leading plotters were the earl of Northumbria, Robert de Mowbray (the slayer of Malcolm Canmore) and Count William of Eu, and their plan allegedly was to murder Rufus and install as king Count Stephen of Aumale, the son of another of the rebels, Odo of Champagne, lord of Holderness in Yorkshire, and a nephew of William I. Earl Robert may have felt frustrated by his failure to establish his pre-eminence within his earldom; the bishop of Durham was a rival for influence there. Beyond this, however, the motives of the conspirators are obscure.[11] Nevertheless, the King took the plot very seriously. He marched north, forced the surrender of Newcastle, Robert's principal fortress, and then besieged the Earl himself at Bamburgh. Robert escaped but the King's men finally captured him at Tynemouth Priory. He was tried early in 1096 along with some of the other conspirators, forfeited his estates and was imprisoned for the rest of his life. The King's kinsman, Stephen of Aumale, by contrast, was treated relatively leniently. After going on the First Crusade, he had his lands restored, and became lord of Holderness after the fall of Arnulf of Montgomery in 1102. Rufus's pursuit of the other plotters in the aftermath of the conspiracy, however, was ruthless. Some paid heavy fines in order to escape the banishment or mutilation suffered by others, whilst the count of Eu, having been defeated in a trial by battle, died from the blinding and castration he was sentenced to undergo.

It has been suggested that Rufus's reaction to the conspiracy of 1095 revealed his insecurity and was tantamount to an admission of his weakness.[12] He had certainly been under pressure in Wales, Scotland, England and Normandy since 1093, and the revolt may have been the last straw. Alternatively, it is also possible to argue that he had emerged relatively unscathed from a very testing three years. To be sure he was brutal in 1095, but in political terms, his authority in England was unchallenged thereafter, his position in Wales and Scotland was soon to be consolidated, and his control over Normandy was on the verge of being confirmed.

Normandy and its frontiers, 1094–1099

Normandy dominated Rufus's concerns during the second half of his reign. The quarrel with his brother Robert, which had simmered since the two parted late in 1091, had boiled over again in 1093. Both men repudiated the agreement they had previously reached, and in February 1094 Rufus returned to Normandy. Robert recruited the support of King Philip I of France, and Rufus summoned his brother Henry to his side. From this point on until 1100, Rufus and Henry were allies and the latter was able to reassert the control he had exercised over western Normandy in the early part of the reign. However, despite the enormous cost of the Norman expedition of 1094, nothing decisive occurred and Rufus remained in Normandy until the end of the year.

Rufus's acquisition of Normandy eventually came down to good fortune as much as anything else. On 27 November 1095, Pope Urban II preached the sermon at Clermont in the Auvergne which launched what is now known as the First Crusade. Duke Robert had no hesitation about taking the cross, and he was to become one of the Crusade's most famous participants. Before he could leave for the Holy Land, however, he needed to raise sufficient funds for what would be a very expensive expedition, and make arrangements for the safe-keeping of his lands. His solution addressed both problems directly. In return for £6,666 13s 4d (10,000 marks), Robert gave Rufus control of Normandy until he returned and a promise of the succession if he did not. In September 1096, Rufus crossed the Channel and handed over the funds. When Robert left the duchy soon afterwards, there was a very strong possibility that he would never return.

For the rest of his reign, apart from the occasional trip to England (Rufus attended the official opening of his great hall at Westminster in May 1099, for example, only to complain that it was still too small) or campaign in Wales, the consolidation of his position within Normandy and the protection of its frontiers preoccupied the King. There is no evidence that he faced opposition within the duchy – the Norman lay and ecclesiastical hierarchy seem to have accepted his rule without question. Count Henry was confirmed in his control of western Normandy – the Cotentin, Avranchin and Bessin, save for the cities of Bayeux and Caen. The fact that England and Normandy were finally united under a single lord once again may even have reconciled any waverers to the potential harshness of Rufus's ruling style. It was from Normandy's neighbours in Maine and the Vexin that Rufus faced the greatest challenges. The allegiance of some local barons in the Vexin was secured with money; but when Rufus also invaded the French Vexin in 1097–8 and 1098–9, he was strenuously opposed there by the heir to the French throne, the future Louis VI, who held the territory as an appanage. By 1099, the only concrete achievement Rufus had made in the Vexin was the construction of a strategically vital castle designed by Robert de Bellême at Gisors on the river Epte. There is no reason to think that Rufus had abandoned his ambition to secure control of the French Vexin, but his sudden death meant that he would never be able to use this launch pad for further campaigns against the French kings.

In Maine, by contrast, the successes were more immediate. Count Elias de la Flèche of Maine was captured in a campaign led by Robert de Bellême in 1098 and imprisoned at Bayeux. Before Rufus was able to move on Le Mans, however, the city was captured by Count Fulk of Anjou, who was alarmed at the prospect of Norman rule (the Normans were the traditional enemies of the Angevins) being consolidated in Maine. In the end a truce was made between Rufus and Fulk: Le Mans and the castles built in Maine by William I were recognised as Rufus's, in return for which Elias was released. In July 1098, Rufus entered Le Mans in triumph. When Rufus returned to England in April 1099, Count Elias re-entered Le Mans. On receiving the news whilst hunting in the New Forest, Rufus immediately spurred his horse and made for Southampton. He crossed the Channel during a storm (the reluctant captain of the ship appears to have been more scared of the King's ferocity than the weather) and on landing immediately rode off to raise an army with which he retook Le Mans. Elias was forced to flee, and Rufus could not pin him down tightly enough to capture him. The Count remained a threat, but when Rufus returned to England in September 1099 he could feel reasonably confident about the future security of his French lands.

A bolt from the blue

The cloud lowering on Rufus's horizon by this time, however, was the return of his brother Robert from the Crusade. Robert's achievements on the expedition which had eventually recaptured Jerusalem in July 1099 were already becoming legendary. He was coming home as a hero; and, what is more, during his return journey Robert had married Sibyl, the daughter of the lord of Brindisi in Apulia, and a member of that adventurous Norman dynasty which had made such a success of controlling southern Italy since the mid eleventh century. More practically, however, and although he was perhaps already 50, this marriage raised the prospect of Robert producing a legitimate heir, whose claim to Normandy it would be difficult to gainsay. Sibyl also provided Robert with a large dowry, perhaps enough on its own to repay the loan Rufus had made him.

Rufus must have known that Robert was on his way back to Normandy, and he must have assumed that he would want his duchy back. After he landed in England in the autumn of 1099, however, the King did surprisingly little to try to entrench his authority across the Channel. It is possible that he was willing to accept Robert's recovery of Normandy without a struggle. Perhaps he had a longer-term strategy, and there were certainly rumours that Rufus's attention had already wandered elsewhere. Duke William IX of Aquitaine was planning to go on crusade and may have been prepared to pawn Poitou to Rufus as Robert had pawned Normandy. On the day before Rufus died, William of Malmesbury claims, he was asked where he would be spending Christmas: 'Poitiers', he replied.[13]

By Christmas 1100, however, William Rufus was dead. He woke up on Thursday 2 August in a New Forest hunting lodge. Unusually the King and his party, which included his brother Henry, did not go out hunting until the afternoon. They split up into groups and took up their positions waiting for the beaters to drive the deer towards them. Standing alongside the King was Walter Tirel, a French nobleman from the Vexin who may have defected to Rufus during the recent campaigns there. As a deer ran between the two men, Tirel fired his arrow. It grazed the back of the beast and pierced the king through the heart. He tried to pull the arrow out, but only managed to snap the shaft. As he fell forward on to the ground, the broken stump of the arrow was driven further into his chest. Rufus was dead; Tirel fled and, in the confusion, Henry was already thinking about what to do next. Pursuing Tirel and burying his brother were not high on his list of immediate priorities. This was his chance to become king.

As the dust settled after Rufus's death, contemporaries began to dwell on the portents and omens which appeared to have presaged it. In July 1099, whilst he had been besieging Count Elias in his castle of Mayet, a stone thrown from the ramparts had narrowly missed the King and killed the man standing next to him. Next, in May 1100, Rufus's nephew Richard, the illegitimate son of Duke Robert, had himself been killed in a hunting accident in the New Forest. Then, in July, at Hamstead Marshall in Berkshire, blood had bubbled out of the ground from a spring. Several men close to the King had had disturbing dreams which Rufus himself laughed off, rather too casually it was later thought. In the end, though, the twelfth-century consensus was that Rufus had paid the price for a morally lax life which had been spent oppressing his people (the creation of the New Forest was a particularly sore point), exploiting the Church (his quarrel with Archbishop Anselm will be discussed more fully in Chapter 11) and disrespecting the divine will. The idea that he was assassinated, perhaps at the instigation of his brother Henry who wished to secure the throne before Duke Robert arrived to claim it himself, or perhaps by a cabal of his French rivals, is of much more recent origin.[14] Hunting was dangerous (his own elder brother Richard had been killed whilst hunting in the New Forest when Rufus was still in his teens), and the likelihood is that Rufus's death was simply an accident. The greater unknown is how he would have fared had he lived longer.

Notes

1 *WMGR*, i p.567.

2 *EHD* II, p.662.

3 *WMGR*, i p.559.

4 *OV*, iv p.173.

5 A.A.M. Duncan, *The Kingship of the Scots 842–1292: Succession and independence* (Edinburgh University Press, 2002), pp.46–9.

6 *ASC* 'E', s.a.1092.

7 R.R. Davies, *The Age of Conquest: Wales 1063–1415* (Oxford University Press, 1991), pp.34–5; I.W. Rowlands, 'The Making of the March: Aspects of the Norman Settlement in Dyfed', *ANS* 3 (1981), pp.142–57.

8 *Brut y Tywysogyon or The Chronicle of the Princes. Peniarth MS. 20 Version*, ed. and trans. T. Jones, 2 vols (Cardiff: University of Wales Press, 1941–1952), p.19.

9 *OV*, ii pp.139–43; *Brut y Tywysogyon. Peniarth MS. 20*, p.19.

10 Davies, *The Age of Conquest*, p.36.

11 *ODNB*, 'Mowbray, Robert de'.

12 David Crouch, *The Normans. The History of a Dynasty* (London: Hambledon, 2002), pp.149–50.

13 *WMGR*, i p.577.

14 Emma Mason, 'William Rufus and the Historians', *Medieval History*, 1 (1991), pp.6–22.

CHAPTER 7

The English conquest of Normandy, 1100–1106

Henry, king of the English, 1100–1102

Only three days after the death of William Rufus, on 5 August 1100 in Westminster Abbey, his younger brother Henry was consecrated king of England. Maurice, bishop of London, conducted the ceremony in the absence of Archbishop Anselm of Canterbury, who was in exile. Henry had already visited Winchester to secure the royal treasury and, with the advice of his closest advisers, the brothers Robert, count of Meulan and Henry, earl of Warwick, he appears either to have overcome, or simply ignored, any immediate objections to his accession. Even so, Henry's own brother, Duke Robert of Normandy, the eldest surviving son of William the Conqueror and now a crusading hero, remained a viable and arguably more credible candidate for kingship. Henry still needed to take steps both to widen the base of his support and to emphasise his legitimacy.

He began to do so as soon as his coronation was over. Henry wrote to Archbishop Anselm apologising for rushing to his consecration without him, and imploring him to return to England. He had Ranulf Flambard, the unpopular representative of the previous regime, arrested and imprisoned in the Tower of London. He even 'purged his court of effeminates, restoring the use of lamps at night which had been given up in his brother's time'.[1] The new king also issued his so-called Coronation Charter, in which he made various promises to rule well and justly. Henry's purpose in these early days of his new reign was to distance himself as far as possible from his predecessor's regime and to identify himself as a king who knew how to rule well and justly. The fact that he had worked enthusiastically alongside Rufus for at least the previous six years was an inconvenience which he hoped others would choose to forget if he made it worth their while to do so. Thus, in his charter, Henry promised not to keep bishoprics and abbacies vacant for his own financial gain; that the reliefs payable by his tenants-in-chief on succeeding to their estates would be 'just and lawful'; to exercise fairly his rights over wardships and marriages; and to forgive 'all pleas and all debts' which were owed to Rufus at the time of his death. In general terms he undertook to 'abolish all the evil customs by which the kingdom of England has been unjustly oppressed' and to restore 'the law of King Edward together with such emendations to it as my father made with the counsel of his barons'.[2]

The charter was indeed a masterpiece of political spin. It appeared to herald a new age of fairness and justice in royal government; in reality, however, it promised nothing specific. It did not make clear which 'evil customs' were to be abolished; neither did it explain what was meant by a 'just and lawful' relief. Similarly, debts owed to Rufus were to be pardoned, 'except', Henry said, 'my own proper dues'. More ominous was the final clause of all:

If, since the death of my brother, King William, anyone shall have seized any of my property, or the property of any other man, let him speedily return the whole of it. If he does this no penalty will be exacted, but if he retains any part of it he shall, when discovered, pay a heavy penalty to me.[3]

In the end, it was his own rights, not the rights of his subjects, which mattered most to the new king; and in this respect his priorities were the same as his predecessors'.

Henry took another step towards consolidating his position when he married in November 1100. The new queen was Edith, daughter of King Malcolm III and Queen Margaret of Scotland. She had been brought up at Romsey Abbey in Hampshire, although it seems she had never become a nun herself. Any qualms about marriage to someone with this background were anyway soon dealt with by a tribunal of sympathetic Anglo-Norman prelates; and certainly the now-returned Archbishop Anselm officiated at the wedding with no hint of a dilemma. William of Malmesbury suggests that Henry was infatuated with Edith and was determined to marry her despite her modest means.[4] For Henry, however, the match was politically attractive, too. A direct link was established between the thrones of England and Scotland (the new queen was King Edgar's sister), and Henry's new wife gave him a link with the ancient ruling house of England. Through her mother, Edith was the direct descendant of Alfred, Edgar and Edward the Confessor, and any children born to her and Henry would have the blood of the Anglo-Saxon royal line mingling in their veins with that of William the Conqueror. Perhaps in part further to emphasise this new connection between her Anglo-Saxon origins and her new Norman family, and perhaps also in an attempt to reassure the Anglo-Norman élite about her qualifications as a royal consort, Edith adopted a Norman name, Matilda, on becoming queen. It was the first evidence of those acute political instincts which would enable her to play a prominent role in the affairs of the Anglo-Norman realm until her death in 1118.

At the end of 1100, however, despite all his efforts to win support, Henry's future on the English throne looked anything but certain. Duke Robert had arrived back in Normandy in September, and Ranulf Flambard joined him there after a daring escape from captivity in the Tower early in 1101. It is likely that the Duke himself was already determined to pursue his claim to the English throne, and it is hard to accept at face value Orderic Vitalis's assertion that Robert had to be persuaded to take assertive action against Henry by the aggrieved Ranulf and by those magnates on both sides of the Channel who were 'alarmed by the energy of king Henry' and preferred 'the mildness of the sluggard duke'.[5] Robert's support in 1101 extended across England and Normandy: Count William of Mortain, the son of William I's half-brother Robert; the earl of Surrey, William de Warenne; the earl of Buckingham, Walter Giffard; and the earl of Shrewsbury, Robert de Bellême, were all his partisans, as were Robert's brothers, Arnulf and Roger. They may have been motivated by a hatred of the Beaumonts, Henry's chief advisers, as much as by a liking for Robert.

On 20 July 1101, therefore, when Duke Robert's fleet of perhaps two hundred ships landed at Portsmouth, his chances of seizing power were good. Henry meanwhile had stationed himself at Pevensey, and had to march quickly westwards to intercept Robert's force before it got to London. The two armies eventually confronted each other at Alton in

Hampshire. Preparations for battle had been made on both sides but, in the end, negotiations resulted in a settlement at the beginning of August, which closely resembled that made by Robert and William Rufus in 1091.[6] In return for an annual payment of £3,000, Duke Robert agreed to abandon his claims to the English throne. For his part, Henry undertook to surrender his lands in western Normandy and elsewhere on the continent, except for Domfront, which he had previously sworn never to abandon. Both promised not to support each other's enemies in the future; and it was also agreed that, if either of the brothers died without heirs, the survivor would inherit the entire Anglo-Norman realm.

There is little doubt, given in particular the scale of influential support Duke Robert enjoyed on his arrival in England and the relative weakness of King Henry's position, that the Treaty of Alton was something of a triumph for the younger brother. On the face of things, Robert had played a winning hand ineptly. It may be, however, that pressure to settle the dispute without a pitched battle came from those same magnates who had urged Robert to invade England in the first place. Most of them would probably have preferred the rule of a single lord; but they also knew that battles were unpredictable and dangerous, and that, if they ended up on the losing side, their lands and their freedom would be at risk. They had secured from Henry and Robert at Alton a promise that the supporters of both sides should be permitted to keep or recover their lands; and, in an attempt to bind the cross-Channel aristocracy together under the rule of two different lords, it was also agreed that any baron who in the future was charged with treason by one brother should be regarded as a traitor by the other.

Henry was soon able to use this part of the agreement to his advantage. He was convinced that some of his great men were too powerful and could not be trusted. Most prominent amongst these were two of the sons of Roger de Montgomery, Robert de Bellême, earl of Shrewsbury, and his brother Arnulf. The latter controlled much of south-western Wales from his base at Pembroke by the early 1100s, and the former was the most powerful Anglo-Norman magnate outside the royal family. They had both been prominent supporters of Duke Robert in 1101, and in 1102 Henry charged them both with offences against him and his brother. Arnulf fled to Wales, where he tried to enlist support from

Ireland; and Robert, who sought to recruit Welsh help in his attempt to defy Henry, retreated to his English castles which were systematically besieged and reduced by the King. In the end both Robert and Arnulf, along with their brother Roger, who was lord of extensive lands in Lancashire, Yorkshire and East Anglia, were forced to flee to Normandy, and their English and Welsh lands were confiscated. The King called upon his brother to enforce the terms of their agreement for mutual help by taking action against the Norman property of Robert de Bellême. The Duke dutifully besieged Robert's castle at Vignats, but the campaign collapsed, having achieved nothing beyond provoking Robert's supporters in central Normandy into disorder. Henry had, therefore, not only managed to rid himself of an over-mighty family; he had begun the process of destabilising his brother's rule in Normandy, too. His display of masterful authority impressed contemporaries. After the fall of the Montgomery brothers in 1102, Orderic Vitalis noted, with only some exaggeration, that there was peace in England for the rest of Henry's reign.[7]

Henry, Wales and Scotland, 1102–c.1110

For the native Welsh chronicler, Henry I was 'the man who had subdued under his authority all the island of Britain and its mighty ones' and 'against whom no one could be of avail except God himself'.[8] This probably goes too far and, in any event, a full analysis of Henry's dealing with the north and west of Britain lies beyond the scope of this book. The first decade or so of his reign, however, witnessed important developments within Wales and Scotland and it provides further evidence of the extent to which Anglo-Norman influence played a part in the politics of those regions.

Following the fall of Robert de Bellême and Arnulf of Pembroke, Shropshire and those areas of Dyfed centred on the castle of Pembroke came into the King's hands and he never let them go. A sheriff was appointed for Shropshire, which soon became fully integrated into the English county structure, and loyal constables at Pembroke exercised royal power there, most notably Gerald of Windsor, who married the King's former mistress Nest, the daughter of Rhys ap Tewdwr. Between 1107 and 1110, moreover, many Flemings ('a folk of strange origins and custom', according to the *Brut*) who had left their own lands because of overpopulation and the threat of an encroaching sea, settled at the King's invitation in western Dyfed.[9] English royal power in south Wales was further extended when lands were granted to some of Henry's most loyal supporters (to Henry de Beaumont, earl of Warwick in Gower in 1106–7, for example, and to Roger, bishop of Salisbury in Kidwelly in about 1107), and when the first royal castle was established at Carmarthen in 1109.

In north Wales meanwhile, the deaths of the earl of Shrewsbury at the hands of King Magnus of Norway in 1098 and the minority which followed the death of Earl Hugh of Chester in 1102, meant that extensive estates came into the King's hands through his rights of wardship, and that a power vacuum arose in Gwynedd. The chief beneficiary of these changed circumstances was Gruffudd ap Cynan, who finally managed to acquire that dominant authority over north Wales which he had been striving for since the 1070s. From 1099, Gruffudd was allowed to build up his power in Gwynedd, first by William II, but principally by Henry I, who, having put aside the possibility of direct royal intervention in Wales for the time being, 'was looking for a prince to sponsor' and granted him lands there.[10] Whilst enjoying the favour of the English king, Gruffudd nevertheless worked hard to consolidate his power west of the river Conwy, and then to extend it east and south. By the time he died in 1137 he had succeeded in re-establishing a dynasty which would last until native rule in Gwynedd was finally brought to an end in 1283.

In Scotland during the early 1100s, there was even less need than in Wales for Henry to intervene directly. King Edgar, who had become king of Scots with the help of William Rufus and Edgar *atheling* in 1097, was an obedient client ruler who looked to England for protection, support and example. It is likely that in 1098, after the invasion of Magnus Barelegs, he had already accepted the fact of Norwegian control over the Western Isles, the Shetlands and the Isle of Man. By giving up royal control of Iona, however, the traditional burial place of the kings of Scots, and through the generosity of his grants to Durham and St Cuthbert (his surviving writ and charters are all Anglo-Norman in phraseology and form), Edgar revealed his priorities. He was not interested in fruitlessly trying to keep control of areas far from the Scottish lowlands and Lothian in which his meaningful authority was peripheral at best. 'Edgar seems to have cared little for *Scotia*, little for his Celtic inheritance in state and church' – he was happy to concentrate on ruling south of the Clyde–Forth line and to stay as close to his English neighbour as he could.[11] The extent of his subordination to his English neighbour was shown more or less directly on several occasions during his reign. When William II held a great crown-wearing ceremony at Westminster in May 1099, Edgar carried the sword in the procession – 'a position of great honour, but also the duty of a great *fidelis*'.[12] Thereafter, Edgar appears to have played no part at all in arranging the marriages of his sisters Edith (Matilda) to Henry I, and Mary to Count Eustace III of Boulogne. Mary's marriage, John of Worcester makes clear, was arranged by the English king.[13]

Duke Robert undermined

As soon as he became king, Henry I set about establishing a network of continental alliances with which he could spin a web of diplomatic silk around his brother. At Dover in March 1101, in return for an annual payment of £267, Count Robert II of Flanders promised to help Henry defend his kingdom against all men.[14] This agreement was renewed in 1103 and 1110, and similar arrangements were made with the counts of Maine, Anjou and Brittany. Contingents from Maine and Brittany were to contribute decisively to Henry's victory at the Battle of Tinchebray in 1106. In England and Normandy, meanwhile, Henry used a range of strategies to build up his support. He rewarded those men who had been his long-term supporters. Robert de Beaumont had become earl of Leicester by 1107, for example, whilst others such as Geoffrey de Clinton and Richard Basset pursued their careers in royal service in possession of new lands and wealth. Henry was also able to see the merits of individuals even if they had not always been loyal to him. The earl of Surrey, William de Warenne, had supported Duke Robert in 1101, but he was courted by Henry thereafter and became a staunch supporter of the English king.

On the other side of the Channel, Henry followed his brother William's example and won friends through flattery and patronage. Generous grants of land and marriages to high-status women, including sometimes Henry's illegitimate daughters, made the prospect of his rule ever more attractive and served in turn to weaken Duke Robert's authority. When Robert's old ally William de Breteuil died in 1103, for example, Henry arranged the marriage of his own illegitimate daughter Juliana to William's illegitimate son, Eustace. With the active assistance of Robert of Meulan, Henry managed to manipulate the situation to ensure that Eustace inherited his father's honour and that Henry, as Eustace's father-in-law was able to intervene in its affairs. Duke Robert was simply outmanoeuvred. Another of the King's illegitimate daughters, Matilda, was married to Rotrou of Mortagne, count of Perche. Mortagne was a key lordship on the southern border of Normandy. And, as has been seen already, Henry arranged the union between Count Eustace III of Boulogne, who had also supported Duke Robert in 1101, and Mary, the sister of King Edgar of Scots. This was a significant marriage in the longer term, as the only daughter of Eustace and Mary was Matilda, who married Stephen of Blois, Henry's successor as king in 1135.

Duke Robert's position in Normandy was not helped by his own actions either. In 1102 his support for Henry's campaign against Robert de Bellême had backfired and served only to antagonise Robert's supporters in central Normandy, not to mention Robert himself. When he returned to Normandy in 1102, Robert de Bellême proceeded to incite disorder in the heart of the duchy, and in June 1103 his forces defeated Duke Robert's outside Exmes. With the Duke unable to rein in his most powerful magnate, the chaos in central Normandy only deepened. The two men did manage to make peace, but even their reconciliation only played further into Henry's hands, as he was now able to claim that his brother had broken the agreement of mutual support against their common enemies which had been part of the Treaty of Alton in 1101. And when in 1104 Henry came to Normandy, his resounding condemnation of Robert's actions and the appearance he gave of confident authority probably struck a chord amongst those barons, particularly those with lands in England too, who must have been feeling increasingly concerned at the instability which was taking hold in the duchy.

In 1105 when he came to the duchy once again, Henry claimed for himself the role of protector of the Norman Church. It was also necessary, however, for Henry to settle his ongoing quarrel with Archbishop Anselm. Anselm had returned to England after Henry's coronation, but the two had soon quarrelled over the issue of investiture and the Archbishop had gone back into exile in 1103. Without the support of the head of the English Church, Henry's campaigns in Normandy would lack moral force and give ammunition to his enemies. What was worse, there were hints coming from Rome that the King might be excommunicated if he did not act quickly to end the dispute. Therefore, in July 1105 at Laigle in Normandy, with significant mediation from Henry's sister Adela of Blois, the King and the Archbishop were reconciled. With this potential obstacle out of his way, Henry returned to Normandy again in the spring of 1106 and began his final campaign to seize control of the duchy. He burnt Bayeux and moved on to Caen, where he awaited the now unavoidable confrontation with his brother.

The Battle of Tinchebray

The positions of the two brothers in 1101 had been reversed. Then it was Duke Robert who had the support, wealth and prestige required to take Henry on. In 1106 by contrast, Henry had the backing of the bulk of the Anglo-Norman baronage, he had used his resources adeptly to recruit support; and the respective leadership qualities of the two brothers had been starkly contrasted by their dealings with Robert de Bellême. Orderic Vitalis's allegation that Duke Robert was by now spending his time with courtesans and clowns and finding it difficult to get out of bed is difficult to credit; but if the Norman magnates had not begun to view him with contempt, many had serious concerns about his ability to rule effectively.[15] By 1106, Robert's best chance of reasserting his legitimacy, restoring his reputation and salvaging something from the wreckage of his rule was to defeat his brother and his supporters in battle.

During the summer of 1106, the two sides jockeyed for position and tactical advantage. The decisive encounter was finally provoked by King Henry, however, when he set about systematically attacking the castles of one of Robert's most die-hard followers, Count William of Mortain. Henry's purpose, as his father's had been after Hastings in 1066 when he devastated parts of southern England, was to demonstrate to his opponents' supporters that they could no longer protect them. William and Robert would have to respond or be deemed bad lords by default. When Henry laid siege to William's castle at Tinchebray in September

1106, the Count demanded Henry's withdrawal; of course he refused to oblige, and on Friday 28 September, in a battle which lasted little more than an hour and which produced few casualties, the fate of the Anglo-Norman realm was settled in King Henry's favour. Initially an infantry battle, Tinchebray was won for Henry by Count Elias of Maine who used his cavalry to attack an exposed flank of Robert's line after the foot soldiers' encounter had ground to a messy halt. The ducal troops panicked and fled. Robert de Bellême managed to escape from the battlefield, but the Duke himself and most of his supporters were captured. Henry kept his brother imprisoned at various castles in England until Robert's death in 1134. It did not escape the notice of contemporaries that the Battle of Tinchebray was fought almost exactly 40 years after the Battle of Hastings. After nearly 20 years of fratricidal warfare, England and Normandy were finally reunited under a son of William I.

Notes

1 *WMGR*, i p.715.

2 *EHD* II, pp.432–4.

3 *EHD* II, pp.432–4.

4 *WMGR*, i pp.715–17.

5 *OV*, v pp.313, 309.

6 *OV*, v pp.319–21.

7 *OV*, vi p.31.

8 *Brut y Tywysogyon or The Chronicle of the Princes. Peniarth MS. 20 Version*, ed. and trans. T. Jones, 2 vols (Cardiff: University of Wales Press, 1941–1952), p.42.

9 *Brut y Tywysogyon. Peniarth MS. 20*, p.27; Rowland, 'The Making of the March', pp.146–8.

10 C.P. Lewis, 'Gruffudd ap Cynan and the Normans', in *Gruffudd ap Cynan. A Collaborative Biography*, ed. K.L. Maund (Woodbridge: Boydell Press, 1996), pp.61–77, at p.77.

11 A.A.M. Duncan, *Scotland: The making of the kingdom* (Edinburgh: Oliver & Boyd, 1975), p.127.

12 A.A.M. Duncan, *The Kingship of the Scots 842–1292: Succession and independence* (Edinburgh University Press, 2002), p.58.

13 *JW*, iii p.103.

14 Elisabeth van Houts, 'The Anglo-Flemish Treaty of 1101', *ANS* 21 (1998), pp.169–74.

15 *OV*, v p.308.

PART THREE

The impact of conquest

CHAPTER 8

Government and law

W illiam I and his sons were assisted in the pursuit of their political and military ambitions in Britain and France when they assumed control of England's relatively sophisticated legal system and its comparatively well-developed structures of central and local administration. Not surprisingly, they left intact much of what they found, and the basic make-up of English government and law in 1106 was largely the same as it had been a century before. There were changes after 1066, however, which were usually necessitated by the military and political needs of the Norman kings. For most of the 40 years after Hastings, they were unwelcome occupiers of a foreign and unfamiliar land; they also faced hostile neighbours within Britain and covetous invaders from beyond its shores. Moreover, as duke of Normandy as well as king of England, William I had to divide his time between his two principalities, and both had to cope with his prolonged absences. And the determination of William II and Henry I to reunite England and Normandy under their exclusive rule meant that they, too, were regularly absent from Britain in the decade or so before 1106, and that Normandy was placed under severe political and military strain. Control had to be enforced when they were away and money had to be raised for their campaigns: these two imperatives prompted improvisation and compelled change, and it is certainly right to say that 'the whole history of the development of Anglo-Norman administration is intelligible only in terms of the scale and pressing needs of war finance'.[1]

Kings and magnates

After 1066 there was little change to the theoretical authority of the English king. Only he could make laws which applied to the whole of his kingdom. Only he could raise money on a national scale to fight wars. Certain types of legal case ('royal pleas') could only be heard by the king or his judges. He was also set apart by special ceremonies and symbols. Central to the coronation ceremony (more important indeed than the placing of the crown on the king's head) was his anointing with holy oil on his chest and arms, and chrism on his head. This established the sacred nature of his office and divine approval for his rule. Next, the king was girded with a sword with which to defend the Church and protect the weak, and then he was crowned and invested with ring, sceptre and rod. This image of the king enthroned in majesty was imprinted on one side of his seal; on the other he rode his warhorse, sword in hand. It was at the coronation, too, that the king made certain solemn promises: to protect the Church, to act justly towards his people and to abolish bad laws and maintain good ones. Henry I embodied these promises in a written charter at the start of his reign; William I and William II may have done something similar.[2]

Periodically, these or similar rituals (except the anointing, which only happened once) were repeated. Usually known as 'crown-wearings', the king used these special occasions to display himself in an atmosphere of public splendour. Edward the Confessor may have begun to celebrate in this way, but the *Anglo-Saxon Chronicle* records that William I wore his crown three times a year, at Easter at Winchester, at Whitsun at Westminster and at Christmas at Gloucester; and William of Malmesbury describes how the Conqueror saw his crown-wearings as opportunities to feast magnificently and, presumably, discuss affairs, with his leading subjects.[3] On these occasions, all the great men of the realm would gather with the king, and the so-called *Laudes Regiae* were sung, as they had been at the coronation. These asked for 'peace, safety and victory for the king of the English, crowned by God'. Such rituals were designed to bind together the king and the members of the ruling élite; but they also served to remind the latter of the uniqueness of the king's position, and of the divine favour he enjoyed.

Ceremonies and symbolism aside, the personality of the ruler remained crucial in determining how effectively he could put his theoretical powers into practice. Contemporaries expected a successful ruler to be pious, generous, just and a strong warrior. And in post-conquest England particularly, where the king was in effect the commander of an occupying army, it was essential that he was determined, ruthless and domineering. To be sure, William I and his sons were all capable politicians; but they were soldiers above all else, prepared to be brutal and violent when necessary. After William I had made it clear between 1066 and 1072 that he was in England for the long haul, his subjects quickly if grudgingly came to respect his authority and fear his wrath. And while William II and Henry I were both tested at the start of their reigns, they soon stamped their authority on the kingdom. For the *Anglo-Saxon Chronicle*, William I 'was a very wise man, and very powerful . . . and stronger than any predecessor of his had been. He was gentle to the good men who loved God, and stern beyond all measure to those people who resisted his will.' William II, by contrast, 'was very strong and fierce to his country and his men and to his neighbours, and very terrible . . . he was always harassing this nation with military service and excessive taxes, for in his days all justice was in abeyance'. However, contemporaries could not deny that he was generous. According to William of Malmesbury, Rufus was 'by the knights in his pay much to be admired for his lavish generosity'. In other words, he taxed his subjects so that he could pay mercenaries. This was pragmatic military leadership not loose prodigality. And as for Henry I, 'He was a good man', the *Anglo-Saxon Chronicle* said, 'and people were in great awe of him. No one dared injure another in his time. He made peace for man and beast.'[4]

Whilst there were differences between them, therefore, William I, William II and Henry I were all forceful, intimidating and resolute. Opponents were dealt with decisively. Lands might be confiscated, as William de Warenne's were by Henry I after he had supported Robert Curthose in 1101. Violence was also an option: the brutality of William I's treatment of northern England in 1069–70 quickly became legendary; and after supporting Robert de Mowbray during the revolt of 1095, William of Eu was blinded and castrated on the orders of William II.[5] Even members of the royal family were not spared: Odo of Bayeux got what he was thought to deserve in 1082 as did Robert Curthose after 1106. Robert, indeed, was widely viewed as weak, impressionable and an unworthy successor to his father. According to Orderic, 'he was sunk beyond redemption in indolence and voluptuousness, which made him an object of contempt to the restless and lawless Normans'.[6] This judgement is unduly harsh, but it is still true that, under his leadership after 1087, Normandy descended into chaos.

Opinions amongst the duchy's aristocracy in 1087 and 1100 were divided on which of the brothers would make the best ruler. A forceful personality and a high level of military ability were important, but would only count for so much. An aspiring ruler had to manage those men who mattered politically, and he needed to convince them that he had the resources and political skill required to keep their own ambitions satisfied. High politics during this period was the preserve of no more than about two hundred rich, landed laymen in addition to the king and his leading churchmen. And the test for the Norman kings remained the same as it had been for their Anglo-Saxon predecessors: could they dominate their magnates without losing their support? One way of doing this was through the exercise of military discipline and the effective suppression of opposition. Another, however, which required more subtle and nuanced skills, was through the allocation of patronage, particularly the distribution of land, the control of heiresses and wardships and the grant of offices, especially sheriffdoms. Yet another way of keeping members of this new nobility loyal was by including them within the process of decision-making. Anglo-Saxon kings had relied on their *witan*, and the Norman dukes had of course relied on their leading subjects before 1066, too. Thereafter, little changed in this respect. The king-duke was obliged to listen to and heed the advice of his great men. All the rulers of this period had their favourite advisers: Roger de Montgomery attested more of William I's surviving charters than any other baron, a sure sign of his importance to the king; Odo of Bayeux (until his fall in 1082), Geoffrey of Coutances, Robert of Mortain and Count Alan of Brittany also regularly acted as witnesses to William's charters. All these men were also 'Class A' landholders in Domesday Book, and there was a clear connection before 1087 between levels of wealth and closeness to the king.[7] After 1087, lesser landholders rather than great magnates, men like Robert FitzHaimon and William d'Aubigny, were William II's most prominent advisers; and in the early part of his reign, Henry I relied heavily on Robert de Meulan and his brother Henry, earl of Warwick. Advice could not be drawn from too shallow a well, however, and it was important to give the impression that opinions were being more widely sought. William of Malmesbury records how the Conqueror ordered 'all great men of whatever walk of life' to attend the great banquets he held after his crown-wearing ceremonies. Other gatherings were more select and designed to meet the needs of a particular occasion. According to the *Anglo-Saxon Chronicle*, for example, the Domesday survey was commissioned by William I after he had had 'much thought and very deep discussion' with his advisers at Gloucester at Christmas 1085, and its findings may have been confirmed at Salisbury the following year when 'his councillors came to him' along with all the landholders 'who were of any account over all England' and swore allegiance to the King. And Orderic's view of Henry I was that: 'Because he humbly deferred to men of experience he deservedly governed many provinces and peoples.'[8]

The maintenance of stable relationships between the ruler and his great men, and the establishment of some sort of consensus between them, were thus essential if the former wanted to avoid serious opposition and secure powerful support in the pursuit of his wider political and military ambitions. Such stability was often elusive, and it is right to remember that ruler and aristocracy 'were at once collaborators and competitors in the pursuit of power'.[9] Robert Curthose certainly found this to be the case in Normandy after 1087, and it is here that Orderic Vitalis's simplistic views about Robert's character as the cause of his failures need to be most carefully treated. Robert inherited a set of tensions within Normandy which even his father, with the resources of England at his disposal, had been barely able to contain. Resistance from Maine and pressure from the French king meant that Robert required the support of his nobles if he was to rule effectively. However, they were looking to him to relax the authoritarian and uncompromising ways of his father, and a succession dispute within the ducal family provided powerful magnates like William de Breteuil and Robert de Bellême with the opportunity to play one brother off against the other in the pursuit of their own private grievances. There was serious violence in southern and central Normandy in the late 1080s and early 1090s as Robert sought to establish his authority over warring families, and when William II invaded at the start of 1091, Robert was forced to rule the duchy jointly with him. When that agreement collapsed a year later, Robert was confronted with another formidable problem in the person of his younger brother, Henry.

Also crucial to his eventual failure was Robert's relative lack of funds. Orderic claimed that 'he often lacked bread in spite of the wealth of his extensive duchy', that ducal resources were lavished on mercenaries and knights, and that Robert surrendered the Cotentin to his brother Henry in 1088 'when his treasure was exhausted', and in return for the £3,000.[10] This suggests that Robert simply frittered away what he had and spent imprudently. However, it was perfectly usual to buy support; and Robert's success on the First Crusade, combined with a more objective assessment of his career in Normandy than Orderic provides, suggest that Robert has been harshly treated. It is certainly the case that the English resources available to Robert's brothers far outstripped the Norman ones available to him. Put another way, 'he had little to give, making it harder to win and keep support'; and, personal qualities aside, it is arguable that Robert never stood a chance against two skilled, determined, well-supported and, most crucially, well-funded opponents.[11] It was the sheer number and range of the challenges he faced which accounts at least in part for his eventual failure.

And in England, too, relationships between king and magnates regularly broke down after 1066. Between 1066 and 1072, William I alienated the surviving members of the Anglo-Saxon aristocracy because he chose to favour his Norman supporters at their expense. In 1075 and 1095, more opposition arose from formidable men with individual grievances, who used revolt as a way of trying to extract concessions. And in 1088 and during the early 1100s, doubts over the succession provided a cloak of legitimacy for those who saw an opportunity to sell their support to the highest bidder. Overall, however, William I, William II and Henry I dealt with such problems very effectively indeed. Revolts and the transitions from one reign to another were certainly destabilising, but no such upheaval between 1066 and 1106 seriously damaged their authority. Indeed, their invariably successful handling of the opposition they faced only served to make them stronger. By 1106, within England and Normandy at least, there was no doubt who was in charge.

Household government

If the great men of kingdom and duchy expected to be present when questions of high policy were discussed, however, it was the household (*familia*) of William I and his sons which remained the constantly beating heart of royal and ducal authority in England and Normandy after 1066. Every lord had his own household. It contained his family members, friends, followers, armed men, officials, chaplains and servants. The king-duke's household was bigger and more powerful than any other, however, and either directly or at a distance it controlled every aspect of his domestic life and of government more widely. It had no fixed form or membership, so whilst some individuals would spend their time more or less permanently with the king, others would come and go, depending on where the king was and how pressing their own needs were. Lay and ecclesiastical barons would attend the king in Normandy or England according to whether their interests lay more on one side of the Channel than the other. There were also no clear lines separating one part of the household from another; individuals could perform more than one role within it and there was considerable overlap between its different functions. In its most formal and public capacity, the household formed the king's court (*curia regis*). This was where the king listened to his advisers on questions of war and diplomacy, received important visitors, made important announcements and dispensed justice to his tenants and the rest of his subjects. This happened most regularly on the great religious festivals of the year, Christmas, Easter and Whitsun, when the household was augmented by the presence of great lay and ecclesiastical magnates.

At the other extreme, by contrast, and at its most basic level, the household was responsible for meeting the daily needs of the king and of those members of his immediate family who were with him at any particular time. Like their predecessors, the rulers of England and Normandy after 1066 were constantly on the move. After 1066, of course, they had to travel further than before, and regularly cross and re-cross the Channel. Wherever the king went, his domestic household (*domus*) travelled with him. Its job was to ensure that the royal family was fed, clothed, cleaned and adequately sheltered from day to day. This required planning and careful organisation. The *domus* had other functions, too. It contained the king's hunting establishment, his huntsmen, dog-handlers and horn-blowers. It also contained the king's chapel, headed by the chancellor and manned by his priests. They took care of the king's spiritual needs, saying mass, hearing confession and keeping his relics; and they also met his secretarial needs and dealt with much of the routine work of government. At the start of this period, as had been the case under the Anglo-Saxon kings, a large proportion of royal documents, principally charters and writs, were drafted by the royal priests supervised by the chancellor. Under William I, Regenbald, referred to as 'chancellor' towards the end of Edward the Confessor's reign, kept his place for a while, but by the end of 1067 one Herfast was holding the post. He was succeeded by Osmund who in turn was replaced by Maurice and then Gerard. All of these men were rewarded for their services with bishoprics. Gerard did particularly well. Having continued to serve William II as chancellor, he became bishop of Hereford in about 1096 and was made archbishop of York by Henry I in 1101. Henry I's chancellors were Roger, Waldric, Ranulf and Geoffrey. Only one of these, Ranulf, did not become a bishop, and Roger did best of all, becoming bishop of Salisbury and the king's chief minster in England for the rest of the reign. The chancellor had his subordinates within the chancery, most important amongst whom was the master of the writing office. He had the custody of the king's great seal, an impression of which was attached to every document issued in the king's name. The most important of the holders of this office during this period was Ranulf Flambard, who served under Chancellor Maurice during William I's reign and went on to dominate royal government under William II and become bishop of Durham in 1099.

The chamber, where the king's clothes and bathing equipment were kept, was also part of the *domus*, and the officials of the chamber were also responsible for the safe-keeping of the king's valuables, his robes, plate and jewels. In addition, the chamber was the financial office of the itinerant household and, therefore, the government's chief spending department. By the reign of Henry I, it was presided over by the treasurer (probably Nigel, nephew of Bishop Roger of Salisbury) and the chamberlains, and wherever the king went he would be accompanied by them and followed by carts loaded with barrels and sacks full of silver pennies. In England, most of this money was supplied to the household from the principal royal treasury at Winchester and later London. In 1087, according to the *Anglo-Saxon Chronicle*, immediately after becoming king, William II 'sent to Winchester and scrutinised the treasury that his father had accumulated. It was impossible for anyone to describe how much was accumulated there in gold and silver and costly robes and jewels, and many other precious things that are hard to recount.' Henry of Huntingdon tried to do so, however, and claimed that the royal treasury contained £60,000 of silver as well as gold, jewels, plate and robes, in 1087.[12] The king also kept smaller reserves of cash at some of his castles, so that he could draw on them during his travels. Such castle treasuries could be found at Gloucester, Colchester, Salisbury, Oxford and Guildford. Other sums might simply be paid into the chamber as and when they were received, from suitors and petitioners who met the king *en route*. Clear evidence of the existence of a central treasury in Normandy both before and after 1066 is lacking; but stores of cash and valuables may have been kept at ducal strongholds such as Rouen and Falaise. When William I died having bequeathed money to his son Henry, the latter hurried away and had his bequest 'carefully weighed to make sure that nothing was withheld'. It would be interesting to know where Henry went and who did the weighing.[13]

Beyond the *domus* and constantly in attendance upon the king would have been his household knights, his military *familia*. These men, whose role was little if at all different from that performed by the *housecarls* of the Anglo-Saxon kings, were central to the military organisation of the kingdom and formed 'something between a royal bodyguard . . . and a small standing army'.[14] Some of these were great men of the realm in their own right, who attended the court from time to time. William FitzOsbern served in the military household of William I, for example; and Henry I's illegitimate son, Robert, served in his father's *familia*. However, at the heart of the military *familia* were knights of more lowly status, perhaps penniless younger sons of minor landed families, who were paid wages by the king and provided with food and shelter at his court. These men were well-trained professional soldiers who provided the core of the royal army in wartime (in 1084–6, 1089–90 and 1105–6, for example), and garrisoned castles. Their chances in life depended on the rewards they might receive from the king in return for the service they performed, and they were aware of the consequences of failing him. One of Henry I's knights, according to Orderic Vitalis, expressed the sort of anxieties on the eve of battle in 1124 which could have been felt by anyone in his position after 1066: if we fail to do our duty, he said, 'how shall we ever dare to enter the king's presence? We shall forfeit both our wages and our honour, and . . . shall never again be entitled to eat the king's bread.'[15]

Cross-Channel government

After 1066, the king-duke and his entourage remained involved in all aspects of governance on both sides of the English Channel. Inevitably, however, it was difficult if not impossible for William I and his sons to exercise power as directly as they might have liked over Normandy when they were in Britain or over Britain when they were in Normandy. Ways had to be found to keep both territories stable and productive whilst the ruler was elsewhere. The introduction of absentee rule, indeed, was a fundamental, perhaps the single most important, change in the way government worked in England and Normandy in the post-conquest period. After 1072, William I spent approximately three-quarters of the rest of his reign outside England: he made only four visits to England after this date and spent 40 months there, as opposed to 130 in France.[16] In these circumstances, he was content largely to delegate responsibility for the kingdom to members of his family or his closest supporters. Thus when he returned to Normandy in 1067, England was left under the control of his half-brother Odo of Bayeux and his friend William FitzOsbern. William de Warenne and Richard FitzGilbert also served as regents in England during the revolt of 1075, and Robert de Mortain along with Robert of Eu were left in charge of Lindsey in about 1069.[17] When William was in England, however, and until her death in 1083, his wife Matilda shouldered much of the responsibility for the government of Normandy. Whilst William was in England in 1066–7, the duchy had been left in her care, and 'its government had been carried on smoothly'. She was ably assisted by Roger de Beaumont, who supervised domestic affairs, and his son Robert, who oversaw military matters.[18] Robert, William's eldest son, also played a prominent role in the protection of Normandy before he fell out with his father in the 1080s. Under William II there was less need for a regent because the King made no long visits to Normandy until 1096. However, when he left England for the duchy in 1097, he 'committed the kingdom' to Bishop Walkelin of Winchester and to Ranulf Flambard.[19] Flambard certainly appears to have controlled the day-to-day operations of English government during the last years of the reign whilst the King was abroad, and Orderic Vitalis described him as the 'chief manager of the King's wealth and justice'. He authorised royal documents, raised money and acted as a judge.[20]

It has been argued that the prolonged absences of the Norman kings did not lead to any weakening of royal control in England. Their absenteeism 'solidified rather than sapped royal government since it engendered structures both to maintain peace and extract money in the king's absence'.[21] Moreover, the argument goes, as the rulers' time was divided between their different territories, and as the demand for resources grew, government became too complex for one individual (whether king-duke or regent) and his immediate associates to manage. By the early 1100s, as a result, there had emerged 'a clearly identifiable body of viceregal administrators' headed by Henry I's chief minister Roger, bishop of Salisbury. It would be misleading to give too much emphasis to the precocity of these developments, however. For one thing, there is little evidence to show clearly and convincingly what the reality of Anglo-Norman administration was by 1100. The pipe roll of 1130 is of only limited value here. And in any event, William II and Henry I were not desk-bound bureaucrats; like their predecessors and contemporaries, they remained in the end itinerant warlords who fed off the lands they controlled and kept their subjects in line through force and intimidation rather than through writs and charters. They dominated more than they governed. Nevertheless, Ranulf Flambard and Roger of Salisbury were different kinds of regent from those who had preceded them: not members of the ruler's family, but low-born careerists who had made their way to the top of the royal administration through hard work and on merit. They were the forerunners of the Angevins' 'chief justiciars' in the second half of the twelfth century. There are also some signs that the personnel of royal government was beginning to change by the end of the eleventh century. Some of those dedicated royal servants who worked alongside Bishop Roger, for example, were, according to Orderic, 'of base stock' and raised 'from the dust' by Henry I. Orderic also accused William II of replacing those magnates who died during his reign with 'certain underlings whom he exalted by the grant of extensive honours as a reward for their flattery'.[22] There is certainly some evidence for this. Rufus's court was not frequented by the great magnates as his father's had been, but by 'middling landholders and household officials', men like Eudo *dapifer*, the most regular witness to Rufus's charters, Robert FitzHaimon and Urse d'Abetot.[23] Henry I was to continue using men from humbler backgrounds during his reign. This is far from saying that Rufus and Henry ignored their magnates, however, or pursued 'anti-baronial' strategies. Both kings were conventional in their appreciation of the need to keep their great men on side and in line through a judicious mixture of promises, threats and rewards.

Government in writing

The Anglo-Saxon kings had almost certainly issued orders and made concessions in writing, and other information about estates and tax obligations were also written down before 1066. However, a notable feature of the post-conquest period was the increased use of documentation by the king-duke's government. Various reasons lay behind this. As has been seen, the ruler needed to keep in touch with the different parts of his extended territories after 1066; his officials in turn needed to communicate with their subordinates in the localities. Records also had to be more systematic if a track on the growing number of debts owed to the king was to be kept. At the heart of this development was the king's chancery staffed, as has been seen, by his priests under the supervision of the chancellor.

Until the early twelfth century the royal chancery was small and its organisation rudimentary. How far the priests of the chapel continued to draft documents as simply one amongst a number of other duties is difficult to tell. The most important documents they prepared were the king's diplomas, writs and writ-charters. A diploma, or *boc* in Old English, was the most portentous of these. Large, imposing and highly formulaic documents, addressed neither generally nor to individuals, they opened with solemn invocations and closed with solemn sanctions in Latin, and were witnessed by those whose names were included on the documents themselves. They recorded a grant of land or privileges by the king to a particular person or religious house, and the boundaries of the land in question were described in English. The 'writ' by contrast, derived from the Old English word *gewrit*, was short, far less grand than a diploma in appearance, addressed by the king to individuals and sealed. Written in English, it was usually a notification of some kind; but it might potentially contain orders, as well. A third category of document, the 'writ-charter' (a historian's term, not a contemporary one), has been defined as 'a writ addressed generally by the king to the officers and suitors of the shire court', which usually notified the recipients of a grant or confirmation of land, but which might contain orders, too.[24] In other words, it performed the function of later royal charters, but it was addressed and delivered like a writ. Almost all surviving royal *acta* from pre-conquest England are writ-charters, probably because, dealing with land as they did, the recipients thought it prudent to keep them safe.

By the end of the twelfth century, the Anglo-Saxon diploma in its traditional form was obsolete. The development of the writ as a multifunctional document accounts for this to some extent, although it has been argued that the changing political, social and cultural circumstances of the eleventh century may also have played their part.[25] For the first few years after 1066, royal documents continued to be written in English, almost certainly by English scribes. One of the most famous was William I's writ of 1067 confirming the ancient privileges of the city of London.[26] But from 1070 onwards Latin became the official language of royal government and England was brought into line with the continental standard. Why this happened at this time is unclear. It may be attributable to a change of chancellor (Osmund replaced Herfast in 1070), but it may also reflect William I's loss of patience with his restive English subjects after the rebellions of the previous years. There were other changes to the form of the writ, too. They carried the name of at least one witness from the early 1070s, and by the end of the eleventh century places and dates of issue were regularly included. These features added to the writ, 'increased its administrative value and gave it a better guarantee of authenticity'.[27]

Given that the writ was such a versatile device, it is striking that, whilst the number of writs issued by the government in England increased significantly after 1066, as did the range of functions a writ could serve, English-style writs do not appear to have been used in Normandy before 1106. One reason for this difference in the pace and nature of administrative developments on either side of the Channel, it has been suggested, was that 'the redistribution of property and the definition of service required in England after 1066 must have required an administrative effort which was never needed in Normandy'.[28] In England before 1066, to judge from the surviving examples, the writ had served almost exclusively as a title deed to land, announcing a new grant or confirming a previous one. William I and his sons used writs in this way, but they also used them as a means of giving orders and instructions to royal officers and private individuals. Thus a single writ might notify a sheriff of a particular grant *and* include an order to give possession of the land to the beneficiary.[29] The distinction between writs and writ-charters, therefore, becomes increasingly meaningless when considering the kinds of document being produced by the English royal chancery by the end of the eleventh century. A rough comparison of what survives from the pre- and post-conquest periods suggests how much more documentation was being produced by the royal government after 1066. Less than 2,000 royal documents of any kind survive from the entire Anglo-Saxon period, either as originals or later copies, but for William II's reign there is an average of 15 survivals per year, whilst for Henry I's reign the figure rises to 41. There are over 100 survivals for the period between 1100 and 1102 alone. Many hundreds more were certainly issued and have been lost, and it has been suggested (perhaps rather extravagantly) that Henry I's government may have been producing as many as 4,500 documents per year by the 1130s.[30]

However, one written record from this period testifies more than anything else to the power and reach of English royal government after 1066. Domesday Book is unique in medieval Europe. In the aftermath of an abortive Danish invasion of England, and after discussing matters with his advisers at his Christmas court at Gloucester in 1085, William I ordered a great survey of England to be carried out. According to John of Worcester, the King wanted to know:

how much land each of his barons possessed, how many enfeoffed knights,
how many carucates, villeins, beasts, indeed how much livestock each man

*owned in his whole kingdom, from the greatest to the lowest, and how much
each estate was able to render.*

The *Anglo-Saxon Chronicle* went further: so detailed was the survey

*that there was no single hide nor virgate of land, nor indeed (it is a shame
to relate but it seemed no shame to him to do) one ox nor one cow nor one
pig which was there left out, and not put down in his record; and all these
records were brought to him afterwards.*[31]

To carry out the survey, the country was divided into at least seven
circuits, each with its own commissioners. Material was collected from
tenants-in-chief and juries of local men and was presented at the shire
court. The name of each manor had to be given, the name of its
holder before the Conquest, the name of its present holder and detailed
information on a range of other matters.[32] How many slaves and freemen did the manor contain, for example, how much woodland and
pasture? What was it worth in 1066 and what was it worth at the time of
the survey? And in addition, all this information had to be given for
three separate dates: when Edward the Confessor died, when William I
re-granted the land and 1085. Some time soon after the survey was
completed, its details having been edited and arranged in a systematic
and consistent form, they were copied up into what is known as
Domesday Book. Precisely when this happened is a matter of ongoing
debate. It has traditionally been thought that the compilation of
Domesday Book took place as the natural and intended culmination of
the survey. More recently, however, it has been argued that the production of Domesday Book was an afterthought, and that it did not take
place until early in the reign of William II, perhaps at the command of
his chief minister, Ranulf Flambard, and in the aftermath of the revolt
of 1088.[33] The complex, diverse and voluminous returns from the survey would have been extremely difficult to use had they not been edited
in some way, however, and it is hard to believe that it was not intended
from the start to bring the essentials together in a manageable and convenient format.

Domesday Book is actually in two parts. Its first volume, 'Great
Domesday', contains the abbreviated and condensed results of the
surveys of all the English shires south of the Tees except Norfolk, Suffolk

and Essex. The returns for these counties, which were never edited and written up in the standardised form of Great Domesday, make up volume two, 'Little Domesday'. There are other gaps, too: London was never surveyed, for example, and nor was Winchester, probably because such projects were too complex to undertake in the available time. Despite this, the wealth of detail the survey gives about landholding both before and after the Norman Conquest is extraordinary. The information in Great Domesday is arranged county by county, and within each county by landholder. A list of the King's lands in the county always comes first, followed by those of the churches and then the lay lords in ranking order. It thus gave the King an accessible and coherently-arranged record of his own estates, those of his vassals and their own tenants, and it recorded their value. William needed to pay for the mercenaries he had recruited to defend England from Danish attack in 1085, and his need for cash may have prompted him to undertake the survey in the first instance. He must have had wider motives, too. The survey recorded in unambiguous and exhaustive detail the impact of the Norman Conquest on England, and it gave the King the information he needed to control his people, particularly his tenants-in-chief and their families, and to exploit his own and their resources when they came into his hands through forfeiture or escheat. In turn it gave the members of England's new landholding élite something like a written title to their lands, a title which may have been confirmed by the giving of oaths to the King at Salisbury in August 1086. It is no wonder that the survey acquired its ominous name: contemporaries could think of nothing as final and conclusive other than the Last Judgement itself.

Regional government

One obvious if not immediate change to the English political landscape after 1066 was in the status and role of the earls. During the early years of his reign William I allowed earls Edwin, Morcar and Waltheof to survive with their lands and titles largely intact. The new king's original plan may even have been to recreate the recently vacated Anglo-Saxon earldoms on a new basis.[34] Until his death in 1071 Earl William FitzOsbern controlled a swathe of territory, the so-called 'march' of Hereford, along the southern frontier with England from his great castle at Chepstow. His title, however, was personal rather than territorial and his earldom comprised much more than Herefordshire alone and appears to have been modelled on Harold Godwineson's earldom of Wessex. It may have been granted to FitzOsbern on such a scale because, when he received it soon after the victory at Hastings, King William was still attempting to stress a high degree of continuity with Edward the Confessor's regime, and 'it was both desirable and necessary to rule England by English methods'. Similar considerations may have been behind the creation of the earldom of Kent for Odo of Bayeux, William's half-brother. That county was a strategically vital area which guarded the route to the English Channel and Normandy, but the earldom was probably granted to Odo early in 1066–7 to bolster his authority in England during the King's absence in Normandy, and it may have comprised lands in other southern counties, specifically those held in 1066 by Earl Leofwine Godwineson.

However, after the upheavals of 1068–71, the King abandoned his attempt to conciliate the English and decided to get tough with his new subjects. More pragmatic considerations came to the fore as far as the English earldoms were concerned. For the rest of William I's reign there were no more than seven earls at any one time and only four in 1087. These earldoms were all small, too, confined to single counties, as he and his sons had no intention of being dominated by their leading subjects in the way Edward the Confessor had been. The earldom of Kent fell into abeyance after the fall of Odo of Bayeux in 1082; and by 1100, indeed, the great earldoms of Wessex, Mercia and Northumbria had also finally disappeared. When William FitzOsbern died in 1071, his son Roger had become earl of Hereford; but he enjoyed little of his father's extensive authority across England. After the rebellions of Edwin of Mercia in the early 1070s and of Robert de Mowbray of Northumbria in 1095, nobody succeeded to their titles or their power. More immediately, William I's appointments reflected the new realities of Norman England. His earls were military governors with authority over more compact areas which were dangerous and vulnerable, particularly in the marches alongside Hereford on the borders of Wales, all of which were exposed to the constant threat of Welsh attacks. Thus Roger de Montgomery and Hugh d'Avranches had become respectively earls of Shrewsbury and Chester by the early 1070s. This met an immediate military need as well as splitting in two the monolithic Anglo-Saxon earldom of Mercia.

William I eventually transformed the status and nature of English earldoms in part by recreating arrangements familiar to him from Normandy. There the counts had tended to be connected closely to the dukes, either through family links or long service; their *comtés* were smaller than English earldoms and had covered regions which were important to the defence of the duchy, on the coasts or the internal frontiers. Thus it has been said that 'the earldom which in 1065 had been in England the normal unit of provincial government had by 1087 become an exceptional jurisdiction created like the Norman *comtés* on certain frontiers for special purposes of security and defence'.[35] This is essentially correct, but the Norman origins of the post-conquest English earldoms should not be emphasised too strongly. They evolved in response to changing circumstances in England and acquired a unique character of their own as a result.[36]

Below the earls the Normans introduced new categories of official into the system of local government. Most important amongst these were those men who had custody of royal castles ('castellans') and those who supervised the royal forest. There was nothing particularly systematic about the appointment of castellans, but they had to be loyal and dependable. Sometimes the sheriff did the job, sometimes the local lord. At other times, men were specifically appointed to these posts. Colchester Castle was placed in the custody of Eudo *dapiter* in 1101, for example. Where the sheriff did not carry out these new responsibilities himself, some realignment of jurisdictions was probably necessary in individual cases. However, the sheriff retained his place as by far the most important royal officer in the localities. In theory, the sheriff was still the earl's deputy, and in the areas where an earl retained meaningful authority, on the frontiers in the years after Hastings, for example, his authority over the sheriff was maintained. At other times, and as the number of earls and the size of earldoms shrank, the sheriffs' authority increased: 'indeed, their power was never greater than between 1066 and 1100'.[37] The sheriff was responsible for making the annual payment (the 'farm') which each county owed to the king, and he presided over the shire court. He also collected taxes, raised armies, repaired royal castles, transported treasure, and more. Essentially, the sheriff was the principal link between the king and the localities. Several English sheriffs retained their posts after 1066, such as Tofi of Somerset and Edmund of Hertfordshire, but they were all eventually replaced because the king needed loyal men in these important and politically sensitive posts.

Being a sheriff was attractive because it gave a man great status and influence within a local community. All the kings of this period appointed members of their household as sheriffs; but many of the Conqueror's sheriffs were already substantial barons. Geoffrey de Mandeville, for example, held lands worth £800 a year; but he was also sheriff of Middlesex, and clearly thought the office was worth having. It was accepted that during the course of a year the sheriff would collect much more money from the people of his shire than he owed the king by way of his farm. The sheriff could keep the surplus for himself. Not surprisingly, therefore, men were willing to act less than scrupulously in carrying out their responsibilities. Urse d'Abetot, for example, became sheriff of Worcestershire shortly after 1066 and acquired a reputation for preying on monastic lands in his county. This did not prevent him from becoming one of the most prominent of William II's administrators, however; and he remained sheriff of Worcestershire until his death in 1108. He was succeeded as sheriff by his son Roger and then by Osbert, who was probably Urse's brother. This reveals the danger for the king of allowing their sheriffs too much power: shrievalties might slip from their control and become hereditary. And it was partly with this in mind that, in about 1108, Henry I issued a writ criticising those sheriffs who summoned the shire court when they wished and not according to the traditional customs. Only 'I myself', the King said, 'if ever I shall wish it, will cause them to be summoned at my own pleasure'.[38]

Shires remained subdivided into hundreds and wapentakes after 1066, just as they had been before. The role of the hundred remained largely the same, too. Domesday Book records about 730 hundreds and wapentakes. The hundred had its own court which met every month. It was presided over by a reeve appointed by the sheriff (or by the lord's reeve if the hundred was in private hands), and was attended by local landowners who were obliged to attend. Twice a year a special meeting of the hundred court was presided over by the sheriff himself. His principal job was to check that the frankpledge system was working properly and that every free adult male was a member of a tithing. By the early

twelfth century, too, he had acquired the responsibility for the operation of the *murdrum* fine, the origins of which are discussed below.

The royal forest

Kings had always hunted. The activity was seen as good training for
warfare as well as a source of food for the royal household. Edward the
Confessor is reputed to have been a very keen huntsman, but the importance of the royal hunting lands took on a new importance after 1066.
Areas suitable for hunting were designated by William I and his sons as
royal preserves, 'forests', and collectively as 'the forest', where the beasts
of the chase (the red deer, fallow deer, roe and wild boar) were protected
for the king's benefit. Some of the forest was on the king's own land,
but much of it was on the lands of other lords, whose rights over those
lands were consequently restricted. The largest concentration was in
Hampshire (the 'New Forest'), Wiltshire, Dorset and Somerset. Eventually,
most of Essex was forest and there were other extended areas in
Nottinghamshire ('Sherwood Forest'). The forest supplied the king with
food and timber. It also supplied him with money. In 1129–30, more
than £400 of forest income was demanded by the King, and over half of
this was paid. Rights to graze cattle or feed pigs had to be paid for, as did
the right to cut down trees.

The forest soon developed its own system of law, too. It was harsh
and arbitrary, a matter purely for the king's will. Landholders could
not hunt deer on their own lands if they were within the forest, and
they could not farm their lands in the same way as other landholders.
Breaches of forest law were punished with large fines. Whilst it was a
source of valuable funds, therefore, because of the severity and unpre-
dictability of the forest system, it also provoked criticism and resentment. It was thus an obvious source of concessions for a king with his
back to the wall. As part of his bid to gain popular support against the
rebels of 1088, for example, William II 'forbade every unjust tax and
granted people their woods and hunting rights'. In his Coronation
Charter, Henry I promised to reduce the extent of the forest to its size in
1087. However, by the end of his reign there were royal forests in 25
counties; and for those living within its boundaries, the administration
of the forest was a constant reminder of the power of their king.

Royal wealth

It was the king's task to exploit the resources of his territories, not least the royal forest, as effectively as he could. After all, no matter what his powers might be in theory, he could do little without money. His daily needs had to be met, and a king was constantly on show: the luxuries and display associated with courtly life were expensive. The king also had to reward his followers and act charitably, and sometimes there were unexpected costs, such as the £6,666 William II agreed to pay his brother Robert for control of Normandy in 1095. Most importantly, though, the king needed money to meet the costs of warfare of one kind or another. There were regular outgoings, such as the wages of the king's knightly *familia*. But all of the kings of this period spent lengthy periods on campaign, and when a campaign was under way and mercenary troops needed payment, the king's expenses rocketed. The payment of troops was just one item of expenditure, however. Castles had to be built and maintained and alliances had to be paid for. In 1101, for example, Henry I agreed to pay the count of Flanders an annuity of £500 in return for the service of 1,000 knights in time of war. Robert Curthose's lack of funds, as has been seen, is a recurring theme in con-temporary accounts of his rule in Normandy after 1087.[39] Orderic Vitalis reported claims that William I 'received each day in sterling money a thousand and sixty-one pounds ten shillings and three halfpence from the ordinary revenue of England, not counting royal tribute and judicial fines and many other sources of revenue which daily swelled the royal treasures'.[40] Precise as it is, this figure is certainly exaggerated: Henry I was a famously rich king and the pipe roll records his revenue in 1130 as approximately £24,500. Nevertheless, Orderic's statement gives a good idea of how lucrative the conquest of England was thought to have been.

Most of the king-duke's regular income was derived from his lands. As has been seen already, William the Conqueror had Harold to thank for his massive landed wealth in England; the latter had united the Godwine family lands with the royal lands when he became king in 1066. According to the Domesday survey of 1086 the king possessed over 18 per cent (by value) of the landed estates listed. There were four shires in which the king held more than 30 per cent of the land, and another eight in which he held between 20 and 30 per cent. Almost everywhere he held more than 10 per cent. This gave the king money and power, and 'meant that the monarchy was drawing revenue from every part of the kingdom and that royal estates gave a local physical focus of royal power everywhere'.[41]

The king could collect the profits and rents from the farms and income from the sale of crops and livestock on his demesne lands. But it would have been a job of almighty complexity for the king personally to manage all his lands throughout the country. The usual practice, therefore, inherited from the Anglo-Saxon kings, was for him to devolve responsibility for the administration of the royal lands and the exercise of royal rights within individual counties to the sheriff. In return for this privilege, the sheriff paid his annual 'farm'. As has been seen, he often collected more than he owed and kept the surplus for himself. The advantage of the system for the king was that the county farms provided him with a regular and predictable income without the problems of having to administer the lands themselves. In 1130, when thorough, quantifiable evidence about royal income becomes available for the first time, over £9,900 was due to the king from this source for the year in question and over £6,000 of this was actually paid.

The Norman kings were extremely fortunate in having gained control over a huge amount of profitable English territory in 1066. They were also the beneficiaries of a system of government, integral to which was the only approximation to a nation-wide system of regular taxation, geld, in Western Europe. They may not have levied geld every year after 1066, but the burden was weighty nevertheless. The geld of 1084 was set at the rate of six shillings for every hide of land, and in 1096 William II imposed a geld of four shillings per hide to raise the money he had promised to pay his brother for Normandy. William I probably levied it more often at the lower rate of two shillings. Nevertheless, the urge to tax heavily had to be resisted if opposition was not to be provoked. Taxation such as that imposed by William I in 1067, for example, was probably one of the reasons why the English resisted the Normans so determinedly in the early years after Hastings.[42] And there were repeated complaints in the *Anglo-Saxon Chronicle* and elsewhere for the rest of this period about the oppressive weight of royal taxes. In 1088, as part of his effort to secure the throne against the claims of Robert Curthose,

William II 'forbade every unjust tax . . . but it did not last any time'.[43] Nevertheless, there are signs that, by the second quarter of the twelfth century, the Norman kings were failing to exploit the geld as effectively as their Anglo-Saxon predecessors. The year 1129–30 may or may not have been representative, but payments of geld into the royal coffers amounted to less than £2,400, according to the pipe roll of that year.[44] This was a small sum by pre-1066 standards and may reflect the number of exemptions from geld which had been granted by that date. It might also suggest, of course, that the references made by the *Anglo-Saxon Chronicle* to huge geld payments in the first half of the eleventh century were exaggerated.

The Norman kings also continued to manipulate and profit from the English coinage in much the same way as their Anglo-Saxon predecessors. Control of the coinage remained a royal monopoly and no foreign coin was allowed to circulate within the kingdom. After 1066 silver pennies of standard weight and design were produced, and periodically until at least 1125 a new coinage was issued and the king pocketed the profits. New mints were opened, too, as royal authority spread to the remoter parts of England. Before 1066, there was no mint further north than York, but one was opened after in Durham, and several in Wales during the reign of William II, at Rhuddlan, Cardiff and St David's. Significantly, the moneyers who produced the coins remained overwhelmingly English, certainly until at least 1100. The king needed good quality silver pennies to meet his expenses, and he needed to maintain royal control over the coinage as a demonstration of his authority. This explains why the Norman kings were so harsh to those who abused the system. In 1100, Henry I announced that anyone found in possession of false coin should lose a hand and be castrated. In 1108 he extended the punishment to loss of eyes and lower limbs. Most famously, in 1124, after complaints from his mercenaries about the quality of the coin with which he was paying them, Henry ordered that all the moneyers in England should have their right hands cut off.

After 1066, the king drew a further significant proportion of his regular revenue from the exercise of his rights as a feudal lord. As will be seen in Chapter 9, this was a quite new source of revenue for the English kings, and derived from the tenurial changes made by the Normans. Used wisely, the system could foster ties of loyalty and dependence.

However, royal failure to exploit these sources of income fairly could create tension and, ultimately, provoke opposition. It was in the fields of inheritances and the descent of land, in the handling of reliefs, wardships and marriages, where most money could be made and where most sensitivity was required. The ways in which William II administered this system gave rise to grievances and complaints. Consequently, in his Coronation Charter, Henry I promised that reliefs should be 'just and lawful' and that other feudal dues would be levied fairly.[45] In practice, however, the amounts paid and payable continued to depend on the bargain an individual could strike with the king. In 1130, payments owed by an heir for having his father's lands appear regularly in the pipe roll: in Essex, for example, Geoffrey II de Mandeville paid £133 6s 8d of the £866 13s 4d he owed 'for the land of his father'; and Ranulf II, the new earl of Chester, owed £1,000 from the relief his father had promised. Other feudal dues are prevalent, too: also in Essex, Ralf FitzWilliam owed the king £6 13s 4d for Juliana, the daughter of Richard of Winchester, and her land.[46] Overall in 1130, £1,300 was received by the King from reliefs and payments for wardships and marriages. Another £5,500 remained outstanding from these sources.

There were other ways the king could raise money from his tenants, too. In place of actual military service, for example, and because ready cash was often more useful in war than someone else's mounted knights, a money payment known as scutage (literally 'shield money') was often substituted by tenants. Such payments are first recorded during Henry I's reign, but were probably being made before then. Consent was not required before a scutage was levied by the king, although there was supposed to be an immediate military need to be met. The tenant-in-chief was entitled to recoup the cost of the scutage from his own tenants. At other times, if a tenant-in-chief rebelled or died without heirs, his lands would return or 'escheat' to the king. He could administer them, grant them away as a gift or sell them off as he pleased, thus creating new bonds of loyalty but also the potential for fresh resentment in the minds of those dispossessed and their heirs.

In the same way as the king controlled succession to the lands of his tenants-in-chief in his capacity as a feudal lord, he controlled the lands of bishoprics and abbeys during 'vacancies'. Like any other tenant-in-chief, when a bishop or an abbot died, the lands his church held from the king were administered by their royal lord until a successor was appointed. The king was supposed to allow the church as much money as it needed properly to function, but he kept any profits for himself. Given that it was the king who appointed the next bishop or abbot, the system was clearly open to abuse by an unscrupulous ruler. William II, aided and abetted by Ranulf Flambard, acquired a reputation for allowing churches to remain vacant for unreasonably long periods so that he could keep the profits. According to Orderic Vitalis, 'When bishops and abbots died the king's officers seized all the property and wealth of the churches, and for three years or more administered them entirely as part of the royal demesne.'[47] Such claims may have been exaggerated, although there is no doubt that William II did obtain funds by such means: he retained custody of Canterbury's estates from after Lanfranc's death in 1089 until 1093, and, whilst Anselm was in exile, from 1097 until his own death. And as Barlow has said, 'Rufus' wars were largely financed by the church'. It has been estimated that, over the course of his reign, he collected over £31,000 from vacant bishoprics and monasteries, an average of £2,400 per year.[48] Henry I for his part promised in his Coronation Charter of 1100, and again as part of his settlement with Anselm in 1106, that such practices would end, but he was later as guilty as his brother of exploiting the churches which came under his control.[49]

The administration of justice was also highly profitable for the king. *Murdrum* fines produced regular payments from sheriffs. Payments might be made to secure the king's assistance in a particular lawsuit. The 1130 pipe roll records that nearly £800 was demanded by the King for his help in judicial matters; just over £100 of this was actually paid. The royal writs which came to dominate civil cases in the royal courts as this period went on had to be paid for, too. Local communities were fined if they failed to carry out their local law enforcement responsibilities. Those who acted as sureties for the appearance of a party in court were fined if that party failed to appear. The belongings of convicted criminals were confiscated by the king's officers and sold. Most sums from such sources were small, but because there were so many of them, large amounts could be raised for the royal coffers. In total in 1130, over £3,600 was owed in respect of royal involvement in one kind of judicial matter or another. In Bartlett's words: 'The king was the fount of justice, but his waters did not run freely.'[50]

Collecting the funds

By 1130, the exchequer had taken the place it was to keep for the rest of the Middle Ages and beyond as the main financial department of English government. Overseeing its operations was Henry I's chief minister, Bishop Roger of Salisbury. He may have been responsible for developing the exchequer's procedures and increasing its powers as Henry's reign went on, but he almost certainly did not invent or create the institution. Something like it, based around the royal treasury at Winchester, may well have been in existence to collect and audit royal revenues during William I's reign. It is not credible to suggest that neither he nor William II had any formalised ways of recording what they were paid and owed. A later twelfth-century source, *The Dialogue of the Exchequer*, suggested that the exchequer was indeed William I's creation, and that its procedures were based on those of the Norman exchequer. Others claimed, the same source went on, that the exchequer's origins were ultimately Anglo-Saxon. To be sure, the pre-conquest kings had collected large quantities of geld before 1066, and there must have been some mechanism for dealing with the huge piles of silver pennies brought to the treasury at Winchester by their sheriffs.[51] It is also important to remember that only the chance survival of the 1130 pipe roll confirms the maturity of the exchequer by that date; and it is in the end impossible to know the extent to which the exchequer had by the early 1100s developed any of the elaborate structures and systems revealed by that singular record.

In its original form, 'the exchequer was not a government department but an object'. According to the *Dialogue of the Exchequer*, which describes how the exchequer worked by the 1170s, 'it is an oblong board measuring about ten feet by five, used as a table by those who sit at it, and with a rim round it about four finger-breadths in height, to prevent anything set on it from falling off'. It derived its Latin name, *scaccarium*, from the chequered cloth which covered it.[52] The cloth served as a gigantic abacus, and different columns and squares on the cloth represented different amounts of money. When the sheriff handed over his money it was set out on the cloth alongside what he owed. Surpluses and deficits could then be calculated. The system was simple and allowed for thorough accounting of the monies owed to the king. The sessions of the exchequer were held twice a year, at Easter and Michaelmas, at the royal treasury at Winchester and, later, Westminster. What happened at these sessions is described in great detail in the *Dialogue*. Presiding over the sessions would be the chief justiciar (or Bishop Roger of Salisbury under Henry I), who would be assisted by numerous other royal officials, the chancellor, the constable, the marshal, the treasurer, two treasury chamberlains and several clerks. At the Easter session, the sheriff would appear and a preliminary 'view' of his accounts would take place. He would pay over such money as he had and would receive a receipt in the form of carved wooden tallies in return. At Michaelmas the main account was held when the sheriff presented himself before the barons to be examined, first by the treasurer about the county farm, and then by the chancellor's clerk (who later evolved into the chancellor of the exchequer) about 'pleas and agreements', money which the sheriff had been ordered by the king to collect from individuals. Such sums may have been feudal dues owed to the king, whilst others might be sums offered to the king by individuals looking for royal support in some legal dispute or other. Those sums which the sheriff had been ordered to pay out by the king during the course of the year were then subtracted from the sums he owed. Then when all the sheriff's debts had been calculated, a final calculation of what he still owed or of what he was owed by the king was worked out on the chequered cloth. The money the sheriff had brought to the exchequer was put into sealed bags, and he was given more wooden tallies as receipts. The quality of the coin he had produced was then tested, either by measuring it against a standard weight, or by the process of 'assay', melting it down to ascertain its precise silver content.

Details of everything accounted for and either owed by or owing to the sheriff were entered on the pipe roll for that year. The roll of 1130 has been described as 'by far the earliest surviving kingdomwide financial survey in the history of humankind'.[53] It records the amounts paid into the exchequer, some of which were owed in respect of the financial year 1129–30 and some of which were left owing from previous years. Any debts left unpaid at the end of this year were carried forward to the next and added to the debts still unpaid which had been carried forward from previous years. In total, at the end of the 1129–30 audit, the outstanding debt owed to the government was a colossal £68,850. It was through the exchequer that the king and his officials could keep track of these sums and maintain pressure on those who owed them. It was also through the exchequer that the king kept his officials honest and accountable. The exchequer, it is fair to say, 'was central to the exaction of revenue, the control of local officials and the web of political control the king could spin over the country'.[54]

The English exchequer is only mentioned by name for the first time in 1110. There is no convincing evidence for the existence of a Norman exchequer at this time or before it; indeed, no Norman equivalent to the English pipe roll of 1130 survives from before 1180. Nevertheless, a Norman exchequer, or some sort of centralised audit, may have existed in the duchy by the early twelfth century, with Bishop John of Lisieux holding a position to some extent analogous with that of Roger of Salisbury in England. It is impossible to be certain, of course, and there is room for serious doubt about this. Indeed, a Norman exchequer may not have existed before the 1130s, and Bishop John's pre-eminence in Norman administration cannot be taken for granted.[55] However, given the absenteeism of the Norman king-dukes after 1066 and their insatiable appetite for funds – as the number of debts owed to the kings grew out of the new mechanisms of feudalism, and as the demands of constant campaigning continued to bite – two offices dedicated to the thorough collection and auditing of royal and ducal revenues may have become increasingly necessary to meet the needs of William I and William II as well as Henry I.

The law

As in government, there was a good deal of continuity between the legal systems of pre- and post-conquest England. William I and his successors preserved the Anglo-Saxon system of shires and shire courts, hundreds and hundred courts, and they also accepted important elements of English custom. This was partly because the system worked well. But the stress upon continuity suited the Norman kings' view of their own legitimacy, too: they saw themselves as the rightful heirs of Edward the Confessor, and so in the so-called *Laws of William the Conqueror* (probably a twelfth-century document, reflecting the laws it was thought William had made), it was proclaimed that 'all shall have and hold the law of King Edward in respect of their lands and all their possessions, with the addition of those decrees I have ordained for the welfare of the English people'. And at his coronation, one of the promises made by Henry I was to restore to his people 'the law of King Edward, with such emendations as my father made to it with the counsel of his barons'.[56]

But although many of the elements of the post-conquest legal system were of Anglo-Saxon origin, there were important advances in legal thought and practice under the Norman kings. The structures under-pinning the authority of the later Anglo-Saxon kings were strong by wider eleventh-century standards, but there were still considerable limits to their coercive power. On an everyday level, for most of the king's subjects, the substance of law, especially that relating to land, was based on local custom and tradition, and its enforcement was locally con-trolled. The established laws varied considerably between neighbouring areas, and especially between different parts of the kingdom. Cnut's law-code had recognised that differences existed between the laws of Wessex, Mercia and the Danelaw, and the so-called *Laws of Henry I*, written in about 1115, did the same. One achievement of the Anglo-Norman period was the start of the introduction of more consistent and regular legal procedures across the kingdom. Just as significantly, new *types* of law were introduced alongside the new systems which administered it. The traditional view is that 'feudal' law was brought to England by the Normans and operated in tandem with and alongside traditional Anglo-Saxon 'customary' law. Matters were not as straight-forward as this, but the maintenance and protection of Norman rule did necessitate innovations in the criminal law, whilst a new system of landholding after 1066 meant that ways had to be found to regulate the relations between landlords and tenants and to solve problems concern-ing land. Underlying both of these dynamics, meanwhile, was the king's need for money to fight his wars: royal justice was profitable, and this in itself was a powerful stimulus to experiment.

After 1066 just as before, the most important courts were the king's own court, the shire court and the hundred court. A new type of court also appeared after the arrival of the Norman kings, the court of the local lord. Kings made some attempts to clarify which courts should hear particular types of cases. In the early 1070s, for example, William I issued a writ stating, amongst other things, that ecclesiastical cases (which encompassed disputes about marriages, wills and legitimacy) should not be heard in hundred courts or by lay judges; rather they should be heard in church courts before ecclesiastical judges. And in about 1108 Henry I issued a writ which purported to set out the limits of the jurisdiction of certain courts.[57] Shire courts and hundred courts were to meet at the same places and at the same times as they had done in the time of Edward the Confessor 'and not otherwise'. If there was a dispute about land between two of the king's tenants-in-chief, it went on, the hearing should be in the king's court (because he was their lord); if the dispute was between two of the men of one of his tenants-in-chief, it should be heard in their lord's court; and if the dispute was between the tenants of different lords, it should be heard in the shire court. In practice, though, matters were more fluid than this and there were no hard and fast rules dictating the court to which every dispute should come.

Fundamental amongst the duties of a medieval ruler was the doing of justice, both between his tenants-in-chief in his capacity as their lord and between his subjects in his capacity as their king or, in Normandy, their duke. Robert Curthose was a poor ruler, Orderic Vitalis claims, in part because he was not able to prevent his duchy descending into lawlessness: he 'made no attempt to bring the malefactors to justice, and for eight years under the weak duke scoundrels were free to treat the innocent with the utmost brutality'.[58] In England, the king was the ultimate fount of justice, and his decisions were binding and authoritative potentially on all matters. Thus he was sought out wherever he went by those eager for an audience and for a conclusive decision in their favour. There was nothing new about this, and also by 1066 the concept of a national 'peace' which it was the king's duty to preserve was a familiar one. In his Coronation Charter, for example, Henry I promised to 'establish a firm peace in all my kingdom', and to order 'that this peace shall henceforth be kept'.[59] Also, at least by Henry I's reign and perhaps much earlier, before 1066, certain types of case ('royal pleas' or 'pleas of the crown') were considered to be a special royal preserve, and could only be heard by the king or his representative. A list of these (by no means definitive) was given in the *Leges Henrici Primi*, a legal tract dating from about 1115, and included all the most serious offences, such as murder, treason, arson, robbery, rape, and 'theft punishable by death'. Other matters (treasure trove, rights over wrecks, destruction of the highway) were also included in the list as, significantly, was the royal right to hear appeals from other courts over claims of unjust judgment or 'default of justice' in other courts.[60] In other words, the king claimed a supervisory jurisdiction over the decisions reached by and between his subjects in lower courts.

Whilst the king would hear cases brought before him in person, royal courts had to be held in his absence, too. When the king was away from England, as he was frequently after 1066, his deputies or his officials heard cases in his name. So that the king's pleas could be heard across the country, moreover, it was necessary that there be local officials to hear them. Anglo-Saxon kings had sent men into the shires to hear particular cases, and the Norman kings continued to do some-thing similar, sending specially appointed justices out into the localities to deal with cases which required royal involvement. However, the Norman kings also began (it is not clear precisely when, but it was certainly happening under Henry I) to use so-called 'local justices', men permanently resident in particular shires whose job it was to hear cases in the king's name. More importantly still for the future, the reign of Henry I saw the developing importance of 'itinerant' (travelling) justices, who were sent to particular counties to hear a wide variety of cases. At this stage these royal judges did not give judgments in the courts they supervised; this remained the job of the suitors to the court, those local people who were obliged to attend the sessions of the court. Moreover, each shire court continued to have its own customs which were applied even when a royal judge presided; as yet these were not local sessions of a national royal court.

Shire courts were well-established features of the English legal landscape before 1066, and after the Conquest they continued to func-tion much as they had always done. However, they came to sit more frequently as time went on; every four weeks by the early thirteenth century, as opposed to twice a year before 1066. This may suggest that they were popular and effective; or, alternatively, that they were seen by the royal government as increasingly efficient mechanisms for assert-ing authority and raising funds. Usually, the shire court was presided over by the local sheriff. The local bishop may occasionally have presided, too, but his influence was probably reduced from the 1070s, as the official policy of the Church was to extricate itself from the administration of secular affairs.[61] And as has been seen, a royal justice may occasionally have supervised sessions of the shire court. There were no fixed rules about who the suitors to the court should be. The *Leges Henrici Primi* stipulated that, amongst others, bishops, earls, sheriffs, hundredmen, reeves, barons, village reeves and other lords of lands should attend, but in practice there was probably much local variation concerning attendance, and an obligation to attend the court probably rested more than anything else on status as indicated by landholding. The shire court dealt with a wide range of matters, many of which concerned non-legal business. Important royal announcements might be made there, and high-status land transactions witnessed. The bulk of the disputes heard there concerned land claims and offences involving violence or theft. If the offences involved breaches of the king's peace, a royal representative would need to be present.

In the early twelfth century, England's shires were subdivided into about 600 hundreds or wapentakes. Some counties contained more than others, and the hundreds themselves varied considerably in size. Many of these hundreds, moreover, were in private hands, having been granted to individuals by the king. The conventional wisdom has been that private hundreds existed in England before 1066. The jurisdiction enjoyed in the twelfth century by the abbey of Bury St Edmunds over 8½ hundreds in Suffolk, and by the church at Ely over five and a half hundreds in the same county by 1066 was thought to pre-date the Conquest, therefore. It has been argued very strongly more recently, however, that the creation of private hundreds was a post-conquest phenomenon.[62] Either way, each hundred in theory had its own court. Like the shire court, the hundred court was a legacy of pre-conquest England, where it was probably held once a month. It has been suggested, however, that, by the early thirteenth century, hundreds were being held every fortnight, but there is no evidence about this from a century before.[63] Presiding over the court, which sat for one day at a time, was a bailiff, appointed by the sheriff, or by the lord if the hundred was in private hands. The obligation to attend rested on the larger landholders of the hundred. It has been calculated that 20,000 men (perhaps one per cent of the estimated population in 1086, or one in twenty adult males) was obliged regularly to attend the hundred court. Shire and hundred courts had similar jurisdictions, and the same case might be dealt with at different stages in both courts. Generally, the hundred probably dealt with less serious disputes than the shire court. And for most people, especially if they had different lords but lived in the same hundred, the hundred would be their court of first resort. Twice a year, there was a special session of the hundred, which was to be attended by all freemen of the hundred. These sessions were presided over by the sheriff himself and, amongst other things, he checked the functioning of the frankpledge system (see below).

Lords' courts, also known as 'honourial' or 'seignorial' courts by historians, were a Norman innovation in England after 1066. Unfortunately, very little is known about how they worked. In theory, every lord held a court for the tenants of his scattered lands or 'honour' who had been given land by him in return for military service. The honourial court was the forum where disputes between the tenants, or between them and their lord, could be heard and settled. The giving of judgment was a vital requirement of good lordship, and an obvious example of one aspect of the 'feudal system' in operation. On one level, indeed, when hearing disputes between his tenants-in-chief, the king's court was functioning simply as the grandest honourial court of all. The lord did not simply hear disputes and make judgments on them, however. After all, 'honourial courts were the key venue for the management of seignorial resources and personal relations'.[64] Property transactions could be witnessed there, the lord made important announcements to his tenants there, and they gave him advice. Just as the king's tenants-in-chief expected their lord to listen to and heed their counsel, so the vassals of lesser lords expected that justice would be done to them and that their opinions would be given due weight. The honourial court could also be used to deal with certain types of offence against the person or goods, if the lord had acquired the right to have such cases heard there. Sometimes these rights were expressly set out in the documents recording the grant of land to the lord; at other times, the origins of the rights claimed were more obscure. Most important amongst these were the ancient forms of jurisdiction called 'sake and soke' and 'infangentheof'. The latter gave the lord the right summarily to execute thieves caught red-handed on his lands. The former gave the lord a wider, less precisely definable right to enforce order within his lands. He could also enforce order amongst the lesser men of his lands in the manor court. There the lord's steward would extract fines from his master's employees if they had carried out their ploughing badly or failed to meet their obligation to supply him with labour; male villeins paid for licences to marry; petty misdemeanours and minor offences of disorder could be tried there, too. There were few clear lines between the overlapping authority and powers of the courts of manor, honour and hundred.

In the eleventh century, the threat and reality of violence permeated society at all levels. The aristocratic élite was brought up to fight, and lower down the social scale the rigours of daily life, and the inescapable grind of poverty, made a high degree of criminality inevitable. This was a knife-carrying society, too. Trivial arguments could easily turn nasty and brutal, and could ultimately lead to the most serious charges. The biggest problem for those interested in keeping violence and disorder to a minimum was the difficulty of apprehending offenders. Unless they were caught red-handed, it was easy for them to escape undetected, and other methods of instilling respect for the law had to be found. William I, for example, introduced the *murdrum* fine, a penalty imposed on a local community (the hundred or village or perhaps the lord of the land where the killing took place) for failure to produce the secret killer of a Norman. Such penalties were designed to give an incentive to produce murderers after the event, but also to prevent killings in the first place.

The introduction of the *murdrum* fine probably reveals much about the native hostility faced by the Norman newcomers in England after 1066. But in setting out to deal with such problems William was only extending a principle that would have been familiar to the local communities of Anglo-Saxon England, that of communal responsibility for the wrongdoing of individuals. This principle was best expressed through the operation of the tithing or 'frankpledge' system, which probably continued to function after 1066 much as it had done before. A tithing was a group of ten or twelve freemen who acted as mutual guarantors that they would not commit offences, and that they would produce the guilty party if an offence was committed by one of their number. Evidence for the way tithings worked before 1066 is scarce, but by the early twelfth century it is possible to see the system working in some detail and it is unlikely that it had been changed significantly after the Conquest. If the members of a tithing failed to fulfil their duties, they were punished financially. If an offence was committed and it was found that the offender was not in a tithing, the whole vill would be fined for having failed to regulate itself properly. Certain areas and groups were never included in this system, and there appears to have been no such structure at all in the northern and western border counties. But, these exceptions apart, by the mid eleventh century it was established that every freeman over a certain age (probably 12) had to belong to a tithing. Unfortunately, there is no quantifiable evidence by which to judge the effectiveness of this system of local policing. When the identity of the offender was unknown, it could not have been helpful at all. Plenty of offenders must have fled, too, even though they believed that they had acted violently in self-defence or that death or injury had been caused by accident. An alternative option for the offender was to seek sanctuary in a monastery or church. This provided a respite, usually of 30 or 40 days, but then it is likely that he would have to leave the country anyway. Otherwise, if the identity of the offender was known, but he had not been apprehended, he would be summoned repeatedly to appear in court and, when he failed to do so, he would be formally outlawed. This placed him outside the normal workings of the law. If captured, he could be executed immediately upon outlawry being proved, and if he resisted arrest he could be killed with impunity.

Depending upon the nature of the offence in question, a trial would usually take place either in the court of a lord with sake and soke, the hundred or shire court. The most serious cases, where breaches of the king's peace or pleas of the crown were concerned, would be heard in the presence of a royal justice or perhaps of the sheriff acting in that capacity. There was no national prosecuting authority, and most accusations were brought by an individual (usually the victim or a member of their kin) through the process of 'appeal'. If both parties appeared on the appointed day, the accuser would formally state the charge and offer to prove it; the defendant would formally deny the accusation. Claims and counter-claims would then be made (an alibi, perhaps, or a claim of self-defence) and evidence brought forward. The defendant's reputation would then be considered: notorious wrongdoers had a much more difficult job than men of previously good character. In hard cases, a form of proof had to be decided upon by the suitors. Three main methods were used: oath, ordeal and battle, all of which introduced a spiritual component into the judicial framework. Oaths sworn on the Gospels or on holy relics were another legacy from pre-conquest England. They continued in use after 1066, but their popularity in relation to serious offences appears to have diminished over this period. Ordeals by hot iron and cold water were regularly used in criminal cases after 1066, however. In trial by cold water, the accused was lowered into a pit full of water which had been blessed by a priest. Guilt was established if he floated, on the basis that holy water would not receive a sinner by allowing him to sink. In trial by hot iron, the accused had to carry a piece of red-hot iron for three paces. The burnt hand was then bound and examined three days after the trial. If the wound was infected, guilt was certain; if it was clean, he was innocent. There is no reason to doubt that, for most people, the outcome of the ordeal was a reliable demonstration of God's preference for one party or another. But almost certainly, the mere prospect of the ordeal would have been enough to push many accused towards confession and a lesser penalty: mutilation, perhaps.

In addition to water and fire, the Normans introduced a new form of the ordeal to England: trial by battle. Trial by battle had a long history in Europe but was unknown in Anglo-Saxon England. However, by the later twelfth century it had become the preferred method of proof in appeals concerning serious offences; and (unlike the ordeals of hot iron and cold water) it was also available to litigants involved in disputes over land. The battle was fought between the accused and the accuser if both were fit and, unlike in battles concerning land where swords were used, the combatants in criminal cases would have employed hammers or staffs with sharpened and reinforced ends. The popularity of this method of proof may testify to a genuinely held belief that God would intervene on the right side. However, this is hard to substantiate, and there was considerable room for interpretation in assessing the results of any particular ordeal, especially those used in criminal cases. Whether someone had sunk or floated, or whether their wounds had healed must often have been nice judgments to make.

If the accuser did fail to prove his case against the accused, he would be punished for having brought a false claim. He would have to pay a sum to the king, and probably something by way of compensation to the accused. More seriously, if the accused failed to establish his innocence, he would have to face the appropriate penalty. For lesser offences, a system of compensation, familiar to the Anglo-Saxons, continued to operate. The victim of a crime might be paid if his belongings had been stolen or damaged, but he would also be paid if he had been physically injured. The amount of compensation would depend on the position and extent of his wounds, and there were complex tariffs setting out the value of specific wounds. Deals would have been struck between the parties as well. All freemen, moreover, had a monetary value placed upon their lives, a *wergild* (literally 'man price'). This was payable in several different types of case, but it was awarded principally to the family of a person who had been killed, and was paid either by the killer or his kin to avoid the carrying out of a feud or vendetta by the dead victim's kin. The amount payable in a particular case depended on the rank of the victim. The king's *wergild* was largest of all. It is impossible to determine how extensively this system of financial penalties was in operation across England between 1042 and 1066, and there have been suggestions that its importance was declining as kings sought to enforce more direct control over the workings of the courts. However, the Norman kings certainly did much to sweep away the Anglo-Saxon system of compensatory justice. For serious offences, the accused would face death, usually by hanging; or occasionally, if he was luckier, physical mutilation of some sort, perhaps the loss of a limb, blinding or castration. At Christmas 1124, the royal justice Ralph Basset hanged 44 thieves in one sitting of his court in Leicestershire, whilst he had six others blinded and castrated. Punishments were so severe because, first, it was thought that the perpetrators deserved such treatment, and, second, they would act as a deterrent.

In medieval England, land was the ultimate source of wealth and prestige. The more land a man had, the greater his standing in local society and the greater his influence within political society. In other words, together with the possession of land went power and influence over individuals and communities. Not surprisingly, therefore, rights over land were jealously guarded, and there were innumerable disputes about it. A new lord might seek to introduce his own followers into lands already held by others, for example, or there might be controversy about who was the closest heir to a deceased tenant. Sometimes grantors even gave the same lands to more than one person. Such disputes could involve violence, which gave rise to subsidiary legal issues. The forum for the hearing of such disputes depended on a variety of factors, and disputes over land could be held in all of the courts mentioned above. Henry I's writ of 1108 is helpful here, but it is not exhaustive. An honourial court could deal with disputes between a lord's men, for example, but also with complaints made by a tenant against the lord himself and with disputes between the lord's tenants and their own men. Royal involvement in lower courts was increasingly common, too, and a litigant could obtain a royal writ issued to the court-holder ordering him to 'do right' in a certain matter. If a disappointed party complained of the justice he had received in a lower court, moreover, he could obtain a royal writ ordering the case to come before the king or his justices. Once the parties were both in court, claims would be made and denied; sworn testimony or documentary evidence might be used, custom and land-holding practice might be referred to. Where the merits of the dispute were unclear, a method of proof again had to be decided upon. Ordeals by fire or water were very unusual in disputes over land, but trial by battle was once again an option. It may have been a more dignified affair than the procedure used in criminal cases: swords were used, for example, rather than staffs or hammers, and the parties could employ champions to fight on their behalf. The winner of the case ended up in possession of the land, although settlements made 'out of court' were by no means unusual.

It would be unwise to overstate the degree to which the English legal system achieved uniformity and coherence in the half-century or so after 1066. One Norman innovation, the honourial court, may actually have served to restrict the reach of royal justice by taking business out of the shire and hundred courts. And even where royal justice was exercised most effectively it was still developing, and large parts of the kingdom remained outside the system altogether. The Church and the royal forest had their own laws and procedures; and their respective jurisdictions only increased as the twelfth century went on. After 1066 if not before, moreover, many hundreds were in private hands. And other individuals or institutions had special powers which reflected the realities of royal power after 1066. The abbey William I founded on the site of the Battle of Hastings, for example, had the right to exclude royal justices from its lands. And more extensively, in vulnerable frontier areas such as the county of Chester or the bishopric of Durham, the earl and the bishop possessed what were, in effect, royal powers: they appointed their own sheriffs who did not account at the royal exchequer, and royal justices could not operate within their jurisdictions. Nevertheless, political and military necessity had combined with a continuously evolving sense of the king as supreme judge and the guarantor of a national peace to ensure that royal influence within and over the legal system would continue to increase. And the more the operation of the legal system could be brought under royal control, the greater the opportunity for financial profit as well as political power.

Conclusion

The focus in this chapter has been on the effect of the Norman Conquest on England's and, to a lesser extent, Normandy's systems of law and government. It was not until well after the end of the period covered by this book that significant changes were introduced into the administrative and legal systems of Wales and Scotland; and they were at best only an indirect and remote consequence of the Conquest. Within England, by contrast, although much remained the same within the systems of law and government after 1066, the following decades also saw innovation and evolution. However, change rarely came about as a result of any preconceived plan; it usually happened pragmatically in response to circumstances and events. Thus, since the Norman kings liked hunting so much, a system of forest administration gradually emerged; because parts of England were more vulnerable or valuable than others, special administrative units like the marcher earldoms and the Sussex rapes developed; because the king could not always be in England, someone had to run the country in his absence. But even this description risks crediting the kings and their servants with too much conscious planning. The keynote of this period was not the deliberate creation of institutions and administrative systems but the extension and intensification of royal activity. This served to consolidate the gains made by William I in 1066, but, most importantly, it served to increase royal revenue. William I and his sons won their victories in part because they were able soldiers, but largely because they were rich. Kings could not win their wars without money, and 'the king's wealth was the product of a vast foraging operation'.[65] More specifically, they needed to administer their lands efficiently, exploit their tenants ruthlessly and supervise the legal system closely. To do all these things successfully, moreover, records had to be kept of what the king was owed and by whom, and instructions had to be given to royal officials more often and in more detail than ever before. It needs to be emphasised that these developments had only just begun by the start of the twelfth century, but there is no reason to doubt that William I, William II and Henry I all appreciated that the more organised and thoroughgoing the system of royal government became, the more effectively their subjects could be fleeced.

Notes

1 J.O. Prestwich, 'War and Finance in the Anglo-Norman State', *TRHS*, 5th series, 4, pp.19–43; repr. in *Anglo-Norman Warfare*, ed. M. Strickland (Woodbridge: Boydell Press, 1992), pp.59–83, at p.76.

2 *EHD* II, pp.432–6.

3 *ASC* 'E', s.a.1087; *WMGR*, i p.509.

4 *ASC* 'E', s.a.1087, 1100, 1135; *WMGR*, i p.577.

5 *JW*, iii pp.82–3.

6 *OV*, v pp.300–3.

7 C. Warren Hollister, 'Magnates and "Curiales" in Early Norman England', *Viator* 4 (1973), pp.63–81; repr. in Hollister, *Monarchy, Magnates and Institutions in the Anglo-Norman World* (London: Hambledon Press, 1986), pp.97–115, at pp.98–9.

8 *WMGR*, i p.509; *ASC* 'E', s.a.1085, 1086; *OV*, v pp.298–9; John Hudson, 'Henry I and Counsel' in *The Medieval State. Essays Presented to James Campbell*, ed. J.R. Maddicott and D.M. Palliser (London: Hambledon Press, 2000), pp.109–26.

9 Judith Green, *The Aristocracy of Norman England* (Cambridge University Press, 1997), p.221.

10 *OV*, iv pp.119–21, v p.309.

11 Judith A. Green, 'Robert Curthose Reassessed', *ANS* 22 (1999), pp.95–116, at p.114; D. Bates, 'Normandy and England after 1066', *EHR* 104 (1989), p.868.

12 *ASC* 'E', s.a.1087; *HH*, p.33.

13 *OV*, iv p.97.

14 C. Warren Hollister, *Henry I* (New Haven; London: Yale University Press, 2001), p.258.

15 *OV*, vi pp.346–50.

16 Bates, 'Normandy and England after 1066', p.872; idem., *William the Conqueror* (London: G.Philip, 1989), pp.109–11.

17 *ASC*, s.a.1066; *OV*, ii pp.231, 317.

18 *WP*, p.179.

19 'Annales Monasterii de Wintonia, 519–1277', in *Annales Monastici*, ed. H.R. Luard (Rolls series, 1864–9), 4 vols., ii p.39.

20 *OV*, v p.311.

21 David Carpenter, *The Struggle for Mastery: Britain 1066–1284* (Oxford University Press, 2003), p.91.

22 *OV*, vi p.16, v p.203.

23 Hollister, 'Magnates and "Curiales"', pp.102–10.

24 Richard Sharpe, 'The use of writs in the eleventh century', *Anglo-Saxon England*, 32 (2003), pp.247–91, at p.250.

25 Charles Insley, 'Where Did All the Charters Go? Anglo-Saxon Charters and the New Politics of the Eleventh Century', *ANS* 24 (2001), pp.109–27.

26 *EHD* II, p.1012.

27 *Facsimiles of English Royal Writs to AD 1100 Presented to Vivian Hunter Galbraith*, ed. T.A.M. Bishop and P. Chaplais (Oxford University Press, 1957), pp.xiii–xiv.

28 David Bates, 'The earliest Norman writs', *EHR* 100 (1985), pp.266–84, at p.282.

29 For example, *Facsimiles of English Royal Writs*, ed. Bishop and Chaplais, Plate XXV(a).

30 Bates, 'The earliest Norman writs', p.267; M.T. Clanchy, *From Memory to Written Record. England, 1066–1307*, 2nd edn (Oxford: Clarendon Press, 1993), p.58.

31 *JW*, iii p.45; *ASC* 'E', s.a.1085.

32 *EHD* II, p.946.

33 David Roffe, *Domesday. The Inquest and the Book* (Oxford University Press, 2000), pp.242–8.

34 For what follows in this and the following paragraph, see C.P. Lewis, 'The Early Earls of Norman England', *ANS* 13 (1990), pp.207–23, at pp.216–23.

35 David C. Douglas, *William the Conqueror* (London: Eyre & Spottiswoode, 1964), p.296. See also Robin Fleming, *Kings and Lords in Conquest England* (Cambridge University Press, 1991), p.148: 'The real precedent for the marcher lordships is to be found in Normandy not England.'

36 Lewis, 'The Early Earls of Norman England', pp.222–3.

37 Brian Golding, *Conquest and Colonisation: The Normans in Britain, 1066–1100* (Basingstoke: Macmillan, 1994), p.105.

38 *EHD* II, p.465.

39 Above, p.192.

40 *OV*, ii p.267.

41 Robert Bartlett, *England under the Norman and Angevin Kings, 1075–1225* (Oxford: Clarendon Press, 2000), p.160.

42 *ASC* 'D', s.a.1067; 'E', s.a.1083.

43 *ASC* 'E', s.a.1088.

44 Judith A. Green, *The Government of England Under Henry I* (Cambridge, 1986), p.223.

45 *EHD* II, p.433.

46 *Pipe Roll 31 Henry I*, ed. J. Hunter (London: HMSO, 1888), pp.55, 59.

47 *OV*, v p.203. See also, *WMGR*, i p.577.

48 Frank Barlow, *The Feudal Kingdom of England, 1042–1216*, 5th edn (London: Longman, 1999), p.121; idem, *William Rufus* (New Haven; London: Yale University Press, 2000), p.239.

49 M. Brett, *The English Church Under Henry I* (Oxford University Press, 1975), pp.105–6.

50 Bartlett, *England under the Norman and Angevin Kings*, p.168.

51 *Dialogus de Scaccario*, ed. and trans. C. Johnson, with corrections by F.E.L. Carter and D.E. Greenway (Oxford: Clarendon Press, 1983), p.14.

52 M.T. Clanchy, *England and its Rulers, 1066–1307*, 3rd edn (Oxford: Blackwell, 2006), p.55; *Dialogus de Scaccario*, pp.5–7.

53 Hollister, *Henry I*, p.369.

54 Carpenter, *The Struggle for Mastery*, p.154.

55 Judith A. Green, 'Unity and Disunity in the Anglo-Norman State', *Historical Research*, 62 (1989), pp.116–23.

56 *EHD* II, pp.432, 434.

57 *EHD* II, pp.647–8, 465.

58 *OV*, iv p.147.

59 *EHD* II, p.434.

60 *EHD* II, pp.491–5.

61 See below, p.293.

62 Patrick Wormald, *Legal Culture in the Early Medieval West: Law as text, image and experience* (London: Hambledon Press, 1999), ch.12.

63 J. Hudson, *The Formation of the English Common Law: Law and society in England from the Norman Conquest to Magna Carta* (London: Longman, 1996), p.38.

64 Hudson, *The Formation of the English Common Law*, p.43.

65 W.L. Warren, *The Governance of Norman and Angevin England, 1086–1272* (London: Edward Arnold, 1987), p.85.

CHAPTER 9

Lands and armies

Between 1066 and 1106, as a result of the Norman Conquest, political, social and military structures in England were changed in profound and fundamental ways. The Anglo-Saxon ruling élite was replaced by a French one, and both the English survivors and the Norman newcomers were compelled to adapt and conform as new systems of landholding and military organisation evolved in the novel circumstances of conquered England. Little about this was premeditated, consistent or uniform; and by no means was every memory of Anglo-Saxon England swept away. Moreover, the effects of these developments on Wales, Scotland and Normandy were limited and deferred. Nevertheless, in England at least, this was a time of radical, arguably unprecedented, upheaval.

A new aristocracy

The year 1066 was a catastrophic one for the aristocracy of Anglo-Saxon England. King Harold and his brothers were only the most prominent amongst the numberless thegns who were killed at the battles of Fulford, Stamford Bridge and Hastings. The following decade was just as destructive in its own way. By the end of 1076, earls Edwin, Morcar and Waltheof were either dead or permanently imprisoned; and other members of the Anglo-Saxon ruling élite had disappeared from sight. In 1086, the Domesday survey recorded the names of only four English landholders of any note. This does not mean that Englishmen did not continue to hold land after 1066; as will be seen, plenty managed to keep their footing on the lower rungs of the property ladder. However, they did so in conditions that were quite changed, and at the mercy of new, French lords.

However, if the Norman Conquest of England eventually resulted in the wholesale dispossession of the Anglo-Saxon ruling class and their replacement by Frenchmen, this may not have been the original plan. William the Conqueror tried hard to conciliate the likes of Edwin, Morcar and Waltheof at the start of his reign; the latter even married the Conqueror's niece Judith, and a marriage between Edwin and the King's daughter may also have been discussed.[1] William wanted to stress the legitimacy of his position as Edward the Confessor's rightful heir, and an emphasis upon continuity would help him to do this. Meanwhile, the writ William issued, probably in 1067, which confirmed the traditional privileges of the City of London, clearly demonstrates how keen the new king was to underline the links between his reign and previous ones: as well as allowing London to retain its liberties, the writ was written in English, presumably by an English scribe, and it took the same form as similar documents from earlier reigns. However, that it was addressed to an official called Geoffrey (who was almost certainly a Norman) and to both the English and French burgesses of the city shows that circumstances had already begun to change.[2]

Indeed, by the end of the 1060s, William's plan to minimise disruption had failed. The English survivors did not help themselves by rebelling as often as they did in the years up to 1075. However, the pressure on King William to reward his own followers probably accounts more for the eventual scale and nature of the redistribution of English land. Even William de Poitiers was frank enough to admit that William's men urged him to be crowned as soon as possible after his victory at Hastings, not just because they thought he would be a good king, but also because 'they wished their gains and honours to be increased by his elevation'. And when the 'E' text of the *Anglo-Saxon Chronicle* claimed that William 'gave away every man's land' on his return from Normandy to England at the end of 1067, it was only the rather early date that was wrong, not the substance of the allegation.[3]

Barons and below

William had promised great prizes to those who came with him in 1066, and he was helped in meeting their expectations by having more territorial resources at his disposal than any previous English king. He claimed that the whole kingdom of England was his by right of conquest, but he also benefited from the way the lands of the Godwinesons had been united with the royal demesne when Harold had become king. The extent of the Conqueror's lands has already been described; his demesne was probably twice the size of Edward the Confessor's, whilst many of his estates were in areas hitherto untouched by direct royal influence.[4] This gave the King unprecedented amounts of influence across his kingdom and a seemingly bottomless well of patronage from which to draw. During his reign, moreover, because of confiscations following rebellions (by Frenchmen as well as English: the earls of Hereford and Norfolk in 1075 and Odo of Bayeux in 1082, for example), that well was regularly replenished. And after 1087, new careers continued to be made: William de Warenne became earl of Surrey and Henry de Beaumont earl of Warwick; and the fall of Robert de Mowbray in 1095 led to fresh confiscations.

As will be seen later, there were various means by which men might come into possession of land after 1066; and it would be wrong to assume that the processes involved were straightforward and consistent ones. However, those who were given land or a 'fief' directly by the king (it was usually called a *feodum* in Latin; hence 'feudalism') or who had their possession of it confirmed by him, religious houses as well as laymen, are usually referred to by historians as his tenants-in-chief or barons. Using the information contained in Domesday Book, it has been calculated that by 1086, whilst approximately a quarter of the landed wealth of the kingdom was in the hands of the Church, no less than half of it was under the control of about two hundred of these barons. About half was held in turn by just ten men, whose names are worth giving in full: Odo of Bayeux (described by Orderic Vitalis as 'like a second king'[5]) and Robert of Mortain, the King's half-brothers, Roger de Montgomery, William de Warenne, Hugh FitzRichard, Count Eustace II of Boulogne, Count Alan of Brittany, Richard FitzGilbert, Bishop Geoffrey of Coutances and Geoffrey de Mandeville. All except counts Eustace and Alan were Normans, and all except Count Alan and Geoffrey de Mandeville had made their careers alongside Duke William as he established his authority in Normandy after 1040. According to Domesday Book, Robert of Mortain's English lands comprised 793 manors in 1086, with an annual value of over £2,100; and Bishop Odo's lands were worth some £3,000.[6] For them the conquest of England had been worth the risk.

Since W.J. Corbett developed the idea in the 1920s, these men have conventionally been referred to by historians as the Class A barons of Domesday England; that is, tenants-in-chief whose lands, according to Domesday Book, had an annual value of more than £750.[7] Below them in Corbett's system were the Class B barons, of whom there were 10, with lands worth between £400 and £650 annually; the 24 barons in Class C in 1087 held lands worth between £200 and £400 per year; the 36 in Class D held land with an annual value between £100 and £200; and finally the 100 or so barons in Class E had holdings worth less than £100 per year. Such numbers only serve to reinforce the view that, after 1066, control over vast tracts of land was placed in the hands of a very small élite of Frenchman. Usually they were Normans, but not invariably. Men such as Alan of Brittany, whose lands around Richmond in Yorkshire formed only part of his extensive English estates, and Gerbod the Fleming, who held the county of Chester until 1071, were only the best rewarded amongst significant numbers of their fellow countrymen. And lower down the league table of Domesday tenants-in-chief, for those like Roger Bigod and William de Braose in Class B, and the Mortimers, Beaumonts and Beauchamps in Class C, all of whom established successful aristocratic dynasties from the profits of 1066, fortunes were transformed.

Despite the apparent clarity of Domesday Book, however, its figures need to be interpreted with great care.[8] Corbett used only 170 barons to arrive at his conclusions, whilst Domesday Book in fact records the names of no less than 846 tenants-in-chief, of whom a mere 13 were English. It has also been argued that Corbett's method, which assesses an individual's wealth by combining the value of his demesne and tenanted lands, 'vastly exaggerates the economic resources of the great magnates'.[9] Therefore, whilst Domesday Book records that Robert of Mortain was the lord of nearly 800 manors spread across England in

1087, it needs to be emphasised that neither he nor any other great lord was able or willing to control such extensive estates directly. For one thing, they had their own followers to reward. Consequently, a proportion of any baron's lands was granted to tenants of his own. Once such 'subinfeudation' had taken place, the baron would no longer receive income from the lands now controlled by his tenant. Domesday Book records the names of 6,300 landholders in all, and nearly 90 per cent of them were not tenants-in-chief and held all their lands from someone other than the king. About half of these men, it is thought, held land with an annual value of no more than £5; but this did not mean that they or their richer fellows were not important politically; and anyway, some of these so-called 'mesne tenants' were wealthier than barons in Class C at least. Below this level, moreover, there must have been a large number of individuals, unrecorded in Domesday Book, who occupied land in some capacity or another. Domesday does not give a complete picture of landholding in England either in 1066 or 1086, because it was never intended to do so.[10]

Honours and incidents

The great estates of the barons after 1066 were known as 'fees' or 'honours'. They were made up of the lands held in demesne by the baron and those held by his tenants in return for military service. An honour would be centred on a particular place, perhaps the chief residence of the lord in the area where the bulk of his lands lay. The honour might be compact and self-contained: those held in Yorkshire at Richmond, Pontefract, Holderness and Tickhill by, respectively, Alan of Brittany, Ilbert de Lacy, Drogo de la Beuvrière and Roger de Bully were of this kind by 1086.[11] But it might also consist, as did the huge honour of Wallingford, not just of lands in the vicinity of its nominal centre, but also of other lands scattered across number of different counties. What bound these lands together, whether they were compactly arranged or widely spread, was the person of the lord. There were thus tensions inherent in these new arrangements: a landholder would have obligations to his county community, to attend the shire court, perhaps, or to provide equipment for a member of the *fyrd*. But, as will be seen, he would also have duties to his lord as a tenant of his honour. Of course the character of honours varied along with the different arrangements made between lords and their men, and tenants in the further-flung parts of a lord's honour might not be burdened as heavily as those nearer to the centre of a lord's power. Moreover, a man might well be the tenant of more than one lord, inevitably diluting the strength of his loyalty to each. To regard the tenants of any particular honour as 'a self-contained feudal community', therefore, which regulated its own affairs with the lord of the honour at its head, may be misleading.[12] Nevertheless, it is important to remember that bonds of lordship were made potentially very strong as a result of the tenurial changes brought about by the Norman Conquest, and that they might cut across other lines of allegiance and loyalty, to family, locality and even, perhaps, to the king.

These bonds were reinforced by meaningful powers which enabled a lord to discipline his tenants and which served to tie the landholders of England together in new kinds of ways after 1066. It is true that they lost out financially when they granted land to their tenants (no longer could the lord derive any monetary profit directly from the running of these estates). But what was gained from these arrangements more than compensated for this. When he was granted his lands, a tenant performed homage to his lord in a solemn ceremony, and promised to provide his lord with loyalty, support and service of some kind. Such service was usually military, although it is wise to remember both that 'not all properties were given out as tidily as the [feudal] myth requires', and that 'there is absolutely no evidence that a "precise definition of service" formed an automatic part of each grant'.[13] By 1100, however, as will be seen below, it does seem that, in return for their lands, all of the king's tenants-in-chief were obliged to provide him with knights to fight in the royal army or to garrison royal castles. Similarly, most sub-tenants probably held their lands from their lords in return for a specified amount of military service. The key moment in this connection may have come after the completion of the Domesday survey, on 1 August 1086 at Salisbury, when 'all the people occupying land who were of any account over all England, no matter whose vassals they might be' appeared before King William, 'submitted to him and became his vassals and swore oaths of allegiance to him, that they would be loyal to him against all other men'.[14] J.C. Holt has suggested that these oaths formalised the grip of the barons and their own tenants over the lands they had acquired or been granted during the preceding 20 years, and that Domesday Book was the official record of their tenure.[15]

Lords could also continue to expect more from their tenants than the occasional provision of a fixed number of troops. Tenants might be obliged to serve in their lord's household, for example, and attendance at the lord's court was probably expected. And in place of actual military service, because ready cash was often more useful in war than someone else's mounted knights, the king, as we have seen, might levy a scutage from his barons who, in turn, could recoup the costs of this from their sub-tenants, and so on down the chain. Such payments are first recorded during Henry I's reign, but were probably being made before 1100. At other times, if a tenant rebelled or died without heirs, his lands would return or 'escheat' to his lord. The lord could keep them, grant them away as a gift or sell them off as he pleased, thus creating new bonds of loyalty but also potentially fresh resentment in the minds of those dispossessed and their heirs. And there were other controls exercised by lords over the lives of their tenants' relatives. If a tenant died leaving an heir, that heir could not enter into his inheritance without the lord's permission and until he had paid the lord a so-called 'relief'. The amount of the payment was negotiable but often large and at the lord's discretion. Further, if a tenant died when his heir was under age, the lord was entitled to take possession of the lands, administer the so-called 'wardship' and take the profits from the land until the heir was old enough to succeed. He could also sell the right to exploit the lands to someone else. The lord's permission had to be sought by a tenant, too, before he could marry off his daughter. A small payment would make the granting of that permission more likely, and if permission was not sought, the tenant would be exposed to some kind of penalty. And if the tenant died leaving a widow of marriageable age or unmarried sons and daughters, it was the lord's prerogative to arrange (or sell) their marriages.

These so-called 'feudal incidents' were a quite new source of revenue and power for the English kings and the landholding élite after 1066. There was nothing like them in Normandy before then, and they derived squarely from the nature of the landed settlement imposed on England by the Normans.[16] Because they also gave lords a continuing say in how their tenants' lands descended from one generation to the next, and how the members of a tenant's family could live, they were also open to exploitation by any post-conquest landholder, not least the king. William II's handling of the system in particular gave rise to grievances and complaints. Consequently, in his Coronation Charter, Henry I promised that reliefs should be 'just and lawful' and that other dues payable by a tenant-in-chief to the King would be levied fairly.[17] In practice, however, the amounts paid and payable continued to depend on the bargain an individual could strike with his lord. On one level, of course, the king was simply one lord amongst many. However, because he had more tenants than anyone else, and because those tenants were of high status, generally rich and politically important, the way he handled them dictated to a significant extent how stable his rule would be. In other words:

> what feudalism gave the king was thus military service, money, sources of patronage (in the marriage of widows and – best of all – of heiresses), and also social and political control . . . The king's exploitation of his new feudal rights was absolutely central to the workings of politics and society in the century and a half after the Conquest.[18]

Landholders were given a great deal of power over their tenants by these new arrangements. However, this was not at the expense of the king, whose power over his own barons was hugely strengthened by the way lands were held after 1066. The lands of an honour might be widely dispersed, but after 1066 the core of most honours tended to be in a single place or region. Thus, the Domesday survey records, Geoffrey de Mandeville's lands were mainly in Middlesex, Essex and Hertfordshire, whilst Geoffrey de Coutances's principal holdings were in south-western England. This meant that the lands of the post-conquest aristocracy tended to be more geographically confined than the widely dispersed lands of their Anglo-Saxon predecessors. What is more, William I was careful to ensure that no baron outside the Welsh marches was given all of the land in a particular shire; any baron wishing to expand his holdings in a particular county, therefore, would find himself confronted by rivals of similar if not equal status. And even the greatest of the Conqueror's subjects in England, his half-brothers Odo and Robert, were no match for the King in terms of landed wealth after 1066: the value of their demesne land, according to Domesday Book, was only

15 per cent of the value of the King's. The Godwinesons' lands in 1066 by contrast had been worth between 125 per cent and 140 per cent of Edward the Confessor's. Plenty of Frenchmen made their fortunes in England after 1066, and they wielded greater authority over their own tenants than most Anglo-Saxon landholders had done. Nevertheless, as far as the English King and his aristocracy were concerned, the events of the Conquest had shifted the balance of power dramatically and decisively in favour of William I and his sons.[19]

In the end, therefore, the awesome power of the Norman kings was founded on the unprecedented scale of their landholdings. However, that power was exercised in practice through the king's ability legitimately to interfere in and control the lives of his tenants. It was 'the king's position, unique in Europe, at the head of a tenurial hierarchy with all its attendant rights and revenues', which fundamentally changed the nature of English political life after 1066.[20] Before then, bonds between lords and men might have been established on a variety of bases; land was only one of these, and ties of neighbourhood, kinship as well as personal commendation might be just as important. After 1066 by contrast, whilst other factors remained significant in determining loyalty and allegiance, it was ties of mutual dependence based on land which counted far more than anything else. William I may not have set out to create a wholly new social and political system in 1066, but by 1106 this is more or less what he and his sons had done.

The English survivors

As has been seen, the native aristocracy was almost entirely dispossessed in the two decades after Hastings. Only 13 tenants-in-chief with English names are recorded in Domesday Book, and only 4 of these are in Corbett's top four classes of landholders, with lands worth more than £100 annually: Edward of Salisbury ('by a long way, the richest of the English survivors'[21]), Gospatric son of Arnkell, Thorkell of Warwick and Colswein of Lincoln. Other barons with less obviously English names may have been natives, too, but probably not many. The men in this small group tended to be either relatives of Edward the Confessor (such as Harold, the son of Earl Ralph of Hereford, who held 36 hides in Gloucestershire, Worcestershire and Warwickshire in 1086), or royal

servants and officials like Thorkell of Warwick, who may have succeeded his father as sheriff of Warwickshire, and Edward of Salisbury,
who served as sheriff of Wiltshire.[22] Other royal servants survived,
too, although not as tenants-in-chief in the new regime. Eadnoth the
Staller, for example, formerly a steward of Edward the Confessor, was
eventually killed fighting against the sons of Harold II in 1068, but
his loyalty to the new regime had secured estates for his family. His
son Hearding held lands in Somerset in 1086 and his family wielded
influence in Gloucestershire during the twelfth century.[23]

It was below this level, however, amongst the ordinary thegns, and
in the face of extensive dispossession amongst their fellow countrymen
and Norman encroachment on their lands, that the bulk of the English
survivors managed to hang on. A certain Augi was confirmed in possession of his lands in Bedfordshire by a royal writ from King William,
for example, whilst in the same shire two English burgesses of Bedford
had writs for land once held by their fathers.[24] Further afield, as Ann
Williams has shown, in counties such as Dorset, Cambridgeshire and
Shropshire, 'it was the lesser men who had managed to salvage something from the wreckage'.[25] William de Poitiers's claim that William I confirmed in their lands and offices all those Englishmen 'who submitted
to him and sought his peace', is not to be dismissed as propaganda,
because there is some evidence to support it. It must have been a peril-
ous business, however; and although clear evidence is lacking, it seems
likely that many Englishmen would have attempted to recover some if
not all of their lands soon after 1066, and deals would have been struck
either with the King or with the new French lord of those lands.

Sometimes a pragmatic motive may have been behind the decision
to allow an Englishman to hold on to his lands. Men with Anglo-
Saxon names continued to serve as sheriff, for example, as has been
seen, if only for a few years after 1066: Tofi in Somerset, Edmund
in Hertfordshire, Aethelwine in Staffordshire and Cyneweard in
Worcestershire. The new regime needed men like this, and others at this
level of local administration, who could act as huntsmen, foresters or
geld-collectors, because they knew how things worked in their regions.
Godric the steward, one of the 13 English tenants-in-chief in 1086, may
have been permitted to retain his lands because of the knowledge of
local affairs in East Anglia he had gained from administering royal

manors there before 1066.[26] Nevertheless, it is still likely that such men held on to lands only after agreeing to pay or continue paying significant sums to their new French lords for the privilege; and it was almost certain that their estates, wealth and social standing were significantly reduced as a result. Aethelric had held his lands in Marsh Gibbon in Buckinghamshire as a free tenant in 1066. He survived the upheavals of conquest and still held his lands in 1086, but of a Norman lord, William FitzAnsculf, for a rent and 'in heaviness and misery'.[27] This was 'survival with suppressed status', and it was probably the fate of the vast majority of those Englishmen who retained any part of their lands after 1066.[28]

The mechanics of settlement

In its account of the lands of Robert d'Oilly in Oxfordshire, Domesday Book records that Robert was given Ludwell by King William at the siege of St Suzanne, which took place in 1083.[29] Such a clear statement of how a tenant-in-chief came into possession of some of his lands after 1066 is rare and remarkable. It is usually much more difficult, and often impossible, to discover how English lands came into the hands of their new French lords in the years after the Norman invasion when, Orderic Vitalis declared, 'foreigners grew wealthy with the spoils of England, whilst her own sons were either shamefully slain or driven as exiles to wander hopelessly through foreign kingdoms'.[30]

Although Domesday Book reveals much about who held land in 1086, it cannot tell the whole story of how that land had been redistributed in the preceding 20 years. There is much ongoing debate about this, and there was certainly no single method of creating new estates. The Church held on to its lands after the Conquest and, as will be seen below, the position of the great religious houses, William's ecclesiastical tenants-in-chief, was clarified by the early 1070s. By contrast, the process of land distribution amongst the laity after 1066 took place over a longer period and was not so straightforward. The Norman advance across England took place broadly, and with some degree of overlap, in stages. The south-east and south-west had been brought under control by the end of 1068, and first steps had also been taken in the Welsh marches, the midlands and at York by then. Norman authority was brutally stamped on northern England in 1069–70, and long-term changes were imposed on eastern England after the fall of Earl Ralph of East Anglia in 1075.[31] There was significant Norman settlement in Yorkshire and parts of Lancashire by 1087, but whilst William II further consolidated Norman control over Yorkshire during his reign, the wider pacification of the north was arguably not even begun until after the death of Malcolm Canmore in 1091. Therefore, if the changes imposed were irreversible by 1100, they were far from complete; moreover, a chronological overview does little to explain how settlement took place.

On a grander scale, some arrangements, like those made in Sussex and the marcher earldoms, were essentially new after 1066, dictated by military needs, and cut across pre-conquest tenurial patterns. After 1066 Sussex was a frontier zone as well as the link between England and France. The strategic importance of the county for the Normans, therefore, cannot be overstated. The Domesday survey shows that, by 1086, Sussex was divided into five separate areas or 'rapes', namely Hastings, Pevensey, Lewes, Bramber and Arundel. Each was a strip of land running from the northern border of the shire to the south coast, and it has been suggested that this shape was adopted to allow the King and his followers easy access from London to the sea and, thence, to Normandy. The rapes were all organised along similar lines. Each was under the control of one of William's leading tenants: Hastings was held by Robert, count of Eu, Pevensey by Robert of Mortain, Bramber by William de Braose, Arundel by Roger de Montgomery and Lewes by William de Warenne. Each of these men was a member of the King's inner circle, and had close personal ties to the royal family. Each rape also had a major castle, which was sited near the coast. Meanwhile in the Welsh marches, that is along the frontier between England and Wales, a radical reorganisation of landholding took place which bore little or no relation to anything that had existed before 1066. Great swathes of territory based around Hereford, Shrewsbury and Chester, all of which had become earldoms by the early 1070s, were controlled respectively by William FitzOsbern (until his death in 1071), Roger de Montgomery and Hugh d'Avranches. These men were military governors, whose principal responsibilities were to protect western England from Welsh attack and to keep their volatile territories pacified. In completely discounting pre-conquest tenurial arrangements in these areas, however, problems could arise. Earl Edwin of Mercia may have revolted in 1068 because he resented the arrival of Roger de Montgomery in Shropshire and his building of a castle at Shrewsbury within Edwin's Mercian earldom.

These new units of landed administration were novel, modelled in part on arrangements current in Normandy before 1066, but created in response to the pressing military needs of the Normans during their early years in England thereafter.[32] Others who had profited from the confiscation and redistribution of estates after 1066, however, preferred to try to legitimise their claims by stressing continuity with the pre-conquest past: Robert d'Oilly, for example, married Eadgyth, the daughter of Wigod of Wallingford, and acquired his lands in Berkshire, Hertfordshire and Oxfordshire as well as an Anglo-Saxon ancestry for his family.[33] More generally, however, it has long been the prevailing view amongst historians of the Norman Conquest that most estates were allocated in this way: when an Englishman lost his lands in or after 1066, he was deemed to be the so-called 'antecessor' of a newly arrived Frenchman, who took over all of the Englishman's lands, as well as the rights and responsibilities that went with them, across the kingdom. In other words, every Frenchman who acquired lands in England after 1066 was the legitimate heir of an English predecessor. In addition, it has more recently been argued by Peter Sawyer that, as well as succeeding to the antecessor's lands, in many cases the successor also obtained the lands of the antecessor's men.[34] There is plenty of evidence in Domesday Book which supports both of these views. The list in Domesday Book of lands held by Ralph Paynel in Somerset concludes with the statement: 'These above-mentioned lands Marlswein held in the time of King Edward.' And in Middlesex, Geoffrey de Mandeville held not only all the land of his antecessor, Asgar the Staller, but also the lands held by Asgar's men in 1066. Similarly, in the same county, Walter FitzOther inherited the lands of Azur, one of Edward the Confessor's *housecarls*, as well as the lands held by Azur's men.[35] Notification of land transfers such as these, it is thought, would have been sent to the shire court by means of a royal writ.

The grant or purchase of an antecessor's lands to or by a French successor may have been characteristic of the early stages of post-conquest settlement. The great Yorkshire lordship of Conisborough, for example, which had been held by King Harold in 1066, was passed intact by

William I to one of his trusted associates, William de Warenne. It has been suggested that this happened in the aftermath of the northern revolt of 1068, both because of Conisborough's strategic importance and because it was a centre of local administration and population.[36] The ready availability of Harold's lands enabled William to meet a military and political need and reward a loyal follower. However, the idea that, in the longer term, there was more continuity than change in landholding arrangements after 1066 has been criticised, particularly by Robin Fleming. Few Norman lords received the lands of just a single antecessor, for example; so their collections of lands, their 'honours', were inevitably new creations. In addition, there were plenty of Anglo-Saxon lordships which did not survive intact in the hands of a single successor after 1066: they fragmented and descended into the possession of multiple new holders. And overall, according to Fleming, only about a fifth of all secular land descended smoothly from English antecessor to Norman successor after 1066. Such transfers had tended to dry up by the mid 1070s, moreover, in part because most wealthy English landholders had been dispossessed by then and because the spate of English revolts against Norman rule came to an end. And so whilst significant antecessorial grants could still be made, after the rebellion of 1075 for example, they necessarily became less frequent. At this point, Fleming argues, as his supply of conveniently-packaged estates began to dry up, William I began to grant land out to his followers, not by reference to antecessor, but territorially, county by county and hundred by hundred. In other words, all the lands within hundreds which had not already been allocated to a successor, and which belonged neither to the royal demesne nor the Church, were granted entirely to an individual baron. These 'hundredal' acquisitions would have formed compact lordships and consisted of the lands of several pre-conquest landholders. They would also have entailed mass dispossession at the level of the current English landholder during the second half of William's reign and massive disruption of established patterns of landholding; but Normans like William Peverel in Nottinghamshire and Henry de Ferrers in Derbyshire at least had royal approval for the acquisition of their compact honours based on castles.[37]

Such analysis has led Dr Fleming to describe 'the 1060s, 70s and 80s as a period of jarring and violent tenurial discontinuity'.[38] But whilst her examination of Domesday Book is detailed and comprehensive, the incompleteness of the record itself, and the inconsistencies and ambiguities within it, mean that there remains ample room for different readings of the same evidence. Judith Green, for example, has recently argued that the transfer of land from English into French hands was intended where possible to be both orderly and controlled; that the aim was for antecessorial succession to be the norm; and that Fleming has underestimated the degree of continuity after 1066, especially in eastern England. Nevertheless, 'where the needs of security of the new regime were at stake, however, there were radical changes'; Dr Green has the marches and the rapes in mind here.[39] It is also possible to argue, however, that the changing nature of redistribution after the early 1070s may have resulted at least in part from developments other than the reduced number of available antecessorial holdings. King William was significantly constrained in the years immediately after 1066 by his desire to stress the legitimacy of his succession and placate the surviving Anglo-Saxon nobility: Edwin, Morcar, Waltheof and others held on to their estates until they eventually forfeited them through rebellion. Only then were their lands available for redistribution. It is right to say, therefore, that 'William's need to make careful calculations between 1066 and c.1071 precluded wholesale and cataclysmic appropriation.'[40] Having abandoned his policy of conciliating the English, by the early 1070s the King was free to redistribute land on a much more extensive scale and make a statement about the permanence of the new Norman presence in England. After the estates of Edwin and Morcar were confiscated, for example, they were used to establish a protective network of great honours in Yorkshire, designed to safeguard the north from Scottish attack, under the control of Drogo de la Beuvrière at Holderness, Alan of Brittany at Richmond, Roger de Bully at Tickhill and Ilbert de Lacy at Pontefract.[41]

From this time, the King was also free finally to satisfy the greed of his own men, who had come to England to get rich. Some of them may have been growing frustrated at the relatively slow pace of change, and even begun to ask whether it was worth staying in England. This impulse might underlie Orderic Vitalis's famous description of how the wives of some of William's supporters urged their husbands to return home soon after 1066, 'adding that unless they did so with all speed they would take other husbands for themselves'. It is hard to take this account literally; but Orderic does use it in part to explain why 'the king, with so much fighting on his hands, was most anxious to keep all his knights about him, and made them a friendly offer of lands and revenues and great authority, promising them more when he had completely rid the kingdom of all his enemies'. At least two prominent Normans, Hugh de Grandmesnil and his brother-in-law Humphrey of Tilleul, could not be persuaded to stay, however.[42] And they were not the only ones to return: Gerbod left his county of Chester and went back to Flanders in 1071, and Drogo de la Beuvrière, lord of the honour of Holderness, left for home before the end of William I's reign. If more men were not to abandon him, the King needed large amounts of land quickly, and the easiest way to do this, he may have thought, was to begin making grants along administrative rather than established tenurial lines. This is important because it serves as a reminder of how varied and complex the range of motivations was amongst the Norman invaders after 1066. The King wanted security quickly, some of his followers wanted to put down roots in England and were there to stay, others wanted to take the money and run.

Whatever lay behind it, however, it seems clear that, from the early 1070s onwards there was a marked change in the scale and character of land distribution in England. Fleming's view is that the 'hundredal' acquisitions which exemplify this change account for something like a third of all the secular land transfers which had taken place by 1086. Another third is perhaps accounted for by antecessorial acquisitions and the arrangements made in the marches and the rapes, which have already been mentioned. Elsewhere, however, there is little evidence of a straightforward or even lawful transition from one group of land-holders to another. Many individual Frenchmen after 1066 appear to have been happy simply to take land and hold on to it until their possession of it could be confirmed by a higher authority. Domesday Book contains plenty of complaints about how great Norman magnates like Odo of Bayeux and Richard FitzGilbert, as well as lesser men, had obtained possession of land they were not entitled to hold. Fleming argues that in certain parts of England after 1066, there was little more than a French 'kleptocracy' in control of much of the land, and that 'these acts of private despoliation explain why the overwhelming majority of land of thousands of freemen and thegns fell to the Normans in just twenty years'.[43]

Military power

For 40 years after 1066, the rulers of England and Normandy were pre-occupied with military matters. England had to be subdued and pacified in the short term, controlled more permanently thereafter and then protected from foreign invasion. The spread of Norman power into Wales and the defence of northern England against Scottish attack could only be effected by force. Rebellion on both sides of the English Channel was a recurrent problem for William I and his sons; and the conquest of Normandy in the decade or so either side of 1100 dominated the concerns of William II and Henry I. In these circumstances, the martial abilities of the kings themselves were severely tested, as were the resources available to them in the pursuit of their military objectives. Few aspects of the Norman Conquest have generated more debate amongst historians than the ways in which the military structures of late eleventh-century England and Normandy were developed and adapted to meet the challenges of cross-Channel rule.

Military organisation was therefore crucial to the success of the Norman Conquest. With strong armies, the kings could defeat their internal and external enemies on campaign. With enduring symbols of military power and might, they could intimidate them into lasting submission. The most potent of such symbols was the castle. As has been seen already in Chapter 2, castles were not built by the Anglo-Saxons, whilst their use in Normandy, although more common, may not have been as widespread before 1066 as has been traditionally thought. Duke William's first acts on landing in England, however, were the erection of fortified structures at Pevensey and Hastings. More such structures were then built as he proceeded to London after his victory over Harold. In 1068–9, castles were constructed on the King's orders as far apart as Exeter and York, with many in between, as William travelled across England. Greatest of all were the huge stone keep at Colchester and the White Tower at London. There is no good reason to doubt Orderic Vitalis's famous assertion about the contribution of castle-building to the ultimate success of the Norman Conquest: before 1066, 'such fortified structures were scarcely known in the English provinces, and so the English – in spite of their courage and love of fighting – could put up only a weak resistance to their enemies'.[44]

During the period immediately after 1066, most castles in England would have been simple structures made of earth and timber, and the most common form was the motte and bailey. The motte was a mound made of earth and surrounded by a ditch. On top of the motte, or even built into the structure of the motte in more complicated cases, a wooden fortification of some kind would usually be erected, perhaps a tower surrounded by a palisade. The Bayeux Tapestry depicts several mottes: in France, at Dol, Rennes and Dinan in Brittany, and at Bayeux in Normandy; and in England, where men are shown building the castle at Hastings on Duke William's orders immediately after the Normans' landing.[45] The bailey was the area immediately surrounding the motte, which would be protected by a wooden palisade on top of an embankment. Although the motte and bailey is the type of castle most frequently associated with the Norman Conquest, however, it was not the only kind of castle built in England after 1066. There were also ringworks: defended enclosures, banked and fenced, with structures of some kind, perhaps a tower or a fortified house, inside them. William FitzOsbern's great keep at Chepstow is essentially an elaborate ringwork – a motte was not deemed necessary presumably because the enclosed keep was so well defended naturally, high on a promontory overlooking the river Wye.

Still more castles were built by the Conqueror's sons, by Robert Curthose at Newcastle in 1080–1, for example, and by William II at Carlisle from 1092; and stone curtain walls and keeps gradually began to replace earth banks and timber stockades. However, castles were not exclusively royal creations. In the marcher earldoms and in the Sussex rapes, castles were built by the men with delegated responsibility for the area. William FitzOsbern's keep at Chepstow and William de Warenne's towering double motte at Lewes are testaments to their determination and staying power. Great men in general, too, like Count Alan of Brittany at Richmond in Yorkshire, preferred to set the seal on their local power with the construction of a castle. The king, of course, had to try to ensure that private castles were constructed only within limits set by him, but this was a secondary concern in the early years after

1066 as the King and his followers sought to tighten their grip on England. Indeed, 'in the early days after 1066, there can have been no objection and every encouragement to building castles, as the Normans needed all the help they could get to make their rule secure'.[46] The fifty or so castles recorded in Domesday Book were almost certainly only a fraction of the ones completed or under construction by 1086; and 'by the end of the Conqueror's reign he and his great vassals had literally dug themselves in and planted their castles across the length and breadth of the lands to rivet their rule upon it'. It has been estimated that there were probably about five hundred castles of one form or another in England by the start of the twelfth century.[47]

As urban areas were ruthlessly cleared to make way for them, castles became permanent signs of Norman domination to a hostile and restless native population: 'built by English labour, paid for by English taxes and dues, lived in by Frenchmen, these were the monuments of a deeply divided society'. The *Anglo-Saxon Chronicle*'s obituary of William I concludes with the comment that, 'He had castles built and poor men hard oppressed.' And when William II's sheriff of Worcestershire, Urse d'Abetot, constructed his castle so close to the monastery in Worcester that its moat caused part of the monastic cemetery to collapse, Bishop Ealdred's response was famously uncompromising: 'You are called Urse, receive God's curse.'[48] However, castles were more than simply blunt instruments of oppression. Managed by a reliable castellan and manned by a professional garrison made up often of household troops, they were important as places which could be retreated to and defended in times of revolt, as centres of local government and administration, as focal points for settlement, as bases for further advance, and as store-houses for royal treasure. But castles came into their own in wartime: controlling one's own and taking control of the enemy's were essential if victory was to be achieved, as William II found in 1088 and Henry I in 1101.

Armies and fleets

The castle has been seen as an essential element of 'the feudal system' which the Normans, according to some, introduced into England after 1066. The castle 'belongs uniquely to feudal society as the creation and manifestation thereof', it has been argued, because they were the focal points of a lord's power and because their offensive and defensive effectiveness depended on them being manned by that other prerequisite of feudalism, contingents of armed and mounted warriors who held their lands from their lords.[49] Historians tend now to be less categorical about such matters; discussions about what constitute the essentials of 'the feudal system' are now unfashionable. Nevertheless, castles and troops were important, and the ability to raise and deploy military power was central to any ruler's concerns. After 1066, as has been seen, the king's tenants-in-chief were obliged to provide him with mounted knights to fight in the royal army or to garrison royal castles. It is generally thought that, once summoned to serve, tenants were obliged to stay with their lord's force for 40 days, although the precise length of service is not known for certain.

The Latin term for the total number of knights owed to the king by his barons was the *servitium debitum* (literally 'service owed'). A fixed, specified number of knights (a 'quota') seems to have been requested by William I early on in his reign, perhaps by 1070, from his ecclesiastical tenants-in-chief, the great cathedrals and abbeys. It has already been seen that the number of knights expected from lay tenants-in-chief was ill-defined and flexible in the immediate aftermath of 1066, and that the process of fixing their quotas was a much slower business. As land came into the king's possession after 1066 through rebellion, forfeiture and failure of heirs, he could redistribute it and make individual arrangements as to the amount of 'knight service' due from his new tenants. Some quotas were small; only one or two knights were owed by some lay tenants-in-chief, but most in the beginning appear to have been fixed in multiples of five or ten. Once these deals were struck and quotas were imposed, a tenant-in-chief then had to be sure he could fulfil his military obligations to the king when called upon to do so. He might simply hire knights to serve with him and the king when service was demanded or, like Abbot Adelelm of Abingdon (1071–83), he might maintain a corps of paid troops permanently in his own household. But this was expensive and the knights might be difficult to control. In the end, Adelelm granted his knights land and allowed them to settle in return for the continued provision of military service.

As time went on, therefore, and as conditions in England became more settled, most knights were probably recruited in this way, from the ranks of those sub-tenants to whom the tenant-in-chief had granted estates.[50] However, as lands changed hands and were further divided up, the situation gradually became more complicated: individual land-holders might owe a fraction of a knight, for example, which begins to hint at the increasingly notional character of these obligations. By 1100, however, there was almost certainly a more-or-less fixed number of mounted knights whose service the king was 'owed' by his tenants-in-chief. Orderic's estimate that the king was owed 60,000 knights on this basis is surely a gross exaggeration; the real figure was probably no higher than 5,000.[51] But the *servitium debitum* was probably considerably greater than any force the king in wartime would actually need. There is certainly no evidence that the entire *servitium debitum* ever turned up for service in England or Normandy. For one thing, it would be difficult for a lord to provide the service of half a knight if he owed, say, five and a half for his lands. It fulfilled another purpose, however, as the basis upon which payments of scutage could be assessed, and the king's position as a lord with many rich barons enabled him intensively to raise those 'feudal incidents' discussed previously.[52]

Another question concerns the extent to which the military changes imposed on England influenced the military system already in existence in Normandy. As has been seen in a previous chapter, theories that Normandy was 'one of the most developed feudal societies in Europe' by 1066, that the military duties of the duke's great men were precisely formulated and regularly enforced by then, and that this fully-fledged system was imposed on England almost at a stroke after 1066, have been largely discredited.[53] And even those who have argued for the relatively advanced nature of Normandy's 'feudal' development before 1066 have accepted that the process of formalising the military obligations owed by the Norman magnates to their duke had, at best, only just begun by then.[54] To be sure, the solutions the Norman kings found to their military problems in England were derived in part from those arrangements with which they were already familiar. But the establishment in the newly conquered kingdom of fixed quotas and tenure by knight service across the landholding classes was a novel, pragmatic response to particular military, political and financial needs. Normandy did not experience such needs so intensely as England after 1066, and thereafter land continued to be held on a variety of bases whilst 'ties of personal dependence could be expressed in many ways'.[55] So, just as the pace of change in other areas (government and administration, for example) was slower in Normandy than in England after 1066 because there was no need for it to quicken, it seems likely that changes in military organisation also took longer to occur in the duchy because no compelling urgency prompted their rapid imposition. Norman knightly quotas with their attendant rights and responsibilities, it seems, were not being fixed precisely until the 1120s or 1130s; and when they were, England provided the model.[56]

The Norman kings introduced significant new elements into the ways English armies were organised, and these changes eventually had an impact on the Norman military system, too. Nevertheless, it is very important to remember that key elements of the military systems of both England and Normandy did not change after 1066, that ' "feudal military service" was never the only military service owed, let alone performed, in post-conquest England and Normandy, and that those who served William I and his sons were not all members of a noble élite'.[57] After 1066 the core of the king-duke's army in wartime, on both sides of the Channel, was still made up of the knights of his household and the household knights of his great men. Some of these men might have been tenants of their lord, but they were not necessarily so: some would have served for wages, and others in the hope of future reward of some kind. This system would have been familiar to the Anglo-Saxon kings, who relied on their *housecarls*. So would the service of the *fyrd*, which the Norman kings continued to use, probably in the same way as their predecessors, with local areas fulfilling their traditional obligations to select troops for the royal army, perhaps one warrior per five hides of land, as in Berkshire before 1066. William I used Englishmen in his armies in Maine in 1073 and 1081, and in the army which fought against Robert Curthose at Gerberoi in 1079; William II summoned the *fyrd* to serve in Normandy in 1094, and Henry I had English troops in his army at Tinchebray.[58]

Naval power and mercenary troops were also important. The *Anglo-Saxon Chronicle* records how, in 1072, 'King William led a naval force and a land force to Scotland and blockaded that country from the sea with ships.' And in 1088, Robert Curthose's plans to invade England were ruined when an advance party was wiped out by 'the English, who guarded the sea'.[59] As for mercenaries, they remained key members of royal armies during this period. The men in the contingents from Maine, Brittany and Flanders who fought with Duke William at Hastings had been paid. William II and Robert Curthose were notorious for lavishing huge sums on their mercenaries; and hired contingents from Brittany and Maine were crucial to Henry I's success in the Battle of Tinchebray in 1106. There was nothing dishonourable or inappropriate about this; it was realistic military leadership. The knights sent by Archbishop Anselm of Canterbury to fight with William II in Wales in 1097 were useless as, in the King's opinion, they were 'not properly trained nor suitable for war'. And in 1094, having summoned 20,000 troops from the *fyrd* to serve with him in Normandy, the same king had simply sent them home once he had relieved them of the ten shillings they had each been given for their daily expenses. This money was probably used to pay experienced professional soldiers, who would always be more attractive to a general than the potentially ramshackle outfits that his barons and other subjects might produce.[60]

The military system that emerged to meet the needs of England and Normandy after 1066 was a hybrid comprised of established and novel elements. Some of those elements, such as the *fyrd*, were inherited from pre-conquest England and others, most notably castles, were imported from ducal Normandy. The system also developed over time in response to circumstances to take on a character of its own. In the past, historians have sought to locate the origins of such institutions as the marcher earldoms and the rapes of Sussex, and devices such as fixed quotas of knight service, in pre-conquest Normandy. More recently, however, less emphasis has been placed on the obvious directness of such links, and the originality of these solutions to immediate and pressing problems has been stressed. They all reflect the predominantly military priorities of the new rulers of England after 1066. It is impossible to know how the military structures of England and Normandy might have evolved had the invasion of 1066 failed or never taken place. Technological change, which would affect the way wars, battles and campaigns were fought in the twelfth and thirteenth centuries, followed hard upon population growth, increased pressure on land and the spread of markets. Neither territory would have remained immune to these wider trends. Nevertheless, what happened on either side of the Channel after 1066, particularly in England, was a largely self-contained phenomenon. In response to a particular set of circumstances, and with striking rapidity, a unique system of military organisation emerged.

'Feudal' England?

The Norman Conquest affected England more immediately, more profoundly and more diversely than it did Wales, Scotland or Normandy. After 1066, the English were ruled by a new French-speaking aristocracy; the English landscape was dominated by new styles of military and ecclesiastical architecture; and England was linked to continental Europe through political, economic and cultural links more directly than ever before. There was something more important than any of this, however, according to J.H. Round, writing over a century ago: 'in approaching the consideration of the institutional changes and modifications of policy resulting from the Norman Conquest, the most conspicuous phenomenon to attract attention is undoubtedly the introduction of what it is convenient to term the feudal system'.[61]

The words 'feudal' and 'feudalism' have appeared regularly in this chapter, although they have usually been safely confined within quotation marks. It is hard to avoid them in any discussion of the way society functioned in post-conquest England. They are easy to use carelessly, however, and it is important to clarify what they might mean. Unfortunately, settled definitions of such controversial terms have never been agreed. For his part, by 'the feudal system', Round meant a structure of landholding and of military and social organisation, imported more or less intact from Normandy, wherein one man (the tenant or 'vassal') received some land (a 'fief') from another (the 'lord'), performed homage to him and undertook to provide him with military service expressed in terms of a fixed number of mounted warriors or knights. The tenant could in turn grant all or part of the lands he had received from his lord to his own 'sub-tenants', who could in due course find tenants of their own. For over half a century after Round put forward his famous thesis, historians accepted and depended upon it without much serious question. As late as 1969, for example, R. Allen Brown asserted that 'the introduction of feudalism into England . . . must be listed among the most important results of the Norman

Conquest'.[62] However, since the 1960s, serious doubts have been raised about the validity of 'feudalism' as a concept; and the idea that the Normans simply imposed on England, almost overnight, a wholly new system of landholding and military organisation has looked increasingly unconvincing. By 1986, J.C. Holt felt able to write that: 'We seem no longer to believe in feudalism, let alone the notion that it was established at a single stroke'; and, according to John Gillingham, 'the notion that the Normans introduced a new framework of lordship, the "feudal system" or "feudalism" is a myth'.[63]

Concepts of 'feudalism', it appeared, had become a dangerous obstacle in the way of a genuine understanding of what really happened in England and Normandy after 1066. And it should be clear by now that the 'perfect feudal pyramid' as constructed by Round and others is far too simplistic a device to do justice to the intricacies of politics, society and landholding in post-conquest England. Having said this, there are examples in the Domesday survey and elsewhere from the later eleventh century which largely comply with this basic model. In Oxfordshire, Domesday Book records, 'Berengar de Tosny holds of the king twenty hides in Broughton, and Robert and Reginald and Gilbert hold of him'; in Middlesex, 'William FitzAnsculf holds Cranford of the king and Hugh holds of him'; and in Somerset, 'Matthew [de Mortagne] holds of the king in Clevedon and Ildebert holds of him'.[64] There are other moments of clarity, too. With so much of post-conquest England under the control of the Church, for example, it was certain that the King would want reliable men in charge of its extensive and widely scattered resources. By the early 1070s, therefore, the obligations of these religious houses to the king were already being clearly defined. According to the twelfth-century *Book of Ely*, by about 1072, 'King William had given orders to both the abbots and the bishops of all England that their obligations regarding military provision should be fulfilled, [and] he laid down that, from then on, garrisons for the king of England were to be paid for, as a perpetual legal requirement, out of their resources, with a view to military campaigning.'[65] The bishops and abbots were the King's ecclesiastical tenants-in-chief and a fixed, specified quota of knights was demanded by William in return for their lands. Another example of the system in practice is given by a writ addressed by the King to the abbot of Evesham, probably in about 1072, instructing him to come to the King with the five knights that he owed.[66] The size of a quota for a particular church, usually in multiples of five or ten (perhaps a legacy of the five-hide system used by the Anglo-Saxon kings), appears to have been fixed arbitrarily by the King. It would have depended on a number of factors: the extent of the land in question, the wealth of the church, its strategic significance and favouritism. Glastonbury and Peterborough may have owed 60 knights each, for example, not just because their estates were large but because they were the main centres of authority in the potentially turbulent Somerset marshes and Fenlands of East Anglia.

The imposition of military quotas on the lay tenants-in-chief, however, as has been seen, was a much more gradual, piecemeal process. Outside the ranks of the ecclesiastical tenants-in-chief, indeed, the picture painted by Domesday Book in particular is both complex and incomplete. The lands of individual lords and tenants might be concentrated in one part of the kingdom and scattered across the rest. At the same time, a single individual might hold different pieces of land from different lords; the tenant of one lord might be the lord of his own tenants elsewhere; or a tenant who held one piece of land from a lord might have the lord as his tenant for another. With such intricacies inherent in the system, it is very difficult to reduce it to a single paradigm. What is more, Domesday Book does not give a comprehensive picture of the state of landed society in 1086: the names of innumerable individuals who occupied land below the highest levels of propertied society are largely unrecorded.[67] Given such difficulties, it is impossible to arrive at definitive or general conclusions about what happened to tenurial structures and the ownership of land after 1066; and so entirely to dismiss the idea of change after 1066 would be just as misleading as the idea that William arrived in England in 1066 with a feudal blueprint in his tunic pocket.

It is also important to remember that, by the end of the eleventh century, parts of England were only just being exposed to Norman influence. After overcoming the challenges he faced in Yorkshire at the start of his reign, William I had brought the area firmly under royal control by 1087; and, as Paul Dalton has shown, the extent of Norman settlement and control there was considerable.[68] William II, perhaps prompted by his experiences of colonisation in Cumbria in 1092, and assisted by having in his possession the lands of those who had rebelled against him in 1095, took this process further. Holderness and Tickhill were given to two of the sons of Roger de Montgomery, Arnulf and Robert de Bellême. Other estates in Yorkshire were granted by Rufus to Robert de Stuteville around Thirsk, Kirkby Malzeard and Burton in Lonsdale, for example, and castles had been built at all these places by 1130. Another Yorkshire lordship was granted to Guy de Balliol in upper Teesdale, and the construction of a great castle was begun by him at Barnard. Overall, 'the Yorkshire honours reorganised or created by William Rufus formed a network of castleries extending from the southern fringe of the North Yorkshire Moors in the east, to Lonsdale and the Ribble Valley in the west'.[69] Further north, a vast lordship was given to another of the sons of Roger de Montgomery, Roger the Poitevin, in what was to become Lancashire: this was 'another great march to buttress Norman power in the north-west'.[70] Despite this, however, the Norman hold on much of northern England, on Cumbria, Northumberland and Durham in particular, remained tenuous and Rufus's achievements have been described as 'fragile and easily reversible'.[71] The process of subjecting these areas to southern control and of fully incorporating them into royal government had barely begun by the time Henry I became king. What is more, whilst for those amongst the English who weathered the storm of conquest the trauma of losing family, friends, lands and status must have been intense, the fact is that, albeit in new and frightening circumstances, most of the native population did survive. And it is worth remembering that 'in all this confusion the continuation at the level of the shire of an English community did not merely ease the conquerors into their new territories; it also ensured the continuance of English customs and traditions'.[72]

None of this should be read as an attempt to minimise the significance of what occurred across England in the 40 years or so after 1066, however. During that period it is beyond question that there was a revolution in English landholding. It did not happen everywhere to the same extent; but if the Normans' advance into northern England took time, their takeover of southern and midland England was rapid and comprehensive. The old earldoms disappeared and one ruling group was entirely displaced by another. Long-established patterns of landholding and time-honoured relationships between landholders, their tenants and their families were simply ignored and overridden, sometimes with a veneer of legality to justify the change, but often with violence and probably, it is easy to think, with an air of superiority and disdain on the part of the new arrivals. The extent to which this revolution can helpfully be described as 'feudal' remains open to question. Nevertheless, as has been seen, there were developments in the organisation of landholding and society in England after 1066 which were 'still immensely significant'.[73] In post-conquest England, chains of mutual obligation based on tenurial relationships and nothing else were forged between the king, his barons and their tenants; and, for all the progress towards establishing hereditary rights in land, estates could not be passed from one generation to the next without the permission of a superior lord. In Anglo-Saxon England, one man might be loyal to another and serve him for a number of reasons. In Anglo-Norman England, by contrast, service was owed by one man to another usually because the former had been given lands by the latter. This gave the king and other landholders much more power over their tenants and their families than their Anglo-Saxon predecessors had ever enjoyed over their men, and much more than they had enjoyed in France before 1066. They could interfere with and manipulate the descent of land – the defining currency of status and wealth control the lives of rich widows, heirs and heiresses, and so make or break the fortunes of those who wished to make their way up the ladder of Anglo-Norman society. It was this 'tenurial content to lordship' which made the changes to landholding caused by the Norman Conquest so important and which changed the ways in which politics and society functioned after 1066.[74]

Wales and Scotland

The sorts of radical social, political and economic change which affected England after 1066 were not replicated in Wales to anything like the same extent; and in Scotland hardly at all before the middle third of the twelfth century. This was because 'the conquest of Wales and Scotland was no part of William's plan' in 1066, and because the achievements of his sons there by the early 1100s, whilst significant, were limited.[75] Nevertheless, Wales and Scotland were deeply and permanently changed by the arrival of the Normans in Britain; and England, too, entered into a new phase in its continuously troubled relationship with its closest neighbours.

Harold and Tostig Godwineson's invasion of Wales in 1063 had come to a successful end with the death of Gruffudd ap Llewelyn at the hands of his own men and the installation of two of his half-brothers, Bleddyn and Rhiwallon, as puppet rulers of Gwynedd and Powys respectively. They 'swore oaths and gave hostages' to King Edward and Earl Harold 'promising that they would be faithful to him [*sic*] in everything'.[76] When William I became king three years later, therefore, and in so far as he thought about Wales at all at this stage, he probably would have assumed an entitlement to the same overlordship there as Edward and Harold had enjoyed. The situation in Wales in 1066, however, was more complicated than William might have appreciated. Bleddyn and Rhiwallon may have controlled Gwynedd and Powys, but Deheubarth was in the hands of Maredudd ab Owain and Glamorgan was ruled by Cadwgan ap Meurig. After the brief period when more or less the whole of Wales had acknowledged the authority of Gruffudd ap Llewelyn, therefore, the land was politically fragmented once again. Traditionally, this was how the rulers of England had preferred Wales to be; but in 1066 'the spirit of the Welsh was still unbroken and their independence was scarcely less ample than before'.[77] Already in 1065, the hunting lodge built by Earl Harold at Portskewett had been destroyed by Caradog ap Gruffudd, another ambitious Welsh princeling, and in 1067 Bleddyn and Rhiwallon were to be found fighting with Eadric 'the Wild' against the Normans, whilst Bleddyn also joined in with the rebellion of Edwin and Morcar in 1068. The Welsh were certainly not intending to submit quietly to the Norman newcomers; their arrival presented rivals for power within Wales with an opportunity to further their own political and military objectives.

William's first priority as far as Wales was concerned, therefore, was to keep the frontier with England stable and secure. It was in order to do this that he sent some of his most trusted lieutenants to the border between England and Wales to establish Norman authority there. Perhaps as early as 1067, William FitzOsbern was sent to Herefordshire where he assumed responsibility for much of the southern frontier or 'march'. After the King himself had visited Chester in 1069–70, he gave control of the county, and of the northern march with Wales, first, to a

Fleming, Gerbod and shortly after to Hugh d'Avranches, who was also given the title of earl. Similarly, by 1071, Roger de Montgomery had become earl of Shrewsbury and been given control over Shropshire and the middle march. It was the job of these men to stop Welsh encroachment into English territory: to put a stop to the sort of raiding that had so troubled Edward the Confessor in the 1050s, and which was threatening to become a problem once again. It was not their job to conquer Wales. However, the Norman governors of these marcher lordships of Chester, Shropshire and Hereford were ambitious men. Their brief may have been to protect the areas under their direct control; but it is not surprising that they saw attack as the best form of defence, and they all made significant advances into Welsh territory. With royal acquiescence and approval usually given at a distance if at all, 'the Norman conquest of Wales was rarely more than the sum of individual baronial enterprises'.[78] By the time he died in 1071, William FitzOsbern had successfully invaded Gwent, and he had begun the construction of a line of castles extending from Wigmore in the north through Clifford, Ewyas Harold and Monmouth to his great castle at Chepstow in the south. In so doing, by installing his men to control them, and by encouraging the establishment of settlement around them, 'he had sketched out the strategy for the subjugation of south-east Wales'.[79] Only when William's son Roger de Breteuil failed in his rebellion against William I in 1075 did the Norman advance into south Wales falter somewhat; but after King William's visit to St David's in 1081 the new ruler of south Wales, Rhys ap Tewdwr, acknowledged his subordination to the English King by agreeing to pay him tribute. Domesday Book records towards the start of its section on Herefordshire that Rhys made an annual payment to the King of £40.[80] This laid a platform for further Norman progress in south Wales later in the century.

In the central march from the early 1070s, meanwhile, Roger de Montgomery was also beginning the Norman advance from the castle he constructed at Montgomery. He and his men worked together to harry the Welsh and extend their control down the Severn valley into Powys. When he died in 1094, Norman control of central Wales was a realistic prospect. But it was in north Wales that the most spectacular early progress was made by the Normans, as a result of the efforts of Earl Hugh of Chester and his cousin Robert de Tilleul, more usually known as Robert of Rhuddlan. Hugh attracted the attention of contemporaries for more than his military achievements alone: he was extravagantly generous to his followers, and his appetite for women, fighting and food was huge, as was his sheer physical size by the time of his death. He was a ferocious fighter, though, known to the Welsh as Hugh 'the Wolf'. As for Robert of Rhuddlan, he is 'the exemplar of the swashbuckling Norman warrior: endless in ambition, pride and greed, combining the most ruthless butchery with the most conventional piety, insatiable in his lust for adventure and battle'.[81] Together they extended their control over north Wales westwards from Chester and beyond the river Clwyd from the castle the King ordered them to build at Rhuddlan in about 1073. It was from this base that Robert assumed the leading role in the further extension of Norman power into north Wales. He had built another castle at Deganwy on the river Conwy by about 1078 and, in due course, Robert came to claim the right to rule over the whole of north Wales. The ruler of Gwynedd since 1075, Trahaearn ap Caradog, had been killed at the battle of Mynydd Carn in 1081. Gruffudd ap Cynan, Trahaearn's rival for control of Gwynedd, who had emerged victorious from the battle along with Rhys ap Tewdwr, was subsequently captured and imprisoned by Earl Hugh. Robert of Rhuddlan was now able to fill the power vacuum caused by these events, and Domesday Book records how, by 1086, he held 'North Wales' from the King for an annual payment of £40.[82] He was, in effect, the first non-Welsh prince of Gwynedd.

When Robert of Rhuddlan died at the hands of the Welsh, probably in 1093, Earl Hugh was able to take up where his cousin had left off in north Wales. A Breton, Hervé, had already been appointed bishop of Bangor in 1092; Hugh also began the construction of a castle there, and of another on Anglesey. During the 1090s, however, as has been seen in Chapter 6, the Normans also suffered serious reverses across Wales, particularly in the north at the hands of the now freed Gruffudd ap Cynan, and Cadwgan ap Bleddyn ap Cynfyn of Powys. The events of 1093–4, 1098 and 1102 meant that any chance of there being a complete conquest of Wales was ruined for the time being. Norman gains proved permanent, however, not just because of the castles they imposed on the Welsh landscape, but also because of the changes they made to the social and economic infrastructures of the Welsh lands they came to control. Norman achievements in Wales in the four decades after

1066 were not just the work of the great marcher lords of Hereford, Shropshire and Chester. The achievements of men like Robert FitzHaimon in Glamorgan, Bernard de Neufmarché in Brecon and Arnulf of Montgomery in Pembrokeshire showed what could still be accomplished by those with a sufficiently remorseless drive to succeed. All of these great men relied in turn on their own followers, however, to hold down territory and impose Norman rule; to do 'the detailed work of conquest'.[83] Orderic Vitalis records, and Domesday Book confirms, how the whole of the county of Chester was held of the King by Earl Hugh in 1086, and how all the other landholders in the county were therefore Hugh's men. A similar situation existed in Shropshire, where most of the leading men of the county were Earl Roger's tenants.[84] As they moved beyond the lands they had been granted on the English side of the frontier, moreover, the swathes of Welsh territory claimed by their lords were also divided up between such subordinates, and feudal ties were used to bind these pioneers together in a common enterprise. By 1135, the Vale of Glamorgan was divided into knights' fees on the English model: this process was almost certainly begun by Robert FitzHaimon in the 1090s; Bernard de Neufmarché did something similar in his lordship of Brecon.[85]

As in England, moreover, the main instruments of domination and of colonisation in the marches and beyond were the castles. These acted as centres of military and political power, and as bases from which to progress deeper into Welsh territory; but they were also magnets for trade and settlement. Boroughs were soon established around the castles built at Cardiff and Brecon, for example; whilst at Rhuddlan by 1086, there were 18 burgesses.[86] The Normans and their followers in Wales did not just gather in safe clusters around their castles, however. Much of the Welsh countryside was colonised, too. This was not so much the case in the more hostile and relatively unproductive uplands of north Wales, but in lowland south Wales the soil was more fertile and the prospects more enticing. Even more so than in England, the means by which such settlement occurred are obscure; doubtless violence and expropriation of the native population played a part. Most of the newcomers were certainly not Welsh. Most famous are the Flemings who settled in Dyfed in the first decade of the twelfth century, after escaping difficult circumstances in their native lands. The mass of the settlers in rural Wales by the end of the twelfth century, however, would have been English; and many of these had probably been imported from a lord's English estates. In the areas they colonised, known as 'Englishries', manorial structures with villages and churches began to develop; in those neighbouring areas, or 'Welshries', where the Welsh remained in possession (or perhaps to where they had been forced to go if the settlers thought some lands more attractive than others), scattered farms and settlements remained the norm, and Welsh customs and usages remained in force.

The Normans' attempt to control Wales in the 40 years or so after 1066 shared many of the characteristics of their attempt to subjugate England. Military power based on the castle was central to their strategy in both lands, as was the sharing out of land amongst those who had played a part in its seizure. However, the Normans' experience in Wales was also very different from their English one. Most obviously, the king was directly involved in the process of conquest only occasionally – William I in 1081, William II in 1095 and 1097, Henry I in 1102; it was a predominantly baronial enterprise with little if any overall or centrally controlled direction. There was certainly no attempt in any way to incorporate Wales into a wider English kingdom. In Wales, unlike England, moreover, the Norman newcomers had to deal with an aristocracy that had not been almost entirely wiped out by the early 1070s. This meant that the Normans in Wales had to be flexible and adaptable in their dealings with the native Welsh rulers and their extended families. Sometimes they attempted to play off one Welsh prince against another. In 1072, for example, Caradog ap Gruffudd defeated the ruler of Deheubarth, Maredudd ab Owain with the help of the 'French' in his army; whilst in 1075 Gruffudd ap Cynan seized control of Gwynedd from Trahaearn ap Caradog (albeit only for a short time), with the help of Robert of Rhuddlan.[87] This did not prevent Robert and Hugh d'Avranches thinking it prudent to capture and imprison their erstwhile ally Gruffudd after his victory at Mynydd Carn in 1081, however. Gruffudd's turbulent career can be contrasted to some degree with that of Rhys ap Tewdwr, who ruled largely peacefully in Deheubarth as a pliable client-king of the Normans until his death in 1093. Only Robert of Rhuddlan in Gwynedd actually managed to take the place of a native Welsh ruler; but his success did not outlast him and a resurgent

Gruffudd ap Cynan eventually came to dominate north Wales. Most importantly, however, in Wales unlike in England, the process of conquest was never completed by the Normans and large parts of the country remained in the hands of native Welsh rulers until the end of the thirteenth century. Nevertheless, despite their inability to make the most of the circumstances they had created by the early 1090s, the Normans left an indelible mark on Wales. In Scotland, meanwhile, events followed a different course again.

By 1093, William I and William II had done little themselves to extend direct Norman rule into Scotland. In 1072 at Abernethy, Malcolm III had been bullied into making a formal submission to the English King. He became William's vassal and gave him hostages, the *Anglo-Saxon Chronicle* records, although it is unlikely that this meant much more in practice than a vague acceptance of overlordship. Malcolm did something similar in 1091, when he 'came to our king [William II] and became his tenant to the extent of such allegiance as he had done to his father, and confirmed it with an oath'.[88] Malcolm, a man 'of the greatest ferocity and with a bestial deposition', Symeon of Durham claimed, had invaded northern England on numerous occasions since becoming king in the 1050s.[89] Both of these English expeditions to the north were made in response to such attacks and as reminders to Malcolm that he would always struggle to make permanent gains at the expense of a strong English king. Beyond requiring such occasional acknowledgements of superiority, however, the first two Norman kings showed no appetite for asserting themselves more forcefully over their Scottish neighbour. William II seized Cumbria in 1092, ejected Dolfin who ruled there under the authority of the king of Scots, had began the construction of a castle at Carlisle and the settlement of Cumbria with peasants from the south. It has also been suggested that these events may have spurred Rufus on to the establishment of a series of new lordships in Northumberland and Cumbria, as well as those he established in Yorkshire which have already been mentioned.[90] Ranulf le Meschin, who was eventually made earl of Chester by Henry I, may have been one of a series of 'strong men' appointed to govern in Cumbria by Rufus after 1092.[91] But their power there was considerably less extensive than that enjoyed by Ranulf's uncle, Hugh d'Avranches, in his lordship of Chester. Earl Robert de Mowbray of Northumbria exercised extensive authority between the rivers Tyne and Tweed during the first half of the 1090s, and it was at the hands of his men that Malcolm III was finally killed in 1093. Nevertheless, with a Norman rival for influence in the north like Bishop William de St Calais of Durham, Earl Robert was not dominant in his earldom in the way that Roger de Montgomery or Hugh d'Avranches were in theirs. There were no Anglo-Scottish equivalents of the Anglo-Welsh marcher earldoms.

Defence of the frontier was the first priority for Ranulf and Robert. They may have tried to consolidate their power within the areas they were given to control by the King; but, unlike their Welsh marcher colleagues, they were not able to take their men into lands beyond those limits. Perhaps this was too difficult; Malcolm III was an experienced and wily opponent. But perhaps it was more because Scotland, unlike Wales, was a single kingdom and the Normans respected that. Political circumstances did not necessarily mean that there was no English or Norman influence in Scotland before 1093, however. When Malcolm III was killed in that year, his brother Donald Bàn was chosen as king and the Scots, in what was almost certainly a reaction against Malcolm's English queen, Margaret (who died within a week of Malcolm's death), 'drove out all the English who had been with king Malcolm'.[92] How substantial this English presence was is impossible to say. Meanwhile Duncan, Malcolm's eldest son from his first marriage, who had lived in comfortable captivity as a hostage in Normandy and England for over 20 years, secured William II's backing and English military assistance for an attempt to overthrow Donald Bàn. Whether Rufus had the deposition of Macbeth in mind here is unclear; if he did think about the events of 1054–5, he must have assumed that Duncan II would be easier for him to control than Malcolm III had been for Edward the Confessor and William I. Duncan did manage to wrest the kingship from his uncle's grasp, and he was allowed to remain as king by the Scots, John of Worcester claims, 'on condition that he would no longer bring English or Normans into Scotland and allow them to serve him'.[93] This certainly supports the idea that there was a resented foreign presence within Scotland before 1093. However, despite this agreement, Duncan II was soon ousted and killed by Donald Bàn and his supporters.

Rufus's first attempt to install a cooperative, dependent and manifestly subordinate king of Scots as Malcolm's successor failed, therefore, and there seemed every chance by the end of 1094 that the tension, suspicion and hostility which had characterised the relations between England and Scotland during the eleventh century would continue. By the end of 1097, however, the situation had been transformed. Donald Bàn was deposed by an English force under Edgar *atheling*, acting on William II's orders, and another of Malcolm III's sons, Edgar, was installed, this time successfully, as king of Scots.[94] This time there was no native Scottish response, and as a result of these developments, the entire tone of the relationship between the rulers of the northern and southern British kingdoms changed. Both Duncan and Edgar had spent much of their early lives at the court of the English kings, the former as a hostage and the latter as a political exile. Both would have been exposed as young men to the ways of Anglo-Norman politics, culture and society. They would also have been impressed by the obvious strength and wealth of the English king. When they were returned to power in Scotland with English help, it was probably with a clear sense of the debt they owed their overwhelmingly powerful southern neighbour. Before he went to Scotland in 1093, Duncan visited William II and 'did such homage as the king wished to have from him'. Similarly, in 1097, Edgar was 'established as king in allegiance to King William'.[95] Anglo-Norman settlement on and beyond the borders of Scotland had barely begun by the early twelfth century, however, and the story of that process belongs to the latter part of the reign of Henry I and that of his Scottish counterpart and protégé David I (1124–53). But the events of the 1090s and early 1100s were crucial in laying a platform for what was to come.

Notes

1   Above, p.138.

2   *EHD* II, p.1012: for 'Gosfrith', read 'Geoffrey'.

3   *WP*, p.149; *ASC* 'E', s.a.1067.

4   Above, pp.207–8.

5   *OV*, ii p.267.

6   C. Warren Hollister, 'Magnates and "Curiales" in Early Norman England', *Viator* 4 (1973), pp.63–81; repr. in Hollister, *Monarchy, Magnates and*

Institutions in the Anglo-Norman World (London: Hambledon Press, 1986), pp.97–115, at p.99.

7 W.J. Corbett, 'The development of the duchy of Normandy and the Norman Conquest of England', *Cambridge Medieval History*, vol.5, ed. J.R. Tanner and others (Cambridge University Press, 1926), pp.510–11.

8 For most of what follows in this paragraph, see J.J.N. Palmer, 'The Wealth of the Secular Aristocracy in 1086', *ANS* 22 (2000), pp.279–91.

9 Palmer, 'The Wealth of the Secular Aristocracy', p.280.

10 'Domesday provides comprehensive evidence only for tenurial levels one and two: tenancies-in-chief and undertenancies': C.P. Lewis, 'The Domesday Jurors', *Haskins Society Journal* 5 (1993), pp.17–44 at p.32.

11 Paul Dalton, *Conquest, Anarchy and Lordship: Yorkshire, 1066–1154* (Cambridge University Press, 1994), pp.39–49.

12 Frank Stenton, *The First Century of English Feudalism*, 2nd edn (Oxford University Press, 1961), p.55.

13 Susan Reynolds, *Fiefs and Vassals: The medieval evidence reinterpreted* (Oxford University Press, 1994), pp.345, 351, quoting Stenton, *First Century*, p.130.

14 *ASC* 'E', s.a.1086.

15 J.C. Holt, '1086', in *Domesday Studies*, ed. J.C. Holt (Woodbridge: Boydell Press, 1987), pp.41–64.

16 David C. Douglas, *William the Conqueror* (London: Eyre & Spottiswoode, 1964), p.97.

17 *EHD* II, p.433.

18 David Carpenter, *The Struggle for Mastery: Britain 1066–1284* (Oxford University Press, 2003), p.85.

19 Robin Fleming, *Kings and Lords in Conquest England* (Cambridge University Press, 1991), pp.217–31.

20 Carpenter, *The Struggle for Mastery*, p.86.

21 Ann Williams, *The English and the Norman Conquest* (Woodbridge: Boydell Press, 1995), p.105.

22 Williams, *The English and the Norman Conquest*, ch.V.

23 *DB*, p.274; Williams, *The English and the Norman Conquest*, pp.119–20, 201; Hugh M. Thomas, *The English and the Normans: Ethnic hostility, assimilation and identity 1066–c.1220* (Oxford University Press, 2003), pp.196–8.

24 Williams, *The English and the Norman Conquest*, pp.8, 77 and ch.IV generally.

25 Williams, *The English and the Norman Conquest*, ch.IV, p.77.

26 Williams, *The English and the Norman Conquest*, pp.108–9.

27 *DB*, p.409.

28 Marjorie Chibnall, *The Debate on the Norman Conquest* (Manchester University Press, 1999), p.88.

29 *DB*, p.435.

30 *OV*, ii p.267.

31 Judith Green, *The Aristocracy of Norman England* (Cambridge University Press, 1997), pp.48–9; ch.2 *passim*.

32 For the Norman origins of the marcher earldoms, see above, p.204.

33 Williams, *The English and the Norman Conquest*, p.101. And more generally, see Eleanor Searle, 'Women and the Legitimization of Succession at the Norman Conquest', *ANS* 3 (1980), pp.159–70.

34 Peter Sawyer, '1066–1086: A Tenurial Revolution?', in *Domesday Book: A reassessment*, ed. Peter Sawyer (London: Edward Arnold, 1985), pp.71–85.

35 *DB*, pp.267, 364–5.

36 Dalton, *Conquest, Anarchy and Lordship*, pp.33–4, 64–5.

37 Fleming, *Kings and Lords in Conquest England*, ch.5.

38 Fleming, *Kings and Lords in Conquest England*, pp.184–5.

39 Green, *The Aristocracy of Norman England*, p.48 and ch.2 *passim*.

40 Brian Golding, *Conquest and Colonisation: The Normans in Britain, 1066–1100* (Basingstoke: Macmillan, 1994), pp.71–2.

41 Green, *The Aristocracy of Norman England*, pp.106–7; Dalton, *Conquest, Anarchy and Lordship*, pp.39–49.

42 *OV*, ii pp.219–21.

43 Fleming, *Kings and Lords in Conquest England*, p.210.

44 *OV*, ii p.219.

45 *BT*, pls.21–3, 25, 49–50.

46 Green, *The Aristocracy of Norman England*, pp.177–8.

47 R. Allen Brown, *The Normans and the Norman Conquest*, 2nd edn (Woodbridge: Boydell Press, 1985), pp.202–3; Richard Eales, 'Royal Power

and Castles in Norman England', in *The Ideals and Practice of Medieval Knighthood, III*, ed. Christopher Harper-Bill and Ruth Harvey (Woodbridge: Boydell Press, 1990), pp.49–78.

48 J. Gillingham in *From the Vikings to the Normans*, ed. W. Davies (Oxford University Press, 2003), p.215; *ASC* 'E', s.a.1087; *WMGP*, p.169.

49 R. Allen Brown, *The Origins of English Feudalism* (London: Allen & Unwin, 1973), p.30.

50 Robert Bartlett, *England under the Norman and Angevin Kings* (Oxford University Press, 2002), p.266.

51 *OV*, ii p.267.

52 Above, pp.209–11.

53 C.H. Haskins, *Norman Institutions* (Cambridge, Mass.: Harvard University Press, 1918), pp.5–30 at p.5. Above, pp.42–4.

54 Douglas, *William the Conqueror*, pp.96–104; Brown, *The Normans and the Norman Conquest*, pp.32–41.

55 Golding, *Conquest and Colonisation*, p.121.

56 Marjorie Chibnall, 'Military Service in Normandy Before 1066', *ANS* 5 (1983), pp.65–77; repr. in *Anglo-Norman Warfare. Studies in Late Anglo-Saxon and Anglo-Norman Military Organisation and Warfare*, ed. Matthew Strickland (Woodbridge: Boydell Press, 1992), pp.28–40, at pp.35, 40.

57 Susan Reynolds, *Fiefs and Vassals: The medieval evidence reinterpreted* (Oxford University Press, 1994), p.352.

58 John Le Patourel, *The Norman Empire* (Oxford: Clarendon Press, 1976), pp.201–2.

59 *ASC* 'D', s.a.1072; 'E' s.a.1088.

60 *HN*, p.79; *ASC* 'E', s.a.1094.

61 J.H. Round, *Feudal England* (London: Sonnenschein, 1909), p.317.

62 Brown, *The Normans and the Norman Conquest*, p.187.

63 Holt, '1086', pp.42–3; Gillingham in *From the Vikings to the Normans*, ed. Davies, p.218.

64 *DB*, pp.437, 366, 272.

65 *Liber Eliensis. A History of the Isle of Ely From the Seventh Century to the Twelfth*, trans. Janet Fairweather (Woodbridge: Boydell Press, 2005), p.258.

66 *EHD* II, p.960.

67 C.P. Lewis, 'The Domesday Jurors', *Haskins Society Journal* 5 (1993), pp.17–44, p.32.

68 Dalton, *Conquest, Anarchy and Lordship*, ch.1.

69 Dalton, *Conquest, Anarchy and Lordship*, p.83.

70 Green, *The Aristocracy of Norman England*, p.112.

71 W.E. Kappelle, *The Norman Conquest of the North: The region and its transformation 1000–1135* (London: Croom Helm, 1980), p.192.

72 Williams, *The English and the Norman Conquest*, p.96.

73 Carpenter, *The Struggle for Mastery*, pp.81–7.

74 Carpenter, *The Struggle for Mastery*, p.87.

75 A.D. Carr, *Medieval Wales* (London, 1995), p.31.

76 *ASC* 'D', s.a.1063.

77 John Edward Lloyd, *A History of Wales from the Earliest Times to the Norman Conquest*, 2 vols (1911), ii p.373.

78 R.R. Davies, *The Age of Conquest. Wales 1063–1415* (Oxford University Press, 1991), p.87.

79 Davies, *The Age of Conquest*, pp.28–9.

80 *DB*, p.494.

81 Davies, *The Age of Conquest*, pp.30–1.

82 *DB*, p.737.

83 Davies, *The Age of Conquest*, p.85.

84 *OV*, ii pp.261–3; *DB*, pp.717, 688. Herefordshire was different: see C.P. Lewis, 'The Norman Settlement of Herefordshire under William I', *ANS* 7 (1984), pp.195–213.

85 Davies, *The Age of Conquest*, pp.94–5.

86 Below, ch.12; *DB*, pp.736.

87 *Brut y Tywysogyon or The Chronicle of the Princes. Peniarth MS. 20 Version*, ed. and trans. T. Jones, 2 vols (Cardiff: University of Wales Press, 1941–1952), p.16.

88 *ASC* 'D', 'E', s.a.1072; 'E', s.a.1091.

89 Alan O. Anderson, *Scottish Annals from English Chroniclers, AD 500 to 1286* (London: D.N. Nutt, 1908; repr. with corrections, Stamford, 1991), p.102.

90 Dalton, *Conquest, Anarchy and Lordship*, p.82.

91 Richard Sharpe, 'Norman Rule in Cumbria, 1092–1136', *Cumberland and Westmorland Antiquarian and Archaeological Society*, Tract Series, vol. XXI (2006), pp.34–52.

92 *ASC* 'E', s.a.1093.

93 *JW*, iii p.69.

94 For these events, see above, pp.164–5.

95 *ASC* 'E', s.a.1093, 1097.

CHAPTER 10

Economies and families

Town and country

The effects of the Norman Conquest on the urban and rural economies of England, Wales and Normandy have, like other aspects of the Conquest, been the subject of much debate. In any such discussion, it is important to remember that all of the territories under discussion here were affected by economic changes that were taking place across Europe well before 1066. Populations grew steadily from about the tenth century to the thirteenth; new land was cleared and cultivated for the first time; trade was stimulated; prices rose; the use of money increased. As has been seen in Chapter 2, a degree of urbanisation had occurred in England and Normandy by the middle of the eleventh century, although nothing comparable had taken place in Scotland and Wales by 1066. Urban life in Scotland did not really begin to flourish until the second quarter of the twelfth century, when King David I was active in the establishment of new towns or burghs. There were early examples of non-rural settlement there, however, and by 1100 burghs of some kind had been established at Edinburgh, Stirling, Dunfermline and Perth. It was a similar story in Wales, where significant urban development did not take place until the twelfth century. However, Chepstow was founded in the first half of the 1070s, Cardiff between 1081 and 1093, and Carmarthen, Kidwelly, Pembroke and Tenby were all established as new towns by the 1120s. Certainly in Wales, and also, despite royal involvement, in Scotland to some extent, urban growth depended on an influx of settlers from England. Many of these came with or on the heels of new Norman lords like William FitzOsbern at Chepstow or Arnulf of Montgomery at Pembroke. In this sense, the Norman Conquest played a significant part in bringing urban life to these parts of England and Wales for the first time.[1]

Domesday Book lists 112 English boroughs, a sure sign of the kingdom's high status as a major European trader by the late eleventh century.[2] In the short term, however, the Norman Conquest may in fact have interrupted urban expansion in England. After the Harrying of the North, for example, the population of York plummeted. Other towns were destroyed at least in part, either as a result of the invaders' ravaging tactics or, as at Lincoln and Shrewsbury, where 166 and 51 houses respectively were demolished, in order to make space for new castles.[3] However, in the longer term, the impact of the Conquest on English towns and local economies was probably a positive one and the brake it put on urban growth only temporary. The building of new castles, churches and cathedrals boosted the demand for skilled and unskilled labour; materials had to be bought and transported and, once the new buildings had been completed, their residents required clothes, food, horses and luxuries. New towns inevitably grew up around post-conquest churches: at Battle in Sussex, for example. And Little Domesday records that there were 342 houses on the demesne land of the abbey of Bury St Edmunds in 1086, 'which was arable' twenty years before.[4] Castles, too, were magnets for new settlement: Newcastle is an obvious example. Other new communities were founded with at least a degree of awareness of the economic significance of events: when William II ordered the construction of a castle at Carlisle in 1092, for example, and the settlement and cultivation of that region.[5] And towns along the south coast, Southampton, Pevensey, Sandwich and Chichester, all benefited from an increase in cross-Channel trade. London also grew in part as a consequence of the expansion of England's trading horizons.

The increase in the number of towns was to be a marked charac-teristic of Britain in the twelfth and thirteenth centuries. So was the establishment within them of authorised public markets, held every week on the same day, and fairs, held annually over a number of days. Domesday Book already refers to 'new markets' at Bolingbroke in Lincolnshire, Cirencester in Gloucestershire and Cookham in Berkshire;

and William I's queen, Matilda, set up the market at Tewkesbury. It is hard to know how formally organised these occasions were at this time, however; and, the last example notwithstanding, how much their establishment owed to the arrival of the Normans.[6] Domesday Book regularly records details of foreign occupants of English towns, and many of these were probably merchants or traders. French quarters were established at Southampton, Norwich, Shrewsbury and Northampton, and developments like these could have eased the process of ethnic integration after the upheaval of 1066. The English almost certainly remained in the majority in urban centres, though, and continued to occupy prominent positions in the urban élite.[7] These foreigners may also have come to England anyway, of course, whether the Normans had invaded or not; and some may even have been in the kingdom since before 1066.

England's first Jewish community came from Rouen to settle in London shortly after 1066, however, almost certainly because the Duke of Normandy, the protector of the Jews there, was now also king of England. There is nothing from William I's reign to prove that the Jewish plantation in England was his idea, but William of Malmesbury thought that the King was responsible for their importation.[8] This is probably correct; after all, the Jewish community in Rouen was successful and prosperous, and William may have wanted to see the Jews' enterprising skills put to use in his new kingdom. A hundred years after this, by which time Jewish settlements had been established in towns across England (there is little if any compelling evidence to suggest that significant numbers of Jews dwelt anywhere other than in towns), their main occupation was moneylending. Initially, however, they dealt in bullion, bought and sold silver plate and, by exchanging foreign coins for English ones, facilitated cross-Channel trade. William of Malmesbury again, writing in the 1120s and 1130s, described what happened when representatives of London's Jewish community appeared before William II to present him with gifts on a religious festival. The irreverent King insisted that the Jews take part in a religious debate with members of his own clergy; if the Jews won, he said, 'he would become one of their sect'.[9] The primary purpose of such a tale was to demonstrate the King's scandalously flippant attitude to religion, and it would be unwise to give it too much credence. However, at least it clearly suggests that the London Jewry had been established in some form by the end of the eleventh century. But if William I initially encouraged it, the main impetus behind Jewish migration across the Channel may have been the violent persecution suffered by Jews at Rouen during the opening stages of the First Crusade in the mid 1090s.

New French lay and ecclesiastical lords controlled the land after 1066, and they needed a workforce if their new estates were to be exploited efficiently. The extent to which English landholders were affected by the arrival of the Normans has already been discussed. At the lower levels of society, however, where Domesday evidence in particular is lacking, it is hard to know what the Conquest meant for most individuals and families. It is not unreasonable to assume, however, that the greater part of the pre-conquest English population probably continued tilling the soil as it had always done after 1066. Nevertheless, in the English countryside, there were important changes. For one thing, it has been suggested that several thousand settlers may have accompanied the new Norman lords of England after 1066. This is impossible to substantiate, but an influx of French peasants into the English countryside on any meaningful scale could have had significant implications. It might have increased ethnic tension, of course; but these newcomers could also have served to bridge the gap between the Norman rulers and the conquered English and to ease the process of acculturation.[10]

Other changes to rural life may perhaps be attributed to the Conquest with a little more confidence. Fleming's analysis of the less than smooth and consistent ways in which English lands came into the possession of new French lords after 1066 has already been mentioned. According to her, in addition, the 'rapid decay of old lordships had a startling effect on the vill and the local economy'.[11] Where tenurial discontinuity was prevalent, that is in those areas where pre-conquest lordships fragmented the most after 1066, land values fell significantly between then and 1086. In Cambridgeshire, for example, the overall value of land fell by 14 per cent over the course of these two decades. Some of this decline is probably attributable to damage caused by the invading army during the campaigns of the 1060s and 1070s. However, Fleming has shown how 'the holdings hardest hit correlate very closely with the vills where the pattern of Anglo-Saxon tenure has been disrupted'. She identifies similar phenomena in Herefordshire, Nottinghamshire and, to a lesser extent, Dorset. What this meant for the peasants who worked the lands is more difficult to say. In some areas, where lands passed relatively smoothly from a pre-conquest antecessor to a post-conquest successor, probably little would have changed except the name of the lord. Elsewhere, however, extensive blocks of territory were broken up, redistributed amongst several foreign newcomers and reorganised internally. The very shape of the landscape was changed as castles, manor houses and churches were built on lands previously occupied by peasant farmers. Anglo-Saxon inlands were increased in size and evolved into what came to be called the lord's demesne.[12] The Normans were consumers, too, and with their vine-yards, mills and deer parks, more land than before was turned over to meeting their material demands, which left less land available for peasant farming. It has been argued that such developments, along with the thirst for a quick cash return on their investment in the invasion of 1066 and a lack of sympathy for their new English tenants, may have led to an intensification of lordship and the imposition of more onerous burdens and restrictions on peasants who had been more loosely tied to their lords before 1066. These changes, however, such as they were, would not have been as significant had the demand for land not been heightened by a rising population. In other words, there were more peasants competing for less land by the end of the eleventh century, and the Normans needed more people to cultivate their territories than had their Anglo-Saxon predecessors. Peasant farmers therefore had little choice but to sell themselves more cheaply and submit themselves to harsher regimes.

Such trends may have required more than just adaptation on the part of most English peasants. They also led to a decline in their formal status and a loss of autonomy. It has long been recognised that between 1066 and 1086 the number of free peasants in England fell. Whereas there were nearly 900 sokemen in Cambridgeshire in 1066, there were only 177 at the time of the Domesday survey. And more than this, much of the land the free peasants had held now formed part of the demesnes of the new foreign lords. In Maitland's words, 'The sokemen have fallen, and their fall has brought with it the consolidation of manorial husbandry and seigniorial power.'[13] Something similar appears to have happened to other free peasants, too. In 1066, 4 of the 34 hides which made up the manor of Bramley in Surrey had belonged to free men. By 1086, however, when the manor was held by Odo of Bayeux, there were only villeins, cottars and slaves on the land.[14] There are plenty of similar examples scattered throughout Domesday Book which together serve to indicate how the size of the free peasantry was reduced after 1066. This could be little more than a matter of terminology: the life of a free peasant before 1066 may have been very similar to that of a villein thereafter. However, it is hard to avoid the conclusion that there was more to it than this, and that the new lords of these lands were implementing a deliberate policy. A free peasant who could 'withdraw' from serving his lord or 'go where he pleases' (in the words of Domesday Book) was of little use to a landholder intent on finding the quickest and most efficient way to exploit his new estates. It was surely much simpler either to eject and replace such men with less independent peasants who knew their place, or to redefine the status and obligations of those they found on their lands under the threat of expulsion or worse. Many pre-conquest sokemen or other free peasants, aware perhaps of the increasing scarcity of available land, would have found themselves having to strike bargains with foreign lords after 1066, and the power in that relationship inevitably lay with the newcomers. There would have been little choice other than simply to become villeins and agree to perform labour services of a more or less onerous kind. Such a loss of status might lie behind the complaint already heard from Aethelric of Marsh Gibbon in Buckinghamshire.[15]

More concretely, by the start of the twelfth century, slavery was in terminal decline in England. It has been estimated that the 28,000 slaves mentioned in Domesday Book, along with their families, may have made up as much as 10 per cent of the rural population of England in 1086. The system was certainly well entrenched, although slaves were not evenly distributed across the kingdom: the population of western England contained a higher proportion of slaves than elsewhere, an indication perhaps of the importance of the slave trade between Bristol and Ireland.[16] Attitudes were changing, however: in 1102, for example, at the Council of Westminster, it was ordered that 'henceforth no one is to dare to carry on that shameful trade by which in England people used to be sold like animals'.[17] In the end, though, it is likely that slavery disappeared from England for economic rather than religious or moral reasons. Slaves had to be supported by their lords because they had no land of their own. It was easier and probably more cost-effective simply to give them land in return for labour services and rent.[18] How much such changes had to do with the arrival of the Normans in England is, of course, open to question. It may be argued that, because slavery appears to have disappeared from Normandy well before 1066, because Norman lords after 1066 were more often absentees than their Anglo-Saxon predecessors, and because money rents were therefore more attractive to them than other forms of service, it was indeed the Normans who dealt a mortal blow to slavery in England. However, William of Malmesbury reveals that the English Bishop Wulfstan was as opposed to slavery just as much as the Italian Lanfranc; and, even though William I himself was initially reluctant to forgo the profits he recouped from the slave trade with Ireland, the commercial sense of turning expensive slaves into lucrative tenants must have been as apparent to most Anglo-Saxon landholders as it was to Norman ones.[19] This is all highly speculative, of course; but it seems likely that slavery would probably have disappeared from England anyway, regardless of what happened in and after 1066.

Families and female power

It has been argued that, hand in hand with the introduction of a new ruling class and the establishment of new systems of landholding in England after 1066, went changes in the structure and perception of family relationships at the highest levels of English society.[20] In Anglo-Saxon England, the theory goes, central authority and local lordship were weak, and the most important relationship an individual had was with the members of his or her kin group. Before 1066, moreover, an individual's 'kin' extended well beyond the nuclear unit of husband, wife and children: his wider 'clan' could include other relatives as well as others with no ties of blood at all to the immediate family. Consequently, when bequests came to be made, land was often divided between the members of this extended kinship network. In Normandy, by contrast, where, by the middle of the eleventh century, ducal authority was increasingly strong, and great families had established themselves in control of extensive estates, there was no urge to divide lands widely amongst heirs, and a system known as *parage* was developing. This meant that only the testator's chattels needed to be bequeathed form-ally in writing, because the family lands would descend automatically and lineally to the sons of the deceased, with the younger brothers holding from the eldest. Increasingly, the eldest brother would take con-trol of the core of the family lands, the patrimony, whilst the younger brothers might share those lands which their father had acquired during his lifetime. This distinction between patrimonial and acquired lands, which William I relied on in 1087 when Robert Curthose and William II received Normandy and England respectively, was thus already recognised and of some importance in Normandy before 1066.[21] Such importance, indeed, is suggested if not proved by the increasing use of hereditary French toponymic surnames (names which identified an individual and their family with a particular place or set of lands), amongst propertied Norman families in the generation or two before 1066.[22] As far as family structures in pre-conquest England and Normandy were concerned therefore, 'the distinction is between clan and lineage, between the extended and the dynastic family'.[23]

After 1066, the argument continues, the new lords of England brought with them from Normandy their ideas about the indivisibility of family property and their preference for lineal over collateral descent of land.[24] Over time, these ideas, along with a wider recognition of the distinction between patrimonial and acquired lands, took hold in England and led eventually to the replacement of pre-conquest assump-tions about kin and property by settled notions of hereditary right and primogeniture. When William FitzOsbern died in 1071, for example, his eldest son William inherited his Norman lands whilst his second son, Roger, became earl of Hereford.[25] As usual, however, the reality was much more complex than this simplification of some difficult arguments suggests. For one thing, these post-conquest trends are inevitably visible only at the highest levels of Anglo-Norman society. Moreover, before 1066, the Anglo-Saxons did bequeath land to direct descendants, usually males; and this may have been a growing tendency as 1066 approached. In general, too, bonds based on extended kinship remained strong across Britain well into the post-conquest period, especially in Wales and Scotland.[26] And in England, when land did descend lineally to heirs after 1066, sometimes both patrimony and acquisitions descended together as a single inheritance, sometimes the heir in question was not the eldest son, and sometimes the Normans did divide their patrimonies between sons, although this tended to be in cases where the acquisitions were larger than the patrimony, or for other special reasons, where there were twin eldest sons, for example.[27] And more generally, the conditions in England after 1066, where lands were regularly and unpredictably being distributed, confiscated and distributed again, hardly made for a smooth transition from one set of property and family relationships to another.

Nevertheless, by 1100, in his Coronation Charter, Henry I assumed that his tenants-in-chief and their tenants in turn would be succeeded by their heirs, and the so-called *Leges Henrici Primi*, written during Henry's reign, also acknowledged the distinction between patrimonial lands, which went to the eldest son and the acquisitions, which could be disposed of at will. And it has also been observed that, by 1100, 'land which had been an acquisition in 1066 was considered a patrimony by many men' and that these tendencies were reinforced during Henry I's reign: the Anglo-Norman baronage 'enjoyed fairly secure inheritance . . . as long as they remained loyal to the king'.[28] It has even been suggested that it was the post-conquest kings who had a vested interest in encouraging these trends and in ensuring that the lands of their tenants were kept together and intact, even though their division would provide them with a deeper well of patronage from which to draw: 'for kings did not wish to see lands on which military service was owed fragmented as generation succeeded generation. By taking homage from only one heir, they could ensure impartibility.'[29] It has been argued in the seminal work on this subject by J.C. Holt that 'the Norman Conquest must be seen as involving not simply the replacement of one aristocracy by another but also the replacement of one set of family relationships by another'.[30] This is surely right, but that process of change and development, like so many others, was still a long way from completion in 1106.

If notions of kinship and family within England's ruling class changed as a result of the Norman Conquest, however, there are serious questions about the extent to which 1066 marked a turning-point in the history of English women. Little is known about the female populations of pre-conquest Wales and Scotland, but this is probably in part because these societies 'systematically privileged agnatically related male relatives', and women there 'were landowners only in exceptional circumstances'. Welsh women, it has been said, 'had no political voice' in the early Middle Ages; although this does not rule out the possibility that they played a role in community affairs by other less formal means.[31] As for Anglo-Saxon England, the long-held orthodoxy that women lived during a 'golden age' in which they were privileged in the eyes of the law and lived on terms of 'rough equality' with men has been challenged and no longer holds sway; the same goes for the associated idea that the Norman Conquest 'meant the end of many things in England, not least among them the independent status of the noble English lady'.[32] It is hard, in fact, to discern how, if at all, the position of English women changed either side of 1066, and the few tentative conclusions which have been put forward can only be applied with any confidence to noblewomen, because this is all that the available sources allow. Moreover, to regard even this class of women as a homogeneous group, all with the same concerns and subject to the same pressures, 'may itself be as misleading as it is helpful'.[33]

Some pre-conquest women, like Alfred's daughter Aethelflaed in the tenth century and Emma of Normandy in the eleventh, played prominent roles in English political life. This continued to be the case after the arrival of the Normans: King Harold's mother, Gytha, was the focus of resistance to the Normans at Exeter in 1067, for example. She may not have been alone, either, as when she left England following the siege, she took 'many distinguished men's wives with her'.[34] As for royal women of the new regime, William I's queen, Matilda, acted on her husband's behalf in Normandy during his absences; Henry I's queen, Matilda, attended meetings of the King's council, and often chaired them in her husband's absence. And in 1105, when Pope Paschal II came close to excommunicating Henry I over his refusal to come to terms on the issue of lay investiture, Adela, countess of Blois, Henry's sister and a friend of Archbishop Anselm, helped to arrange a meeting that led to a temporary truce between the King and his Archbishop.[35] These were women of the highest status, however, and members of an exclusive club. And despite their involvement, the public sphere of events and policies remained overwhelmingly the preserve of men who 'alone played an active part in the groups and communities which debated and implemented society's rules'.[36] Having said this, most women could expect to wield power informally, within the confines of their family and wider kinship and social networks; and aristocratic women might also do so through the patronage of ecclesiastics, authors and other artists. Queen Matilda, Henry I's first wife, commissioned a biography of her mother, Queen Margaret of Scotland, and she may also have inspired and helped to pay for the writing of William of Malmesbury's *Deeds of the Kings of England*. There was nothing new about this after 1066, however: Edward the Confessor's queen, Edith, had commissioned the *Vita Edwardi*. Such activity must have enabled these women, albeit mostly indirectly, to exercise some degree of influence over the men who dominated public political affairs and over the image of them bequeathed to later generations.

Women were also important politically because of the rights they could enjoy over property. Anglo-Saxon women had held property and bequeathed it by will, but it is hard to know how much independence of thought and action they exercised in doing so. Some were very rich, however, like Gytha, the mother of Harold II, who held lands in most of the shires south of the Thames in 1066.[37] Thereafter, women continued to acquire property and retained the right, in certain circumstances, to deal with it as they wished. The daughters of noblemen might acquire land in several ways. When they married, they would expect to receive a dowry or marriage portion from their family. They could also expect to be allotted a share of his own lands, known as dower, by their new husband. However, in the early decades after 1066, neither an entitlement to dower and a marriage portion nor their size were fixed by law; much would depend on the resources of the families entering into the marriage alliance, the calls which might be made on them by other children and the attractiveness of the proposed union. What is more, once the marriage had taken place, control over the wife's lands passed in practice to her husband. However, if she outlived him, a widow was entitled to hold her dower and, at least until the middle of the twelfth century, her marriage portion, too, in her own right, with no interference from anyone else. This was the state of affairs in 1100, at least according to the Coronation Charter of Henry I.[38]

It was as widows that women were in theory able to exercise personal control over land. Most of the women landholders who appear in Domesday Book were widows, notably Judith, the widow of Earl

Waltheof. Precisely because they could have extensive resources at their immediate disposal, however, there was heavy pressure on them to remarry quickly, and most if not all did so at least once. Thus control of their lands passed into the hands of their new husbands, and widows' autonomy tended to be short-lived.[39] Women could also inherit property. Some women did so even when they had elder brothers, but this was probably unusual. By the end of the twelfth century, if a landholder died leaving only daughters as heirs, the inheritance would be divided between them, and their husbands would acquire *de facto* control of their wives' shares. Before this, however, the practice was more flexible and varied and one daughter might inherit all of the lands.[40]

Heiresses and widows were thus highly marketable and desirable commodities in post-conquest England. Through them their lords and husbands could gain access to lands and wealth; they could also receive a helping hand up the social ladder if the woman in question was from a particularly prestigious family. Marriage was also a way of establishing a political alliance between families. As a result, it is hardly surprising that the king wanted to be involved in the marriage strategies of his great men and their female relatives. As has been seen, the king could control the marriages of his tenants-in-chief, their sons, daughters and widows. He might do this in order to reward a loyal follower; but, if he did so at all, he needed to step delicately, and the prominence given to such matters in Henry I's Coronation Charter demonstrates just how politically sensitive an issue this was. The King stipulated that no baron should give his daughter, sister, niece or cousin in marriage without royal consent. The baron would get that consent 'unless he wishes to give her in marriage to one of my enemies'. If a baron died leaving a daughter as his heir, she would be given by the King in marriage 'according to the counsel given me by my barons'. And if a baron died leaving a childless widow or a widow with minor children, the King would not give her in marriage without her consent.[41] The tone and content of this document suggest strongly that the rules and conventions governing a woman's role in the descent of land were still being worked out in 1100. This is not surprising given that some of the situations covered by the charter arose out of the rights over marriage which had only come under royal and seigniorial control since 1066. Such rights gave women the occasional walk-on part in the high dramas of politics and society. But they had few lines of their own and, in this sense, little had changed since 1066.

Notes

1 Richard Britnell, *Britain and Ireland 1050–1530. Economy and Society* (Oxford University Press, 2004), pp.120, 139–43.

2 H.C. Darby, *Domesday England* (Cambridge University Press, 1977), pp.289, 296–7.

3 Darby, *Domesday England*, pp.295–8.

4 *DB*, pp.1248–9.

5 *ASC* 'E', s.a.1092.

6 Darby, *Domesday England*, pp.318–19.

7 Hugh M. Thomas, *The English and the Normans: Ethnic hostility, assimilation and identity 1066–c.1220* (Oxford University Press, 2003), ch.12.

8 *WMGR*, i p.563.

9 *WMGR*, i p.563.

10 Thomas, *The English and the Normans*, pp.161–6.

11 Robin Fleming, *Kings and Lords in Conquest England* (Cambridge University Press, 1991), pp.120–5.

12 Rosamund Faith, *The English Peasantry and the Growth of Lordship* (Leicester University Press, 1997), pp.49–50; and ibid., ch.7, for what follows in the rest of this paragraph.

13 Darby, *Domesday England*, pp.61–3; Fleming, *Kings and Lords in Conquest England*, pp.122–3; Faith, *The English Peasantry and the Growth of Lordship*, chs.7–9 generally and pp.215–18 in particular; F.W. Maitland, *Domesday Book and Beyond: Three essays in the early history of England* (Cambridge University Press, 1897; repr. London, 1969), p.91.

14 *DB*, p.74.

15 *DB*, p.409; above p.241.

16 Darby, *Domesday England*, pp.72–4, 76–7.

17 *Councils and Synods, with Other Documents Relating to the English Church*, ed. D. Whitelock, M. Brett and C.N.L. Brooke, 2 vols (Oxford: Clarendon Press, 1964, 1981), I part ii, p.678.

18 David Carpenter, *The Struggle for Mastery: Britain 1066–1284* (Oxford University Press, 2003), p.51.

19 *WMGR*, ii pp.496–9.

20 This paragraph draws heavily on J.C. Holt, 'Politics and Property in Early Medieval England', *Past and Present*, 57 (1972), pp.3–52; repr. in idem, *Colonial England, 1066–1215* (London: Hambledon Press, 1997), ch.8.

21 Holt, 'Politics and Property', pp.45–8; Emily Zack Tabuteau, 'The Role of Law in the Succession to Normandy and England, 1087', *Haskins Society Journal* 3 (1991), pp.141–69, at pp.155–68. Both of these authorities differ on this point from John Le Patourel, 'The Norman Succession 996–1135', *EHR* 86 (1971), pp.225–50.

22 Marjorie Chibnall, *Anglo-Norman England* (Oxford: Basil Blackwell, 1986), pp.165–6; J.C. Holt, 'Feudal Society and the Family in Early Medieval England: I, The Revolution of 1066', *TRHS*, 5th series, 32 (1982), pp.193–212, at pp.200–1; repr. in idem., *Colonial England*, ch.9; idem, 'Politics and Property', pp.7–8; David Bates, *Normandy Before 1066* (London: Longman,1982), pp.126–7; Judith A. Green, *The Aristocracy of Norman England* (Cambridge University Press, 1997), pp.342–4.

23 Holt, 'Feudal Society and the Family I', p.199.

24 Holt, 'Politics and Property', pp.1–13.

25 Above, p.148.

26 Richard Britnell, 'Social Bonds and Economic Change', in *The Twelfth and Thirteenth Centuries*, ed. Barbara Harvey (Oxford University Press, 2001), pp.101–33, at pp.123–7.

27 Green, *The Aristocracy of Norman England*, p.339; Holt, 'Politics and Property', pp.14–15, 49–51.

28 *EHD* II, p.432 (cap.2); *Leges Henrici Primi*, ed. L.J. Downer (Oxford: Clarendon Press, 1972), p.225 (caps.70, 21); RáGena DeAragon, 'The growth of secure inheritance in Anglo-Norman England', *Journal of Medieval History*, 8 (1982), pp.381–91, quotations at p.389.

29 Green, *The Aristocracy of Norman England*, p.339.

30 Holt, 'Feudal Society and the Family I', p.200.

31 Britnell, 'Social Bonds and Economic Change', in *The Twelfth and Thirteenth Centuries*, ed. Harvey, p.126; Wendy Davies, *Wales in the Early Middle Ages* (Leicester University Press, 1982), p.79.

32 Doris Mary Stenton, *The English Woman in History* (London: Macmillan, 1957; repr. New York: Schocken Books, 1977), p.28; P. Stafford, 'Women and the Norman Conquest', *TRHS*, 6th series, 4 (1994), pp.221–49.

33 Pauline Stafford, *Unification and Conquest. A Political and Social History of England in the Tenth and Eleventh Centuries* (London: Edward Arnold, 1989), p.173.

34 *ASC* 'D', s.a.1067.

35 *WP*, p.179; *HN*, pp.175–6; *The Letters of St Anselm*, trans. Walter Fröhlich, Cistercian Studies Series 96, 97, 142 (Kalamazoo, Mich.: Cistercian Publications, 1990, 1993, 1994), nos.286, 287, 388.

36 Stafford, *Unification and Conquest*, p.173.

37 Stafford, *Unification and Conquest*, p.176.

38 *EHD* II, p.433 (cap.4).

39 Green, *The Aristocracy of Norman England*, pp.370–2.

40 Green, *The Aristocracy of Norman England*, pp.373–81.

41 *EHD* II, p.433 (caps.3–4).

CHAPTER 11

The Church

One result of the Norman victory in 1066, claimed William of Malmesbury, was that 'the standard of religion, dead everywhere in England, has been raised by their arrival: you may see everywhere churches in villages, in towns and cities monasteries rising in a new style of architecture; and with new devotion our country flourishes'.[1] To be sure, the Norman Conquest profoundly affected the English Church and it had an impact on religious structures and organisation in Scotland and Wales, too. After all, contemporaries would have had little doubt that, with divine backing for his invasion and divine help during the Battle of Hastings, William I had proved the righteousness of his cause. After 1066, therefore, the process of bringing the supposedly backward and isolated Churches of Britain into the mainstream of continental Christianity was justified and could proceed in tandem with political and military domination. William of Poitiers, indeed, went so far as to argue that William of Normandy's motive for invading England in 1066 'was not so much to increase his own power and glory as to reform Christian observance in those regions'.[2] However, such comments are hard to accept at face value, and it suited the Duke and his propagandists both to denigrate the religious practices and traditions of their newly conquered territories, and to portray William as a missionary as well as a warrior, more concerned with the spiritual welfare of his new people than their lands. It has already been seen in Chapter 2 how unfair it would be to claim that the Churches of Britain on the eve of the Conquest were moribund; and it would be just as misleading to argue that the Normans swept away all of the customs and institutions they found in the Churches of Britain and began to reform them from scratch.

The post-conquest English Church

Every king needed the support of the local Church before he could be crowned. It was Archbishop Lanfranc who ensured that William I's wishes were carried out in 1087, for example, and who smoothed the path to William II's accession. For his part, William I had not set about imposing his will on the English Church immediately after Hastings. Partly this was because dealing first with the political and military opposition he faced after 1066 was a more urgent priority. But he also needed to obtain the backing of the ecclesiastical establishment and the stamp of legitimacy which that would give him. In 1069, however, Archbishop Ealdred of York died, leaving an important vacancy to be filled, and by early 1070 William appeared to have dealt with a major Danish invasion and to have brutalised northern England into submission with the Harrying of the North. At Easter 1070, therefore, at Winchester, William set about addressing the shortcomings of the English Church.[3] A papal deputation, led by Ermenfrid, bishop of Sion in Switzerland, had arrived in England, and he re-crowned the King before several English bishops were deposed. The bishops of Selsey, Lichfield, Durham and Elmham were all removed from their posts as, most notably, was Stigand, archbishop of Canterbury and bishop of Winchester. The vacancies were filled mostly by Normans. Thomas of Bayeux became archbishop of York, Walkelin bishop of Winchester, Herfast bishop of Elmham and Walcher bishop of Durham. But most important of all was the appointment of Lanfranc, an Italian and abbot of William's foundation of St Stephen's, Caen, as archbishop of Canterbury.

The depositions of 1070 sprang from William I's need, in John of Worcester's words, to 'strengthen his position in the newly acquired kingdom'.[4] By 1087, this process had gone even further: 11 of the 15 English bishops were Normans, and only one, Wulfstan of Worcester, was English. The Church's power over land and people was the key reason behind the King's determination to control appointments. When a bishop was elected, he 'would immediately become a major landlord, a local, perhaps regional, and possibly national potentate, and a master of knights, castles, and money as well as religious director of his see'.[5] At the time of the Domesday survey in 1086, between a quarter and a third of the landed wealth of the kingdom was held by the Church, and it goes without saying that the king would want reliable men in charge of such extensive and widely scattered resources. By the early 1070s, therefore, as has been seen in Chapter 9, the obligations of these religious houses to the king were already being clearly redefined. Bishops and abbots would probably have been obliged to provide military service to the Anglo-Saxon kings under the five-hide system or something similar. After the Conquest, however, they became the king's ecclesiastical tenants-in-chief, and by the early 1070s a fixed, specified quota of knights had been demanded from them by William in return for their lands.[6] The King clearly took his tenants' obligations seriously. When in 1082 Bishop Odo of Bayeux was accused of treason against William I, he claimed that his status as a bishop meant that he could only be tried by the pope. Archbishop Lanfranc replied that, on the contrary, he would be tried just like any other tenant-in-chief in the royal court. According to William of Malmesbury, when Odo was arrested, William I 'put him in chains, having explained that his fetters were not for the bishop of Bayeux but for the earl of Kent'.[7] Similarly in 1088, as has been seen, when Bishop William of Durham was accused of having supported William II's opponents during the revolt of 1088, he was tried in his capacity as a royal vassal, not as a bishop.[8]

As well as legitimacy, political support and military resources, the Church also provided the king with funds. Rufus for one, it has been said, 'had absolutely no interest in the church save as a source of profit'.[9] Individual religious houses paid geld, of course, and this was levied frequently by the Norman kings, much to the distress of the English sources. Alternatively, the king might simply help himself to whatever he could get. According to the *Anglo-Saxon Chronicle* and John of Worcester, for example, in 1070 William I ordered that every English monastery should surrender its cash reserves to the King.[10] Kings could take money from ambitious churchmen, too. Notoriously, Herbert Losinga paid William II for the privilege of becoming bishop of East Anglia in 1091, and in 1095, on the death of Bishop Wulfstan of Worcester, the same King demanded a payment from all of the bishop's tenants. A more regular source of royal income was ecclesiastical vacancies. These had probably been open to exploitation by the kings of Anglo-Saxon England, too. However, the extent to which William II, assisted by Ranulf Flambard, and Henry I, took advantage of this source of revenue became infamous.

English monastic chroniclers universally criticised Ranulf Flambard because he was so successful in raising money for the King. William of Malmesbury, for example, described how he 'skinned the rich, ground down the poor, and swept other men's inheritances into his net'. However, for the *Anglo-Saxon Chronicle*, he was more than a mere financial enforcer; it was Ranulf 'who had managed [the King's] councils over all England and superintended them'.[11] Flambard's reward for his loyal service was the traditional one of a bishopric: in 1099 he became bishop of Durham, albeit after paying £1,000 to the King for the privilege. Thus the Church was also a source of patronage for the king as well as funds. Of the 15 bishops appointed by William I, 10 were royal clerks. According to Orderic Vitalis, William II 'bestowed ecclesiastical honours, like hireling's wages, on clerks and monks of the court, looking less for piety in these men than for obsequiousness and willing service in secular affairs'.[12] In fact six out of the eight appointments to bishoprics made by Rufus were of royal clerks. Then, between 1100 and 1125 every new bishop was appointed from amongst the ranks of the king's servants. Posts within the royal administration were sought after by the ambitious because this was an avenue to status and wealth in the highest reaches of the English Church; and their success in obtaining bishoprics is evidence of how highly valued they were by the king. Royal priests ministered to the king's spiritual needs, but they also drafted his documents. The chancellors of the Anglo-Norman kings were almost certain to obtain bishoprics, the most notable example being Gerard, chancellor of William I and Rufus, and bishop of Hereford (1096–1101) and archbishop of York (1101–8). And by 1110 a bishop, Roger of Salisbury (1107–39), was in overall charge of royal government.

As well as running the royal administration itself, the leading churchmen of the day were also expected to advise the king on great affairs of state as well as on matters of direct relevance to the Church. Archbishop Lanfranc performed all of these functions for William I – regent, judge, adviser; his closeness to the King is most obviously revealed by the series of letters he wrote to William in Normandy in

1075, which kept the latter informed of the progress of the revolt of that year. Later, in 1085 at Gloucester, the leading churchmen as a group contributed to the discussions which led to the commissioning of the Domesday survey, and several, such as Remigius, bishop of Lincoln (1072–92), and Walcher, bishop of Durham (1071–80), took leading roles in the execution of the survey. And it was not just the highest affairs of state with which the leading churchmen were involved. They continued to have local military responsibilities, for example. In 1075, Bishop Wulfstan of Worcester and Abbot Aethelwig of Evesham played leading roles in dealing with the revolt of Earl Roger of Hereford; Gundulf, bishop of Rochester (1077–1108), supervised the building of the White Tower in London; in 1088, the garrison of Worcester Castle was under the command of Bishop Wulfstan and was instrumental in suppressing the rising against William II in that part of the country.

Bishops continued to preside over the shire courts, too, as they had done before 1066, along with the earl or his deputy. But changes were made to the way in which different types of cases were heard locally. At some time between 1072 and 1076, William I and Lanfranc ordered that there should henceforward be a much clearer distinction between the respective jurisdictions of lay and church courts. In a famous writ, the King announced that 'by the common council and counsel of the archbishops, bishops, abbots and of all the magnates of my kingdom' no spiritual offences (which included adultery and incest, for example) should be tried in a hundred court or by laymen. And anyone accused of such an offence should only be tried and judged in 'the place where the bishop shall choose and name'.[13] The writ leaves many questions unanswered, of course. It does not mention the shire court, where the bishop was probably still able to hear spiritual cases, and there is no compelling evidence to show whether its terms were observed in practice. Also, it does not amount to the complete surrender of lay rights over the Church which it might superficially resemble. Sheriffs were expressly authorised by the writ forcibly to bring any reluctant accused to the church court. More importantly, as has been seen, the kings continued to treat the cases of disloyal bishops as their own particular preserve; and William I at least would not allow his tenants-in-chief or his royal servants to be examined or punished by a church court without his consent. The King was prepared to go some way towards meeting the particular needs of the Church, therefore, but he remained in over-all control and insistent that his royal rights prevailed above all others.

Questions of primacy

The changes made to the leadership of the English Church by William I in 1070 were designed in part to ensure that trustworthy men of Norman extraction were placed in control of ecclesiastical affairs in the newly conquered kingdom. This did not mean that such men did not argue amongst themselves, however; and perhaps the most heated dispute of all after 1070 was between the archbishops of Canterbury and York over the question of which, if either, of them had precedence over the other. Two later sources deal at some length with the struggle which took place in the 1070s over the primacy: the *History of Recent Events in England* by Eadmer, which was principally intended to be a record of the public life of St Anselm, and *The History of the Church of York* by Hugh the Chanter, which was written after 1127 to celebrate the triumph of Archbishop Thurstan of York over the claims of Canterbury. Another record made at Canterbury much nearer the time also outlined what had happened as far as the southern province was concerned.[14] Each of these sources describes the controversy from a specific southern or northern perspective, therefore; indeed, Hugh's account has been described as 'demonstrably unreliable for the earlier period'.[15] Nevertheless, they provide unique insights into the machinations of late eleventh-century ecclesiastical politics.

Both Lanfranc of Canterbury and Thomas of York were keen to defend and extend their own rights and the powers of their churches within England and beyond.[16] Lanfranc may have felt a particular pressure to do so from his own monks at Canterbury, however. After all, Canterbury's reputation had been stained by Stigand, and if both Harold II and William I had indeed been consecrated by Archbishop Ealdred of York, it may have been felt in the southern province that there was much lost ground to recover. Archbishop Thomas was immediately at a disadvantage in his dealings with Lanfranc, largely because of the latter's prestige and reputation, but also because of the timing of events. Archbishop Ealdred of York had died on 11 September 1069, but it was not until 24 May 1070 that Thomas was nominated as his successor; and even then nothing was done about his consecration until after Lanfranc had been consecrated archbishop of Canterbury on 29 August 1070. Thomas then travelled to Canterbury for his consecration, but, before he would consecrate him, Lanfranc demanded that Thomas should give him a written profession of obedience reinforced by an oath of loyalty, 'following the practice of his predecessors', Lanfranc later claimed.[17] Thomas refused and left Canterbury without having been consecrated. King William's anger at what he perceived as the archbishop of Canterbury's unnecessarily confrontational approach was soon allayed by Lanfranc's skilful persuasion. He argued amongst other things that 'it was expedient for the union and solidarity of the kingdom that all Britain should be subject to one primate'. Otherwise, Lanfranc went on, at some time in the future a disloyal archbishop of York might take it upon himself to consecrate a foreign invader as king. The King then turned on Thomas and forced him to return to Canterbury for consecration; which he did, albeit reluctantly, in late 1070 or early 1071.[18] According to the evidence from Canterbury sources, Thomas also made a personal profession of obedience to Lanfranc, although he maintained that he would not repeat such a profession to Lanfranc's successors until it was proved that his own predecessors had done the same.[19]

The dispute resumed when Lanfranc and Thomas both travelled to Rome to receive their pallia from the Pope in autumn 1071. During their audience with Alexander II, it was alleged that both Thomas (the son of a priest) and Remigius, bishop of Dorchester (who was also present), had been appointed uncanonically. Each pleaded for the Pope's mercy, and when Lanfranc spoke for them on the grounds of their learning, experience and usefulness to the King, Alexander allowed Lanfranc in his own presence to restore the bishops' insignia.[20] Thomas also took this opportunity to press the claims of the church of York: he argued that the churches of Canterbury and York were of equal status. Relying on what Gregory the Great was supposed to have ordered, moreover, he claimed that neither archdiocese should be in any way subject to the other, except that precedence for the time being should be given to the archbishop who had been consecrated earliest. He also argued that the three bishops of Dorchester, Worcester and Lichfield owed obedience to York, not Canterbury. Eventually, after much argument,

Alexander ruled that the whole matter should be dealt with in England by the bishops and abbots of the whole kingdom. The Pope was in a difficult position: he did not want to offend William I or Lanfranc, but neither did he approve of the idea of primacy. He was probably happy to leave the decision to others.[21]

Accordingly, in the course of two separate meetings held at Winchester and Windsor during April and May 1072, the questions at issue between York and Canterbury were considered once again by the English bishops and abbots in the presence of a papal legate. During the course of the debate, Lanfranc argued that the stipulations of Pope Gregory I, on which Thomas relied, were irrelevant because they referred to the churches of London and York, not Canterbury and York. It is hard to be sure about the tone and course these debates took, and about the precise details of what was eventually agreed, because evidence about them continues to come mainly from Canterbury sources. In the end, however, under royal pressure as much as anything else, Thomas submitted. He accepted that York should be subject to Canterbury and should obey its archbishop as 'primate of the whole of Britain' in all matters relating to the Christian religion. The archbishop of York and his suffragans must obey the primate's summons to a council, wherever convened, and must also obey his lawful instructions. On the death of an archbishop of Canterbury, the archbishop of York should come to Canterbury and duly consecrate his successor, with the help of the other suffragans of the church of Canterbury, as his own primate; if the archbishop of York died, his successor should, however, come for consecration to Canterbury or to wherever the archbishop of Canterbury might direct. Thomas's claim to jurisdiction over the three disputed dioceses was also rejected, and the southern boundary of his province was fixed at the river Humber. He was granted nominal jurisdiction further north, however, 'to the furthest limits of Scotland'.[22]

For the rest of Thomas's lifetime (he died in 1100), the issue of the primacy lay largely dormant. During the vacancy at Canterbury which followed Lanfranc's death, between 1089 and 1093, Thomas was of course the senior English prelate, and he consecrated bishops usually subject to the authority of the southern metropolitan (Chichester and Thetford in 1091 and Bangor in 1092). There is nothing to suggest that Thomas sought to make anything of this, but when Anselm was chosen by William II to succeed Lanfranc as archbishop of Canterbury in 1093, Thomas may have felt the need to revisit old ground once again. It was Thomas's responsibility to consecrate the new archbishop, but evidence from York sources claims that he objected to consecrating Anselm as 'primate of all Britain' and required the phrase 'metropolitan of Canterbury' to be used instead. The Canterbury sources, by contrast, describe how Thomas objected to the description 'metropolitan of all Britain', but agreed to 'primate of all Britain'.[23] Whatever actually happened in 1093, the arguments had reached an aridly semantic level and interested few beyond those directly involved. In the longer term, however, the dispute was damaging to the integrity of the English Church, to the extent that, for much of the twelfth century, the two archbishops could not travel into each other's provinces without risk of causing serious offence.

Parishes and councils

Arguments over the primacy were on one level narrowly concerned only with the particular relationship between the churches of York and Canterbury. More widely, however, clear lines of authority within the Church were desirable if reforms to ecclesiastical structures and practices within England were to be implemented efficiently and consistently. The English Church in 1066 was already in a state of ongoing and long-term development. Many of the minster churches which had dominated the ecclesiastical landscape since the seventh and eighth centuries still existed. However, the network of rural parishes which was to supplant the minster system and survive until the twenty-first century was also well on the way to being constructed. Domesday Book lists over two thousand village churches in England, many of which, the survey said, had their own priest.[24] It is likely that many other local churches went unrecorded in 1086, and it also makes sense to conclude, given the numbers involved, that most of these predated the arrival of the Normans. Indeed, it has been said in this context that 'the Norman settlement was more a stimulus to an existing trend than a new beginning' and that 'the critical shift can be located during c.1030–1080, when local churches were rebuilt to last, equipped with stone fonts and endowed with land, and when the minsters' monopoly over church dues went into drastic decline'. This is not to dismiss the contribution of the Conquest to the process of parochialisation, however. The number of village churches in England may have doubled between c.1070 and c.1170.[25]

Such developments also facilitated other changes, such as the establishment within dioceses of archdeaconries and rural deaneries. At one of Lanfranc's councils of the 1070s all bishops were ordered to appoint archdeacons; and very soon it seems that individual dioceses were being divided territorially above the level of the parish. In larger dioceses, often each shire was made an archdeaconry. There had been archdeacons in the late Anglo-Saxon church, but there is no indication that they administered on a similarly territorial basis. The archdeaconries were divided in turn into deaneries, which tended to correspond with the boundaries of hundreds. Thus new levels of authority were interposed between the parish and the bishop, and it was the responsibility of the archdeacons and deans to 'police' their areas, and to ensure that standards were being maintained and that no offences were being committed against canon law. According to Barlow, 'by 1120 archdeacons had secured an established and important place within the English church', and the complaints raised against them can be used as one measure of the way in which 'the Church was exercising an ever more intrusive and effective government'. Similarly by 1135, rural deans 'had emerged as a significant and well-defined element in the ecclesiastical hierarchy, holding courts in the bishop's name, enforcing judgements, collecting episcopal revenues and even collecting fines for breaches of the king's peace when ecclesiastical or spiritual matters impinged on the royal'.[26] Archdeacons and deans, in other words, were essential agents in enabling a bishop to control parochial affairs in his diocese.

The same or similar changes may have been implemented in England without Norman interference, of course; although it is hard to think that they would have happened as quickly. However, one practice was imported to England from Normandy after 1066, namely the regular holding of ecclesiastical councils or synods. This was also intended to further the process of streamlining administration and spreading the message of reform. Admittedly, no such council was convened during the reign of William II (he 'had no interest in the church's ideals'[27]), but under Henry I councils were held at Westminster (1102 and 1127) and

London (1107, 1125 and 1129). However, the most important councils of all were those which took place whilst William I was king and Lanfranc was archbishop of Canterbury. After two were held in 1070, the one held in 1072 dealt with the primacy dispute between Canterbury and York. Thereafter, councils were convened by William and Lanfranc on seven occasions between 1075 and 1086. Just as in Normandy before 1066, the aim of these meetings was to update the practices of the local church and to bring them into line with church or 'canon' law. Thus, repeatedly at the councils of the 1070s, the practice of simony was condemned; and at Winchester in 1076 it was decreed that no one was to be ordained as a deacon or a priest unless his unmarried status or celibacy was first proven. Those parish priests who were already married could remain so, but none could marry in the future. Higher standards were obviously expected of cathedral clergy: if they were already married, they were either to forsake their wives or give up their positions.

These councils were intended to establish effective, accountable mechanisms for controlling the personnel and the machinery of the Church. Further steps towards restructuring and updating ecclesiastical organisation were taken during the 1070s, when several episcopal centres were transferred to important towns within the diocese. Before 1066, most Anglo-Saxon bishops had tended not to have a permanent base within their sees, but to move around from church to church. Two of the Lotharingian bishops brought to England by Edward the Confessor, Herman of Ramsbury and Leofric of Devon and Cornwall, had established permanent diocesan centres, and accompanying cathedrals, in major towns: Leofric in Exeter (from Crediton, with papal approval) and Herman in Sherborne. After 1070, however, such transfers were much more frequent. Thus Bishop Herman moved his see (again) from Sherborne to (Old) Sarum or Salisbury after the London council of 1075, Herfast from Elmham to Thetford, Stigand II from Selsey to Chichester, Peter from Lichfield to Chester and Remigius from Dorchester to Lincoln. There were further transfers under Rufus, too: John moved from Wells to the monastery of Bath in about 1090, and Herbert Losinga moved from Thetford to Norwich in 1095. Such changes were in accordance with canon law, but they also aided the process of centralisation within individual dioceses and within the Church as a whole. It was significant, for example, that one of Lanfranc's councils of the early 1070s ordered bishops to hold their own councils twice a year. Standards needed to be maintained, but so did control. The more regular and consistent the structure of the Church became, the easier it would be to administer; a matter of no little concern to the king as well as the archbishops and bishops.

Conquest and cloister

The English abbots did not receive the same treatment at the hands of the Normans as the bishops. In 1070, only those of St Augustine's Canterbury and St Albans were deposed. Others were removed later (Wulfric of the New Minster, Winchester in 1072, for example), but William I seems to have been content to replace the heads of England's monasteries gradually. Initially, too, the King was not determined to import Norman successors: thus, Abbot Leofric of Peterborough, who was present at the Battle of Hastings, 'fell ill there, and came home and died soon after', was replaced by an Englishman, Brand. And when Brand sided with Edgar *atheling*, he was allowed to keep his position after a payment to the King of 40 gold marks.[28] And of the 21 abbots who attended Lanfranc's council at London in 1075, 13 were Anglo-Saxons. In contrast, by 1086, only three Anglo-Saxon abbots remained, and Norman influence had begun to spread across England's monasteries in other ways, too. Archbishop Lanfranc introduced a new set of *Constitutions* at Christ Church, Canterbury, which reformed liturgical practice and regulated domestic life within the monastery. His example was followed, and his regulations were adopted, at other English monasteries, such as St Albans, Rochester and Durham. Sometimes, however, the attempt to introduce continental practices was not so successful. By 1083, the new abbot of Glastonbury, Thurstan, who had been a monk at Caen, had alienated his monks by insisting that they used a chant from Fécamp. Thurstan proceeded to threaten the monks and then sent armed knights into the church to force them into submission. According to the horrified account in the *Anglo-Saxon Cronicle*, 3 monks were killed and 18 were injured during the assault. Ethnic tensions and a resistance to the imposition of foreign practices cannot have lain far below the surface of this superficially theological argument.[29]

There is more evidence to suggest that England's monasteries were abused and exploited in other ways by the Norman newcomers. In 1070, as has been seen already, King William ordered the plundering of religious houses across his kingdom.[30] Some monasteries, Domesday Book shows, also lost lands to rapacious Normans like Picot, the sheriff of Cambridgeshire, in the confused aftermath of conquest. In 1077, indeed, the King was compelled to order his sheriffs to return all the demesne lands they had acquired from the Church, whether they had been freely granted 'or which they had seized by violence'.[31] However, it would be misleading to suggest that the changes imposed on the English monastic landscape after 1066 were either thoroughgoing or wholly destructive. Whilst there are isolated examples of lay expropriation of monastic lands after 1066, it has been said that 'there is no widespread deprivation evident' from Domesday Book.[32] There is also plenty to suggest that the Normans were interested in and even enthusiastic about certain aspects of Anglo-Saxon religious history and practice. The cults of certain Anglo-Saxon saints were maintained and promoted at some monasteries under Norman leadership. This emphasis on the Anglo-Saxon past served to stress continuity and to raise revenue in the case of particularly popular saints. When Turold, the Norman abbot of Peterborough, set about retrieving the relics of St Oswald from Ramsey Abbey, he may have been thinking of the financial profit to be gained from turning Peterborough into a pilgrimage destination. Such enthusiasm may also have been sincere, of course, and the way in which the Normans treated those anomalies of the Anglo-Saxon ecclesiastical system, the monastic cathedrals, suggests that they found something to admire in the way the English conducted their religious affairs. There were four monastic cathedrals in 1066: at Canterbury, Winchester, Worcester and Sherborne. When the last of these sees was moved to Old Sarum, it did not remain monastic; but the other three survived and more monastic cathedrals were established at Durham, Rochester, Norwich and elsewhere. By 1135, indeed, 10 out of England's 19 cathedrals were served by monks.

Given the importance and influence of monasticism in eleventh-century Normandy, it is not surprising that the monastic cathedrals of England appealed to Lanfranc and his fellow Norman monks. There was more to their spread than this, however. In 1083, when the Norman bishop, William de St Calais, replaced the secular clerks who served at the shrine of St Cuthbert in Durham with Benedictine monks from nearby Monkwearmouth and Jarrow (monasteries which had themselves been restored with Norman help), the new rulers of the English Church were displaying their reverence for the great saint of northern England and for Anglo-Saxon history as written by Bede. There were political and cultural concerns at stake here as well as religious ones.

None of this is to say that the Normans did not introduce significant changes to English monastic life, however. Many of those Normans who acquired English lands between 1066 and 1086 gave some of it to one or more continental religious houses. This led to the establishment in England of so-called alien priories, outposts of the senior house across the Channel staffed by foreign monks. Such things were not entirely novel: the Norman monastery of Fécamp, for example, had acquired lands in England before 1066. However, the scale of such activity increased significantly after the Norman invasion: by 1086, over thirty continental houses held English lands. Brand new monasteries were also founded in England after 1066. William I himself founded a great monastery on the site of his victory over Harold II. Monks from Marmoutier on the river Loire colonised Battle, whilst others from Sées and Bec arrived to serve the new foundations at Shrewsbury and Chester respectively. But not least amongst the new English foundations were those made by monks from Cluny in Burgundy. At the end of the eleventh century, Cluny was the most prestigious monastery in Europe. The abbot of Cluny presided over a network of monasteries which followed Cluniac customs and liturgy. They all acknowledged the abbot of Cluny as their own abbot and styled themselves priories rather than abbies as a result. Norman monasteries had been heavily influenced by Cluny well before 1066, but the first Cluniac priory in England was only established in 1077, by William de Warenne at Lewes in Sussex. Other Cluniac foundations were soon made at Castle Acre and Thetford in Norfolk, and at Bermondsey in London.[33] It was in ways like this that the English Church was exposed to current continental practices and brought increasingly into the mainstream of European religious observance. These new monastic foundations were also the spiritual arm of military conquest. At sites across the kingdom, new religious houses and new castles were constructed side by side, to demonstrate that Norman domination of England had divine blessing.

Kings, archbishops and popes

Papal influence was by no means unknown in Anglo-Saxon England, as has been seen in Chapter 2. But to Edward the Confessor and Harold, the pope was a remote albeit respected figure. William I and Pope Alexander II (1061–73), by contrast, were on closer terms because their objectives in Normandy and England coincided to a significant degree. The popes of the mid eleventh century had been concerned to stamp out abuses within the Church, to eradicate simony and to establish a celibate clergy. William as both king and duke was happy to support these reforming principles as long as they did not impinge upon his royal rights. In return, Alexander may have supplied him with a papal banner at Hastings, and he sent his representatives to re-crown William in 1070. The relationship changed when Gregory VII became pope in 1073. He adopted a more radical reforming stance than his predecessors and advocated the idea that ecclesiastical authority was superior to secular (in other words, that popes had authority over kings) and that the pope was entitled to enforce direct control over the entire Church in matters of doctrine, discipline and law. Such ideas were bound to find little favour with William I, and during the second half of his reign, Anglo-papal relations worsened steadily. Gregory was insistent that English bishops should attend papal councils and that he should be able to communicate freely with them. He also made repeated demands for Lanfranc's attendance at Rome after the Archbishop had reluctantly travelled to receive his pallium there in 1071, and that papal legates should be allowed to hold councils in England and Normandy. Most provocatively, he wanted William to perform homage to him for the kingdom of England and declare himself a vassal of the papacy. Gregory claimed that William had agreed to do this before 1066 in order to obtain papal support for his invasion of England. The implications of such a claim for the King's authority within his lands could not be countenanced by William, and in 1080 he firmly but politely rejected the pope's demands. In a letter to Gregory, he said 'I have never desired to do fealty, nor do I desire it now; for I neither promised on my own behalf nor can I discover that my predecessors ever performed it to yours.' The King did allow the payment of Peter's Pence to be resumed after it had lapsed, because this was a long-standing custom, not a sign of subjection.[34]

After 1080, Gregory VII's interest in England waned as his relationship with the Emperor Henry IV became increasingly acrimonious. In 1084 he was driven out of Rome by the Emperor and his place was taken by the anti-pope Clement III who had been appointed by Gregory's opponents in 1080. These political difficulties relieved the pressure on William I, and William II was able to take advantage of them, too. Rufus had little time for the claims of the papacy in any event, and he was able further to reduce papal influence in England by refusing to come down on the side of one or another claimant to the papal throne. Pope Urban II, who had to deal with Henry IV and Clement III just as Gregory VII had done, was not recognised by Rufus until 1095, in return for an acknowledgement that papal legates and papal letters could only enter England with royal consent.

By this time, the English Church had a new leader. The see of Canterbury had been left vacant by the King after Lanfranc's death in 1089, but William II fell seriously ill in 1093 and appeared to be dying. Amongst his acts of repentance was the appointment of Anselm as the new archbishop. Anselm had a Europe-wide reputation as a scholar and as the saintly prior and then abbot of the great Norman monastery of Bec. Temperamentally, therefore, he and the King could not have been more different, and the cooperation that had characterised the relationship between William I and Lanfranc was never present between William II and Anselm. For one thing, Anselm was much more heedful of the demands of the reform papacy than his predecessor had been. However, it was only after having his traditional rights over the Church acknowledged by Urban II that Rufus allowed Anselm to receive his pallium. More tension arose from the King's unwillingness to hold church councils in England as Anselm repeatedly asked him to do. A final quarrel arose in 1097 after the King's unsuccessful campaign against the Welsh: he criticised Anselm for having supplied him with inadequate knights in his capacity as a tenant-in-chief. This prompted Anselm to seek permission to leave the kingdom and go to Rome, perhaps to resign his archbishopric. Finally, the King gave his consent, Anselm departed and they never met again. This allowed Rufus once more to exploit the revenues of the vacant archbishopric; but whilst this benefited him in the short term, the long-term implications of this dispute for royal authority in England were significant. By 1100 the king was not inevitably the ultimate source of all authority in England; and the papacy, revived by Urban II whose stock had risen dramatically since he had preached the First Crusade in 1095, was beginning to provide a meaningful and credible alternative focus for loyalty. The English king no longer had an exclusive claim on the allegiance of the English clergy.

Henry I's political weakness at the start of his reign, and his desire to distance himself from the excesses of his brother, led to him immediately recalling Anselm to England in 1100. During his absence, however, Anselm had absorbed the latest ideas of the reform papacy, in particular its renewed stress on the unacceptability of 'lay investiture'. In other words, the reformers wanted to eradicate the practice of lay rulers giving the emblems of their office, the ring and the staff, to new bishops at their consecration. The symbolism of this practice, which seemed to imply that a bishop was dependent on a secular ruler for his spiritual power, was intolerable, and so lay investiture was condemned at papal councils held at Clermont and Bari in 1098 and at Rome in 1099, as was the performance of homage by a churchman to a layman. Such ideas, if put into effect, would have impinged seriously on the king's authority over his ecclesiastical tenants-in-chief, and Henry I was determined to retain what he saw as his traditional rights. For his part, Anselm was determined loyally to enforce the Pope's reforming decrees, and on his return he refused investiture at the King's hands and would not perform homage to him. Anselm was thus forced into exile again in 1103, but Henry was brought to the negotiating table after he was threatened with excommunication during his Norman campaign of 1105. By March 1106, a settlement had been reached, and it was publicly proclaimed in a church council at Westminster in 1107. The King agreed to give up his right to invest bishops with ring and staff, but he retained the right to receive homage from the bishops and abbots before they were consecrated.

The King did well by the compromise of 1107. He lost little of practical value by surrendering the right of investiture. He could still expect his leading churchmen to profess obedience to him and perform their feudal obligations; and he retained huge influence over the choice of bishops and abbots in practice. Henry's chief minister, Roger, became bishop of Salisbury in 1107, and his chaplain, Thurstan, archbishop of York in 1114. Indeed, every new bishop appointed until 1125 was a royal servant of some kind, and ecclesiastical vacancies continued to be exploited by the King, not least at Canterbury for the five years after the death of Anselm in 1109. The King also managed to retain his control over the holding of church councils, and he restricted papal influence by regulating the visits of papal legates to England. But, whether he realised it or not, Henry was swimming against the reforming tide, and the theories which justified papal supremacy within the Church were now part of the intellectual mainstream across Europe. The reluctance of the English kings to accept the realities of this new situation would lead to further confrontations with the Church during the course of the following century.

Reconstruction

It was in its architecture that perhaps the most obvious and permanent change affected the English Church after 1066. As has been seen, if Anglo-Saxon England was not completely insulated from advances in continental building styles and techniques before 1066, it was something of an architectural backwater. Normandy, by contrast, was very much at the centre of current trends. Nevertheless, although it is right to say that English architecture was transformed after 1066, this was not by a simple process of importing Norman practices and preferences into England. No single model was used in England; influences from beyond Normandy were at play, and there were variations in the approaches to these major undertakings across the kingdom. Some things are clear, however: in the half-century or so after the arrival of the Normans in England, with the exception of Westminster Abbey which had already been built in the Romanesque style, every major Anglo-Saxon cathedral or abbey was replaced. And, with the exception of Bishop Wulfstan of Worcester, all those responsible for undertaking these rebuilding programmes were new to the kingdom. Perhaps not surprisingly, Canterbury Cathedral, which was entirely rebuilt after a fire from c.1070, appears to have followed in size and arrangement Archbishop Lanfranc's former church of St Stephen at Caen, which has been described as 'one of the most consummate statements in Romanesque architecture'.[35] Even at Canterbury, however, features were incorporated which suggest influences from beyond Normandy. In eastern England,

meanwhile, at Ely, London, Norwich, Bury St Edmunds and, in particular, at Winchester, size mattered. These churches were far bigger
than any built in eleventh-century Normandy; indeed, when the new
cathedral at Winchester was designed, it was the largest church built
since antiquity, and Bishop Walkelin's expressed desire was to model his
new church on Old St Peter's in Rome. Unfortunately only the transepts
remain to give an impression of what was intended.[36] In the west, at
Gloucester and Tewkesbury, churches were constructed on a comparatively less grand scale; whilst the unusual plan of cathedral constructed
at York, it has been suggested, may have resulted from Archbishop
Thomas I's wish to distinguish his church from Canterbury as much
as possible. And to facilitate these grand schemes, new architectural
methods were pioneered, most notably in the use of ribbed stone vaults
to support roof, walls, transepts and aisles at Durham, where construction began in 1093.

A range of priorities and motivations underlay this extensive and
varied building programme. England's wealth provided the new French
ecclesiastical hierarchy with the means to retain skilled designers and
craftsmen to oversee their display of conspicuous power and prestige;
whilst a ready supply of forced labour was on hand to execute their
plans. And new side altars, transepts and aisles served to meet specific
liturgical needs. These great new churches had functions beyond the
purely religious and symbolic, however. Durham and Winchester were
expressions of 'religious triumphalism' and served as 'an overpowering
reminder of the conquest which had just taken place'. And Bishop
Remigius's new church at Lincoln, built close to the castle, had a military
function, too. Henry of Huntingdon described it as 'strong in a strong
place, beautiful in a beautiful place, dedicated to the Virgin of virgins,
which would be pleasing to God's servants and, as time went on,
impregnable to enemies'. The vast masonry façade of the cathedral, with
great arches seemingly tunnelled through it, still bears his assessment
out.[37]

By the early twelfth century, therefore, the architectural landscape
of England had been transformed, not just by Norman castles, but by
new cathedrals, abbeys and (although this is difficult to discern at such
an early stage) parish churches built increasingly in stone instead of
wood. 'You may see everywhere' (and William of Malmesbury's famous

statement bears repeating here), 'churches in villages, in towns and cities monasteries rising in a new style of architecture.' And Bishop Wulfstan of Worcester was admired for the way in which 'he constructed churches on his own estates and pressed for them to be constructed on others'.[38] Wulfstan was a survivor from an Anglo-Saxon past which was not entirely forgotten in the new era either. Perhaps under the influence of illustrations from Anglo-Saxon manuscripts in the cathedral library, the capitals built in the crypt at Canterbury whilst Anselm was archbishop contain Anglo-Saxon motifs in the foliage carving; and something similar may have happened in the transepts at Ely Cathedral, which were constructed in the 1090s.[39] Given what had already happened by 1066, it is likely that England's great churches would have been significantly affected by wider European architectural trends in any event. However, the Norman Conquest speeded up these developments dramatically and resulted in the development of a unique hybrid Anglo-Norman architectural style, neither purely Romanesque nor purely Norman, and with an eye on the pre-conquest past.

Wales, Scotland and Normandy

The impact of the Norman Conquest on the Churches of Scotland, Wales and Normandy was less direct and less immediate than in England. In Normandy, as has been seen in Chapter 2, an ongoing campaign of ecclesiastical reform was well under way before 1066. Hand in hand with the spread of monasticism through the duchy in the eleventh century and the improvement of standards within the ranks of the Norman episcopate went the beginning of a systematic reorganisation of individual dioceses and the further strengthening of episcopal power. The construction of new cathedral churches across Normandy continued, too; lands and cathedral chapters were reorganised, and archdeaconries may have been established in some dioceses by the later 1070s. The reform process was far from complete by 1066, however, as the experiences of Archbishop John of Rouen revealed. According to Orderic Vitalis, John 'was a man who showed his zeal for virtue in both words and deeds, and . . . led a merciless campaign against vice'; but when in 1072 he tried to compel the priests of his archdiocese to abandon their wives and mistresses, he was stoned out of the synod, and fled exclaiming with a loud voice: 'O God, the heathen are come into thine inheritance.'[40] Imposing strict standards of conduct and behaviour was certainly a struggle, but it does seem that the pace of reforming activity in Normandy increased in the 1060s and 1070s. The decrees of the councils of Rouen in 1072 and Lillebonne in 1080 were sophisticated and detailed, combining condemnation of abuses like simony and clerical marriage with provisions about episcopal rights and jurisdiction. The latter have been described as 'a monument to the achievement of the eleventh-century Norman Church'.[41] If these developments were related in any way to what was happening in England, they can only have been so indirectly. Nevertheless, the Norman Church was not left untouched by events across the Channel. The already pervasive control exercised by the Duke over the Norman Church was strengthened further by the events of 1066 as William I's status was elevated to that of a consecrated king. Great prelates like Odo of Bayeux and Geoffrey of Coutances were required to spend considerable amounts of time away from their Norman dioceses dealing with their new responsibilities in England. They, and other Norman churchmen, became very rich indeed as the spoils of conquest were doled out. Before 1086, moreover, more than twenty Norman monasteries had received lands across 25 English shires, and French clergy had come to England to administer them.[42]

A notional supremacy over the Scottish Church was granted to the archbishop of York as part of the compromise over the primacy agreed in 1072. Occasionally this meant something in practice, and York was able to consecrate some Scottish bishops. Ralph I, bishop of Orkney, was consecrated at York in 1073, for example, as were his successors Roger and Ralph II in the early twelfth century. Bishops of Glasgow and St Andrews were consecrated at York, too; and one bishop of St Andrews, Fothadh (d.1093) travelled south to profess obedience to the archbishop of York 'because he had been ordained by the Scots, [and] on the advice and command of King Malcolm [III] and Queen Margaret'. Then in 1102 when Archbishop Gerard of York went to Rome to collect his pallium, he secured a papal bull ordering all the Scottish bishops to obey him as their metropolitan.[43]

In Wales, too, there were signs of increasing Anglo-Norman influence over the native Church. In 1081, William I's journey to St David's may have been designed in part to show respect for Wales's patron saint, but it was surely intended to demonstrate Norman dominance over the Welsh Church, too. And soon after, Archbishop Lanfranc's temporary suspension of the bishops of Llandaff and St David's did the same. Attempts to impose more permanent change took place in north Wales. The transfer of the see of Lichfield to Chester was one result of the Norman advance into Gwynedd, as was the appointment to the see of Bangor in 1092 of Hervé, William II's Breton chaplain. Hervé was forced to leave his diocese when the Welsh revolt broke out in 1095, and he was eventually translated to the new see of Ely in 1109: 'Thus the subjection of the see of Bangor under Hervé was only temporary, as was the Norman conquest of Gwynedd which made it possible.'[44] Nevertheless, during Henry I's reign, the sees of Llandaff, St David's, Bangor and, to a lesser extent, St Asaph were to be brought within the archbishop of Canterbury's sphere of influence.[45]

If political considerations dictated the speed and course of events in Wales, royal involvement in the affairs of the Scottish Church also stimulated further change in Scotland. In 1069 or 1070 at Dunfermline, King Malcolm III married Margaret, the sister of Edgar *atheling*. Edgar, his mother and his two sisters had fled to the Scottish court in 1068. This kind of marriage may have taken place anyway, of course, but this particular union can be said to have come about as a direct result of William of Normandy's invasion of England. The major source for Margaret's life is the hagiographical work written in the early 1100s at the request of Margaret's daughter, Queen Matilda of England, by Turgot, then prior of Durham and later bishop of St Andrew's, but previously Margaret's chaplain. Whose idea the marriage was is not completely clear, although the indications are that Malcolm was keen from the start.[46] According to Turgot, moreover, Margaret was keener on entering the religious life and becoming a nun than she was on becoming queen of Scots. Her interest in the lives and regimes of the Scottish hermits she came to know after her marriage was probably the product of genuine enthusiasm on her part; and she may have had little choice but to marry Malcolm, given her family's dependence on Scottish help. Once she was queen, however, and with the active cooperation of Archbishop Lanfranc, she recruited monks from Canterbury to help convert the church in which she had been married, Holy Trinity at Dunfermline, into the first conventional Benedictine monastery in

Scotland. Margaret appreciated Scottish religious tradition, too: she restored the church at Iona, according to Orderic Vitalis; and as a keen devotee of St Andrew, she persuaded her husband to allow pilgrims free crossing of the Firth of Forth at the place which later became known as Queensferry.[47]

There is no reason to doubt Turgot's portrayal of Margaret as a woman of remarkable piety, with a string of saintly qualities. Her most important achievement, however, was to start the process of bringing the lax procedures of the Scottish Church more into line with those of mainstream western Christianity. She and her husband presided over ecclesiastical councils at which the Scottish people were urged to receive communion more than once a year, to abstain from work on Sundays, to change their marriage practices and to celebrate mass in a common and consistent way. It seems unlikely that these reforms had progressed very far by the time Margaret died in November 1093, of grief at hearing the news of her husband's death three days earlier and exhaustion after years of self-denial and fasting. Margaret was revered in the twelfth century by a wide range of commentators, but she was not canonised until the middle of the thirteenth century. According to the *Anglo-Saxon Chronicle*, she had been divinely chosen 'to increase the glory of God in the land, and set the king right from the path of error, and turn him to the better way, and his people as well; and put down the evil customs that this nation had practised, just as she afterwards did'.[48] This assessment of Margaret's achievements goes too far. Her foundation at Dunfermline did not lead to a Scottish monastic revival, nor did she succeed in modernising the Scottish Church. Arguably, however, through her own personal example and because of the influence she had on her children (three of her sons succeeded in turn to the Scottish crown, her daughter married Henry I of England, and all of them were keen religious reformers), she prepared the Scottish Church for the reform it was to experience under her successors.

Conclusion

Traditional views of the Norman Conquest have tended to highlight the differences in religious and ecclesiastical structures in Normandy and Britain before 1066. The pre-conquest Norman Church was a centre of reforming practice and principle. The pre-conquest Churches of Britain, by contrast, had their shortcomings, and abuses were widespread. In England, Edward the Confessor and Stigand showed no interest in continental reforming trends, whilst Wales and Scotland appear to have been cut off from such developments almost entirely. However, in the decades before 1066 there was nothing unusual about any of this by wider European standards. Across continental Europe, lay rulers, not least the dukes of Normandy, appointed bishops and abbots who played essential roles in central and local government. And whilst the late Anglo-Saxon Church produced no figure equivalent to a Dunstan or an Anselm, someone who might have tried systematically to introduce new ideas and to reinvigorate English religious life, the signs are that the ideas of the reform papacy were gradually beginning to seep into the kingdom by 1066. Serious reform of the English Church was probably inevitable by 1066, just as it was elsewhere; and it may have happened under a pious and vigorous ruler like Harold II, just as it did later in Scotland under David I. Decisions about the precise nature and scale of reform in England were in the event left to the Normans, however, who were not slow to take up the challenge. William the Conqueror, therefore, 'may have accelerated the pace of change, but he did not alter its direction'.[49]

Notes

1 *WMGR*, i p.461.

2 *WP*, p.109.

3 *Councils and Synods, with Other Documents Relating to the English Church*, ed. D. Whitelock, M. Brett and C.N.L. Brooke, 2 vols (Oxford: Clarendon Press, 1964, 1981), I/ii pp.563–76.

4 *JW*, iii p.13.

5 Robert Bartlett, *England under the Norman and Angevin Kings, 1075–1225* (Oxford: Clarendon Press, 2000), p.395.

6 Above, pp.255–6.

7 *WMGR*, i p.507.

8 Above, p.161.

9 David Carpenter, *The Struggle for Mastery. Britain 1066–1284* (Oxford University Press, 2003), p.130.

10 *ASC* 'D', 'E', s.a.1070; *JW*, iii p.11.

11 *WMGR*, i p.559; *ASC* 'E', s.a.1099.

12 *OV*, v p.203.

13 *EHD* II, pp.647–8.

14 *The Letters of Lanfranc Archbishop of Canterbury*, ed. Helen Clover and Margaret Gibson (Oxford: Clarendon Press, 1979), no.3.

15 *Councils and Synods*, I/ii p.587.

16 A good overview of the events described here is given in the introduction to Hugh the Chanter, *History of the Church of York, 1066–1127* ed. and trans. Charles Johnson, rev. M. Brett, C.N.L. Brooke and M. Winterbottom (Oxford: Clarendon Press, 1990), at pp.xxx–xlv.

17 *The Letters of Lanfranc*, ed. Clover and Gibson, no.3 (p.41).

18 Hugh the Chanter, pp.5–7.

19 *The Letters of Lanfranc*, ed. Clover and Gibson, no.3 (pp.41–3).

20 *HN*, pp.11–12.

21 *The Letters of Lanfranc*, ed. Clover and Gibson, no.3 (pp.43–5).

22 *Councils and Synods*, I/ii pp.588–607; *The Letters of Lanfranc*, ed. Clover and Gibson, no.3 (pp.45–8).

23 Hugh the Chanter, pp.13–15; *HN*, p.43.

24 H.C. Darby, *Domesday England* (Cambridge University Press, 1977), pp.52–6, 346.

25 John Blair, *The Church in Anglo-Saxon Society* (Oxford University Press, 2005), pp.498–512; quotations at pp.498, 507.

26 Frank Barlow, *The English Church, 1066–1154* (London: Longman, 1979), p.49; H.R. Loyn, *The English Church, 940–1154* (Harlow: Longman, 2000), p.116; Bartlett, *England under the Norman and Angevin Kings*, p.389.

27 Barlow, *The Feudal Kingdom of England*, p.126.

28 *ASC* 'E', s.a.1066.

29 *ASC* 'E', s.a.1083.

30 Above, p.291 and n.10.

31 *DB*, pp.519, 544–7 *passim*; *EHD* II, p.463.

32 Janet Burton, *Monastic and Religious Orders in Britain, 1000–1300* (Cambridge University Press, 1994), p.26.

33 Brian Golding, 'The Coming of the Cluniacs', *ANS* 3 (1981), pp.65–77.

34 *The Letters of Lanfranc*, ed. Clover and Gibson, no.39.

35 Richard Plant, 'Ecclesiastical Architecture, *c*.1050 to *c*.1200', in *A Companion to the Anglo-Norman World*, ed. Christopher Harper-Bill and Elisabeth van Houts (Woodbridge: Boydell Press, 2003), pp.215–53, at p.253; Richard Gem, 'English Romanesque Architecture', in *English Romanesque Art, 1066–1200* (London: Hayward Gallery, 1984), pp.27–40, at pp.27–8; E.C. Fernie, 'Architecture and the Effects of the Norman Conquest', in *England and Normandy in the Middle Ages*, ed. David Bates and Anne Curry (London: Hambledon Press, 1994), pp.105–16, at pp.109–10.

36 R.D.H. Gem, 'The Romanesque Cathedral of Winchester: Patron and Design in the Eleventh Century', *British Archaeological Association Conference, VI, 1980* (1983), pp.1–12.

37 Gem, 'English Romanesque Architecture', p.32; Henrietta Leyser, 'Cultural Affinities', in *The Twelfth and Thirteenth Centuries*, ed. Barbara Harvey (Oxford University Press, 2001), pp.167–99, at p.188; *HH*, pp.33–4.

38 *WMGR*, i p.461; Bartlett, *England under the Norman and Angevin Kings*, p.386.

39 Leyser, 'Cultural Affinities' in *The Twelfth and Thirteenth Centuries*, ed. Harvey, p.188; Gem, 'English Romanesque Architecture', p.34.

40 *OV*, ii p.201.

41 David Bates, *Normandy Before 1066* (London: Longman, 1982), p.204.

42 David C. Douglas, *William the Conqueror* (London: Eyre & Spottiswoode, 1964), p.320.

43 Hugh the Chanter, pp.xlv–lv, 51–3.

44 John Edward Lloyd, *A History of Wales from the Earliest Times to the Norman Conquest*, 2 vols (1911), ii p.449.

45 Lloyd, *A History of Wales*, i pp.449–59; Barlow, *The English Church 1066–1154*, pp.32–3.

46 *ASC* 'D', s.a.1067.

47 *OV*, iv p.273.

48 *ASC* 'D', s.a.1067.

49 Brian Golding, *Conquest and Colonisation: The Normans in Britain, 1066–1100* (Basingstoke: Macmillan, 1994), p.146.

PART FOUR

Conclusion

CHAPTER 12

Britain and Normandy in 1106 – myths and reality

Myths about the Norman Conquest were very quick to develop. Most persistent and long-standing has been the notion that the events which took place in and after 1066 were a catastrophe for England; that the proud, independent and, most importantly, free English people were beaten down and subjected to 'the Norman yoke' of oppression and subjection. Not surprisingly, English historians took the lead in making this case. The doom-laden response of the *Anglo-Saxon Chronicle* to the Norman invasion, encapsulated in the 'D' text's description of the events of 1066, is well known: the English were a sinful people and deserved their punishment at the hands of Duke William and his men. For William of Malmesbury, 14 October 1066 was 'a day of destiny for England, a fatal disaster for our dear country as she exchanged old masters for new'.[1] Henry of Huntingdon's father was a Norman, but he was born in England in about 1088 and lived there all his life. He was well placed to judge the effects of the Conquest from a distance, and he was uncompromising in his assessment. When William I died in 1087, Henry claimed that:

the Normans had fulfilled the just will of the Lord upon the English people, and there was scarcely a noble of English descent in England, but all had been reduced to servitude and lamentation, and it was even a disgrace to be called English . . . [The Lord] deservedly took away from the English race their safety and honour, and commanded that they should no longer exist as a people.[2]

Other early commentators sometimes took a less gloomy view of the fate which had befallen the English. William de Poitiers was determined to praise the Normans come what may; and as early as the 1070s, Orderic Vitalis later claimed, 'peace reigned over England; and a degree of security returned to its inhabitants now that the brigands had been driven off. English and Normans were living peacefully together in boroughs, towns and cities, and were intermarrying with each other.'[3] However, in 1070, the Harrying of the North had just taken place, and the mass dispossession of English landholders was about to begin. Moreover, at other points in his work, Orderic made his awareness of the sufferings experienced by the English at the hands of the Normans quite clear. Indeed, it was Orderic himself who first described how 'the English groaned aloud for their lost liberty and plotted ceaselessly to find some way of shaking off a yoke that was so intolerable and un-accustomed'; and it is this idea which has kept its hold on the popular imagination for close to nine hundred years.[4]

By the sixteenth and seventeenth centuries, other ideas had developed to make the Conquest appear even more of a disaster for Britain. The Anglo-Saxons, it was held by some, had developed a so-called 'ancient constitution', in which all the nascent and incipient freedoms of Englishmen were contained. These freedoms, embodied by allegedly representative institutions like the *witan* and the courts of shire and hundred, were cruelly stamped on and repressed by the tyrannical Normans, and England's progress towards liberty had been violently blocked. Edward Augustus Freeman, in his massive five-volume *History of the Norman Conquest*, published between 1867 and 1879, saw the Anglo-Saxons as the true founders of the British constitution. The Conquest also strengthened England's ties with the papacy whereas, before 1066, the English Church had been able to govern itself more or less free of interference from Rome. These arguments reveal more about the nature of political and religious debate in Tudor and Stuart England than they do about the reality of the Norman Conquest. Nevertheless, they have struck a resonant chord with many in subsequent generations, and the popular view that 'evil' Normans and 'good' Saxons continued to fight each other throughout the Middle Ages continues to retain much of its power. Walter Scott expressed it clearly in *Ivanhoe*, published in 1819 and set at the time of the Third Crusade at the end of the twelfth century:

[F]our generations had not sufficed to blend the hostile blood of the Normans and Anglo-Saxons, or to unite, by common language and mutual interests, two hostile races, one of whom felt the elation of triumph, while the other groaned under all the consequence of defeat.

And, nearly two centuries after this, Robin Hood, a mythical figure in his own right, still holds his place as the archetypal English freedom fighter, defending the poor and oppressed 'Saxons' from the 'Norman' Prince John and his henchmen.

The popular myth of 'the Norman yoke' developed in the face of scholarly efforts since the eighteenth century to focus minds on serious questions about the extent of continuity and change after 1066. Other myths have been created by the scholars themselves, however. J.H. Round may have argued most famously and forcefully that William I introduced feudalism into England after 1066, but the ultimate origins of the 'myth of feudalism' lie in the work of seventeenth-century lawyers such as Sir Henry Spelman. It was only in the later twentieth century that historians stopped writing unquestioningly about the feudal system; and even today the arguments rumble on.

Another myth of more recent currency, which burnt brightly only to fade almost as quickly as it arose, has been that of 'The Norman Empire'. 'Empire' is, of course, a controversial term loaded with any number of political and ideological connotations; this makes it difficult to define. However, in his 1966 work, *The Norman Empire*, John le Patourel argued that the cross-Channel systems and structures established by William I and his sons to rule England and Normandy after 1066 had some imperial features.[5] The two territories were governed by the same central authority: a single ruler, household and court controlled both for the greater part of the period covered by his analysis, 1066–1145. Another characteristic of an empire is the domination and exploitation of a native majority by an alien minority, and this is what happened in England after 1066: a Norman lay and ecclesiastical aristocracy with lands either side of the English Channel ruled over the English, enriched themselves at their expense, and established common bonds between the two territories which brought the interests of kingdom and duchy together. Those aristocrats were also driven by an expansionist impulse which prompted more settlement and colonisation and irresistibly pushed them to go further into Britain, to dominate Wales, Scotland and, ultimately, Ireland, as they had England, Normandy and its neighbours such as Maine. According to C.W. Hollister, who took Le Patourel's arguments even further, 'England and Normandy became in many respects two parts of a single political unit' by the end of the eleventh century and, at least after 1106, 'Normandy was governed as if it were the southern part of a trans-channel kingdom'.[6]

Neither Le Patourel nor Hollister pushed their analyses too far, and both recognised that there were limits to the connections and links binding England and Normandy together after 1066. Nevertheless, both would have argued that centrifugal tendencies prevailed over centripetal ones, and it is their assumption that developments after 1066 inevitably pulled England and Normandy closer together which has been most strongly challenged.[7] For one thing, there was nothing set in stone about a single ruler controlling both England and Normandy. William I had not wanted this, it seems, and kingdom and duchy were split between three brothers for most of the two decades after 1087. Furthermore, the extent to which England and Normandy developed parallel systems of administration should not be overstated. There was a single court at times, but in the fields of government, finance and the law progress was made at a different pace and it took different forms. And as for a cross-Channel baronage constituting a single political society, there were plenty of Norman families who chose to confine themselves to their established family lands and their exclusively Norman concerns after 1066. Many showed little if any interest in England or in what it had to offer. Put simply, those who have criticised Le Patourel's thesis have stressed how Normandy and England remained linked but separate territories after 1066; there was no desire, even had this been possible, to establish a single Anglo-Norman political entity. Nevertheless, all of the different rulers of England and Normandy during this period did want to rule both territories simultaneously and most of their great subjects felt more secure under the lordship of a single man. The king-dukes also appreciated that control of Normandy was the key to security in England. It is no coincidence that England descended into civil war during the reign of King Stephen (1135–54) only after he had lost control of Normandy.

Myths about the Conquest abound, therefore; and peering into the mists which surround them can be disconcerting and misleading. Despite this, some things can be seen clearly. Britain would have changed after 1066 whether the Norman Conquest had happened or not. Economic, political, social and cultural changes were affecting Europe in the eleventh century and would continue to do so in the twelfth. Britain's position on the edge of Europe did not make it immune to such pervasive trends. Nevertheless, the scale, pace and direction of change in Britain were affected in ultimately indefinable ways by the events of 1066 and their aftermath. England and, to a lesser extent, Wales, Scotland and Normandy itself, were deeply and permanently changed in the 40 years between 1066 and 1106 in ways they would not have been but for the Norman invasion. Systems of social, political, economic and military organisation which had grown up over the course of hundreds of years sustained a jarring and brutal shock. By 1086, the ruling class of Anglo-Saxon England had been all but wiped out through a traumatic series of military defeats, suppressed rebellions and forcible expropriations. Indeed, 'from the point of view of the élite in town and country the Norman Conquest was the greatest disaster so far in the entire course of English history'.[8] Their place was taken by a new ruling class which spoke a different language and which regarded itself as superior to the conquered native population both ethnically and socially. Those English men and women who did survive, therefore, did so as second-class citizens, and Henry of Huntingdon's claim that, 20 years after Hastings, it was a disgrace to be called English, rings true. And even 20 years after this, in 1107, the *Anglo-Saxon Chronicle* could still pointedly record that 'it was the forty-first year after the French had been in control of this country'.[9]

Such observations notwithstanding, the foreign element within the native population always remained small after 1066. Again, it is impossible to establish conclusive figures. It has been claimed both that 'the Conquest had perhaps placed 8,000 Normans throughout the shires of England', and that 'in 1086 the newcomers were probably much less numerous than the 25,000 slaves at the other end of the social scale'.[10] It has also been claimed that the starkness of the divide between English and Norman after 1066 may have been overcome to some extent by intermarriage. In the 1170s, a prominent official at the court of Henry II could confidently declare that 'nowadays, when English and Normans live close together and marry and give in marriage to each other, the nations are so mixed that it can scarcely be decided (I mean in the case of freemen) who is of English birth and who of Norman'.[11] But the accuracy of this view and its applicability to the situation in England 70 years before are both open to question. William of Malmesbury and Henry of Huntingdon were both products of mixed marriages, and the former noted the Normans' willingness to marry 'their inferiors'.[12] So, of course, was Orderic Vitalis, who claimed, as has been seen, that intermarriage was becoming common as early as 1070. There is little hard evidence to support this, however. To be sure, some Normans did marry English women soon after 1066. Robert de la Haye married the daughter of one of the great English survivors, Colswein of Lincoln, and Geoffrey de la Querche's wife was Alfgeofu, the daughter of the Warwickshire thegn, Leofwine. These marriages may have been intended to legitimise a Norman husband's acquisition of his English wife's lands; this motive certainly appears to have been behind Robert d'Oilly's marriage to Eadgyth, daughter of Wigod of Wallingford, for example.[13] And in what was certainly an attempt to reinforce his own legitimacy and that of his ancestral line, Henry I married Edith-Matilda of Scotland. Such cases invariably concern relatively high status individuals or those linked to them; and it was a similar story in Wales, where some Normans, like Gerald of Windsor, married into the houses of ruling Welsh princes. They were not common, either, particularly at the top level of Anglo-Norman society, whose members were prepared to enter into marriages with families outside Normandy but not often, it seems, ones from England. It is hard to know, and beyond the limits of the surviving documentary sources, how prevalent intermarriage was lower down the social scale but most Normans who were married in England after 1066 probably acquired a husband or wife from another settler family.[14] Marriages between English men and Norman women were possibly discouraged. Earl Waltheof was able to marry William I's niece Judith, although he probably regretted having done so when she informed on him to her uncle in 1075; but Earl Edwin of Mercia eventually rebelled, in part because the marriage he had been promised to the Conqueror's daughter never took place. In the absence of clear evidence, it would be wrong to assume that Anglo-Norman intermarriage was common in the generation or two after 1066.[15]

Archbishop Lanfranc (a Lombard by birth) could describe himself only as 'a novice Englishman' (*novus Anglus*) and confess his continuing ignorance of English affairs in one of his letters from 1071.[16] Such sentiments were probably common amongst the first Norman arrivals in England and their immediate successors. A significant obstacle to integration between the peoples of Britain and their new Norman lords was language. Lanfranc again, in late 1072 or early 1073, confessed to Pope Alexander II that he had originally been reluctant to take up his position as archbishop of Canterbury in part because the local language was unknown to him.[17] There was nothing new in 1066 about linguistic barriers within Britain, however: the Welsh and Scottish tongues must have been as mysterious to most Englishmen as they were to the Normans. William of Malmesbury, indeed, even complained that 'the whole speech of the Northumbrians, especially that of the men of York, grates so harshly upon the ear that it is completely unintelligible to us southerners'.[18] After 1066, though, another vernacular language, French, was dominant in the higher reaches of society. Orderic Vitalis claims that William I tried to learn how to read English, but he was too old and too busy to stick at his lessons and soon abandoned them.[19] How representative the King was of his fellow invaders, and how much English William II and Henry I understood, is hard to know; but they and their officials must have established some means of communicating with the occupiers of their new estates. There would have been a small bilingual class, but it is likely that this existed before 1066, too, given the nature of the relationship between England and France in the eleventh century. Merchants and traders would have needed a working knowledge of French, and a few enterprising Englishmen may have realised that there was a market for translators and interpreters. In the end, 'bilingualism spread wherever it was needed for everyday business, or for the advancement of the able and ambitious'.[20] French words certainly entered into English usage, and, by the second half of the twelfth century, few English children were being given Anglo-Saxon names (Edward was the principal exception to this rule); and whilst girls' names tended to change more slowly, French names such as William, Robert, Richard, Roger and Hugh soon became common for boys.

French toponyms, too, were certainly being used to denote higher social status as early as the 1080s, although it was not unknown for lower status men of French origin to use English place names to identify themselves.[21] As far as place names themselves were concerned, however, and unlike the Anglo-Saxon and Scandinavian invasions of previous generations 'the arrival of the Normans left virtually no imprint'; a sure sign of the relatively small number of Norman settlers in England after 1066 and of the restricted circulation of their language.[22]

French remained the spoken language, principally if not exclusively, of the self-contained lay and ecclesiastical élites until it was replaced, by English of course, later in the Middle Ages. When he was sent from Shropshire to Normandy to become a monk at the age of ten in about 1085, Orderic Vitalis later recalled, 'I heard a language which I did not understand.'[23] As the child of a mixed marriage, it might reasonably be assumed that Orderic would have understood at least some French by then. It is striking that he did not, and his negligible exposure to spoken French was probably typical of the experiences of most Englishmen in the years after 1066, for whom their new rulers remained remote, strange and intimidating figures.

As for the English language, the traditional idea that the Norman Conquest was responsible for the shift in the spoken vernacular from Old English to Middle English is simplistic and now discounted. This change was under way before 1066 and was not completed until well into the twelfth century.[24] However, on parchment things were different. William I's writ confirming the liberties of the City of London was written in Old English in about 1067. But this practice was not to last and, after about 1070, Latin began to replace so-called Standard Old English as the language of written royal government. This did not mean that written English died out, of course: the *Anglo-Saxon Chronicle* continued to be written in the vernacular, for example. But it had faded from prominence by the middle of the twelfth century, during which Anglo-Norman and Latin became the dominant literary languages in England. This dominance did not last, and if the Conquest forced written English to go underground for a generation or two, 'the displacement of Anglo-Saxon as the language of government caused written English to diversify into regional dialects' and 'this use of the local vernaculars produces the diversity of language which is the most striking characteristic of Middle English'.[25] In other words, the Norman Conquest in the end deepened the richness and variety of written English and helped clear a path for Langland and Chaucer.

The different ethnic groups within Britain were still speaking different languages and marrying within their own ranks in 1106, and such things remained important markers of status and power as well as nationality. It is notable that, according to William of Malmesbury, some of the barons who supported the claims of Robert Curthose to the English crown in 1101 referred to Henry I and his new Anglo-Scottish wife as 'Godric' and 'Godgifu'. Their use of English nicknames was deliberately contemptuous and, despite the fact that Edith had been courted by illustrious figures such as Count Alan of Brittany and William de Warenne before she married Henry, it suggests that Henry's union with an Englishwoman, albeit a royal one, was considered to be demeaning by at least some of his enemies. And when Henry married, of course, his wife changed her English name Edith to the French Matilda.[26] Such distinctions were no doubt reinforced by different hairstyles and fashions, too. In 1066, it was probably quite easy to tell an Englishman from a Norman just by sight. On the Bayeux Tapestry, for example, the Normans are usually depicted as clean-shaven and with short hair, whereas the English have longer hair and moustaches. And when Cnut of Denmark threatened to invade England in 1086, William I ordered the Englishmen in his army to 'shave their beards, adopt weapons and clothes of the Norman style and become completely like Frenchmen, in order to delude the eyes of the invaders'.[27] Soon after this, the young men at the courts of William II and Henry I were growing their hair long and wearing curved, pointed shoes, much to the horror of monastic commentators who thought such things effeminate. But all the indications are that this was a new fashion confined to part of an aristocratic élite, and there is no reason to think that Norman or French styles and fashions had been adopted by most people in Britain by then, or that the young courtiers' hairstyles were based on English ones.[28]

By 1106, therefore, evidence that the new rulers of England were beginning to regard themselves as English is elusive; and distinctions between them and the people they had conquered remained firm. There is no reason to think, of course, that William I, his sons and their followers were at all interested in any form of assimilation. If they allowed

Englishmen to keep their lands or gave them responsibilities, this was tolerance prompted by pragmatism. Partly as a result of this, it was not until the end of the twelfth century that the cultural, linguistic and social barriers separating English and Normans could be said to have finally broken down.[29] To be sure, amongst the ecclesiastical élite and in the monastic scriptorium there was a growing interest in the saints, cults and history of Anglo-Saxon England, which can only have fostered mutual understanding. However, the effects of this and of other developments only became apparent in the longer term, and on Anglo-Norman society at large they may have been peripheral; whilst those symbols of Norman rule, the castle, the monastery and the cathedral can only have served to remind the native population of their continuing subjection.

What is more, if the English people were only just beginning to get to know their Norman rulers by the end of the eleventh century, this was the case in other parts of Britain to an even greater extent. In northern England, Scotland and Wales, contacts with the newcomers were still a novelty for most of the native population. Significant Norman settlement beyond Yorkshire had only begun in the 1090s, and Scotland's own distinctive process of Normanisation had not even started. In Wales, meanwhile, after rapid early progress, the Norman advance had stalled by 1106. Gruffudd ap Cynan was dominant in north Wales, and in the south Norman aristocratic power had been seriously damaged by the fall of the Montgomery brothers in 1102. The successful revitalisation of Anglo-Norman interest in Wales was to be one of Henry I's most significant achievements.[30] In central, southern and western England, by contrast, the processes of conquest and integration were well advanced if not complete by 1106. Real, lasting transformations had been imposed on these areas beyond the altered personnel of the ruling class. Structures of landholding had been reshaped, not consistently across the kingdom, and in some areas more extensively than others. Nevertheless, despite the varied character and rate of change, these developments were of immense significance. The imposition by the king of tenure by knight service on his lay and ecclesiastical tenants-in-chief had led to the enfeoffment by them of large numbers of men on their own estates in return for military service. This in turn had long-term effects on the way these men and their families came to view their own landed possessions – as heritable commodities, not to be taken away or interfered with at the whim of their lord. At the same time, whilst the holders of estates came increasingly to see their lands as belonging to them permanently (barring escheat or forfeiture), most lords' perceptions of their right to be involved in the inheritances, marriages and minorities of their vassals remained acute. This unresolved tension between the different views of landlords and tenants about their respective rights in and over land was to reshape the ways in which politics and society would operate in the twelfth and thirteenth centuries.

It is arguable, of course, that these developments affected only a very small proportion of the population: those who 'mattered' politically, a few thousand people at the most and, more usually, just a few hundred. And it is only right to say that, below the level of the great English lordships, it is hard to assess the impact of the Norman Conquest on the mass of the British people. Slavery had disappeared from England by the middle of the twelfth century, and those like the Irish, Welsh and Scots who still practised it were increasingly seen as uncivilised 'barbarians' by English commentators.[31] The English may not have had that much to feel superior about, however. To be sure, English people in servile positions were not called 'slaves' anymore; but the lives of many Anglo-Norman villeins were probably very similar to those of the slaves of Anglo-Saxon England. A good proportion of those villeins were probably once free peasants, moreover, and their status declined after 1066. But, once again, it is hard to pin responsibility for such changes on the Conquest alone. Population pressures and economic changes surely had an impact, just as they did on the continuing spread of nucleated villages and urban centres within Britain after 1066. Urbanisation and a growth in the number and size of nucleated settlements in the countryside had been taking place across Europe since the ninth century. But it is still likely that the Norman Conquest ultimately speeded up this process within Britain by fostering contacts with mainland Europe, stimulating trade and creating a need for more boroughs, markets and rural centres to provide them with goods and produce. New towns appeared across the British landscape in the twelfth century, whilst new villages which drew scattered local populations together were established in northern England, Scotland and Wales, all areas subject to new lordship and new methods of estate management.[32]

In other areas, the effects of the Norman Conquest on Britain remain obvious and easier to quantify. The great castles, cathedrals and monasteries built in the half-century or so after 1066 testify to the strength of Norman purpose and to the fluctuating but ultimately total control they exercised over their newly conquered territories. It is possible to argue that such structures would have arrived in England in due course anyway; but it is hard to think they would have done so on the same scale or with the same violent urgency if they had not been the product of prolonged military conflict and deeply felt ethnic tension. Other developments, too, in government, the law and the economy, might also have taken place over time in any case. But events in England, Scotland, Wales and Normandy between 1066 and 1106 acquired their unique character as a result of the interaction in a wholly novel context of Norman and British customs and traditions. Across Britain, however, and even within England, it should be clear by now that the effect of the Conquest was neither consistent nor uniform. Because the Norman impact on England was more immediate and profound than it was on Wales or Scotland, it is not surprising that the kingdom's political and economic orientation shifted away from northern Europe and Scandinavia further west towards France and other parts of central Europe. Trading patterns changed, as the Flemish market for English wool expanded; and commercial contact with the Rhineland was soon to provide English merchants with more new opportunities. More important than perhaps anything else, however, the king of England, at those times when he was also duke of Normandy, was now a vassal of the king of France. What this meant in practice by 1100 was still unclear, and twelfth-century English kings were always keen to minimise the significance of this relationship. Nevertheless, it was to have momentous consequences for the priorities of England's rulers in subsequent generations. Wales and Scotland by contrast retained their links with the Scandinavian and Celtic worlds long after the eleventh century ended. As the twelfth century went on, and as Anglo-Norman influence failed to make itself felt there more than occasionally and superficially, the traditional customs and practices of the Welsh and the Scots were seen increasingly by the English as barbaric and uncivilised. This in turn, it has been argued, led to a hardening perception of racial and cultural differences between the peoples of Britain and, in the end, to 'the creation of an imperialising English culture' which underlay later attempts to bring the whole of Britain under English control.[33]

It also needs to be remembered, however, that, for all the upheaval which shook Britain in so many different ways after 1066, much remained the same. For most Scots, and for most Welsh outside the marcher baronies, everyday life was probably largely unchanged. And at the level of shire and hundred, Henry I's England was not very different to Edward the Confessor's. The extent to which rural society was disrupted after 1066 is in the end unclear; as is the extent to which prevailing economic and demographic trends would have caused dislocation in any event. And after the turbulence of the first few years after the Battle of Hastings, most English men, women and children probably continued to live and work in much the same way as their ancestors had done for centuries – rising with the sun and sleeping when it set, making sure that there was food for the days ahead, performing labour services for their lord and contributing to their community when they were expected to do so, perhaps as the member of a tithing, as a witness in a dispute over land, or in the occasional discharge of a duty to serve in the *fyrd*. And, for all its dynamism and ultimate permanence, it was far from clear at the outset what form and course the Conquest would take. Cnut had arguably been just as dominant and successful a ruler as William I, yet his 'empire' outlived him by less than a decade. If William of Normandy had been killed at Hastings, his conquest would never have begun; if his resolve had been lacking in the difficult early years after 1066, it would have struggled even more than it did to sustain any momentum; and if William's plan to divide his territories between his sons in 1087 had been put permanently into effect, it is difficult to see how Norman influence on England could have remained as intensive and pervasive as it did into the twelfth century. It was only the vigour and determination of William II and Henry I which gave fresh impetus to the process of conquest, maintained the connection between England and Normandy and acquainted new generations of ambitious Frenchmen with what Britain had to offer.

Notes

1 *ASC* 'D', s.a.1066; *WMGR*, i p.457.

2 *HH*, pp.31, 35.

3 *OV*, ii p.257.

4 *OV*, ii p.203.

5 John le Patourel, *The Norman Empire* (Oxford University Press, 1976).

6 C. Warren Hollister, 'Normandy, France and the Anglo-Norman *Regnum*', *Speculum* 51 (1976), pp.202–42; repr. in *Monarchy, Magnates and Institutions in the Anglo-Norman World* (London: Hambledon Press, 1982), pp.17–57, at pp.24, 31.

7 For example, in D. Bates, 'Normandy and England after 1066', *EHR* 104 (1989), pp.851–80; Judith A. Green, 'Unity and Disunity in the Anglo-Norman State', *Historical Research*, 62 (1989), pp.116–23.

8 J. Gillingham in *From the Vikings to the Normans*, ed. W. Davies (Oxford University Press, 2003), p.215.

9 *HH*, p.31; *ASC* 'E', s.a.1107.

10 David Carpenter, *The Struggle for Mastery: Britain 1066–1284* (Oxford University Press, 2003), p.4; Marjorie Chibnall, *Anglo-Norman England* (Oxford: Basil Blackwell, 1986), p.208.

11 *Dialogus de Scaccario*, ed. and trans. C. Johnson, with corrections by F.E.L. Carter and D.E. Greenway (Oxford: Clarendon Press, 1983), p.53.

12 *WMGR*, i p.461.

13 Above, p.243.

14 Judith A. Green, *The Aristocracy of Norman England* (Cambridge University Press, 1997), pp.351–5.

15 *OV*, ii p.320; K.S.B. Keats-Rohan, *Domesday People: A Prosopography of Persons Occurring in English Documents, 1066–1166. Vol. 1: Domesday Book* (Woodbridge: Boydell Press, 1999), p.28; Hugh M. Thomas, *The English and the Normans: Ethnic hostility, assimilation and identity 1066–c.1220* (Oxford University Press, 2003), pp.146–55.

16 *The Letters of Lanfranc Archbishop of Canterbury*, ed. Helen Clover and Margaret Gibson (Oxford: Clarendon Press, 1979) no.2 (p.39).

17 *The Letters of Lanfranc*, ed. Clover and Gibson, no.1 (p.30).

18 *WMGP*, p.139.

19 *OV*, ii p.257.

20 Chibnall, *Anglo-Norman England*, p.212.

21 C.P. Lewis, 'The Domesday Jurors', *Haskins Society Journal* 5 (1993), pp.17–29.

22 Robert Bartlett, *England under the Norman and Angevin Kings, 1075–1225* (Oxford: Clarendon Press, 2000), pp.538–41, 490.

23 *OV*, vi p.555.

24 Bartlett, *England under the Norman and Angevin Kings*, pp.493–7.

25 M.T. Clanchy, *From Memory to Written Record. England, 1066–1307*, 2nd edn (Oxford: Clarendon Press, 1993), pp.212–13; Ann Williams, *The English and the Norman Conquest* (Woodbridge: Boydell Press, 1995), p.213.

26 *WMGR*, i p.717; Eleanor Searle, 'Women and the Legitimization of Succession at the Norman Conquest', *ANS* 3 (1980), pp.166–9; Green, *The Aristocracy of Norman England*, p.354.

27 Bartlett, *England under the Norman and Angevin Kings*, p.573.

28 *WMGR*, i pp.559–61.

29 Thomas, *The English and the Normans*, ch.5.

30 R.R. Davies, *The Age of Conquest: Wales 1063–1415* (Oxford University Press, 1991), pp.40–5.

31 J. Gillingham, 'The Beginnings of English Imperialism', in *The English in the Twelfth Century: Imperialism, national identity and political values* (Woodbridge: Boydell Press, 2000)', pp.13–14.

32 Richard Britnell, *Britain and Ireland 1050–1530: Economy and society* (Oxford University Press, 2004), p.167.

33 J. Gillingham in *From the Vikings to the Normans*, ed. Davies, p.232; and more generally his 'The Beginnings of English Imperialism'.

Suggestions for further reading

This is not a comprehensive bibliography, but merely an introduction to the enormous amount of contemporary and later
scholarly writing about the Norman Conquest. The works mentioned
below are, in my view, the essential ones with which any serious study
of the Conquest should begin. Details of many others, not singled out
here but relied on in my analysis, can be found in the footnotes.

The sources

The best collections of translated primary sources are *English Historical
Documents I c.500–1042*, ed. D. Whitelock, 2nd edn (London: Eyre
Methuen, 1979), and *English Historical Documents II 1042–1189*, ed.
D.C. Douglas and G.W. Greenaway, 2nd edn (London: Eyre Methuen,
1981). Also very useful is *The Norman Conquest of England. Sources and
Documents*, ed. R.A. Brown (Woodbridge: Boydell Press, 1984). Together
these provide a good selection of extracts from many of the principal
narrative sources, as well as administrative and legal sources – writs,
charters, leases, assizes and extracts from Domesday Book and the pipe
rolls. A translated and accessible edition of Domesday Book itself is
now available: *Domesday Book: A Complete Translation*, ed. A. Williams
and G.H. Martin (London: Penguin, 2002), and the slightly less user-
friendly but nevertheless complete text of the pipe roll for the financial
year 1129–30 can be found in *The Pipe Roll of 31 Henry I* (London: HMSO,
1929). The Bayeux Tapestry is reproduced in full in *EHD* II (albeit in
black and white) and, sumptuously, in *The Bayeux Tapestry*, ed. David M.
Wilson (London: Thames and Hudson, 1985).

The indispensable guide to the narrative sources produced in
England during this period is Antonia Gransden, *Historical Writing in*

England: I c.550–c.1307 (Ithaca, NY: Cornell University Press, 1974). The *Anglo-Saxon Chronicle* provides the principal English account of the late Anglo-Saxon and Anglo-Norman period. It is translated in full in *EHD* II, and also in *The Anglo-Saxon Chronicle*, ed. D. Whitelock (London: Eyre and Spottiswoode, 1961). Other English texts include the *Vita Edwardi Regis*, which can be found in *The Life of King Edward who rests at Westminster*, ed. and trans. F. Barlow (London: Nelson, 1962); *The Chronicle of John of Worcester*, ii, ed. R.R. Darlington and P. McGurk, trans. J. Bray and P. McGurk (Oxford: Clarendon Press, 1995), and iii, ed. and trans. P. McGurk (Oxford: Clarendon Press, 1998); William of Malmesbury's *Gesta Regum Anglorum: The History of the English Kings*, 2 vols, ed. and trans. R.A.B. Mynors, R.M. Thomson and M. Winterbottom (Oxford: Clarendon Press, 1998–9), and his *The Deeds of the Bishops of England*, trans. D. Preest (Woodbridge: Boydell Press, 2002); and *Eadmer's History of Recent Events in England*, trans. G. Bosanquet (London: Cresset Press, 1964). A valuable and affordable recent addition to the list of translated sources is *Henry of Huntingdon. The History of the English People, 1000–1154*, trans. D. Greenway (Oxford University Press, 2002). This edition, which I rely on in my footnotes, is a condensed version of *Henry, Archdeacon of Huntingdon, Historia Anglorum The History of the English People*, ed. and trans. D. Greenway (Oxford: Clarendon Press, 1996).

The main Norman accounts of the duchy's early history, and of the Conquest itself, are by Dudo of St Quentin, William de Jumièges and William de Poitiers: respectively, *The History of the Normans*, ed. E. Christiansen (Woodbridge: Boydell Press, 1998), *The Gesta Normannorum Ducum of William of Jumièges, Orderic Vitalis and Robert of Torigni*, 2 vols, ed. and trans. E.M.C. van Houts (Oxford: Clarendon Press, 1992–5), and *The Gesta Guillelmi of William of Poitiers*, ed. and trans. R.H.C. Davis and M. Chibnall (Oxford: Clarendon Press, 1988). A twelfth-century interpretation is *The History of the Norman People, Wace's Roman de Rou*, trans. Glyn S. Burgess (Woodbridge: Boydell Press, 2004). The Battle of Hastings is dealt with in *The Carmen de Hastingae Proelio of Guy Bishop of Amiens*, ed. and trans. Frank Barlow (Oxford: Clarendon Press, 1999). Also essential for Norman history either side of 1066, and for much more besides, is the work of Orderic Vitalis, the whole of whose *Ecclesiastical*

History can now be found in *The Ecclesiastical History of Orderic Vitalis*, 6 vols, ed. and trans. M. Chibnall (Oxford University Press, 1969–90).

Reference works

The Oxford Dictionary of National Biography, in Association with the British Academy. From the earliest times to the year 2000, ed. H.C.G. Matthew and Brian Harrison (Oxford University Press, 2004) is a potentially endless source of reliable detail about the lives of many of those mentioned in this book. It is available in print and online (at http://www. oxforddnb.com), and is regularly updated. For the pre-conquest period, *The Blackwell Encyclopaedia of Anglo-Saxon England*, ed. M. Lapidge, J. Blair, S. Keynes and D. Scragg (Oxford University Press, 1999) is full of useful information and perceptive explanation arranged alphabetically.

Not exactly a work of reference, more an indispensable guide to the latest scholarly thinking on all aspects of eleventh- and twelfth-century England and Normandy, are the annual volumes of *Anglo-Norman Studies* (formerly *Proceedings of the Battle Conference*), ed. R. Allen Brown and, latterly, Marjorie Chibnall, Christopher Harper-Bill, John Gillingham and C.P. Lewis (Woodbridge: Boydell Press, 1979–).

General works

The Norman Conquest

The historiography of the Conquest is illuminatingly evaluated in Marjorie Chibnall, *The Debate on the Norman Conquest* (Manchester University Press, 1999).

E.A. Freeman, *The History of the Norman Conquest of England*, 5 vols (Oxford: Clarendon Press, 1867–79) is the grandest narrative of all, and, despite its age, still merits more than a cursory acknowledgement. Probably more suitable for those new to the subject are Brian Golding, *Conquest and Colonisation: The Normans in Britain, 1066–1100* (Basingstoke: Macmillan, 1994) and N.J. Higham, *The Norman Conquest* (Stroud: Sutton, 1998). D.J.A. Matthew, *The Norman Conquest* (London: Batsford, 1966) still provides a solid introduction; and a robust assertion of older views on the Conquest is found in R.A. Brown, *The Normans and the Norman Conquest*, 2nd edn (Woodbridge: Boydell Press, 1985).

Britain and France

D.A. Carpenter, *The Struggle for Mastery. Britain 1066–1284* (London: Penguin, 2003) is the best single-volume treatment of post-conquest Britain and an essential introduction to the subject. Older, superseded in many ways, but still valuable as a starting point is G.W.S. Barrow, *Feudal Britain. The Completion of the Medieval Kingdoms, 1066–1314* (London: Edward Arnold, 1956). David Walker, *The Normans in Britain* (Oxford: Blackwell, 1995) is clear and wide-ranging; and the chapters by different authors in *From the Vikings to the Normans*, ed. W. Davies (Oxford University Press, 2003) are helpfully comparative on a range of matters across the British Isles.

There are several good introductions to the history of medieval France. Most useful are Elizabeth M. Hallam and Judith Everard, *Capetian France, 987–1328*, 2nd edn (Harlow: Longman, 2001), and Jean Dunbabin, *France in the Making, 843–1180*, 2nd edn (Oxford University Press, 2000).

The regions

England

F.M. Stenton, *Anglo-Saxon England*, 3rd edn (Oxford: Clarendon Press, 1971) retains its status as the classic single-volume account of the period. It extends to the death of William the Conqueror. Another introduction, beautifully illustrated, to all aspects of the Anglo-Saxon period is *The Anglo-Saxons*, ed. J. Campbell (London: Penguin, 1991). Richard Huscroft, *Ruling England, 1042–1217* (Harlow: Pearson, 2005) provides an introduction to the main political developments of this period, as does F. Barlow, *The Feudal Kingdom of England, 1042–1216*, 5th edn (London: Longman, 1999). More challenging is Pauline Stafford, *Unification and Conquest. A Political and Social History of England in the Tenth and Eleventh Centuries* (London: Edward Arnold, 1989), and important insights are provided by Ann Williams, *Kingship and Government in Pre-Conquest England, c.500–1066* (Basingstoke: Macmillan, 1999). Other useful works which deal with the end of the Anglo-Saxon period are N.J. Higham, *The Death of Anglo-Saxon England* (Stroud: Sutton, 1997) and F. Barlow, *The Godwins* (Harlow: Longman, 2002). The works of James Campbell are essential for an understanding of the sophistication and power of the late Anglo-Saxon state: his *Essays in Anglo-Saxon History* (London: Hambledon Press, 1986) and *The Anglo-Saxon State* (London: Hambledon Press, 2000) conveniently collect many of his essays together.

There are several outstanding general works dealing with England after 1066. Most notable, dynamic and full of insight and novelty, is Robert Bartlett, *England under the Norman and Angevin Kings, 1075–1225* (Oxford: Clarendon Press, 2000). Also very stimulating are M.T. Clanchy, *England and its Rulers 1066–1272*, 2nd edn (Oxford: Blackwell, 1998) and Marjorie Chibnall, *Anglo-Norman England, 1066–1166* (Oxford: Blackwell, 1986). The north of England has received particular and differing treatment in two works: W.E. Kappelle, *The Norman Conquest of the North. The Region and its Transformation 1000–1135* (London: Croom Helm, 1980); Paul Dalton, *Conquest, Anarchy and Lordship. Yorkshire, 1066–1154* (Cambridge University Press, 1994). And light has been shed on the contrasting fates of the Norman newcomers to England and the English survivors after 1066 by two significant works: J.A. Green, *The Aristocracy of Norman England* (Cambridge University Press, 1997), and Ann Williams *The English and the Norman Conquest* (Woodbridge: Boydell Press, 1995).

Scotland

Three general works, which deal in passing with the Conquest, together provide the foundation for studies of medieval Scotland: A.A.M. Duncan, *Scotland. The Making of the Kingdom* (Edinburgh: Oliver and Boyd, 1975), the same author's *The Kingship of the Scots, 842–1292: Succession and Independence* (Edinburgh University Press, 2002), and G.W.S. Barrow, *Kingship and Unity: Scotland 1000–1306*, 2nd edn (Edinburgh University Press, 2003). Also useful and recent are Bruce Webster, *Medieval Scotland: The Making of an Identity* (New York: St Martin's Press, 1997), and A.D.M. Barrell, *Medieval Scotland* (Cambridge University Press, 2000). R.L. Graeme Ritchie, *The Normans in Scotland*

(Edinburgh University Press, 1954) is now rather outdated, but it is thorough and of obvious relevance for this period.

Wales

J.E. Lloyd, *A History of Wales from the Earliest Times to the Edwardian Conquest*, 2 vols (1911), remains the starting point for any study of medieval Wales. Volume 2 is particularly relevant here. Wendy Davies, *Wales in the Early Middle Ages* (Leicester University Press, 1982) provides a thorough overview of Welsh society, its economy, politics and ecclesiastical structure from post-Roman times until the eleventh century. R.R. Davies, *Conquest, Coexistence and Change: Wales, 1063–1415* (1987; repr. in paperback as *The Age of Conquest: Wales, 1063–1415* (Oxford: Clarendon Press, 1991)) is a modern classic. D. Walker, *Medieval Wales* (Cambridge University Press, 1990) and A.D. Carr, *Medieval Wales* (Basingstoke: Macmillan, 1995) are useful overviews which consider the impact of the Conquest on Wales amongst other things.

Normandy

C.H. Haskins, *Norman Institutions* (Cambridge, Mass.: Harvard University Press, 1918) underpinned all discussions of Norman power for most of the twentieth century. It has now been surpassed by two contrasting interpretations of the early history of the duchy: David Bates, *Normandy Before 1066* (London: Longman, 1982), and Eleanor Searle, *Predatory Kinship and the Creation of Norman Power, 840–1066* (Berkeley, Cal.: University of California Press, 1988). There are shorter descriptions of the early history of the duchy in David Crouch, *The Normans: The history of a dynasty* (London: Hambledon, 2002), chs 1–2, and Marjorie Chibnall, *The Normans* (Oxford: Blackwell, 2000), chs 1–2.

Individual rulers

ODNB provides relatively short and well-informed accounts of the lives of all the British rulers of this period. There are no full-length modern biographies of any of the Scottish kings of this period; for Wales there is *Gruffudd ap Cynan: A collaborative biography*, ed. K.L. Maund

(Woodbridge: Boydell Press, 1996). As for the English kings, full biographies include: Ann Williams, *Aethelred the Unready: The ill-counselled king* (London: Hambledon, 2003); M.K. Lawson, *Cnut: The Danes in England in the eleventh century* (London: Longman, 1993), repr. as *Cnut: England's Viking King* (Stroud: Tempus, 2004); F. Barlow, *Edward the Confessor*, 2nd edn (London and New York: Yale University Press, 1997); Ian W. Walker, *Harold. The Last Anglo-Saxon King* (Stroud: Sutton, 1997); D. Bates, *William the Conqueror* (London: G. Philip, 1989); D.C. Douglas, *William the Conqueror* (London: Eyre and Spottiswoode, 1964); F. Barlow, *William Rufus* (London: Methuen, 1983); Emma Mason, *William II. Rufus the Red King* (Stroud: Tempus, 2005). The latter's 'William Rufus and the Historians' in *Medieval History* I (1) (1991) provides a stimulating view of the historiography of the reign and includes her discussion of the circumstances surrounding the King's death. C. Warren Hollister, *Henry I* (London and New York Yale: University Press, 2001), published posthumously, is the product of a lifetime's intensive study of its subject and his times; Judith A. Green, *Henry I: King of England and Duke of Normandy* (Cambridge University Press, 2006) is the latest study.

Some specific aspects of the Conquest

Hastings

The standard work on the battle is now M.K. Lawson, *The Battle of Hastings 1066* (Stroud: Tempus, 2003). An earlier thorough account, albeit one heavily dependent on the account of William de Poitiers, is R.A. Brown, 'The Battle of Hastings', in *Anglo-Norman Warfare. Studies in Late Anglo-Saxon and Anglo-Norman Military Organisation and Warfare*, ed. Matthew Strickland (Woodbridge: Boydell Press, 1992). Also useful are the essays in S. Morillo, *The Battle of Hastings. Sources and Interpretations* (Woodbridge: Boydell Press, 1996).

Government and law

The general works already mentioned on Scotland, Wales and Normandy consider government and law in those territories. Three works together deal exclusively with the development of English government before, during and beyond the period covered by this book. These are H.R. Loyn, *The Governance of Anglo-Saxon England 500–1087* (Stanford University Press, 1984), W.L. Warren, *The Governance of Norman and Angevin England 1086–1272* (London: Edward Arnold, 1987), and J.A. Green, *The Government of England under Henry I* (Cambridge University Press, 1986). Richard Huscroft, *Ruling England 1042–1217* (Harlow: Pearson, 2005), is also primarily concerned with developments in government and administration. Seminal as far as the development of written government and literacy in general are concerned is M.T. Clanchy, *From Memory to Written Record: England 1066–1307*, 2nd edn (Oxford: Blackwell, 1993).

F. Pollock and F.W. Maitland, *The History of English Law*, 2 vols, 2nd edn (Cambridge University Press, 1898) remains essential despite its age. R.C. van Caenegem, *The Birth of the English Common Law*, 2nd edn (Cambridge University Press, 1988) also examines developments in the law during this period. The most accessible and comprehensive introduction to developments in the law after 1066, however, is J. Hudson, *The Formation of the English Common Law: Law and society in England from the Norman Conquest to Magna Carta* (London: Longman, 1996).

Domesday Book

Domesday Book has a huge literature of its own. The works of V.H. Galbraith provide a starting point: *The Making of Domesday Book* (Oxford: Clarendon Press, 1961) and *Domesday Book: Its Place in Administrative History* (Oxford: Clarendon Press, 1974). A useful series of essays is contained in *Domesday Book: A Reassessment*, ed. P. Sawyer (London: Edward Arnold, 1985). Sometimes controversial interpretations of the Domesday process have recently been given by David Roffe in *Domesday: The Inquest and the Book* (Oxford University Press, 2000), and *Decoding Domesday* (Woodbridge: Boydell Press, 2007).

Economies

Two books provide overviews of the economies of Britain in the Middle Ages: C. Dyer, *Making a Living in the Middle Ages: The people of Britain 850–1520* (Cambridge University Press, 2002), and Richard Britnell,

Britain and Ireland 1050–1530: Economy and society (Oxford University Press, 2004). For the development of towns, see S. Reynolds, *An Introduction to the History of English Medieval Towns* (Oxford University Press, 1977), and R.H. Britnell, *The Commercialisation of English Society, 1000–1500* (Cambridge University Press, 1993). R.V. Lennard, *Rural England 1086–1135* (Oxford: Clarendon Press, 1959) retains its status as a classic analysis of English rural society at the time of the Domesday survey, whilst R. Faith, *The English Peasantry and the Growth of Lordship* (Leicester University Press, 1997) questions some traditional assumptions about the impact of the Conquest on lordship, manorialisation and the peasantry in England.

For Wales and Scotland (see under 'The regions' above), there are relevant chapters in Davies, *Wales in the Early Middle Ages* (ch. 2), Davies, *Conquest, Coexistence and Change* (ch. 6) and Duncan, *Scotland. The Making of the Kingdom* (ch. 18), although the last two of these extend far beyond the chronological scope of this book. The pre-conquest Norman economy is discussed in David Bates, *Normandy Before 1066* (London: Longman, 1982), ch. 3.

Military organisation

C.W. Hollister, *Anglo-Saxon Military Institutions on the eve of the Norman Conquest* (Oxford: Clarendon Press, 1962) and R.P. Abels, *Lordship and Military Organisation in Late Anglo-Saxon England* (London: British Museum Publications, 1988) are the essential guides to the military systems of late Anglo-Saxon England. M.K. Lawson, *The Battle of Hastings*, (Stroud: Tempus, 2003) also contains an excellent analysis of both English and Norman military capacity at the time of the Conquest. M. Bennett, *Campaigns of the Norman Conquest* (Oxford: Osprey Military, 2001) provides a useful and well-illustrated guide to the military situation in England in the first few years after 1066. Several essays in *Anglo-Norman Warfare*, ed. Strickland are also essential, particularly those by Chibnall ('Military Service in Normandy Before 1066'), Hooper ('The *housecarls* in England in the eleventh century', and 'Some observations on the navy in late Anglo-Saxon England'). Also in this volume, J.O. Prestwich, 'War and Finance in the Anglo-Norman State' is seminal.

The best introduction to castles remains R.A. Brown, *English Castles*, 3rd edn (London: Batsford, 1976). Also very helpful is R. Eales, 'Royal power and castles in Norman England', in *Ideals and Practices of Medieval Knighthood III*, ed. C. Harper-Bill and R. Harvey (Woodbridge: Boydell Press, 1990).

Feudalism

J.H. Round, *Feudal England* (London: Sonnenschein, 1909) gives the most famous, if not the first, statement of the idea that the Normans introduced feudalism into England. Sir Frank Stenton's lectures on *The First Century of English Feudalism 1066–1166*, 2nd edn (Oxford: Clarendon Press, 1961) provide the standard analysis of feudal structures of aristocratic power after 1066 and the picture of the aristocratic honour as 'a feudal state in miniature'. They are robustly supported by R. Allen Brown, *Origins of English Feudalism* (London: Allen and Unwin, 1973). Two essays, one by John Gillingham and the other by Sir James Holt, both entitled 'The Introduction of Knight Service into England', address the arguments from contrasting perspectives: *ANS* 4 (1982); *ANS* 6 (1984). For more general and wide-ranging critiques of the 'feudal' model, see Elizabeth A.R. Brown, 'The Tyranny of a Construct: Feudalism and Historians of Medieval Europe', *American Historical Review* 79 (1974) and Susan Reynolds, *Fiefs and Vassals. The Medieval Evidence Reinterpreted* (Oxford University Press, 1994). The most recent summary of the debate is in Marjorie Chibnall, *The Debate on the Norman Conquest* (Manchester University Press, 1999).

The Anglo-Norman realm

J. Le Patourel, *The Norman Empire* (Oxford: Clarendon Press, 1976) develops the view that England and Normandy formed a single political entity after 1066. C. Warren Hollister, 'Normandy, France and the Anglo-Norman *Regnum*', *Speculum* 51 (1976), which is reprinted as ch. 2 in his *Monarchy, Magnates and Institutions in the Anglo-Norman World* (London: Hambledon Press, 1986), says something similar. D. Bates, 'Normandy and England after 1066', *EHR* 104 (1989) convincingly criticises Le Patourel's thesis, as does Judith A. Green, 'Unity and Disunity in the Anglo-Norman State', *Historical Research*, 62 (1989).

The Church

There are relevant chapters on the Welsh, Scottish and Norman churches in Davies, *Wales in the Early Middle Ages* (chs. 6–7), Davies, *Conquest, Coexistence and Change* (ch. 7), Duncan, *Scotland. The Making of the Kingdom* (chs. 10–11) and Bates, *Normandy Before 1066* (ch. 5) (see above for full details). John Blair, *The Church in Anglo-Saxon Society* (Oxford University Press, 2005) is a ground-breaking work which, amongst many other things, in chapters 6–8 and the Epilogue, addresses the extent to which the Conquest affected the development of England's parochial system. It is not an easy work for the beginner to use, however, and the most straightforward introduction to the history of the pre-conquest English Church remains F. Barlow, *The English Church, 1000–1066*, 2nd edn (London: Longman, 1979). His *The English Church, 1066–1154* (London: Longman, 1979) is similarly essential for the post-conquest period, as is M. Brett, *The English Church under Henry I* (Oxford University Press, 1975). There are also relevant chapters in H.R. Loyn, *The English Church, 940–1154* (Harlow: Longman, 2000), and ch. 2 of J. Burton, *Monastic and Religious Orders in Britain, 1000–1300* (Cambridge University Press, 1994) is very useful, too.

Thorough accounts of the lives of many individual churchmen can be found in *ODNB*. Full-length studies include Margaret Gibson, *Lanfranc of Bec* (Oxford: Clarendon Press, 1978), R.W. Southern, *St Anselm and his Biographer* (Cambridge University Press, 1963) and *Saint Anselm: A Portrait in a Landscape* (Cambridge University Press, 1990) and Emma Mason, *St Wulfstan of Worcester c.1008–1095* (Oxford: Basil Blackwell, 1990).

Identities

English identity before 1066 is discussed by Sarah Foot in 'The Making of *Angelcynn*: English Identity before the Norman Conquest', *TRHS*, 6th series, 6 (1996). For the post-conquest period, Hugh M. Thomas, *The English and the Normans. Ethnic Hostility, Assimilation and Identity*

1066–c.1220 (Oxford University Press, 2003) is already the standard work. John Gillingham, *The English in the Twelfth Century: Imperialism, National Identity and Political Values* (Woodbridge: Boydell Press, 2000) also contains valuable essays on the development of English identity. Chapter 1, 'The Beginnings of English Imperialism' locates the origins of the English view that the Welsh, Scots and Irish were uncivilised 'barbarians' in the twelfth century, and in the work of William of Malmesbury in particular.

For the growth of Scottish national identity, the work of Dauvit Broun is indispensable. It includes *The Irish Identity of the Kingdom of the Scots in the Twelfth and Thirteenth Centuries* (Woodbridge: Boydell Press, 1999), and 'Defining Scotland and the Scots before the Wars of Independence', in *Image and Identity: The Making and Remaking of Scotland through the Ages*, ed. D. Broun, R.J. Finlay and M. Lynch (Edinburgh: John Donald, 1998). Bruce Webster, *Medieval Scotland: The Making of an Identity* (Basingstoke: Macmillan, 1997) is also helpful. R.R. Davies, *Conquest, Coexistence and Change* (Oxford: Clarendon Press, 1987) ch. 1 introduces notions of Welsh identity in the eleventh century, but only scratches at the surface of much wider issues raised by the same author in his seminal works in this area, which include *Domination and Conquest. The Experience of Ireland, Scotland and Wales, 1100–1300* (Cambridge University Press, 1990) and his lectures on 'The Peoples of Britain and Ireland', *TRHS*, 6th series, 4–7 (1994–7).

As for Normandy, G.A. Loud, 'The "Gens Normannorum" – Myth or Reality?' *ANS* 4 (1981) is a good starting point for discussions of Norman ethnic identity. Thomas, *The English and the Normans* ch. 2 also provides a good brief treatment of the early development of 'the Norman myth'.

Women and the family

On the family, the starting point is the work of J.C. Holt, in particular his 'Feudal Society and the Family in Early Medieval England: I, The Revolution of 1066', *TRHS*, 5th series, 32 (1982). It is reprinted as ch. 9 of his *Colonial England 1066–1215* (London: Hambledon Press, 1997). The work of Pauline Stafford on queenship and the position of women is fundamental. It includes *Queen Emma and Queen Edith: Queenship and*

Women's Power in Eleventh-Century England (Oxford: Blackwell, 1997) and 'Women and the Norman Conquest', *TRHS*, 6th series, 4 (1994). Ch. 10 of her *Unification and Conquest* is also very helpful. Susan M. Johns, *Noblewomen, Aristocracy and Power in the Twelfth-Century Anglo-Norman Realm* (Manchester University Press, 2003), is recent and useful, especially chs 1–2.

Art and culture

For a good selection of images of Anglo-Saxon artwork of all kinds, and useful introductions to it, see *The Golden Age of Anglo-Saxon Art, 966–1066*, ed. J. Backhouse, D.H. Turner and L. Webster (London: British Museum Publications, 1984). Michelle P. Brown, *Anglo-Saxon Manuscripts* (London: British Library, 1991) is a very helpful and well-illustrated introduction to its subject. For the post-conquest period, *English Romanesque Art, 1066–1200* (London: Hayward Gallery, 1984) provides excellent illustrations and illuminating essays.

Index

abacus 212
abbies, *see* cathedrals and abbies, monasteries
Abernethy, peace of (1072) 147, 152, 264
acquisitions 280–81
  see also patrimony
acta 16, 199
  see also writing in government
Adela, countess of Blois 181, 282
Adelelm, abbot of Abingdon 250
Adeliza, daughter of William I 104
Aelfgar, earl of Mercia 39, 47, 91, 97–101 *passim*
Aelfgifu of Northampton, royal consort 83
Aelfwold, bishop of Sherborne 62
Aethelflaed, noblewoman 41, 282
Aethelmaer, bishop 59
Aethelred II, king of England 16, 33, 36, 41, 42, 75–6, 79, 80–82, 83, 86
Aethelric, landholder 241, 278
Aethelric, monk 90
Aethelstan, king of the English 22–3, 41, 147
Aethelwig, abbot of Evesham 255–6, 293
Aethelwine, sheriff of Staffordshire 240
Aethelwold, bishop of Winchester and saint 57
Agatha, Hungarian princess 97
Aire, river 143
Alan, count of Brittany 190, 233–4, 235, 245, 248, 325
Alençon 50
Alexander II, pope 68, 137–8, 295–6, 303, 323
  and papal banner in 1066 121–2, 303

Alexander, bishop of Lincoln 8
Alfgeofu, wife of Geoffrey de la Querche 322
Alfred, king of Wessex 4, 25, 28, 33, 41, 51, 57, 83–4, 175, 282
Alfred *atheling* 82, 83, 91
  death of 84, 86
alien priories 302
Almenèches 67
Alnwick 164
Alton, Treaty of (1101) 175–6, 180
'ancient constitution', myth of 318
Andrew, saint 311
Angelcynn 25
  see also Englishness
Angles 23
Anglesey (Mon) 166, 261
Anglo-Saxon Chronicle 4–6, 7, 14, 21, 22, 41–2, 47, 49, 50, 81, 84, 87, 91–2, 93–5, 107–8, 115–17, 132–3, 139, 144, 146, 155, 163, 188, 189, 191, 195, 201, 208–9, 232, 249, 252, 264, 291, 292, 300, 311, 317, 321, 324
Anjou 28, 122, 179
anointing 140, 188
  see also coronation, consecration
Anselm, archbishop of Canterbury and saint 8, 67, 159, 282, 296–7, 304–6, 308, 312
  and Henry I 173, 174, 180–1, 211, 305
  and William II 163–4, 170, 211, 253, 296–7, 304–5, 308
antecessors 242–5
  see also lands and landholding
appeal, process of, *see* law
Apulia 169

Aquitaine 28, 169
arable farming 25, 49, 274
archdeacons and archdeaconries 298, 308
archers 46, 48, 127, 131
  see also military organisation
Argyll 23
aristocracy 152, 176, 181
  lands of, after 1066 238–9
  new after 1066 231–2, 239, 254, 279, 281, 319–20, 321, 326
  Norman 38
armies, see military organisation
Arnulf of Montgomery, baron 166, 175–7, 257, 262, 274
Arnulf of Pembroke, see Arnulf of Montgomery
Arundel 142, 242
Asgar the Staller, landholder 243
Ashingdon, battle of (1016) 82
assaying 213
Athol 35
Augi, landholder 240
Aumale 162, 166
Auvergne 167
Avranchin 28, 162, 168
Azur, housecarl 243

Babylon 47
baileys 45
  see also motte and bailey castles
Baldwin IV, count of Flanders 117
Baldwin V, count of Flanders 89, 92, 117, 122
Baldwin VI, count of Flanders 147–8
Bamburgh 142, 166
Bangor 261, 296, 310
Bari 305
Barlow, Frank, historian 211, 298
Barnard Castle 257
barons 218, 233–5
  see also tenants-in-chief
Bartlett, Robert, historian 211
Barton-on-Humber 63
Bates, David, historian 16, 28, 43–4
Bath 21, 299
Battle 126, 274
  Abbey 224, 302

battle, trial by see trial by battle
Bayeux 11, 13, 45, 92, 162, 168, 181, 248, 290
  see also Odo, bishop of Bayeux
Bayeux Tapestry 12–14, 45–8, 59, 64, 102–4, 108–9, 115, 116, 121–2, 125–9, 142, 248, 325
Beauchamp family 234
Beaumont family 38, 175, 234
  see also Henry de, Robert de, Roger de
Bec, see Le Bec
Bede, historian 7, 25, 30, 302
  Ecclesiastical History of the English People 7–8, 25
Bedford 240
Bedfordshire 240
Benedict X, pope 59, 65
Benedictine communities 57, 164, 302, 310–311
  see also monasteries
Benedictional of St Aethelwold 63
Beorn Estrithson, earl 87, 90
Berengar de Tosny, baron 255
Berkhamsted 133
Berkshire 131, 170, 243, 274
  five-hide system in 40, 252, 256
Bermondsey 302
Bernard de Neufmarché, nobleman 262
Bessin 168
Beverley 62
Bleddyn ap Cynfyn, Welsh prince 102, 140, 259
boc 198
  see also writing in government
Bolingbroke 274
Book of Ely 255
bookland 39–40
bordars 54, 55
bordiers, see bordars
boroughs 262, 274, 327
  see also towns
bowmen see archers
Bramber 142, 242
Bramley 277
Brand, abbot of Peterborough 300
Brecon 165, 262
Bretons, see Brittany
Brindisi 169

Bristol 54, 140, 165, 278
Brittany 88, 103, 121, 122, 149–50, 179,
    190, 233–4, 235, 245, 248, 253,
    310
  Breton retreat at Hastings 127–8
Broughton 255
Brown, R. Allen, historian 254–5
Bruges 84, 95
Brunanburh, battle of (937) 22
Brut y Tywysogyon 14, 165, 177–8
Buchan 35
Buckinghamshire 241, 278
burghs 273
Burgundy 302
burhs 40–41, 44, 51
Burton 61
Burton in Lonsdale 257
Bury St Edmunds 218, 274, 307

Cadwgan ap Bleddyn ap Cynfyn, Welsh
    prince 165–6, 261
Cadwgan ap Meurig, Welsh prince 259
Caen 11, 50, 51, 67, 68, 156, 168, 181,
    290, 300, 306
Caithness 23
Cambridge 141
Cambridgeshire 86, 240, 276, 277, 300
canon law 299
Canterbury 5, 8, 13, 15, 56, 57, 58, 59,
    61, 63, 65, 66, 67, 88, 90, 96, 103,
    108, 131–2, 159, 160, 164, 211,
    290, 294–7, 300, 301, 310, 323
  Cathedral 306, 308
  see also Anselm, Dunstan, Eadsige,
    Lanfranc, Robert de Jumièges,
    Stigand
cantrefs 36
Capetians 28, 76
Caradog ap Gruffudd, Welsh prince 102,
    149, 153, 259, 263
Cardiff 165, 209, 262, 273
Carham on the Tweed, battle of (1018)
    27
Carlisle 163, 248, 264, 274
Carmarthen 178, 273
Carmen de Hastingae Proelio 12, 126, 129
Carolingian Empire 28, 38, 156
castellans 204, 249

  see also castles and castle-building
Castle Acre 302
castles and castle-building 88–9, 98,
    124, 140–42, 152, 153, 163, 165,
    168, 170, 177, 178, 181–2, 195,
    202–3, 204, 207, 236, 242, 253,
    261, 262, 263, 274, 291, 293, 302,
    307, 325, 327–8
  in England after 1066 247–50
  in England and Normandy before
    1066 44–5
  see also fortifications, ring-works
cathedrals and abbies 274, 306–8, 326
  English monastic and secular 57, 301
  rebuilding after 1066 306–8, 327–8
cavalry 44, 47–8, 99, 127–8, 149
  English lack of at Hastings 130–31
  see also military organisation
celibacy 299, 303
Ceredigion 165
chamber and chamberlains 194, 213
  see also household
chancellors 194–5, 198, 213, 292
  of the exchequer 213
  see also Gerard, Herfast, Maurice,
    Osmund, Ranulf, Regenbald,
    Roger, Waldric
chancery, royal 194, 198–9
  see also writing in government
Charlemagne, emperor 27
Charles the Simple, king of the West
    Franks 28
charters 194, 198
  Coronation 188
    see also Henry I
  see also writing in government
Chaucer, Geoffrey, poet 325
Chepstow 142, 153, 203, 248, 260, 273,
    274
Cherbourg 162
Chester 21, 40, 142, 145, 165, 203, 225,
    242, 246, 259–60, 261, 264, 299,
    302, 310
Chichester 274, 296, 299
chief justiciars 197, 213
  see also government
Christ Church, Canterbury 300
Christina, Scottish princess 97

The Chronicle of the Princes, see Brut y Tywysogyon
Chronicon ex Chronicis 6
    see also John of Worcester
Church 55–69, 289–312
    in post-conquest England 145, 163, 181, 217–8, 290–308 *passim*, 311–2, 318
        courts of 215–6, 224, 293–4
        landholdings confirmed by William I 241, 255–6, 291
        lands of 244
            in 1086 233, 291
        and military service after 1066 250, 255–6, 291, 293
        reorganised in 1070 290–1, 299–300
        in royal government 194, 292
        as source of royal funds and patronage 210–1, 291–2
    in post-conquest Normandy 27, 180, 289, 308–9
    in post-conquest Wales and Scotland 27, 289, 308–11
        see also Margaret
    in pre-conquest England 31, 55–7, 58–60, 61–6, 109, 194, 289, 291, 297, 298, 299, 309, 311–2, 318
    in pre-conquest Normandy 66–8, 301, 308–9, 311–2
    in pre-conquest Scotland 57–8, 64, 289, 311–2
    in pre-conquest Wales 57–8, 60–1, 289, 311–2
    see also alien priories, archdeacons, bishoprics, canon law, cathedrals, celibacy, *clas*, church councils, culdees, deans, ecclesiastical vacancies, marriage, minsters, monasteries, monastic revival, pallium, papacy, parishes, Peter's Pence, primacy dispute, Romanesque architecture, simony, synods
church councils 68, 298–9, 299–300, 304, 305, 309, 311
    see also Westminster, London
Cirencester 274
Cistercians 14

clan 279
    as opposed to lineage 280
    see also families
clas, clasau 58, 61
    see also Church
Claudius, Roman emperor 122
Clavering 44
Clement III, anti-pope 304
clerical marriage, *see* marriage
Clermont 167, 305
Clevedon 255
Clifford 260
Cluny 302
Clwyd, river 261
Clyde, river 179
Cnut, king of England 7, 32, 33, 50, 59, 64, 76, 78, 79, 82–7 *passim*, 88, 99, 143, 215, 325, 329
    Laws of 106, 215
Cnut VI, king of Denmark 149, 155, 325
coinage 15, 37, 50, 209, 213
    see also minting, money
Colchester 195, 204, 247
Colman, biographer 60
Cologne 97
Colswein of Lincoln, baron 39, 322
common burdens 40
commotes 36
comtés 204
Conan, count of Brittany 103
Conisborough 243–4
conrois 47
consecration 31, 34, 35, 115, 173, 294, 295, 309
    see also anointing, coronation, crown-wearings
Conwy, river 165, 178, 261
Cookham 274
Copsi, earl of Northumbria 142
Corbett, W.J., historian 234, 239
Cormeilles 67
Cornwall 31, 49, 140–1, 299
coronation 188–9, 215, 283
    see also anointing, consecration, crown-wearings
Coronation Charter, *see* Henry I
Cospatric, Northumbrian thegn 106
cot 54

Cotentin 28, 162, 168
  count of, *see* Henry I
cottars 54, 55, 278
counties, *see* shires
Coutances, *see* Geoffrey, bishop of
Coventry 60, 61
Cranford 255
Crediton 65, 299
cross-Channel government 187, 196–8,
    247, 319–20
  see also government
Crowland Abbey 61, 149–50
crown-wearings 153, 179, 188, 191
  see also anointing, consecration,
    coronation ceremony
culdees 58
Cumberland 98, 106
Cumbria 21, 23, 49, 98, 163, 164, 165,
    256–7, 264
curia regis 193
  see also king's court
Cuthbert, bishop and saint 302
Cymry, see Wales
Cyneweard, sheriff of Worcestershire
    240
Cynsige, archbishop of York 60, 62, 65,
    66

Dalton, Paul, historian 256
Danelaw 25, 32, 40, 215
Danes 82–5, 149, 155–7
  see also Denmark
dapifer, see Eudo
David I, king of Scots 266, 273, 312
De obitu Willelmi 156–7
deans and deaneries 298
decorated manuscripts *see* illuminated
    manuscripts
Dee, river 21
The Deeds of the dukes of the Normans, see
    Gesta Guillelmi ducis Normannorum
    et Regis Anglorum
The Deeds of the English Bishops 7
  see also William of Malmesbury
The Deeds of the kings of the English 7, 283
  see also William of Malmesbury
Deeds of William the Conqueror 9
  see also William de Poitiers

Deganwy 165, 261
Deheubarth 35, 102, 153, 165, 259, 263
De Moribus et Actis Primorum Normanniae
    Ducum 9, 10
  see also Dudo of St Quentin
demesne 54, 233, 235, 244, 274, 277
  meaning of 36
Denmark 81, 83, 89, 116, 138, 143,
    146–7
Devon 81, 95, 140–1, 299
The Dialogue of the Exchequer 212–3
Dinan 248
Dingwall 23
diplomas 198–9
  see also writing in government
Dives, river 123
documents and document production,
  see writing in government
Dol 150, 248
Dolfin, ruler of Cumbria163, 264
Domesday Book 16–17, 24, 34, 40, 52–4,
    88, 100, 145, 153, 155, 161,
    190–1, 200–2, 205, 231, 233–49
    passim, 255–6, 260–2, 274, 275,
    278, 283, 291, 293, 297, 301
  'classes' of landholders in 190, 234–5
  Great Domesday 16–17, 201–2
  limitations of 201–2, 244–5, 256, 276
  Little Domesday 16–17, 202, 274
  meaning of 'waste' in 145
Domesday survey 155, 191, 200–2, 207,
    231, 238, 242, 277–8, 291, 293
Domfront 176
domus 193–4, 195
  see also household
Dorchester 88, 295, 299
Dorset 206, 240, 276
Donald Bàn, king of Scots 97, 164,
    265–6
Dover 91, 103, 104, 131–2, 139, 142,
    179
dower 283
Drogo de la Beuvrière, baron 235, 245–6
Dublin 54, 95
Dudo of St Quentin, chronicler 9–11, 28,
    30
Dumbarton 23
Duncan I, king of Scots 97

Duncan II, king of Scots 163, 164, 265–6
Dunfermline 273, 310
  Holy Trinity 310, 311
Dunsinane 98
Dunstan, archbishop of Canterbury and
    saint 57, 63, 312
Durham 14–15, 142–3, 150, 152, 160–1,
    163, 166, 178, 194, 209, 225, 257,
    290, 292, 300, 301, 302, 307, 310
Dyfed 165, 177, 178
  Flemings in 177–8, 262

Eadgifu, abbess of Leominster 89
Eadgyth, wife of Robert d'Oilly 243, 322
Eadmer, chronicler 7–8, 66, 103–4, 294
Eadnoth the Staller, nobleman 140, 240
Eadric 'the Wild', rebel 140, 259
Eadsige, archbishop of Canterbury 90
Eadwig, king of the English 21
Ealdgyth, see Edith, wife of Gruffudd ap
    Llewelyn and queen of Harold II
ealdormen 33, 78
Ealdred, bishop of Worcester and
    archbishop of York 5, 59–60, 61,
    62, 65, 66, 96–7, 98, 115, 132–3,
    249, 290, 294–5
earl's and earldoms 33–4, 218, 257
  changes in nature and status after
    1066 202–4
    alleged Norman influence on 204,
    243
  marcher 202–3, 203–4, 225, 238, 241,
    242–3, 245, 248, 253, 259–60,
    262, 265, 329
  see also Chester, Hereford,
    Shrewsbury, Shropshire
  see also local government, Revolt of
    the earls
earl's Barton Church, Northamptonshire
    63
earthworks 45, 123
  see also castles; fortifications
East Anglia 33, 58, 86, 87, 91, 99, 100,
    148–9, 177, 240, 241, 256, 291
Ecclesiastical History 10
  see also Orderic Vitalis
Ecclesiastical History of the English People,
  see Bede

ecclesiastical vacancies 164, 174, 210–1,
    291–2, 296, 304, 306
economies 49–55, 273–9, 328
  in post-conquest England 273, 274–6
  in post-conquest Normandy 273
  in post-conquest Scotland 273–4
  in post-conquest Wales 273–4
  in pre-conquest England 49–50
  in pre-conquest Normandy 50–1
  in pre-conquest Scotland 49–50, 52
  in pre-conquest Wales 49–50, 52
  see also coinage, minting, money,
    markets, rural society, towns,
    trade, wealth
Edgar, king of the English 21–2, 41, 57,
    175
Edgar, king of Scots 164–5, 175, 178–9,
    180, 266
Edgar atheling 97, 132–3, 137–43 passim,
    147, 148, 163, 164, 178, 266, 300,
    310
Edinburgh 273
Edith, queen of Edward the Confessor
    6, 62, 79, 87, 91, 96, 97, 99, 106,
    107, 108, 131, 174–5, 179, 283,
    322, 325
Edith-Matilda, queen of Henry I, see
    Matilda
Edith (Ealdgyth), wife of Gruffudd ap
    Llewelyn and queen of Harold II
    100, 107, 131
Edith Swan-neck, consort of Harold II
    131
Edmund 'Ironside', king of England 76,
    77, 82, 97
Edmund, sheriff of Hertfordshire 205,
    240
Edward the Confessor, king of England
    and saint 6, 15, 32, 33, 36, 40, 41,
    42, 44, 47, 63–6, 76, 82, 83,
    85–109 passim, 120, 133, 139,
    140, 175, 188, 194, 201, 203, 206,
    214, 216, 232, 233, 239–40, 243,
    259, 260, 265, 283, 299, 303, 312,
    329
  death and burial 107–9, 115, 120
  and earl Godwine and his family 86,
    89–91, 95–6, 99, 101

lands of 100–1, 239
'law of' 215
marriage and childlessness 87, 90, 97
and Normandy 82, 83, 87–9, 94
and Northumbrian rising 105–7
offers crown to William of Normandy
    91–5, 103–4
position in 1042 85–6
and the succession in 1066 75–9
Westminster Abbey 63–4, 96, 107, 133
see also Vita Edwardi Regis
Edward the Elder, king of Wessex 41
Edward I, king of England 22
Edward 'the Exile', son of Edmund
    'Ironside' 97
Edward, son of Malcolm III, king of
    Scots 164
Edward of Salisbury, sheriff of Wiltshire
    239–40
Edwin, brother of earl Leofric 98
Edwin, earl of Mercia 100, 105, 107, 117,
    119–20, 132–3, 138–46 passim,
    202, 203, 231, 232, 245
  death 146
  rebellion in 1068 141, 243, 259, 322
Elias de la Flèche, count of Maine 168–9,
    170, 182
Elmham 59, 290, 299
Ely 59, 84, 146, 307, 308, 310
Emma, daughter of William FitzOsbern
    148
Emma of Normandy, queen of Aethelred
    II and Cnut, 80, 81, 82, 84, 89, 282
  disgrace and death 87
  marries Aethelred II 75–6
  marries Cnut 82–3
England, Norman Conquest and
    chs. 1–12 passim
  impact on
    English attitudes to Scots and Welsh
      328
    fashions 325
    language 323–5
    names 323–4
      see also toponyms
    see also aristocracy, Church, coinage,
      economies, families and family
      structures, feudalism,
      government, kin and kinship,
      lands and landholding, law,
      military organisation, peasantry,
      population, rulers and rulership,
      rural
    society, wealth
Englishness 8, 25, 317, 321
  see also gens Anglorum
'Englishries' 263
Epte, river 168
Ermenfrid, bishop of Sion 290
escheats 202, 210, 237, 327
Essex 17, 44, 62, 86, 202, 206, 210, 238
Eu 162, 167, 189
Eudo 'the steward' (dapifer) 198, 204
Eustace, son of William de Breteuil 180
Eustace II, count of Boulogne 91, 129,
    139, 142, 179–80, 233–4
Eustace III, count of Boulogne 179, 180
Evesham 62, 255–6, 293
Ewyas Harold 44, 260
exchequer 17, 212–4, 225
  Norman 214
  see also abacus, assaying, chancellors,
    The Dialogue of the Exchequer, pipe
    rolls, scaccarium, tallies, treasurer,
    wealth
Exeter, 41, 65, 81, 140–1, 247, 282, 299
Exmes 180

Falaise 50, 195
familia 193, 195, 207
  see also household
families and family structures 279–82
  in post-conquest England 280–1
  in pre-conquest England 279, 280
  in pre-conquest Normandy 279–80
    see also acquisitions, parage,
      patrimony
  in pre-conquest Scotland and Wales
    281–2
  see also clans, dower, heiresses,
    inheritance, intermarriage,
    kinship ties, marriage portion,
    toponymic surnames, wardships,
    women
farm of shire 32, 208, 213
  see also sheriffs

Fawdon 149
fealty 303
    see also homage
Fécamp 67, 68, 138, 162, 300, 302
fees 235
    see also honours
feigned retreats, see Hastings
feodum, 233
feudal incidents 174, 209–11, 237–8, 251
    see also escheats, heirs and heiresses,
        marriage, minors and minorities,
        reliefs, scutage, wardships, widows
feudalism 215, 233, 236–9
    in England 43, 249–50, 254–8
        debate over 'introduction' after
            1066 254–5, 319
        'myth' of 255, 319
    in post-conquest Wales 262
    in pre-conquest Normandy 42–4,
        251–2
    see also feudal incidents, fealty,
        feodum, fief, homage, knight
        service, lands and landholding,
        mesne tenants, quotas, servitium
        debitum, subinfeudation, vassal
fief 233, 254
Fife 35
First Crusade 47, 166, 167, 169, 173,
    192, 276, 305
Firth of Forth 311
five-hide system 256, 291
Flanders 6, 28, 42, 49, 84, 89, 90, 91, 94,
    117, 121, 147–8, 149, 179, 246,
    253, 328
fleets 41–2, 120–1, 125, 128, 252–3
    see also scipfyrd
Fleming, Robin, historian 244–7, 276
Flemings, see Dyfed
Florence of Worcester, monk, see John of
    Worcester
forest, royal, 204, 206, 224
    see also hunting, law
Forest of Dean 49
fortifications, see castles, ring-works
Forth, river 24, 179
Fothadh, bishop of St Andrews 309
frankpledge 205–6, 219, 220–1
    see also tithings

Freeman, Edward Augustus, historian
    318
freemen 44, 53–4, 201, 219, 220, 247,
    277–8
    see also liberi homines
Fulford, battle of (1066) 47, 119–20, 231
Fulk IV, count of Anjou 148, 150, 153,
    168
fyrd 39, 40, 41, 235, 252, 253, 329
    select 40
    see also scipfyrd

Gaídil 26
Galloway xiv
Galwegians 22
    see also Galloway
geld 36–7, 208–9, 291
    see also taxation, wealth
gens Anglorum 25
    see also Englishness
gens Normannorum 10, 19, 29
    see also Normans
Geoffrey, portreeve of London 232
Geoffrey, count of Anjou 93, 94, 122
Geoffrey de Clinton, baron 179
Geoffrey, bishop of Coutances 67, 68,
    149, 160, 190, 233, 238, 309
Geoffrey, bishop of Durham and
    chancellor 194
Geoffrey de Mandeville, baron 205, 234,
    238, 243
Geoffrey II de Mandeville, baron 210
Geoffrey de la Querche, baron 322
Gerald of Wales, chronicler 60
Gerald of Windsor, baron 177, 322
Gerard, bishop of Hereford, archbishop
    of York and chancellor, 194, 292,
    309
Gerberoy 152, 252
Gerbod the Fleming, baron 234, 246,
    260
Germany 64
Gesta Guillelmi ducis Normannorum et
    Regis Anglorum 9, 13
Gesta Normannorum Ducum, see The
    Deeds of the dukes of the Normans
Gesta Pontificum Anglorum, see The Deeds
    of the English Bishops

Gesta Regum Anglorum, see *The Deeds of the kings of the English*
gewrit 199
    see also writing in government
Gilbert, tenant of Berengar de Tosny 255
Gilbert, count of Brionne 67
Gilingham, John, historian 255
Giso, bishop of Wells 59, 65, 88
Gisors 168
Glamorgan, 149, 153, 165, 259, 262
Glasgow 23, 309
Glastonbury 59, 256, 300
Gloucester 91, 153, 155, 164, 188, 191, 195, 200, 293, 307
Gloucestershire 165, 239, 240, 274
Godric the steward, baron 240
Godwine, earl of Wessex 5, 6, 8, 33, 78, 84–7, 93, 94–101 *passim*, 121
    and Alfred *atheling* 84, 86
    in crisis of 1051 90–1
    death of 8, 98–9
    and Edward the Confessor 86, 89
    return in 1052 95–6
Godwineson family, lands of 100–1, 207, 239
Gospatric son of Arnkell, baron 239
Gospatric, earl of Northumbria 142–3, 163, 239, 263
Gospels 222
government 31–8, 187–214, 320, 328
    in post-conquest England
        absentee rule and use of regents 187, 196–8
        funding of 207–14
        local government 202–6
        men 'raised from the dust' in 197–8
        role of Church in 194, 292
        role of household 193–6
        role of king and aristocracy in 190–2
        writing in 198–202
    in post-conquest Normandy 190, 195, 199–200, 214, 225
    in post-conquest Scotland and Wales 225
    effect of Norman Conquest on 225–6

in pre-conquest England 31–4, 36–7, 188, 190
in pre-conquest Normandy 37–8, 204
in pre-conquest Scotland 34–5
in pre-conquest Wales 35–6
    see also Church, chief justiciars, cross-Channel government, exchequer, forest, kingship, local government, master of the writing office, rulers and rulership, *witan*, writing in government
Gower 178
Gowrie 35
Great Domesday, see Domesday Book
Green, Judith, historian 245
Gregory I ('the Great'), pope 25, 55, 295, 296
Gregory VII, pope 25, 55, 154, 303–4
Grestain 67
Gruffudd ap Cynan, Welsh prince 153, 165–6, 261, 263–4, 326
Gruffudd ap Llewelyn, Welsh prince 39, 47, 98, 99–100, 107, 153, 165–6, 178, 259
    fall and death of 101–2
Guildford 195
Gundulf, bishop of Rochester 293
Guy de Balliol, baron 257
Guy, bishop of Amiens, chronicler 11–12
Guy, count of Ponthieu 43, 103, 104
Gwent 102, 260
Gwynedd xiv, 22, 35, 98, 101, 140, 153, 165–6, 178, 259, 261, 263, 310
Gyrth Godwineson, earl of East Anglia 47, 91, 100, 124
Gytha, mother of Harold II 86, 91, 124, 131, 140, 282, 283

hagiography 6, 310
Haakon, nephew of Harold II 93, 103–4
Hallamshire 52
Halley's Comet 116
Hampshire 91, 131, 174, 176, 206
Hamstead Marshall 170
Harald Hardrada, king of Norway 79, 89, 116, 118–20, 123, 125, 166
    his claim to the English throne 118–9

Harold I 'Harefoot', king of England 75, 76, 77, 83–5
Harold II, king of England (Harold Godwineson, earl of Wessex), 6, 41, 42, 48, 59, 62, 64, 84, 86, 90, 91, 95, 99–109 *passim*, 115–33 *passim*, 142, 203, 207, 243–4, 282, 283, 288, 294, 302, 303, 312
  in Battle of Hastings 126–31
  death 12, 129, 231
  defeats northern invasion at Stamford Bridge 117–9
  during Hastings campaign 124–6
  his marriage 107
  his sons 140–1, 240
  trip to Normandy 8, 12–13, 102–5
    takes oath to William of Normandy 13, 103–4, 117, 124
  and Northumbrian rising 105, 106–7
  preparations in 1066 117–8
  and the succession in 1066 76–9, 108–9
  and Wales 101–2, 140, 259
  see also Godwineson family
Harold, son of earl Ralph of Hereford 239
Harold Godwineson, earl of Wessex, *see* Harold II
Harrying of the North 144–5, 189, 241, 274, 290, 318
Harthacnut, king of England 75, 77, 83–6, 117–8, 143
Hastings, 125
  battle of (1066) 5, 9, 10, 11–12, 13, 41, 46–8, 62, 66, 126–31, 146, 151, 181, 182, 187, 203, 204, 208, 224, 231, 232, 239, 289, 290, 300, 302, 303, 329
  English and Norman armies 126–7
  feigned retreats 128
  numbers of troops at 126
  sources for 126
  campaign 68, 124–6
  castle 247, 248
  rape of 142, 242
  reasons for Norman victory and English defeat 48, 129–31
Hearding, son of Eadnoth the Staller 240

Hebrides 23
heirs and heiresses 190, 210, 223, 237, 238, 250, 258, 279, 280–1, 284
  see also minors and minorities
Henry I, king of England and duke of Normandy 7, 8, 9, 17, 77, 78, 79, 92, 94, 151, 156, 167, 180–82, 187–226 *passim*, 192–5, 205–7, 237, 247, 249, 252–3, 257, 264, 266, 282, 292, 298–9, 305–6, 323, 325–6, 329
  bequest on William I's death 157
  consolidates position as king 173–5
    anti-baronial strategies 198
    and archbishop Anselm 173, 174, 180–1, 211, 282, 305
    conquers Normandy 179–82
    engineers fall of Montgomeries 176–7
    marriage 174–5, 179, 311, 322, 325
    and men 'raised from the dust' 197–8
    obituary 189
    Treaty of Alton with Robert Curthose 175–6
    in Wales and Scotland 177–9, 258, 263, 266, 310, 326
    wealth of 207
    and writ of c.1108 concerning courts 205, 216, 224
  coronation 173, 215
    Charter 173–4, 188, 206, 210, 211, 215, 216, 238, 281, 283, 284
  as 'count of the Cotentin' 162, 168, 192
  at William Rufus's death 170, 195
  see also Laws of Henry I, Leges Henrici Primi, Tinchebray
Henry I, king of France 92, 93, 94, 122
Henry II, king of England 11, 322
Henry III, emperor 42, 89, 96–7
Henry IV, emperor 121, 154, 304
Henry de Beaumont, earl of Warwick 141, 162, 173, 178, 191, 233
Henry of Huntingdon, chronicler 7–8, 76, 99, 195, 307, 317, 321, 322

Herbert Losinga, bishop of Thetford/
    Norwich/East Anglia 291, 299
Hereford 39, 44, 61, 88, 99, 140, 142,
    148, 202, 203, 242, 260, 292
Herefordshire 39, 44, 88, 98, 99, 142,
    148, 259, 260, 276
Herewald, bishop of Llandaff 60
Hereward, rebel 146–7
Herfast, bishop of
    Elmham/Thetford/East Anglia and
    chancellor 194, 199, 290, 299
Herleva, mother of William I 67, 92
Herluin de Conteville, nobleman 67,
    92
Herman, bishop of
    Ramsbury/Sherborne/Salisbury 60,
    61, 62, 65, 88, 299
Hertfordshire 205, 238, 243
Hervé, bishop of Bangor 261, 310
Hexateuch 63
hides 36, 40, 208, 277
*Historia Novorum, see History of Recent
    Events*
Historia Regum 14
    see also Symeon of Durham
History of the Church of York 8, 294
    see also Hugh the Chanter
History of the English People, see Bede *and*
    Henry of Huntingdon
Holderness 166, 235, 245, 246, 257
Hollister, C.W., historian 320
Holt, J.C., historian 236, 255, 281
Holy Land 92, 167
Holy Roman Empire 121
Holy Trinity, Caen 67
Holy Trinity, Dunfermline, *see*
    Dunfermline
homage 236, 254, 266, 281, 303, 305
    see also fealty
honourial courts, 224
    see also honours, lords' courts
honours 219, 235–9, 244, 257
    see also honourial courts
housecarls 39, 105, 124, 131, 195, 243,
    252
household 31, 205, 206, 237, 249, 319
    role in post-conquest English royal
    government 193–6 *passim*

see also chamber, *domus, familia,*
    government, military
    organisation, treasurer, treasury
Hrlófr, viking leader 28
    see also Rollo
Hugh, *ceorl* 81
Hugh, tenant of William FitzAnsculf 255
Hugh 'the Wolf', *see* Hugh d'Avranches
Hugh d'Avranches, earl of Chester 145,
    162, 165, 178, 203, 242, 260–1,
    262, 263, 264
Hugh the Chanter, chronicler 8, 294
Hugh FitzRichard, baron 233
Hugh de Grandmesnil, nobleman 246
Hugh, bishop of Lisieux 67
Hugh de Montgomery, earl of
    Shrewsbury 166, 178
Hugh, count of Ponthieu 11
Humber, river 117, 119, 143–4, 296
Humphrey of Tilleul, nobleman 246
hundred courts 32, 214, 214, 218–19,
    221, 293, 318
    and writ of c.1070 215–6
hundredmen 218
hundreds 32, 36, 205, 218–9, 220, 244, 329
    private 218, 224
    see also hundred courts, local
    government, reeves, shires,
    wapentakes
Hungary 97
hunting 170, 194, 206, 240, 259; *see also*
    royal forest
Huntingdon 7, 141
    see also Henry of Huntingdon

Ilbert de Lacy, baron 235, 245
Ildebert, tenant of Matthew de Mortagne
    255
illuminated manuscripts 63
'infangentheof' 219
inland 53, 277
intermarriage *see* marriage
investiture, *see* lay investiture
Iona 178, 311
Ireland 91, 98, 140, 166, 278, 279,
    320, 327
Isle of Man 178
Isle of Thorns 63

Isle of Wight 42, 82, 95, 116
Italy 154, 169
itinerant justices 217
Ivanhoe 318–9

Jarrow 302
Jersey 11
Jerusalem 169
Jewish settlement in England after 1066
    275–6
John, bishop of Bath/Wells 299
John, bishop of Lisieux 214
John, archbishop of Rouen 149, 308–9
John of Worcester, chronicler 6, 14, 16,
    21, 47, 59, 78, 81, 89, 91, 97,
    108–9, 115–6, 124, 132, 179, 200,
    265, 290, 291
Judith, wife of earl Tostig 89, 117
Judith, wife of earl Waltheof 138, 149,
    232, 283–4, 322
Juliana, daughter of Henry I 180
Juliana, daughter of Richard of
    Winchester 210
Jumièges 9, 64, 67
    see also Robert de, William de
justices, *see* itinerant justices, law

Kenneth, king of Scots 21
Kenneth MacAlpin, king of Scots 33
Kent 13, 52, 91, 95, 131, 142, 161, 203,
    291
Kidwelly 178, 273
king's court 215, 219
    see also curia regis
king's thegns 34
    see also thegns
kin and kinship 38, 78
    in post-conquest Scotland and Wales
    280
    in pre-conquest England 239, 279
    see also families, succession
kingship, *see* rulers and rulership
Kirkby Malzeard 257
knight service 250–1, 326

La Flèche 153
Laigle 151, 181
Lake District 23

Lancashire 177, 242, 257
lands and landholding 231–47 *passim*,
    254–8
    in post-conquest Wales and Scotland
    258–66
    in pre-conquest England 100–1,
    238–9, 280
    revolutionary changes in post-
    conquest England 255, 257–8,
    276–7, 279, 318, 326, 327
    English landholders after 1066
    239–41, 244
    English royal lands after 1066
    207–8, 233, 238–9
    methods of redistribution after 1066
    241–7
    antecessorial 243–4
    hundredal acquisitions 244
    illegal 246–7
        debate on 244–7, 276
    see also feudalism
Lanfranc, archbishop of Canterbury 8,
    15, 65, 67, 137–8, 157, 160–61,
    164, 211, 279, 290, 291, 292–3,
    299–304 *passim*, 306, 310, 323
    Constitutions of 300
    and primacy dispute with York 294–7
Langland, William, poet 325
Last Judgement 17, 202
Laudes Regiae 188
law, system of, in England 32, 187,
    214–26 *passim*, 320
    developments after 1066
    appeal, process of 221–3
    clearer definition of royal pleas
    216–7
    customary and 'feudal' law after
    1066 215
    establishment of private hundreds
    218
    extension of king's role as keeper of
    national 'peace' 216
    importance of tithings in
    peacekeeping 220–1
    introduction of *murdrum* fine 220
    limits of, 224–5, 328
    trial, proof and punishment
    in criminal matters 221–3

in disputes over land 223–4
to system of courts 214–6, 217–20
emergence of lords' courts after
1066 215–6, 219
wider use of local and itinerant
justices by 1135 217
of forest 206, 224
as source of royal funds 211
see also appeal, *curia regis*, feudal law,
frankpledge, hundred courts,
'infangentheof', itinerant justices,
king's court, lords' courts, manor
courts, *murdrum*, mutilation,
oaths, ordeal, outlawry, private
hundreds, royal 'peace', royal
pleas, 'sake and soke', sanctuary,
shire courts, tithings, trial by
battle, *wergild*
Laws of William the Conqueror 214–5
lay investiture 181, 282, 305
Le Bec 9, 67, 164, 302, 304
Leges Henrici Primi 216, 218, 281
see also Laws of Henry I
Le Mans 153, 168–9
Leo IX, pope 62, 65, 92–3
Leofric, bishop of Devon and Cornwall
60, 65, 299
Leofric, earl of Mercia 33, 61, 86, 87, 91,
95, 96, 99, 100, 299–300
Leofric, abbot of Peterborough 61, 300
Leofwine, thegn 322
Leofwine Godwineson, earl 47, 91, 95,
100, 203, 322
Leominster 39, 89, 98
Le Patourel, John, historian 319–20
Lewes 142, 242, 248, 302
Libellus de Exordio 14
see also Symeon of Durham
liberi homines 53
see also freemen
Lichfield 290, 295, 299, 310
Life of king Edward 6, 59–60, 64
see also Vita Edwardi Regis
Lillebonne, council of 309
Lincoln 51, 105, 141, 274, 293, 299, 307,
322
Lincolnshire 52, 62, 146, 274
Lindsey 117, 196

Lire 67
Lisieux 9, 68
Little Domesday, *see* Domesday Book
Llanbadarn Fawr 61
Llandaff 58, 60, 310
local government, 31–2, 33–4, 34–5, 36,
38, 177, 202–6
see also ealdormen, earls and
earldoms, hides, hundreds,
marches, rapes, sheriffs, shires,
wapentakes
Loire, river 302
London 17, 41, 51, 55–6, 65–6, 83, 88,
91, 95, 124, 126, 131–3, 175, 195,
199, 202, 232, 274, 293, 296, 302,
307
council of 298–9, 300
Jewry in 275–6
writ of William I in favour of 138, 199,
232, 324
Lonsdale 257
lords' courts 215, 219–20, 237
and writ of c.1108 216
lordship 219, 255, 327
based on landholding after 1066 236,
257–8
see also lands and landholding,
peasantry
in England before 1066 23, 258
Lorraine, *see* Lotharingia
Lotharingia (Lorraine) 65, 68, 88, 299
Louis VI, king of France 168
Lothian 22, 24, 27, 163, 179
Ludwell 241
Lulach, son of Macbeth 98

Macbeth, king of Scots 64, 97–8, 265
Maccus, king 21
Magnus, king of Norway 42, 83, 84, 86,
89, 100, 118, 178
Magnus ('Barelegs'), king of Norway 166,
178
Maine 122, 147, 153, 154, 168–9, 179,
191, 252, 253, 320
Maitland, F.W., historian 277
Malcolm, king of Cumbria 21
Malcolm II, king of Scots 27, 97, 105–6,
117, 266

Malcolm III 'Canmore', king of Scots 27, 39, 97–98, 105–6, 117, 143, 147, 152, 174, 242, 265, 309, 310
    death 164, 166, 265
    swears oath to William II 163, 264
    see also Abernethy, peace of
Malmesbury 7
    see also William of Malmesbury
manor courts 55, 219–20
manorialisation 54–5
manors 33, 52–3, 201, 234, 278
man price, see wergild
Mantes 155
manuscripts, see illuminated manuscripts
marches, see earls and earldoms
Maredudd ab Owain, Welsh prince 259, 263
Margaret, queen of Scots and saint 15, 97, 143, 174, 265, 283, 309
    death of 164, 265
    and Scottish Church 310–1
    sons and daughter of 311
markets 274–5, 327
Marlswein, landholder 243
Marmoutier 302
marriage 38, 56, 174, 179, 210, 216, 237, 238, 283–4, 311, 327
    clerical 61, 309
    intermarriage 243, 321–3
    portion 283
Marsh Gibbon 241, 278
Mary, sister of Edgar, king of Scots 179, 180
master of the writing office 194
Matilda (Edith-Matilda), queen of Henry I 15, 174–5, 179, 282, 283, 310, 322, 325
Matilda of Flanders, queen of William I, 12–13, 92–3, 94, 117, 140, 147–8, 149, 151–2, 154, 196, 275, 282
Matilda, daughter of Eustace III 180
Matilda, daughter of Henry I 180
Matthew de Mortagne, baron 255
Mauger, archbishop of Rouen 67, 68
Maurice, bishop of London and chancellor 173, 194
Maurilius, archbishop of Rouen 68

Mayet 170
mercenaries 188, 192, 202,207, 208, 209, 253
Mercia 5, 21, 22, 23, 33, 39, 40, 82, 98, 99, 100, 105, 107, 138, 140–1, 203–4, 215, 243
Mersey, river 32
mesne tenants 235
Middlesex 86, 205, 238, 243, 255
military organisation 38–48, 247–66
    in post-conquest England, 236, 249–54, 255
        feudal military service 250–2
        and the Church 250, 291
        fyrd 252
        military household 195–6, 207, 252
        naval power and mercenaries 252–3
    in post-conquest Normandy 251–2
    in pre-conquest England 39–42, 44–5, 46–8, 118, 119–20, 127–8, 253
    five-hide system, see Berkshire
    in pre-conquest Normandy 42–4, 45, 47–8, 131, 253
    in pre-conquest Scotland 38–9
    in pre-conquest Wales 39
    see also armies, cavalry, common burdens, conrois, feudalism, five-hide system, fleets, fyrd, hauberks, housecarls, lands and landholding, mercenaries, quotas, scutage, servitium debitum, shield wall
minors and minorities 284, 327
    see also heirs and heiresses
minsters 51, 56, 297
minting and mints 37, 51, 195, 209
    see also coinage, money
mixed marriages, see intermarriage
monastic revival of tenth century 63
monasteries 57, 58, 66–7, 289, 291, 301, 308
    post-conquest English 300–302, 326, 328
    see also cathedrals, Benedictine communities
money 15, 50, 194–5, 212–13
    see also coinage, minting, wealth

moneyers 208
  see also mints and minting
moneylending 275
Monkwearmouth 302
Monmouth 260
Montfort family 38
Montgomery 260
Montgomery family 38, 67
  fall of 176–7, 326
  see also Arnulf de, Hugh de, Robert de
    Bellême, Roger de, Roger the
    Poitevin
Mont St Michel 9, 67
Moray 97
Moray Firth 23, 27
Morcar, earl of Northumbria 105, 107,
    117, 119–20, 132–3, 138–46
    passim, 202, 231, 232, 245
  rebellion in 1068 141, 259
mormaers 35, 39, 97
  see also government in pre-conquest
    Scotland
Mortagne 180
Mortemer, battle of (1054) 43, 94
Mortimer family 234
motte and bailey castles 44, 45, 248
  see also castles and castle-building
multiple estates 52
murdrum fine 206, 211, 220
  see also law
mutilation 54, 84, 131, 150, 209, 222,
    223
Mynydd Carn, battle of (1091) 153, 261,
    263

Nest, consort of Henry I 177
Newcastle 152, 166, 248, 274
New Forest 169, 170, 206
Nicholas II, pope 66
Nigel, bishop of Ely and treasurer 194
nithing 90
Norfolk 17, 148, 201, 302
Norman Conquest, main events of
    chs. 3–7 *passim*
  effects of chs. 8–11 *passim*,
    321–9
  see also England, Scotland,
    Wales

myths about, 317–21
  see also 'ancient constitution',
    feudalism, 'Norman Empire',
    'Norman myth', 'Norman yoke'
  sources for, *see* sources
  see also England, Normandy, Wales,
    Scotland
Normandy 27–30, 37–8, 42–4, 45, 47–8,
    121, 138–9, 149, 150–2, 162–3,
    167–9, 173–7, 179–82, 190, 195,
    199–200, 203, 204, 207, 214, 216,
    231, 232, 247, 251–2, 253, 254,
    279, 280, 282, 299, 301–2, 306,
    308–9, 311–2, 317–29 *passim*
  described as 'Richard's kingdom', 81
  see also Church, economies, family,
    feudalism, government, military
    organisation, slavery, wealth
'Norman Empire', myth of 319–20
The Norman Empire 319
Normanisation 326
Normanitas 30
  see also gens Normannorum, 'Norman
    myth'
'Norman myth' 10, 30
  see also gens Normannorum
'Norman yoke' 317, 318–9
Northampton 105, 275
Northamptonshire 63, 138
North Sea 89–3
Northumberland 152, 257, 264
Northumbria 24, 27, 82, 97, 99, 105–7,
    116, 138, 142, 150, 152, 163, 164,
    167, 203, 323
Northumbrian rising (1065) 6, 105–7,
    108
Norway 84, 86, 89, 100, 116, 118, 166
Norwich 51, 149, 275, 301, 307
Nottingham 141
Nottinghamshire 206, 276
nucleated village 53, 327
  see also manor, vill

oaths, 259, 295
  in legal disputes 221–2
  see also Harold II, Malcolm III,
    Salisbury
Odda of Deerhurst, earl 91

Odo, bishop of Bayeux and earl of Kent 13, 43, 67, 92, 139, 142, 152, 160–61, 166, 189–91, 203, 233–4, 238, 246, 278, 291, 309
    fall of 153–4, 156, 233, 291
    in revolt of 1088 160–1
Odo, count of Champagne 166
Offa, king of Mercia 23
    see also Offa's Dyke
Offa's Dyke 24, 26, 31, 58
Old English 94, 324
Old Sarum 299, 301
ordeal, 221–222, 224
Orderic Vitalis, chronicler 10–11, 16, 30, 32, 45, 67, 75–6, 108, 124, 132, 140, 142, 144, 146, 150–52, 156–7, 160, 162, 165, 175, 177, 181, 190–92, 196–8, 207, 211, 216, 233, 241, 245–6, 247–8, 251, 262, 292, 308–9, 311, 318, 322, 323, 324
Orkney 23, 64, 309
Orleans 28
Osbern, brother of Swein Estrithson 143
Osbert, sheriff of Worcestershire 205
Osmund, bishop of Salisbury and chancellor, 194, 199
Osulf of Bamburgh, northern magnate 142
Oswald, bishop of Worcester, archbishop of York and saint 57, 61, 301
Ouse, river 119
outlawry 221
Oxford 105, 195
Oxfordshire 241, 243, 255

pagus 38
    see also government in pre-conquest Normandy
pallium, pallia 65, 66, 295, 303, 304, 309
papacy 62–6, 145, 154, 312
    and Britain after 1066 303–6, 309, 318
    and primacy dispute 295–6
    and Britain before 1066 64–6, 303, 318
    papal banner at Battle of Hastings, see William I
parage 279–80
Paris 28
parishes 56, 297–300

churches 289, 297–8, 307–8
parochialisation, see parishes
Paschal II, pope 282
patrimony 280–81, 292
    see also acquisitions
'peace' see royal 'peace'
peasantry, 163, 276
    decline in status and size of free peasantry after 1066 277–8, 327
    English, in 1086 53–5
    intensification of lordship over after 1066 277
    see also bordars, cottars, freemen, manorialisation, slavery, sokemen, villeins
Pembroke 165, 177, 273, 274
Pembrokeshire 262
Pennines 32
Perth 23, 35, 273
Perthshire 98
Peterborough 5, 60, 61, 146, 256, 301
Peter, bishop of Lichfield/Chester 299
Peter's Pence 64–5, 303
Pevensey 120, 123–4, 125, 161, 175, 247, 274
    rape of 142, 242
Philip I, king of France 122, 148, 150, 152, 155, 167
Picot, sheriff of Cambridgeshire 301
Picts 34
pilgrimage 64, 106, 153, 311
pipe rolls, 17, 197, 207, 209–11, 213–14
place names, see English names, toponyms
pleas of the crown, see royal pleas
Poitiers 169
Poitou 169
Pontefract 143, 235, 245
Ponthieu 103, 121
    see also Guy
popes, see papacy
population of Britain, in eleventh century 24–5
    of England, after Harrying of the North 144
    estimated, in 1086
    Norman additions to 321–2
    growth of 253, 273

Portskewett 102, 259
Portsmouth 175
post obitum grant 77–8, 88, 93, 95, 156
primogeniture 75–7, 280
Powys 22, 35, 58, 98, 101, 140, 166, 259, 260, 261
primacy dispute 8, 294–7, 299, 309

Queensferry 311
quotas 43, 250–1, 253, 255–6, 291

Ralf FitzWilliam, baron 210
Ralph Basset, royal justice 223
Ralph de Gael, earl of East Anglia 148–9, 150, 233, 242
Ralph of Mantes ('the Timid'), earl of Hereford 39, 44, 47, 88, 90, 91, 98, 99, 100
Ralph I, bishop of Orkney 309
Ralph II, bishop of Orkney 309
Ralph Paynel, landholder 243
Ralph the Staller, nobleman 88, 148
Ramsbury 60, 61, 62, 88
    see also Herman
Ramsey Abbey 301
Ranulf, chancellor 194
Ranulf I ('le Meschin'), earl of Chester 264–5
Ranulf II, earl of Chester 210
Ranulf Flambard, bishop of Durham 162, 173–5, 194, 197, 201, 211, 292
rapes of Sussex 142, 225, 242, 245–6, 248, 253
reeves 32, 218
Regenbald, chancellor 194
regents, *see* cross-Channel government
Reginald, tenant of Berengar de Tosny 255
reliefs 174, 210, 237, 238
Remigius, bishop of Dorchester/Lincoln 293, 295, 299, 307
Rennes 248
Revolt of the Earls (1075) 15, 148–9, 192, 242, 292–3
Rheims 65
Rhineland 328
Rhiwallon, Welsh prince 102

Rhuddlan 101, 209, 261, 262
Rhys ap Tewdwr, Welsh prince 153, 165, 177, 260, 261, 263
Ribble Valley 257
Richard, son of Robert Curthose 170
Richard Basset, baron 179
Richard FitzGilbert, baron 196, 233, 246
Richard II, duke of Normandy 9, 29–30, 38, 75, 81, 83
Richard III, duke of Normandy 9
Richard I, count of Rouen 28–9, 80
Richard's Castle 44
'Richard's kingdom', *see* Normandy
Richmond 234, 235, 245, 248
ringworks 45, 248
    see also castles, fortifications
Robert, tenant of Berengar de Tosny 255
Robert de Beaumont, count of Meulan and earl of Leicester 179, 191
    see also Beaumont family
Robert de Bellême, earl of Shrewsbury 152, 166, 168, 175–7, 180–82, 191, 257
Robert Bloet, bishop of Lincoln 7–8
Robert Cumin, earl of Northumbria 143
Robert, count of Eu 196, 242
Robert FitzHaimon, baron 165, 190, 198, 262
Robert FitzRichard, baron 143
Robert FitzWimarc, kinsman of Edward the Confessor 88, 108
Robert I ('the Frisian'), count of Flanders 148, 155
Robert II, count of Flanders 179, 207
Robert II ('the Pious'), king of France 140
Robert, earl of Gloucester 195
Robert de la Haye, baron 322
Robert de Jumièges, archbishop of Canterbury 59, 64, 65, 88, 90–1, 93, 94–6
Robert, count of Meulan 173
Robert, count of Mortain 43, 67, 154, 160, 175, 190, 196, 233–5, 238, 242
Robert de Mowbray, earl of Northumbria 164, 264–5
    revolt in 1095 166–7, 189, 192, 203, 233

Robert I ('the Magnificent'), duke of
    Normandy 9, 83, 92
Robert II ('Curthose'), duke of
    Normandy 77–8, 79, 122, 147,
    152, 153, 156–7, 160–63, 166–70,
    173–82, 189–92, 196, 207, 208,
    216, 248, 252, 253, 280, 325
  capture, imprisonment and death 182
  character 151, 181, 190, 191
  First Crusade and marriage 169, 173
  invades England and makes peace
    with Henry I 175–6
  loses Normandy to Henry I 179–82
    reasons for 191–2, 207, 216
  pawns Normandy to William Rufus
    167–8
  relationship with family 151–2, 154,
    163
  revolt of 1088 160–1, 252–3
  undermined by William Rufus in
    Normandy 162–3
Robert d'Oilly, baron 241, 243, 322
Robert of Rhuddlan, baron 165, 261,
    263–4
Robert de Stuteville, baron 257
Robert de Tilleul see Robert of Rhuddlan
Robert of Torigny, chronicler 9
Robin Hood, outlaw 319
Rochester 161, 293, 300, 301
Roger de Beaumont, baron 141, 147,
    149, 196
Roger Bigod, baron 234
Roger de Breteuil, earl of Hereford 145,
    203, 280
  and Revolt of the earls 148–9, 233,
    260, 293
Roger de Bully, baron 235, 245
Roger de Montgomery, earl of
    Shrewsbury 141–2, 145, 147, 152,
    160, 176, 190, 203, 233, 242–3,
    257, 260, 262, 265
Roger, bishop of Orkney 309
Roger the Poitevin, son of Roger de
    Montgomery 175, 177, 257
Roger, bishop of Salisbury and
    chancellor 8, 178, 194, 197,
    212–4, 292, 305
Roger, sheriff of Worcestershire 205

Rollo, viking leader 11, 28
Roman du Rou, 11
  see also Wace
Romanesque architecture 62, 64, 289,
    306, 308
Rome 61, 64–6, 106, 181, 295, 303, 304,
    305, 307, 309
Rome-scot, see Peter's Pence
Romney 131
Romsey Abbey 174
Rotrou of Mortagne, count of Perche
    180
Rouen 28, 50, 51, 68, 103, 138, 151, 154,
    156, 162, 195, 275, 308, 309
  ecclesiastical province of 67
Round, J.H., historian 254–5, 319
Royal Navy 41–2
royal 'peace' 216, 218, 221, 225
royal pleas 188, 216–17, 221
rulers and rulership 188–92
  qualities required 31, 32–3, 34–5,
    78–9, 102 189–90, 216
rural society
  in post-conquest England 276–9
  in post-conquest Wales 49–50, 52
  in pre-conquest England 52–5
  in pre-conquest Scotland 52
  in pre-conquest Wales 52
Rutland 32

St Albans 59, 300
St Andrews 27, 58, 309, 310
St Asaph 310
St Augustine's, Canterbury 59, 300
St Bertin 6
St Cuthbert 178, 302
St David's 58, 60, 61, 153, 165, 209, 260,
    309–310
St Denis 150
St Evroult 10, 68
St Omer 66
St Peter's Church, Barton-on-Humber 63
St Peter's, Rome 307
St Stephen's, Caen 67, 156, 290, 306
St Suzanne 241
St Tysilio 58
St Valéry-sur-Somme 121–2
'sake and soke' 219, 221

Salisbury 161, 178, 195, 292, 299
  Oath of 1086 155, 191, 202, 236–7
  see also Roger, bishop of
sanctuary 221
Sandwich 42, 89, 274
Sawyer, Peter, historian 243
Saxons 23
scaccarium 212
Scandinavia 15, 27–32, 39, 79–85
scipfyrd 41
  see also fleets, fyrd, military
    organisation
Scone 27, 33
Scotia 23, 179
Scott, Walter, novelist 18
Scotland 26–7, 34–5, 38–9, 52, 96, 97–8,
    105–6, 117, 138, 143, 146–7,
    163–5, 167, 174, 177, 178–9, 225,
    231, 245, 247, 252, 254, 258, 273,
    280, 281–2, 289, 296, 308, 309,
    310–1, 312
  Norman impact on 264–6, 320–1,
    326–9 passim
  Scottishness 26–7
  see also burghs, Church, economies,
    feudalism, government, kin,
    military organisation, population,
    rural society, towns, urbanisation,
    women
scutage 210, 237, 251
secular cathedrals, see cathedrals
Sées 67, 302
segmentation 35
seigniorial courts, see lords' courts
Seine, river 28
select fyrd, see fyrd
Selsey 290, 299
servitium debitum 250–51
Severn, river 100, 149, 161
  valley 260
Sherborne 57, 61, 65, 88, 299, 301
sheriffs 17, 32, 33, 177, 200, 208, 211,
    212–4, 217, 218, 221, 240, 293,
    300
  role and growth of power after 1066
    204–5
  see also government
Sherwood Forest 206

Shetland 23, 178
shield wall 46, 48, 126–7
  see also military organisation
shire courts 32, 199, 201, 214, 215, 216,
    217–9, 221, 235, 293, 318
  and writ of c.1108 205, 216
  see also law
shire-reeves, see sheriffs
shires 32, 36, 52, 204–6, 329
  see also local government
Shrewsbury 141, 142, 145, 165, 166,
    203, 242, 243, 260, 274, 275, 302
Shropshire 177, 240, 243, 260, 262, 324
Sibyl, wife of Robert Curthose 169
silver pennies 37, 50, 194, 209, 212
  see also coinage, mints and minting,
    wealth
Simon, count of the Vexin 50, 154
simony 65, 68, 299, 303, 309
Siward, earl of Northumbria 33, 86, 87,
    91, 95, 96, 99, 97–100
slavery 54–5, 201, 321, 327
  decline of in England after 1066
    278–9, 327
  in pre-conquest Normandy 279
  see also peasantry
sokemen 53, 277–8
sokes 52
Solway, river 98
Somerset 95, 205, 206, 240, 255, 256
The Song of the Battle of Hastings, see
    Carmen de Hastingae Proelio
Sources, for the Norman Conquest 3–20
  administrative 15–18
  narrative 4–15
Southampton 84, 169, 274, 275
Southwark 96, 131
Spearhafoc, abbot of Abingdon 65
Spelman, Henry, lawyer 319
Stafford 145
Staffordshire 240
Stamford Bridge, battle of 5, 47, 119–20,
    123, 124, 125, 130, 231
Stephen, king of England 180, 320
Stephen, count of Aumale 166
Stigand, archbishop of Canterbury 58–9,
    60, 61, 65, 87, 96, 108, 115, 132–3,
    138–9, 145–6, 290, 294, 312

Stigand II, bishop of Elmham 299
Stirling 273
The Story of Rollo, see Roman de Rou
Stow 62
Strata Florida 14
Strathclyde xiv, 22
Strathearn 35
subinfeudation 235
succession, royal, in England 75–80
    see also kinship, *verba novissima, post
        obitum* grant
Suffolk 17, 201
Sulien, bishop of St Davids 60–61
surnames, *see* toponyms
Surrey 131, 277
Sussex 95, 120, 125, 142, 161, 225, 242,
    253, 274, 302
Swein Estrithson, king of Denmark 86, 87,
    89, 116, 121, 143–4, 146–7, 149
Swein Forkbeard, king of Denmark 81–2
Swein Godwineson, earl 86, 89–91
Switzerland 290
Symeon of Durham, chronicler 14, 264
synods 298
    see also councils

Taillefer, minstrel 12
tallies 213
    see also exchequer
taxation 142, 155, 161, 208–9
    see also geld
Tay, river 27, 33
Tees, river 32, 17, 201
Teesdale 257
tenants-in-chief 216, 219, 233–4, 236,
    238–41, 250–1, 281, 284, 291,
    293, 304–5, 326
    ecclesiastical 241, 250, 255–6, 291,
        305, 326
    see also barons
Tenby 273
tenure, *see* lands
terra Normannum 29–30
Tewkesbury 275, 307
Thames, river 91, 95, 131–2, 283
thanages 33
    see also government in pre-conquest
        Scotland

thegns 33–4, 39, 78, 105, 240, 247
    see also king's thegns
Thetford 296, 299, 302
Third Crusade 318
Thirsk 257
Thomas I of Bayeux archbishop of York
    8, 290
    and primacy dispute with Canterbury
        294–7, 307
Thorfinn the Mighty, earl of Orkney 64
Thorkell ('the Tall'), viking 81
Thorkell, sheriff of Warwickshire 239–40
Thorney 61
Thurstan, abbot of Glastonbury 300
Thurstan, archbishop of York 294, 300,
    305
Tiberius Psalter 63
Tickhill 235, 245, 257
Tinchebray, battle of (1106) x, 179,
    181–2, 252, 253
    castle 181–2
tithings 205–6, 220–21, 329
    see also frankpledge, law
Tofi, sheriff of Somerset 205, 240
tolls 36
Tonbridge 161
toponyms 280, 324
    see also English names
Tostig Godwineson, earl of Northumbria
    6, 64, 79, 89, 91, 98, 99, 101, 142,
    259
    and invasion of 1066 116–20, 125
    and Northumbrian rising 105–7
Tower of London 133, 173, 175
    see also White Tower
towns 51–2, 321, 327
    in Britain after 1066 273–4
    see also boroughs, burghs, *burhs*,
        economies
trade 49–52, 54, 273, 274–5, 323, 328
    see also economies
Trahaearn ap Caradog, Welsh prince
    261, 263
treasurer 194, 213
    see also household, treasury
treasure trove 216
treasury 195, 212
    see also household, treasury

trial by battle 222, 224
Troarn 67
Turgot, bishop of St Andrew's and
    biographer of St Margaret 15,
    310–311
Turold, abbot of Peterborough 146,
    301
Tweed, river 23, 24, 26, 31, 117, 265
Tyne, river 31, 152, 265
Tynemouth Priory 166

Uhtred, earl of Northumbria 106
Ulf, bishop of Dorchester 88
underfeng, meaning of 94
Urban II, pope 167, 304–5
urbanisation, see towns
Urse d'Abetot, sheriff 198, 205, 249

Val-ès-Dunes, battle of (1047) 38, 92
Varaville, battle of (1057) 94
vassal 254, 264, 291, 303, 328
verba novissima 77–8
Vercelli 65
Vexin 150, 154, 155, 168, 170
vicomtes 38, 67
    see also government in pre-conquest
        Normandy
Vignats 177
vikings 25, 28, 32, 39–41, 50, 51, 56, 57,
    67, 80–81, 82, 290
villeins 53–4, 55, 220, 278, 327
vills 32, 145, 221, 276
vineyards 277
Virgil, poet 11
Vita Edwardi Regis 6, 59–60, 64, 87–8, 91,
    99, 105–8, 283
    see also Life of king Edward

Wace, chronicler 11, 43, 93, 104
Walcher, bishop of Durham 150, 152,
    290, 293
Waldric, bishop of Laon and chancellor
    194
Wales 26, 35–6, 39, 52, 96, 101–2, 105,
    138, 142, 149, 153, 165–6, 167,
    168, 177–8, 203, 209, 225, 231,
    242, 247, 253, 254, 273–4, 280,
    281–2, 289, 309–10, 312

Norman impact on 258–64, 320, 321,
    322, 326–9 passim
Cymry and Welshness 26
see also boroughs, Church,
    economies, feudalism,
    government, kin, military
    organisation, population, rural
    society, towns, women
Walkelin, bishop of Winchester 197,
    290, 307
Wallingford 132, 235, 243, 322
Walter, bishop of Hereford 59, 65, 88
Walter FitzOther, baron 243
Walter Giffard, earl of Buckingham 175
Walter Tirel, nobleman 170
Waltham 62, 131
Waltheof, earl of Northamptonshire
    and Northumbria 98, 138–9, 143,
    152, 202, 231, 232, 245, 283–4,
    322
    execution and cult of 149–50
    in revolt of the earls 148–50
wapentakes 32, 36, 205, 218
    see also hundreds
wardships 174, 178, 190, 210, 237
Warwick 141, 162, 178, 239–40
Warwickshire 239, 322
waste, see Domesday Book
wealth
    post-conquest English royal 206,
        207–214
    of William I 207
    pre-conquest English royal 36–7, 50
    in 1087 195
    in 1130 206, 207, 208–11, 213–4
    see also ecclesiastical vacancies,
        economies, exchequer, feudal
        incidents, geld, money, scutage,
        silver pennies, taxation, towns,
        trade
Wells 59, 65, 88, 299
Welshpool 98
'Welshries' 263
wergild ('man price') 223
Wessex 4–6, 31, 40–41, 57, 79, 82, 86,
    91, 99, 101, 129, 142, 203, 215
Westbury-on-Severn
Western Isles 178

Westminster 116, 179, 188, 213
    councils of 278, 298, 305
Westminster Abbey 6, 63–4, 96, 107–8,
    115, 133, 140, 160, 168, 173, 179,
    306
Westminster Hall 168
West Saxons 22
    see also Wessex
Wherwell 91
White Tower 247, 293
    see also Tower of London
widows 237, 238, 258, 283–4
Wigmore 260
Wigod of Wallingford, landholder 243,
    322
William the Conqueror see William I,
    king
William Rufus, see William II, king
William I ('the Conqueror'), king of
    England and duke of Normandy
    4, 9–10, 11, 12, 13, 15, 16, 17, 32,
    38, 41, 42, 43, 45, 48, 65, 66,
    91–5, 96, 97, 102–5, 107, 117–33
    passim, 137–57 passim, 162, 164,
    165, 166, 173, 175, 182, 187–226
    passim, 236, 240, 241, 244, 247,
    252, 253, 275, 279, 280, 289, 302,
    309–10, 319, 322, 323, 325–6, 329
    alleged wealth 195, 207
    attitude to Wales and Scotland 147,
        152, 153, 258, 259, 260, 263, 264,
        265
    and Battle of Hastings 126–3
    and the Church 290–4 passim, 300,
        303–4, 312
    confirms privileges of City of London
        138, 199, 232, 324
    coronation 133, 145–6, 290, 294, 303
    death and bequests 30, 156–7, 160,
        317, 320
    defines jurisdiction of church and
        hundred courts 215–6, 293–4
    Domesday survey 155, 200–2
        see also Salisbury Oath
    early life 92–3
    and English opposition after 1066
        137–50, 155, 192, 202, 231, 245
    and Harold II 13, 102–5, 117, 124
    after Hastings 131–3

on Hastings campaign 124–6
    his illegitimacy 92
    his marriage 92–3, 94, 154
    negotiates with Harold in 1066 117–8
    obituary 189, 249
    offered crown by Edward the
        Confessor 91–5, 103–4
    and papal banner 121–2, 303
    prepares to invade England 120–2
    relationship with Robert Curthose
        150–2
    sea-crossing to England 122–4
    and the succession in 1066 75–9
    see also Laws of William the Conqueror
William II ('Rufus'), king of England 7,
    9, 15, 17, 38, 75, 76, 77, 78, 151,
    152, 173–4, 178–9, 187–226
    passim, 242, 247, 248, 249, 253,
    264–6, 273, 274, 280, 291–2, 323,
    325–6, 329
    abuses rights over barons 238
    acquires Normandy from Robert
        Curthose 167–8, 207
    alleged anti-baronial strategies 198
    alleged wealth in 1087 195
        and ecclesiastical vacancies 163–4,
        211
    appearance and character 159–60, 275
    as king 160–70
    and Church 290–4 passim, 298, 304
        and archbishop Anselm 170, 211,
        253, 304–5
    death 169–70, 173
    designated king by William I 156–7,
        160
    and Elias de la Flèche 168–9
    and England's Jews 275–6
    and the fyrd 252–3
    illness in 1093 163–4
    and northern England 256–7
    obituary 189
    prefers low-born servants 197–8
    revolt of 1088 160–1, 206, 208–9, 249,
        291, 293
    in Scotland and Wales 163–6, 178,
        258, 263, 264, 265–6, 310
    strengthens position in Normandy
        162–3, 179
    and Wesminster Hall 168

William IX, duke of Aquitaine 169
William, count of Arques 68
William d'Aubigny 190–91
William de Braose, baron 234, 242
William de Breteuil, son of William
    FitzOsbern 148, 152, 180, 191, 280
William, count of Eu 166–7, 189
William FitzAnsculf, baron 241, 255
William FitzOsbern, earl 43, 67, 139,
    142–3, 148, 152, 195, 196, 202–3,
    242, 248, 259–60, 274, 280
    death of 145, 148
William de Jumièges, chronicler 9–11,
    13, 30, 45, 81, 82, 83, 84, 93, 95,
    102, 116, 117, 121–2, 129
William, bishop of London 66, 88
William Malet, baron 141, 143
William of Malmesbury, chronicler 6,
    11, 13, 14, 59, 60, 62, 98–9, 103,
    108, 116, 159, 162, 169, 174–5,
    188, 189, 191, 275, 279, 283, 289,
    291, 292, 307–8, 317, 322, 323,
    325
William, count of Mortain 175, 181
William II, duke of Normandy, see
    William I, king of England and
    duke of Normandy
William Peverel, baron 141
William de Poitiers, chronicler 9–11,
    13–14, 30, 42, 47–8, 68, 77, 93,
    95, 102, 115, 121–30 passim,
    132–3,138–9, 232, 240, 289, 318
William I ('Longsword'), count of Rouen
    28
William de Saint-Calais, bishop of
    Durham 14, 15, 265, 291, 302
    revolt of 1088 and trial 160–1
William of Volpiano, abbot of Fécamp
    67
William de Warenne, earl of Surrey 142,
    175, 179, 189, 196, 233, 242, 244,
    248, 302, 325
Williams, Ann, historian 240
Wilton 62
Wiltshire 206, 240
Winchester 51, 57, 59, 61, 63, 84, 87, 96,
    99, 131–2, 139, 140, 144, 146,
    149, 153, 160, 173, 188, 202,
    212–3, 290, 295, 301, 307

'style' 63
Windsor 295
witan 33, 190, 318
women 179, 281–5
    in post-conquest England 282–5
    in pre-conquest England 282, 283
    in pre-conquest Scotland and Wales
        281–2
    see also dower, families, heiresses,
        marriage, widows
Worcester 5, 6, 57, 60, 61, 62, 66, 96, 98,
    149, 161, 249, 290, 291, 293, 295,
    301, 308
    see also John of Worcester, Wulfstan
Worcestershire 85, 205, 239, 240, 249
writing in government 15–18, 31, 138,
    178, 194, 198–202, 292, 324
    increase in England after 1066 200,
        226
    see also acta, boc, chancery, charters,
        Church, diplomas, Domesday,
        gewrit, writs and writ-charters
writ 'of right', see writs and writ-charters
writs and writ-charters, 16–18, 178, 194,
    198–200, 211, 215–6, 224, 232,
    240, 243, 255–6, 293–4, 324
    writ 'of right' 224
    see also Henry I, William I, writing in
        government
Wulfnoth, thegn 86
Wulfnoth Godwineson, nobleman 93
Wulfric, abbot of Winchester 300
Wulfstan, bishop of Worcester 60, 149,
    161, 279, 290, 291, 293, 306, 308
Wye, river 153, 248

yardland 54
York 37, 51, 55–6, 57, 58, 61, 66, 105,
    119, 141, 143–4, 209, 241, 247,
    274, 290, 292, 294–7, 307, 309,
    323
    Minster 149
    see also Cynsige, Ealdred, Gerard,
        Oswald, Thomas of Bayeux,
        Thurstan
Yorkshire 52, 119, 124, 143, 145, 166,
    177, 234, 235, 242, 243, 245, 248,
    256–7, 264, 326
Yves, bishop of Sées 67